D0849127

Lincoln and Liberty

LINCOLN & LIBERTY

WISDOM FOR THE AGES

Edited by
LUCAS E. MOREL

Introduction by
U.S. Supreme Court Justice Clarence Thomas

UNIVERSITY PRESS OF KENTUCKY

Copyright © 2014 by The University Press of Kentucky

Scholarly publisher for the Commonwealth,
serving Bellarmine University, Berea College, Centre College of Kentucky,
Eastern Kentucky University, The Filson Historical Society, Georgetown College,
Kentucky Historical Society, Kentucky State University, Morehead State
University, Murray State University, Northern Kentucky University, Transylvania
University, University of Kentucky, University of Louisville, and Western
Kentucky University.

Editorial and Sales Offices: The University Press of Kentucky
663 South Limestone Street, Lexington, Kentucky 40508-4008
www.kentuckypress.com

Cataloging-in-Publication data is available from the Library of Congress.

ISBN 978-0-8131-5101-4 (hardcover : alk. paper)
ISBN 978-0-8131-5102-1 (epub)
ISBN 978-0-8131-5103-8 (pdf)

This book is printed on acid-free paper meeting
the requirements of the American National Standard
for Permanence in Paper for Printed Library Materials.

Manufactured in the United States of America.

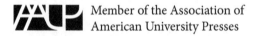

Member of the Association of
American University Presses

The struggle of today, is not altogether for today
—it is for a vast future also.

—Abraham Lincoln, December 3, 1861

Contents

Preface

On the question of liberty, as a principle, we are not what we have been.
— Abraham Lincoln, August 15, 1855

Amid the many books marking the bicentennial of Abraham Lincoln's birth and the sesquicentennial of the American Civil War, it seems the Lincoln most relevant to our times is one whose principal attraction is his openness to change. This progressive Lincoln got better as the nation got worse, with a good number of its white citizens grown indifferent toward the spread of black slavery into federal territory, while others fought to defend a way of life where white supremacy was the rule and not the exception.

Moreover, a Lincoln worthy of our twenty-first-century esteem must exhibit virtues that shine brightest when distanced from his country's slave-holding founders. After all, few of the founders freed their own slaves or strove to rid the new nation of the "peculiar institution." If Lincoln is to be praised, his affinity for the founders, especially Thomas Jefferson, needs to be minimized if not altogether muted.[1]

Thus what makes the Emancipator so great in the eyes of succeeding generations of Americans must be his capacity for growth, a figure embraced by future generations who, presumably, have improved upon the past to the extent they followed Lincoln's example of not being too fixed in one's views and of being open to the light of experience and progress. Lincoln as progressive, as focused on the future, becomes one who did not know early on what he believed about America or what he hoped for the nation.

For example, in a major biography published to commemorate the bicentennial of Lincoln's birth, Ronald C. White Jr. interprets Lincoln as expressing "evolving thoughts on slavery," a man "coming to believe that every generation needed to redefine America for its own time" and one who offered "a new vision for America" that must be something different than the founders envisioned. White acknowledges Lincoln's admiration for the American founding only to mark his shift away from the founders and highlight Lincoln's "ability to articulate a compelling vision for the nation," which White sees as the hallmark of presidential leadership: "For the first year and a half of the war, Lincoln's public rhetoric showed him acting with fidelity to the great ideals of the past, especially as they were enshrined in the Declaration of Independence and the Constitution. By the end of 1862, Lincoln became willing to change the definition of the war in terms of the future." To White's credit, he does identify Lincoln's "moral integrity" and "moral center" as something unambiguous about his character, calling it "the strong trunk from which all the branches of his life grew."[2] Nevertheless, the lesson of his biography is that Lincoln's ambiguity and willingness to change enabled him to accomplish great things for himself and the American people.[3]

Others who read Lincoln's political career as a work in progress and laud him for this include the preeminent professor of African and African American history Henry Louis Gates Jr., Pulitzer Prize–winning historian Eric Foner, and the first African American president, Barack Obama. In an edited volume of excerpts from Lincoln's writings dealing with race and slavery, Gates presents Lincoln as experiencing an "evolution in his own thinking about who blacks were as human beings in relation to whites," which should be juxtaposed with later comments about Lincoln's "skepticism about the nature of the Negro," "the transformation in his attitudes toward blacks," and "how very far Lincoln had come in his thinking about race and the abolition of slavery."[4] Moreover, to bolster how much President Lincoln had progressed from his antebellum days, Donald Yacovone, Gates's coeditor and author of the volume's headnotes to the Lincoln excerpts, states that the Lincoln of the 1850s "revealed . . . striking limits to his conception of black rights," professed "the racial inferiority of African Americans," and "shared [Stephen] Douglas's popular racial attitudes"—that is, white supremacy.[5]

For his part, Eric Foner describes Lincoln as one whose public career "revealed a consistency that allows us to take him at his word," but he emphasizes that Lincoln was a man "whose views changed over time" and, in particular, one who exhibited an "evolution of his ideas and policies about slavery."[6] Similarly President Barack Obama, who did so much to identify his own political career with that other inexperienced Illinois lawyer, praises Lincoln for keeping "his moral compass pointed firm and true," while also noting, "I cannot swallow whole the view of Lincoln as the Great Emancipator. . . . I am fully aware of his limited views on race." Obama adds that it was "precisely those imperfections—and the painful self-awareness of those failings etched in every crease of his face and reflected in those haunted eyes—that make him so compelling." Lincoln's ability to improve, personally and professionally, reminds Obama of "the enduring belief that we can constantly remake ourselves to fit our larger dreams."[7] Apparently our time calls not for heroes and icons but flawed figures and careworn visages.

In Lincoln's time, neither Chief Justice Roger B. Taney nor Illinois senator Stephen A. Douglas saw the American founders as compelling due to any humility regarding their flaws but because they demonstrated the courage of their convictions. But unlike Lincoln, they read the Declaration of Independence as a "whites only" charter and did so in an attempt to protect slaveholding founders from charges of hypocrisy. In 1857 Taney wrote that "the men who framed this declaration were great men—high in literary acquirements, high in their sense of honor, and incapable of asserting principles inconsistent with those on which they were acting."[8] A year later, Stephen Douglas echoed this sentiment: "[I]f they included negroes in that term ['all men'], they were bound, as conscientious men, that day and that hour, not only to have abolished slavery throughout the land, but to have conferred political rights and privileges on the negro, and elevated him to an equality with the white man."[9] To produce consistency between profession and practice at the American founding, thereby establishing an integrity worth admiring for subsequent generations, Taney and Douglas interpreted the profession in light of their practice. If the founders did not free their slaves and abolish the peculiar institution, then they must not have seen Africans as "created equal" to Englishmen.

Commenting on the self-evident truth of human equality stated in the Declaration of Independence, Lincoln observed: "They did not mean to assert the obvious untruth, that all were then actually enjoying that equality, nor yet, that they were about to confer it immediately upon them. In fact, they had no power to confer such a boon. They meant simply to declare the *right*, so that the *enforcement* of it might follow as fast as circumstances should permit."[10] From Lincoln's antebellum vantage point, he understood the reticence of the founders not as hypocrisy but as prudence: they recognized that circumstances, such as British opposition, could impede their attempt "to secure these rights."

Furthermore, Lincoln pointed out that their inaction regarding the black slaves in their midst was no different than their inaction toward white residents on American soil: "[T]hey did not at once, *or ever afterwards,* actually place all white people on an equality with one another. . . . They meant to set up a standard maxim for free society, which could be familiar to all, and revered by all; constantly looked to, constantly labored for, and even though never perfectly attained, constantly approximated, and thereby constantly spreading and deepening its influence, and augmenting the happiness and value of life to all people of all colors everywhere."[11]

Put simply, the founding generation of Americans did not believe they could both free themselves and their slaves without hazarding the success of both their independence and their new way of governing themselves. As Lincoln noted elsewhere, "We had slavery among us, we could not get our Constitution unless we permitted them to remain in slavery, we could not secure the good we did secure if we grasped for more, and having by necessity submitted to that much; it does not destroy the principle that is the charter of our liberties."[12] Time and again, as the controversy over slavery threatened to split the nation, Lincoln returned his audience to the words of the Declaration of Independence; there he hoped they would find clarity regarding the true principles of self-government and thus common ground for promoting a common future as a completely free people.

This book argues for a Lincoln fairly well set in terms of his political philosophy. To keep him relevant, our task should not be to remake him in our image but to render an accurate portrait of him in his age. He spoke to his own era with sufficient transcendence not only to enable Americans then to surmount their difficulties, but also to teach subsequent generations lessons to address the abiding questions that face a free people. The essays that follow seek to understand Lincoln as he understood himself and attempted to make himself clear to his day and age. He "belongs to the ages" as a teacher of profound lessons regarding the nature of the American regime and how Americans from generation to generation could perpetuate their free form of government.

A noteworthy distinction of this volume of essays is the diversity of disciplinary approaches to examining the life and politics of Abraham Lincoln, ranging from law and English literature to history and political theory. The essays address longstanding controversies arising from Lincoln's approach to race, emancipation, civil liberties, and executive power, while exploring less-developed aspects of Lincoln the man and politician—for example, how literature shaped his mindset, his nuanced dealings with public opinion, the role of theology in his view of labor and capital, how he approached electioneering as a party leader, and the use and abuse of Lincoln by progressive politicians and intellectuals. Taking Lincoln seriously as a political thinker as well as practical politician, the contributors show that the most iconic American president still has much to reveal to the modern-day student of politics. Although the crisis through which he steered the ship of state was altogether unique in American history, the challenge it posed was and remains inherent for any people who intend to maintain their freedom from generation to generation.[13]

In an essay that is part historical analysis, part memoir, Associate Justice Clarence Thomas examines how Lincoln addressed the controversial Kansas-Nebraska Act of 1854, showing how his civic engagement serves as a model for today's citizens and politicians alike. Lincoln drew from America's past, in particular the Declaration of Independence, to alert citizens to the threat the 1854 law posed to their future prosperity: the danger that opening new territory to slavery would pose to individual liberty. White indifference regarding the spread of black slavery, under the cover of Stephen Douglas's "popular sovereignty" coupled with Chief Justice Roger B. Taney's infamous 1857 decision in *Dred Scott v. Sandford,* conspired to move the country away from the equal protection of liberty and toward the nationalization of slavery. Justice Thomas astutely notes the significance of free citizens speaking up to sound the alarm to threats to freedom. Like Lincoln in his own day, Thomas warns against "complacency in the citizenry" as well as government malfeasance in the form of "pernicious constitutional rulings by judges." Growing up in a racially segregated America taught Justice Thomas that even "democratic institutions" can "produce policies fundamentally at odds with the core principles that underlie our democracy."

The influence of literature on Lincoln's character is the subject of the next two chapters: one focuses on various works of fiction and nonfiction that shaped Lincoln's moral outlook, the other on what Shakespeare's plays about kings taught Lincoln about democracy's potential for tyranny. Fred Kaplan shows that Lincoln's reading "revealed to him a world of literary brilliance and insight into human character." From economics to poetry, from the obscure (e.g., Thomas Dilworth, William Grimshaw, and James Riley) to the renowned (the Bible, William Shakespeare, and Aesop), what Lincoln drew from his reading was chiefly ethical in content. "Reason, logic, and evidence," according to Kaplan, were for Lincoln "the guides to truth," supplemented by "Christian ethics, classical style, and natural law." Taken together, these produced a mind-set and ethos that charged Lincoln's prose with a moral imperative unlike that of any other American president. Kaplan argues that we ought to "think of Lincoln as an essayist, since the tools and practices he brought to his art were those of a writer and his concern with writing on the practical and philosophical level distinguish him from every other president."

John Channing Briggs focuses on Shakespeare as the writer from whom Lincoln drew his most profound lessons about a free society's potential for tyranny. "The wish to be free, without restraint," Briggs explains, "is the tyrant's wish too." Lincoln learned from the Bard that the tyrant's vices are not such distant possibilities for ordinary white citizens long accustomed to the enslavement of blacks. "Familiarize yourselves with the chains of bondage," Lincoln warned, "and you are preparing your own limbs to wear them. Accustomed to trample on the rights of those around you, you have lost the genius of your own independence, and become the fit subjects of the first cunning tyrant who rises." Briggs argues that Lincoln's favorite Shake-spearean plays held power "to hold the mirror up to tyranny in the human heart as well as in the political world." Even the body politic of a republic could be corrupted by a "false optimism about our ability to keep tyranny in exile" when that tyranny finds its source in the people's own freedom to rule themselves.

At the turn of the nineteenth century, discussion of Lincoln's statesman-ship was muted on the subject of race. In the twenty-first century, it now stands front and center of public and scholarly assessments of Lincoln's legacy. Two authors examine what Lincoln's character teaches about the role of race in American politics. Michael Burlingame defends Lincoln from three criticisms of his reputation as "the Great Emancipator": that he was a "reluctant" emancipator, that he was a firm supporter of black coloniza-tion, and that he was singularly a "white man's president." Contrary to the current trend that interprets Lincoln as having evolving attitudes toward race and emancipation, Burlingame argues that he held early and consistent antislavery convictions. Through reminiscence material, as well as speeches and letters, Burlingame highlights the rampant antiblack sentiment that confronted any politician who sought to do right by black Americans. Lincoln chose to tread lightly on racial matters among constituencies likely to support him on other issues, therefore appearing to dismiss the rights and concerns of black Americans. In actuality his accommodation of white sentiments and prejudices—especially in the border slave states and among Southern unionists—always carries with it an enlightened view of the natural rights of blacks, which he trusts will form the basis of future progress in protecting the rights of all. Burlingame caps his defense of Lincoln as a legitimate defender of black American interests with an account of one of his fiercest wartime critics, Frederick Douglass, who described Lincoln as "the martyr president" and "emphatically the black man's President."

Diana Schaub also looks at Lincoln through Douglass's eyes, offering a close reading of his 1876 "Oration in Memory of Abraham Lincoln," which was delivered upon the unveiling of a statue of Lincoln blessing an emancipated slave, the Freedmen's Monument. Schaub explains that even for a die-hard abolitionist such as Douglass, Lincoln's politics meet "the requirements of democratic statesmanship." Douglass judges him not simply by the partisan viewpoint of abolitionists but by the larger constituency of white America. Schaub argues that Douglass "does not want the black embrace of Lincoln to trigger a white flight from Lincoln." Had Lincoln made abolition more important than saving the Union, Douglass observed, "he would have inevitably driven from him a powerful class of the American people and rendered resistance to rebellion impossible." Douglass concluded, "Viewed from the genuine abolition ground, Mr. Lincoln seemed tardy, cold, dull, and indifferent; but measuring him by the sentiment of his country, a sentiment he was bound as a statesman to consult, he was swift, zealous, radical, and determined." Douglass's rhetorical task in 1876 was to help a still-divided nation "develop a shared perspective on the achievements of Abraham Lincoln." Schaub interprets Lincoln as one who understood the union of the American States to be "a moral project," devoted as it was to the principle of human equality. Hence its preservation was central to the eventual promotion of the rights of black Americans. In his oration, Douglass therefore portrays Lincoln not only as a liberator of black Americans, but also a protector of their newfound freedoms precisely by emphasizing the preservation of the United States of America.

Turning from Lincoln's character to Lincoln's politics, Tom Krannawitter argues that though Lincoln was not a political philosopher, he drew his political principles from "nature, or natural right." Krannawitter highlights that Lincoln sought to "conserve . . . the natural right principles of the American founding," especially the concept of human equality found in the Declaration of Independence. Contrary to "historicism or evolutionary right," Krannawitter identifies three main elements of Lincoln's political thought. The first is egalitarian natural right, where free society and limited government are coeval: "For Lincoln it was impossible to deny the self-evident truth of human equality without denying the very ground of free society and constitutional self-government." Second, Lincoln believed in the timeless nature of the American founding principles, which transcend territory and culture. For him "political legitimacy" was not due to "birth or race or tribal membership or religious dogma." Third, he believed in universal principles "that cut through time and across space." Although Americans understood themselves as embarking on a *novus ordo seclorum* (a "new order for the ages"), they also thought the basis of their regime was applicable to all times.

In my own essay I ask, was Lincoln a union man or liberty man? The definition of liberty complicates this question, as there were several practical definitions of liberty that produced conflicting policies regarding the American union and federal constitution. Slaveholders had one definition, abolitionists another, and popular sovereignty proponents still another. Lincoln's genius was in negotiating this terrain of varying definitions by focusing on the connection between equality and consent. In this context, he saw liberty as an end and the constitutional union as a means to that end. Lincoln strove to teach Americans that preserving the Union was worth doing only if it was a union devoted to liberty. The union of American states, if committed to self-government, presented the best chance for liberty to be extended to all the inhabitants of the United States—blacks as well as whites—and eventually to all human beings. The principle of consent, however, could not be forgotten. This meant that in American's popular form of government, political persuasion was not optional but a requirement of securing progress in liberty. Moreover, the constitutional mechanisms of self-government were necessary but not sufficient; how citizens thought about freedom would help or hinder its preservation. Lincoln's politics were marked by a consistent effort to inform public opinion so that the structures of self-government would operate in light of the principles that gave them birth.

Steven Kautz explores what he calls "the paradox of democratic states-manship"—popular self-government and rule by great men. The art of statesmanship in a republic is "to persuade the people . . . to listen," which entails "the right [of statesmen] to speak harsh truths." The end is to help the citizenry practice "the habits and virtues of self-government." Kautz argues that "Lincoln's common touch" helped him gain the trust of Americans, at least in the North. He sounded the alarm of a nation losing its moral bearings—"to undertake a 'restoration' of the policies and principles of the founders," specifically "to preserve and cultivate, perhaps even to restore, the democratic moral opinion that would one day lead the people themselves to choose to free the slaves." In short, democratic policy needed to be the product of free choice, not compulsion. But in the 1850s, Northern white public sentiment became more open to the expansion of black slavery into federal territories. Lincoln thought that any compromise on slavery, while a necessary part of the political process if union was threatened, could not "retreat from the *principles* of the Declaration of Independence in the moral opinion of *his* people." Making justice the *summum bonum* of democratic politics in the public mind, Lincoln strove to bring reason to bear on public policy formation, which he sought to demonstrate was no distant kin of interest. The tragedy of the Emancipation Proclamation, according to Kautz, was that it was the consequence of military necessity rather than popular discussion. Bullets rather than ballots determined the progress of liberty's march on American soil. This meant that the "new birth of freedom" her-alded so eloquently at Gettysburg remained incomplete, as Douglass noted with his own eloquence upon the dedication of the Freedmen's Monument.

Continuing the theme of Lincoln and public opinion, Allen Guelzo examines how Lincoln viewed the proper role of popular opinion in a re-public. Given the central place of consent in a popular form of government (Lincoln called it "the sheet anchor of American republicanism"), Lincoln gave speeches to shape public opinion as well as spoke of the importance of consent and opinion-making in a self-governing regime. Guelzo explores various meanings of public opinion and its relation to the vote. In doing so, he shows how Lincoln became a deft monitor and shaper of public opinion, one who was careful to show how the public's self-interest rightly understood could facilitate public policy that was also just. This contrasts with Stephen Douglass's paean to "popular sovereignty," which made no attempt to root itself in "the natural rights" of a nation's inhabitants. Herein one sees the democratic tension of majority rule and minority right. "I do not think the people had been quite educated up to it" stands as an apt reflection of Lincoln's approach to shaping public opinion—namely, the engine of popular government that must be respected but also educated in order to promote the common good.

Matthew Pinsker turns our attention to Lincoln's influence on party tactics—political choir directing as opposed to open-air preaching. Lincoln once assessed the place of parties in a free society as follows: "A free people, in times of peace and quiet—when pressed by no common danger—naturally divide into parties. At such times, the man who is of neither party, is not—cannot be, of any consequence." Needless to say, the man once described by his law partner as possessing ambition that was like "a little engine that knew no rest" quickly became a party leader and sought in various ways to direct that party to particular ends. In addition to speeches, Lincoln used letters "to command party legions." Pinsker examines one letter in particular to explore Lincoln's "political ethics" in the heat of a campaign where he himself was not running for office. Not averse to resorting to trickery, though not illegality, Lincoln is seen by Pinsker as one who took seriously the art of electioneering. Given consent's centrality to the rule of a free people, Lincoln approached elections as the best measure of the public's will and therefore worth his attempt to shape it.

Joseph Fornieri contrasts Southern apologists of black slavery (such as John Henry Hammond, George Fitzhugh, and Frederick A. Ross) with Lincoln's belief in universal liberty, human equality, and government by consent as the mainstays of a free, civilized, and industrious society. Fornieri argues that Lincoln derived a theology of labor from Genesis 3:19 and articulates a "synthesis of faith and reason" as the key to Lincoln's political economy. The debate between free labor and slave labor was not always one where slavery was understood to be incompatible with freedom, so Fornieri focuses on the impact of William Paley and James Smith on Lincoln's rational application of revealed religion to American political practice.

Given that Lincoln's presidency was chiefly a war presidency, two chapters focus on the lessons to be drawn from Lincoln's role as commander in chief. Mack Owens argues that President Lincoln fought a war to defend the American union from disintegration in a way that set the nation decisively down the road to emancipation. Lincoln's use of emergency powers, stemming from the rebellion of citizens of several states, was complicated by the "dual nature of the conflict": "both a war and a domestic insurrection." Owens shows how many were the options Lincoln could have chosen and then explains the choices he made that ill suit him for the role of dictator (benevolent or otherwise) or mere "executor" of the will of Congress. Despite his lack of executive experience and a cabinet full of men with professional recommendations to spare, Lincoln was confident in his own judgment, managed his generals (and their respective constituencies) with remarkable equanimity, and balanced "vigilance and responsibility" in protecting civil liberties while ensuring there would be a nation in which to live free—for blacks as well as whites—when the fighting was over. America survived under Lincoln's wartime leadership as the bastion of self-government in the modern age—with its devotion to liberty as the natural possession of every human being and consent as its structural corollary.

Ben Kleinerman views Lincoln's executive discretion as "the preservation of political constitutionalism." How did one of President James K. Polk's most fervent critics and Whig partisans become a strong executive in his own right? Kleinerman argues that a hallmark of Lincoln's executive discretion is his consistent defense of his actions before the bar of public opinion. Kleinerman believes the concept of a "limited constitution" actually empowered Lincoln's exercise of extensive presidential discretion. That said, Lincoln was not one whose presidential powers depended on deference to Congress. Kleinerman notes that the power Lincoln exercises "aims to restore the possibility of politics rather than to overrun the political sphere." He also distinguishes Congress's authority and power during peace and the president's actions during war. The Civil War was a peculiar context for the exercise of congressional and executive authority. Kleinerman concludes that to be "worth the keeping," the Union "must exercise the power it needs without destroying the very foundations of limited government"—a task Lincoln kept foremost in his mind even as he employed war powers derived without almost any precedents to guide him.

With the election of Barack Obama and his use of Lincoln during the presidential campaign, American politics on the Democratic side has taken on a more explicitly progressive cast. This progressive Lincoln shines only as his virtues find distance not only from his own past, but also the nation's founding. R. J. Pestritto and Jason Jividen argue that the progressives' Lincoln and the real Lincoln diverge principally over Lincoln's connection to the American founding. Specifically the progressives seek to depart from the "original constitutionalism" of the founders, while Pestritto and Jividen see Lincoln as "animated by a drive to return the country to its original ideas." That said, the progressives still claim Lincoln as their own because they interpret his Civil War presidency as a significant expansion of national authority over the state. Pestritto and Jividen interpret progressives such as Herbert Croly, Theodore Roosevelt, and especially Woodrow Wilson as enemies of the founders because the founders believed in individual rights as a static concept, with static institutions (such as a constitution of separated powers and federalism) as the primary means of protecting said rights. Progressives believed that a better instrument of progress needed to be a living thing—namely, a living person, a leader (such as a president) who could gauge a people's needs and where history was headed, and thus one who could interpret and breathe life into a static or dead instrument such as a written constitution to make it work on behalf of the people and against the tyranny not of a majority but of a minority. In this light, Wilson and other prominent progressives saw in Lincoln not a devotee of the individual rights of the Declaration of Independence and the mechanisms of the Constitution but an interpreter of the people's spirit and their leader into a grander future. Pestritto and Jividen reject Lincoln the progressive for Lincoln as a man of abstract ideas, an adherent to the rule of law, and a moderate promoter of change through constitutional means.

Notes

1. See Kevin R. C. Gutman, "Abraham Lincoln, Jeffersonian: The Colonization Chimera" and James N. Leiker, "The Difficulties of Understanding Abe: Lincoln's Reconciliation of Racial Inequality and Natural Rights," in *Lincoln Emancipated: The President and the Politics of Race,* ed. Brian R. Dirck (DeKalb: Northern Illinois University Press, 2007), 47–72 and 73–98.

2. Ronald C. White Jr., *A. Lincoln: A Biography* (New York: Random House, 2009), 4, 5, 6 174, 221, 522–23.

3. "A. Lincoln continues to fascinate us because he eludes simple definitions and final judgments"; "As people came to him with their certainties, he responded with his ambiguities"; and "One reason we have never settled on one definition of Lincoln, and, indeed, never will, is that Lincoln never stopped asking questions of himself." Ibid., 3, 512, and 676.

4. Henry Louis Gates Jr., "Introduction," *Lincoln on Race and Slavery,* ed.

Henry Louis Gates Jr. and Donald Yacovone (Princeton, NJ: Princeton University Press, 2009), xxvi, xxxv, xlv, and lxiv.

5. Ibid., 57, 93, and 127.

6. Eric Foner, *The Fiery Trial: Abraham Lincoln and American Slavery* (New York: Norton, 2010), xvi. "If Lincoln achieved greatness," Foner adds wryly, "he grew into it" (xxv).

7. Barack Obama, "What I See in Lincoln's Eyes," *Time*, June 28, 2005, http://www.cnn.com/2005/POLITICS/06/28/obama.lincoln.tm/. The clearest articulation of Obama's progressive mindset can be found in his political manifesto, *The Audacity of Hope: Thoughts on Reclaiming the American Dream* (New York: Random House / Three Rivers Press, 2006), where he claims of the Constitution that "implicit in its structure . . . was a rejection of absolute truth" and of the founders that they "were suspicious of abstraction" (93). For an interpretation of Obama's progressive liberalism as a rejection of the American founding, see Charles R. Kesler, *I Am the Change: Barack Obama and the Future of Liberalism* (New York: HarperCollins / Broadside Books, 2012). Cf. James T. Kloppenberg, *Reading Obama: Dreams, Hope, and the American Political Tradition* (Princeton, NJ: Princeton University Press, 2010).

8. *Dred Scott* v. *John F. A. Sandford*, 60 U.S. 393 (1857), 410.

9. Stephen Douglas, "Speech at Springfield, Illinois" (July 17, 1858), http://teachingamericanhistory.org/library/document/speech-at-springfield-illinois/.

10. Abraham Lincoln, "Speech at Springfield, Illinois" (June 26, 1857), *Collected Works of Abraham Lincoln*, ed. Roy P. Basler, 8 vols. plus index (New Brunswick, NJ: Rutgers University Press, 1953), 2:406. Hereinafter cited as *CW*; emphases in original unless otherwise noted.

11. Ibid., 405, 406.

12. Abraham Lincoln, "Speech at Chicago, Illinois" (July 10, 1858), in *CW*, 2:501.

13. In his first great speech, which he titled "The Perpetuation of Our Political Institutions," Lincoln put the challenge bluntly: "At what point then is the approach of danger to be expected? I answer, if it ever reach us, it must spring up amongst us. It cannot come from abroad. If destruction be our lot, we must ourselves be its author and finisher. As a nation of freemen, we must live through all time, or die by suicide." Abraham Lincoln, "Address before the Young Men's Lyceum of Springfield, Illinois" (January 27, 1838), in *CW*, 1:109.

Introduction

Lincoln, *Dred Scott*, and the Preservation of Liberty

Clarence Thomas

Since my youth, I have admired Abraham Lincoln greatly. Back then, we thought of Lincoln as "the Great Emancipator." In difficult times that would follow in my life, he represented a model of perseverance, and in my early years in Washington he served both as an inspiration and a beacon that highlighted the underlying principles of our country, especially the Declaration of Independence. So, my interest in him has been deeply personal and long-standing.

Lincoln's battle against slavery and the threat it posed to our nation's survival is one of the most important chapters in our nation's history. Lincoln saved the union and ultimately prevailed over the institution of slavery because of his extraordinary understanding of the bedrock principles of our constitutional democracy: that government by consent must be preserved if liberty is to be secured and that to accomplish this the separation of powers between the three branches of the federal government and between the sovereign powers of the national government and those of the states must be maintained.

Lincoln's understanding of how the structure of our government preserves its purpose, liberty, also enabled him to see how the branches of our government could be manipulated to achieve ends inconsistent with that purpose. Specifically it was Lincoln's ability to see how a bad but popular piece of legislation would combine with a bad but popular Supreme Court decision that spurred him to join the battle against slavery in time to ensure

1

a victory. The lessons we can draw from Lincoln's experience are enduring ones. They can help us address some of the most challenging issues we face today, particularly to the extent those issues result from, or are exacerbated by, the ever-increasing role of courts and the growing social and political apathy toward the principles of liberty on which our country is founded. This is particularly true as providing security appears to be displacing the protection of liberty as the government's purpose. How Lincoln used the ideological and structural underpinnings of our Constitution to defeat the evil of slavery is a wonderful story. It illustrates how one of our country's darkest moments produced one of its greatest leaders and also revealed the formidable strength and virtue of our constitutional structure.

The threat created by the Kansas-Nebraska Act in 1854, that slavery would expand into the new American territories of the Louisiana Purchase, was the principal reason Lincoln returned to politics and ultimately ascended to the presidency. After serving a single term in Congress, from 1847 to 1849, Lincoln had decided to return to Illinois and practice law. But when Congress passed the act, which repealed the portion of the Missouri Compromise that prohibited slavery north of the 36° 30' parallel in the Louisiana Purchase territories, except, of course, for Missouri, and opened the door to slavery's expansion into the Kansas territory, Lincoln once again committed to run for office. The Kansas-Nebraska Act signaled a sea change in slavery's future, because before the act's passage, slavery had been barred from most of the existing territories since the time of the founding. The act's proponents tried to understate the impact of this change, arguing that the new legislation would simply allow each new territory to decide for itself whether or not to permit slavery within its borders and that the rest of the country should, as Lincoln later put it, "care not" what each territory decided.[1] This populist rhetoric did not prevent Lincoln from seeing the Kansas-Nebraska Act for what it was: a crucial first step by proslavery forces to expand the institution of slavery across the country. So great were Lincoln's fears about the act and its consequences that he decided to reenter politics, running for the state legislature and campaigning for other anti-Nebraska Whigs.

Lincoln spoke vehemently against slavery, giving nearly two hundred speeches. Perhaps the best early example of these, which also previewed his later arguments, is his speech at Peoria in October of 1854 in which he rebutted a three-hour argument in favor of the Kansas-Nebraska Act by Sen. Stephen Douglas, who led the efforts to pass the act in the Senate. Lincoln set out the basis for his vehement opposition to the inevitable expansion of slavery under this legislation:

> This *declared* indifference, but as I must think, covert *real* zeal for the spread of slavery, I can not but hate. I hate it because of the monstrous injustice of slavery itself. I hate it because it deprives our republican example of its just influence in the world—enables the enemies of free institutions, with plausibility, to taunt us as hypocrites—causes the real friends of freedom to doubt our sincerity, and especially because it forces so many really good men amongst ourselves into an open war with the very fundamental principles of civil liberty—criticising [*sic*] the Declaration of Independence, and insisting that there is no right principle of action but *self-interest*.[2]

Douglas defended the act on the grounds of popular sovereignty, or as Lincoln referred to it, "squatter sovereignty," arguing that the people of each territory should not have their position on slavery dictated to them by the national congress.[3] Lincoln was not persuaded:

> The doctrine of self government is right—absolutely and eternally right—but it has no just application, as here attempted. Or perhaps I should rather say that whether it has such just application depends upon whether a negro is *not* or *is* a man. If he is *not* a man, why in that case, he who *is* a man may, as a matter of self-government, do just as he pleases with him. But if the negro *is* a man, is it not to that extent, a total destruction of self-government, to say that he too shall not govern *himself?* When the white man governs himself that is self-government; but when he governs himself, and also governs *another* man, that is *more* than self government—that is despotism. If the negro is a *man,* why then my ancient faith teaches me that "all men are created equal;" and that there can be no moral right in connection with one man's making a slave of another.[4]

Impassioned, Lincoln continued: "What I do say is, that no man is good enough to govern another man, *without that other's consent.* I say this is the leading principle—the sheet anchor of American republicanism. Our Declaration of Independence says: 'We hold these truths to be self-evident:

that all men are created equal; that they are endowed by their Creator with certain inalienable rights; that among these are life, liberty and the pursuit of happiness. That to secure these rights, governments are instituted among men, DERIVING THEIR JUST POWERS FROM THE CONSENT OF THE GOVERNED."[5] To Lincoln, then, slavery was an evil that deviated from this principle and, thus, from the course set by the founders in the Declaration of Independence.

In 1858 the Republican Party, which Lincoln helped found to oppose slavery, nominated him to run for the US Senate against Douglas. Upon accepting the nomination, Lincoln reiterated his view of the enormous consequences of the spread of slavery on the future of the Union:

> "A house divided against itself cannot stand." I believe this government cannot endure, permanently half *slave* and half *free*. I do not expect the Union to be *dissolved*—I do not expect the house to *fall*—but I *do* expect it will cease to be divided. It will become *all* one thing, or *all* the other. Either the *opponents* of slavery, will arrest the further spread of it, and place it where the public mind shall rest in the belief that it is in course of ultimate extinction; or its *advocates* will push it forward, till it shall become alike lawful in *all* the States, *old* as well as *new*—*North* as well as *South*.[6]

It was in this "House Divided" speech that Lincoln warned the country that slavery would not die off quietly as proponents of the Missouri Compromise might have hoped. Instead, Lincoln knew that the Kansas-Nebraska Act had transformed the question of slavery into the great question of his time. A self-taught student of history, Lincoln understood that all great questions demand answers. Compromise of any sort can delay the inevitable for only so long. The same was true for the question of slavery. Either the institution would be extinguished from every state and territory, or it would endure and ultimately engulf the entire nation and, along with it, the core principles of liberty and democracy on which our nation was founded.

Lincoln vowed to oppose the latter result, which meant fighting not only an act of Congress, the Kansas-Nebraska Act, but also a Supreme Court decision, the court's decision in *Dred Scott*. Dred Scott was a slave who sued for his freedom on the grounds that his master had removed him for several years to the free state of Illinois and the Wisconsin territory before returning to the slave state of Missouri. Chief Justice Roger B. Taney wrote the court's opinion in Scott's case. He concluded that Scott's travels in Illinois and the Wisconsin territory had not made him a free man. But first the court held that Scott could not sue in federal court because the Constitution permitted only citizens to file federal lawsuits, and blacks were not citizens as the Constitution used that term. The court could have left it at that and decided the case on that ground alone. Taney, however, went further. He decided that Congress had exceeded its authority when it prohibited slavery in the territories through the Missouri Compromise. According to Taney, slaves were private property, protected by the Constitution, and the Missouri Compromise infringed this constitutionally protected, substantive property right. Based on this latter rationale, many predicted that the court would rule in a subsequent case that states had no power to prohibit slavery within their borders, because state laws prohibiting slavery would likewise infringe slave owners' constitutional property rights. Well aware of this, Lincoln lamented the court's decision before it was even announced, writing that "so soon as the Supreme court decides that Dred Scott is a slave, the whole community must decide that not only Dred Scott, but that *all* persons in like condition, are rightfully slaves."[7]

Lincoln knew the court's decision in *Dred Scott,* like the Kansas-Nebraska Act, was fundamentally at odds with his understanding of the Declaration of Independence and the Constitution. Lincoln's commitment to end slavery was thus based on more than just the particular evils of slavery. It was based on his conviction that slavery was merely the embodiment of an even greater evil, a philosophy of human relations irreconcilable with the core principle of liberty on which our constitutional democracy rests: the principle that no man is good enough to govern another man without that other's consent. Lincoln recognized that slavery was and is irreconcilable with this principle. He knew that a government that could make slaves of blacks could just as easily restrict the franchise of whatever other category of persons it saw fit, placing large proportions of the populace under the governance of a permanent ruling class.[8] In this way, slavery corrupted our constitutional democracy by breaking the promise that our democracy made in exchange for its legitimacy: the promise that it would be a government by consent of the governed, all of the governed.

Lincoln understood the incongruence between slavery and our country's founding principles in a way many people of his day did not. This understanding is what prompted Lincoln to view the question of whether slavery would expand as synonymous with the question of whether our country would give up the inalienable rights it was founded to protect, including the inalienable right of each of us to eat the bread we earn with our own hands without asking leave of anyone else.[9] Lincoln thus objected to, and opposed, slavery advocates' manipulation of both Congress and the Supreme Court to tilt the scales in their favor. In securing passage of the Kansas-Nebraska Act, the proslavery forces used the elected branches of the federal government to enact a law fundamentally inconsistent with the principle of liberty. They then used populist and democratic rhetoric to lull the public into a sense of ease or complacency about that law, assuring everyone that it would simply allow the people of the new territories to choose whether to adopt slavery or not, limited only by the bounds of the Constitution. But they simultaneously used the courts to constitutionalize certain aspects of that choice and thus removed those aspects from the democratic sphere entirely. Specifically they used the Supreme Court's decision in *Dred Scott* to constitutionalize the notion that slaves were property and, in doing so, all but ensured that the democratic choice contemplated by the Kansas-Nebraska Act, a territory's choice of being slave or free subject only to the bounds of the Constitution, would develop in only one direction—a proslavery direction, irreconcilable with our country's founding principles.

Lincoln's battle cry against this assault on our democracy transcended his day. In his "House Divided" speech, he warned that complacency in the citizenry combined with pernicious constitutional rulings by judges can strike at the heart of our democratic civil society. That is as true now as it was in the 1860s. Although modern threats to our liberty do not come in forms as obvious as slavery, they undermine the same principles that Lincoln fought so hard to preserve. Remembering these principles, and how the structure of our government works to protect them, would serve us well today. By doing so, we can better fulfill the role that all of us as citizens—and also, and particularly, that we federal judges—play in safeguarding our constitutional democracy. Lincoln's understanding of our country's founding documents teaches us the reason this government exists: to honor, as well as protect, our liberty.

This principle, which compelled Lincoln's opposition to slavery, was one of the earliest lessons from Lincoln's time that I was able to relate to my own life and work. I was blessed to be raised by my grandparents. My grandfather was a man who, like Lincoln, staunchly believed in liberty, freedom, and independence at a time when those ideals were far from a reality. Lincoln's work and legacy allowed my grandfather to dream of someday realizing these fundamental human and American promises—if not immediately for himself, then, vicariously, for his progeny. Indeed, it was Lincoln's understanding of the Declaration of Independence that reverberated throughout our country and our lives when Dr. Martin Luther King Jr. stood at the foot of the Lincoln Memorial and delivered his "I Have a Dream" speech, describing the Declaration as "a promissory note to which every American was to fall heir."[10]

Like Lincoln and Dr. King, my grandfather knew that the liberty promised in our Declaration of Independence, though guaranteed by our Constitution, would require vigorous defense. Liberty was not something permanently secured by past generations to be enjoyed without effort by all that came afterward. Liberty was a virtue we would retain only to the extent we understood its importance and fought to preserve and advance it. Lincoln did fight to preserve liberty against "the monstrous injustice of slavery," and we can and should fight to preserve liberty today against threats that, though they do not come in the form of institutions as objectively evil as slavery or of military challenges as great as the Civil War, are no less real.[11]

My grandparents understood this, and their opposition to one of the greatest threats of their time, government-enforced segregation, helped me to appreciate the lesson Lincoln learned in confronting the Kansas-Nebraska Act: that it is possible for our own democratic institutions to produce policies fundamentally at odds with the core principles that underlie our democracy. But it was not until the mid-1980s, during my tenure as chairman of the Equal Employment Opportunity Commission (EEOC), that I was fully able to understand Lincoln's lessons about the importance of our Constitution's structure as a tool for safeguarding democratic principles. These lessons, which I learned through countless hours of reading and discussing the founding documents and leaders such as Lincoln, not only helped me better discharge my duties in the executive branch, but they also helped prepare me to be a judge.

The lesson from Lincoln's battle against slavery that I did not fully appreciate until I was at the EEOC was that the separation of powers between the branches of government and between the federal government and the states is not always enough to safeguard our liberty. As the evils worked by the

Kansas-Nebraska Act and *Dred Scott* make clear, abuses can be perpetrated even within that framework. Lincoln understood that, and his example vividly illustrates how important it is to ensure that the organs of government abide by the limits and principles that govern their constitutional roles.

I began to take the lesson to heart while I was working in the executive branch, and my appreciation for it has only grown since I prepared to become a judge. It was then that I recognized the brilliant scope of Lincoln's objection to the *Dred Scott* decision. Lincoln objected not only because he opposed the result, but also because he recognized the decision for what it was: a judicial aggrandizement that attempted to cloak the institution of slavery in the language of constitutional rights—specifically, a slave-owner's right to treat his slave as his property and his right to have other jurisdictions respect and recognize his property right.[12] Lincoln refused to accept the premise that slaves were not human, knowing full well that the relationship between slave and master violated the principles of the Declaration of Independence. Lincoln thus abhorred the court's attempt to twist these principles, which anchor our Constitution, to advance the proslavery political agenda in a way that would help to insulate it from future democratic choice. Such conduct is wholly inconsistent with a government of separated powers that the framers created and particularly with the judiciary's special role in safeguarding the Constitution's structure as well as its substance. In creating our constitutional republic, the framers endeavored to create a government strong enough to defend itself and the liberties of its people, yet limited enough that it would not destroy those same liberties.

The first mechanism the framers chose to restrain the powers of the federal government was the separation of those powers into three coordinate branches: the executive, the legislative, and the judicial. The founders then complemented this structure by further dividing the federal government. They split the legislature into two separate houses, gave the executive a veto over legislation, and authorized the judiciary to review certain kinds of cases and controversies. In the constitutional structure, the judiciary serves as an important check on the aggrandizement of power by the political branches. The political branches do not, however, necessarily provide as robust a check on the judiciary. This is perhaps because the founders considered the need to check the judiciary less compelling. As Alexander Hamilton explained in *Federalist* No. 78, this "least dangerous" branch gains legitimacy only on the strength of its "judgment" and the recognition that it "must ultimately depend upon the aid of the executive arm even for the efficacy of its judgments."[13] Mr. Hamilton may have underestimated the federal judiciary.

The federal courts, like the *Dred Scott* court Lincoln criticized, have a tendency to assume a larger role in the governance of our nation than the framers intended. This is particularly true today when it is more acceptable for judges to constitutionalize policy choices. To the extent that citizens care not about judges making difficult policy choices for all, they allow judges to foreclose legitimate political discussion and resolution of those problems through democratic processes. This is at odds with the principle of government by consent. It takes away the people's right, and obligation, to decide these questions for themselves. In doing that, Americans follow the dangerous trail blazed by the political society of Lincoln's day. This step is again the more ironic because the federal judiciary bears the special charge of safeguarding liberty and the structural provisions of our Constitution.

The founders understood that adherence to the Constitution would put judges at odds with prevailing public opinions and the preferences of the political branches and with those institutions whose lot it is to shape and pressure certain policy results. Accordingly Article III insulates the federal judiciary from political reprisal by granting its members tenure during good behavior, which essentially amounts to life. In return for granting judges this independence, the Constitution demands that judges discipline themselves and limit their role in the nation's affairs. The Constitution does not ask officers of the other two branches to cultivate this self-discipline because they are subject to the inherent discipline that popular elections provide.

The self-discipline required by unelected, life-tenured judges (like me) is not always easy to maintain. Every judge confronts the temptation to combine the potential power of his office with his moral view of the world and to use the cases before him as opportunities to push national or social policies in whatever direction he deems just. But a judge who gives in to this temptation cannot long remain true to his office. Like a house divided, a judge divided cannot long stand. He becomes one thing, or he becomes another. He either becomes a policymaker or remains a judge who discharges his authority within the confines of the Constitution. Lincoln warned his fellow citizens not to be lulled into a "care not" daze and to guard vigilantly against the judicial usurpation of power like that in the *Dred Scott* case. His advice remains sound.

The business of trying to cement judicial policy preferences into the

Constitution did not begin with *Dred Scott* and, unfortunately, it did not end there. *Dred Scott* is the paradigmatic case of bad judging, because it abused the Constitution to take a political issue out of the democratic sphere. Recall that the court in *Dred Scott* held that slave-owners had substantive property rights in their slaves. This holding invoked the language of the Fifth Amendment's due process clause, which provides that no person shall be deprived of life, liberty, or property without due process of law. This provision was originally conceived as a protection against government interference with our most fundamental rights. The clause secured this protection by preventing the government from interfering with those rights absent appropriate procedural safeguards. It was not conceived as a provision by which the government could define or redefine the scope or substance of a person's property or liberty rights. Yet that is precisely how the *Dred Scott* court used it. Chief Justice Taney read the clause not only to create a substantive constitutional right to treat slaves as property, but also to require free states and territories to recognize this right. In so doing, the *Dred Scott* court relied on a dubious notion of due process divorced from the Constitution's text to create a supposed "right" to spread slavery into territories that had previously been free.

Although no judge today would support the policy result in *Dred Scott*, its method of reading the due process clause as a source of new substantive rights remains in use. This method is often justified on the grounds that the rights they identify serve positive and beneficent ends, but these ends do not justify the means. I do not doubt the good intentions or beneficence of those who support this approach, but even results that everyone would agree are desirable do not justify judges departing from the Constitution so that they, rather than legislators, can make our policy. *Dred Scott* is evidence that this method of judging is dangerous and a clear violation of the structural separation of powers that protects our democracy. The good intentions of those who use this method today do not change that, nor do they protect against the method's abuse tomorrow. What is to be done when we observe our Constitution being used in such a way, even for well-intentioned reasons?

Lincoln was acutely aware that policymaking, including policymaking by judges, succeeds only to the extent that citizens permit it. In his "House Divided" speech, he described proslavery forces and government initiatives such as the Kansas-Nebraska Act working hand in hand to educate and mold public opinion—at least Northern public opinion—not to care whether slavery is voted down or voted up. Lincoln knew that the proponents of slavery could only succeed in imposing the policies they wanted if they lulled the public into indifference about their importance or distracted it with palliations and lullaby arguments. As he explained after *Dred Scott* declared that Congress could not prohibit slavery in the territories, "[W]e may, ere long, see . . . another Supreme Court decision, declaring that the Constitution of the United States does not permit a *state* to exclude slavery from its limits. And this may especially be expected if the doctrine of 'care not whether slavery be voted *down* or voted *up*,' shall gain upon the public mind sufficiently to give promise that such a decision can be maintained when made."[14]

In the end, our house was not divided by slavery, because Lincoln and his countrymen refused to stand by while slavery expanded and the court prepared to take *Dred Scott* a step further. Although the cost of this victory was great—a brutal civil war and over 600,000 dead (some say as many as 750,000 dead)—Lincoln and his generation turned back a mortal threat to our democracy by opposing efforts to convince the public not to care about the question of slavery.[15] Lincoln, joined by countless soldiers and citizens, put their lives on the line to show that they cared indeed, and cared very much. In so doing they taught us that our democracy, our government by consent, can succeed only to the extent that each of us is committed to holding our leaders, all of us, to the task of defending the liberties that our government exists to protect.

As new challenges confront us today, we all, as citizens of this democratic republic, have a duty to live up to the example of our forebearers and ensure that the principles on which our nation was founded continue to endure. When Lincoln dedicated the cemetery at Gettysburg, he famously eulogized the fallen soldiers by stating, "The world will little note, nor long remember what we say here, but it can never forget what they did here."[16] The world may not long remember my grandparents' words of wisdom or what we say. Indeed, even Lincoln's words, with time, may fade into the recesses of history or be lost in the flack of revisionism, but his actions, and those of many small and often anonymous heroes, will live on in the liberty that they preserved for us. What I ask is, What will we be said to have preserved for those who come after us? As proud citizens of this country and descendants of its legacy, with all its difficulties and contradictions, we are part of something far greater than ourselves, far greater than our wants, and far greater than our self-interest. Like those who fought at Gettysburg, we are duty-bound to carry the torch of liberty in our time, to defend it from modern attack, and to preserve it for our children and for their children.

Lincoln said it best: "It is for us the living, rather, to be dedicated here to the unfinished work which they who fought here have thus far so nobly advanced." I encourage all students of Lincoln to rededicate themselves to the principles of liberty that the framers drew upon to found our country, that Lincoln relied upon to end slavery and save the Union, and that we must now draw upon again to preserve and defend the freedoms for which the heroes of our past have given "the last full measure."[17]

Notes

1. Abraham Lincoln, "'A House Divided': Speech at Springfield, Illinois" (June 16, 1858), *Collected Works of Abraham Lincoln,* ed. Roy P. Basler, 8 vols. plus index (New Brunswick, NJ: Rutgers University Press, 1953), 2:467. Hereinafter cited as *CW;* emphases in original unless otherwise noted.

2. Abraham Lincoln, "Speech at Peoria, Illinois" (October 16, 1854), in *CW,* 2:255.

3. Robert W. Johannsen, *Stephen A. Douglas* (New York: Oxford University Press, 1973), 421, 426, and 431, and Lincoln, "'A House Divided,'" 2:462.

4. Lincoln, "Speech at Peoria, Illinois," 2:265–66.

5. Ibid., 2:266.

6. Lincoln, "'A House Divided,'" 2:461–62.

7. Abraham Lincoln, "Fragment on the Dred Scott Case" [January 1857?], in *CW,* 2:388.

8. See Abraham Lincoln, "To Joshua F. Speed" (August 24, 1855) in *CW,* 2:323: "How can any one who abhors the oppression of negroes, be in favor of degrading classes of white people? Our progress in degeneracy appears to me to be pretty rapid. As a nation, we began by declaring that 'all men are created equal.' We now practically read it 'all men are created equal, except negroes.' When the Know-Nothings get control, it will read 'all men are created equal, except negroes, and foreigners, and catholics.' When it comes to this I should prefer emigrating to some country where they make no pretence [sic] of loving liberty—to Russia, for instance, where despotism can be taken pure, and without the base alloy of hypocracy [sic]."

9. Abraham Lincoln, "Speech at Springfield, Illinois" (June 26, 1857), in *CW,* 2:405.

10. Martin Luther King Jr., "I Have a Dream" (August 28, 1963), in *I Have*

A Dream: Writings and Speeches That Changed the World, ed. James M. Washington (San Francisco: HarperSanFrancisco, 1992), 102.

11. Lincoln, "Speech at Peoria, Illinois," 2:255.

12. Lincoln, "Speech at Springfield, Illinois," 2:398–410.

13. Alexander Hamilton, *The Federalist Papers,* ed. Clinton Rossiter (New York: Penguin, 1999), essay no. 78, 464.

14. Lincoln, "'A House Divided,'" 2:467.

15. Guy Gugliotta, "New Estimate Raises Civil War Death Toll," *New York Times* (April 3, 2012), D1, citing J. David Hacker, "A Census-Based Count of the Civil War Dead," *Civil War History*, vol. 57, no. 4 (December 2011), 307–48.

16. Abraham Lincoln, "Address Delivered at the Dedication of the Cemetery at Gettysburg" (November 19, 1863), in *CW*, 7:23.

17. Ibid.

Part I

Lincoln's Character

1

"The Great Invention of the World"

Lincoln and Literature

Fred Kaplan

In February 1859 Abraham Lincoln presented a lecture on "discoveries and inventions" at Illinois College, in Jacksonville, one of the earliest sites of higher education in the state. Lincoln, as is well known, never received formal education even to the level of secondary school.[1] He was now attempting for the second time to elucidate a subject with wide ramifications that had been of interest to him for much of his life. He was addressing a relatively sophisticated audience, the Phi Alpha Society. Lincoln's first effort at a lecture on "discoveries and inventions" had been presented to the Young Men's Association of Bloomington in April 1858.[2] It failed dismally to say much of interest on the subject or even to approach the core of Lincoln's fascination with human creativity and its role in the development of Western civilization. Probably the general nature of the audience in Bloomington had little to do with Lincoln's conceptual failure in the April version of the lecture. In one of his least inspired moments, he had determined to use the Bible as the source for instances of invention and for the chronology of progress that his scenario required. Probably some members of his April 1858 audience were puzzled or even alienated by the notion that the Bible was an adequate, let alone accurate, source for a supposedly rational account of the progress of civilization as represented by improvements over millennia in technological sophistication. The biblical fundamentalists in the audience may have been equally and probably more emotionally discomfited by an analysis that treated the Bible as if it were only a source book for historical information.[3]

Lincoln discarded the April 1858 lecture. Though the February 1859 lecture has the same title, it's a newly conceptualized treatment of the same subject. In it the Bible plays no role. It reflects, as the April 1858 lecture does not, Lincoln's life-long concern with what he considers the primal and causative invention that has made Western civilization what it is. That mother of all inventions is writing. Without it, the idea of "progress," central to Lincoln's and his nineteenth-century contemporaries' Whig view of history, would not even have been conceivable.[4]

Lincoln made it a point to distinguish speech from writing. "Speech alone," he observed, "valuable as it ever has been, and is, has not advanced the condition of the world much." This is a noteworthy view for a man whose achievement was seen, during his lifetime and especially thereafter, to be based on his oratory rather than on the writing process that created the words he spoke. And this of course is the Lincoln who had the previous summer participated in a series of oral performances with Stephen Douglas that pushed speech and the speakers to the limit. Douglas devoted each presentation mostly to a repetition of his main argument rather than to its development or to a direct response to Lincoln. The very format that the candidates had agreed to did not allow for the give-and-take, especially rebuttal, associated with formal debates. I doubt that the Lincoln-Douglas Debates "advanced the condition of the world much." They generated a great deal of heat but little light. They did, of course, advance Lincoln's reputation among the constituency that soon elected him to the presidency.[5]

In making this distinction between speaking and writing, Lincoln was speaking of speech in the general sense: oral utterance of every sort. If pressed, it's likely he would have made the qualification that those special instances of speech that are the oral presentation of a written text qualify not as speech but as writing. For example, dramatic performances on the stage—an actor reciting a Shakespeare soliloquy—do not exemplify the power of speech but the power of writing.

Lincoln the reader and Lincoln the writer had thought carefully about the role of the written language in his own life and in civilization in general. The primal language acts of his legal and political careers were not oral presentations—they were acts of writing, the creation of carefully crafted and revised texts, often but not always for oral presentation and then publication. It isn't much of a stretch to think of Lincoln as an essayist, since the tools and practices he brought to his art were those of a writer and his concern with writing on the practical and philosophical level distinguish him from every other president. He never wanted to speak in public without a written text. What is writing, he asks in his lecture on "discoveries and inventions," and why has it been and continued to be so important to our civilization? "*Writing*," he answers, is "the art of communicating thoughts to the mind, through the eye." It "is the great invention of the world. Great in the astonishing range of analysis and combination which necessarily underlies the most crude and general conception of it—great, very great in enabling us to converse with the dead, the absent, and the unborn, at all distances of time and of space; and great, not only in its direct benefits, but greatest help, to all other inventions. . . . It's [*sic*] utility may be conceived, by the reflection that, to *it* we owe everything which distinguishes us from savages. Take it from us, and the Bible, all history, all science, all government, all commerce, and nearly all social intercourse go with it."[6]

Like most avid and sensitive readers, Lincoln had been conversing with "the dead" and "the absent" from the moment he learned to read. What he read shaped his sensibility, his sense of himself, his worldview (particularly his view of human nature), and especially his language. And for Lincoln, as for most writers, reading literature and creating literature were inseparable.[7] Not surprisingly, there is no one-to-one formulaic connection between Lincoln's reading and any particular political position or philosophical view that he held. There are, though, thematic connections strong enough to see the influence of certain writers in broad political and philosophical terms, which is what I will concentrate on and selectively survey in this essay.

My argument takes its stand on the level of sensibility and worldview, of the impact that Lincoln's reading had on the way he experienced the world and on his basic values. I need not rehearse in full detail the particulars of Lincoln's early reading except to emphasize the importance to the formation of his sensibility and values of Thomas Dilworth's *New Guide to the English Tongue,* popularly known as *Dilworth's Speller.* This was a widely reprinted textbook first published in London in 1740. It provided him with his introduction, other than the Bible, to the power of the written word. Like every British and American textbook in the eighteenth and nineteenth centuries, this *New Guide to the English Tongue* also taught Protestant theology and moral behavior. Its substance is inseparable from its pedagogy. The purpose of literacy was to advance the teaching of religious, moral, and civic value.

For such textbooks, the literature of most value was wisdom literature: the synthesis of language, imagination, and literary devices that taught one how to live as a good and theologically correct Christian.[8]

Dilworth's Speller was a help and a challenge, a formative book whose message influenced Lincoln selectively. Some of the language as language, and its lessons, entered deeply into him. The lessons became touchstones of his temperament and memory, not because they formed him but because they were there as guideposts in his formative years. Dilworth gave him permission, so to speak, to transcend the limits of his frontier community. "It is a commendable thing," Lincoln read, "for a boy to apply his mind to the study of letters; they will be always useful to him; they will procure him the favor and love of good men, which those that are wise value more than riches and pleasure." Dilworth gave the highest value to reading as a repository of social and emotional utility, words of wisdom and words for advancement. Dilworth's selections reinforced the values of Christian homes and of Protestant due diligence. Learning to read and learning moral conduct were one and the same. Since children needed to have no doubt about man's position on earth, Dilworth highlighted that "by the Fall of Adam from that glorious and happy state, wherein he was created, the Divine image in [man's] Mind is quite changed and altered, and he, who was created but a little inferior to the Angels above, is now made but little superior to the Angels below." The phrase, in a significantly altered form, stayed strongly enough in Lincoln's memory to emerge eventually as an expression of post-Calvinist appeal to "the better angels of our nature."[9]

Some of the statements of common wisdom in Dilworth represented values that the adult Lincoln held. For example, it is a short distance from Dilworth's expression of the common wisdom about obedience to Lincoln's adult view. "Obedience comprehendith the whole duty of man," Dilworth writes, "both towards God, his neighbor, and himself; we should therefore let it be engraven on our hearts, that we may be useful in the common-wealth, and loyal to our magistrates." Lincoln was continuously to give highest priority to his duty to the law, as embodied in the Constitution, and to the preservation of the commonwealth. Obedience to the magistrates became the guiding pole of his public life. More or less, he walked in the paths of such communal piety always, except in regard to Christian theology, though even there Dilworth's language remained part of him. Dilworth's Christian and biblical language existed for Lincoln independent of any particular theological beliefs, of which he had few if any. But, as president, he could draw on the values Dilworth conveyed to reinforce and appeal to a common bond in a language and a reference frame that most Americans shared.

As an economic moralist, Dilworth urged boys like Abraham to take the busy ants as their model: "For in their mouths we see them carry home / A stock for winter, which they know must come." And, Dilworth writes, "personal merit is all a man can call his own. Whoever strictly adheres to honesty and truth, and leads a regular and virtuous life, is more truly noble than a debauched abandoned profligate, were he descended from the most illustrious family." Lincoln's private life and his public image merged as an exemplification of the maxim. "Honest Abe" emerged as a fulfillment of this widely held ideal. Better an honest than a clever politician. And Lincoln's life became an embodiment of a widely held economic ideal that Dilworth neatly expressed: "Trade is so noble a master that it is willing to entertain all mankind in its service; and has such a variety of employments adapted to every capacity, that all, but the lazy, may support at least, if not enrich themselves." In search of vocation, Lincoln sampled a variety of employments. In the main, he became a lawyer-businessman, a frugal lender rather than a borrower, who believed that free labor was man's supreme self-definition and that all capital resulted from the sweat of the physical and mental brow. Dilworth's lessons and language, an expression of his culture's values, which were fed to Lincoln from other sources as well, became a part of his selfhood.[10]

Early on, Lincoln got into his hands three books that influenced him considerably: Aesop's fables, John Bunyan's seventeenth-century Puritan allegory *Pilgrim's Progress,* and Daniel Defoe's *Robinson Crusoe. Pilgrim's Progress* was received by Lincoln's Protestant culture much like the Bible, providing moral guidance through what it said and how it said it. And the language was as important as the substance. Its sonorous, intricate sentences embodied the power of words to transcend the ordinary, to raise the moment and the message to higher truths. *Pilgrim's Progress* exposed Lincoln to elevated writing, the weaving together of sound, rhythm, and imagistic language for special occasions, for heightened moments that emphasized the extraordinary. Lincoln seems not to have taken to heart the underlying theology. But the story of a young man struggling on his journey toward a higher life could readily be adapted to his own secular version, particularly how to find a path out of the limitations of the world into which he had been born. *Pilgrim's Progress* could be read as a story about upward mobility.

Robinson Crusoe apparently riveted him: he and his contemporaries identified their own frontier world with the shipwrecked Crusoe's struggle against isolation and adversity. It was a seminal story for dissenting outsiders, separated from the mainstream of American and English polite culture. They saw in Crusoe's survival the triumph of their fundamentalism and their code of self-sufficiency. Crusoe helped himself in order to be helped by God; so did they. Crusoe defeated primitive savages and found subsistence in a primitive world; so did they. It was a culturally confirming story about the superiority of the Protestant worldview and work ethic. Like *Pilgrim's Progress*, *Robinson Crusoe* was read as a didactic book with a moral purpose. A variant of a comment by Crusoe resurfaced years later in one of Lincoln's two most famous compositions: "I ought to leave them," Defoe's hero says, "to the justice of God, who is the Governor of Nations, and knows how, by national punishments to make a just retribution for the national offenses and to bring public judgments upon those who offend him in a public manner by such ways as best please him." When a nation commits offenses, God will make a "just retribution" in his inscrutable way. Lincoln would suggest as much in his Second Inaugural Address: "If we are to suppose that American slavery is one of those offences."[11]

And it was seen as one of America's offenses in two books that the young Lincoln absorbed, William Grimshaw's *History of the United States from their First Settlement as Colonies to the Cession of Florida in Eighteen Hundred and Twenty-One* and James Riley's *An Authentic Narrative of the Loss of the American Brig Commerce, Wrecked on the Western Coast of Africa, In the Month of August, 1816, with an Account of the Sufferings of the Surviving Officers and Crew, Who Were Enslaved by the Wandering Arabs, On the African Desert; and Observations Historical, Geographical, and Made During the Travels of the Author, While a Slave to the Arabs, and in the Empire of Morocco*. Grimshaw reminded readers that the United States had been founded on two primal sins, the appropriation of the land from its native inhabitants and the importation of slaves. Grimshaw believed slavery an embodiment of human greed, incompatible with the humanitarian values of the nation best represented in the claim of universal equality in the Declaration of Independence. "What a climax of human cupidity and turpitude," he wrote, when the Dutch first brought slaves to Virginia, which by 1820 had resulted in a population of over a million and a half black slaves, mainly in the Southern states. "Since the middle of the last century," Lincoln read, "expanded minds have been, with slow gradations, promoting the decrease of slavery in North America" which would eventually remove "the fetters, which are no less alarming to the master, than galling to the slave." He expected that American Negroes eventually would join other "free people of color" in Sierra Leone. Like Jefferson, whom he refers to as a model, Grimshaw believed that slavery would be abolished without bloodshed. Compromise, compensation, and moral principle would make that possible over time. Hence radical abolitionism was unnecessary. Religious antislavery views, such as those of Lincoln's parents,' would bear practical fruit. Enlightened Americans, with their country's best long-term interests at heart, would prevail by consensus, not armed struggle. This was the fountain of hope at which the young Lincoln drank. Over the next decades the water turned increasingly salty and bitter.[12]

If he needed any further fine-tuning of a sensibility that recoiled from cruelty and injustice, he found it in Riley's *An Authentic Narrative*. Riley's narrative is a harrowing true-life story that gives vivid specificity and a white man's voice to the horror of what it means to be a slave. Published in 1817 and frequently reprinted, it appealed to American curiosity about the Arab world and exotic Africa. Its account of suffering, slavery, and freedom attained against formidable obstacles was attractive both as an adventure story and as an embodiment of American ingenuity, courage, and talent. A first-person narrator, the author never forsakes his humanistic loyalty to his crew. He regularly sees the guiding hand of Providence in his survival, and he wants nothing more than to be reunited with his family, which will suffer destitution without him. In Riley his American readers saw, as if looking into a mirror, what they believed to be their own virtues.

In the book's final paragraph, the author states directly what he has been implying throughout his narrative:

My proud-spirited and free countrymen still hold a million and a half, nearly of the human species, in the most cruel bonds of slavery, many of whom are kept at hard labor and smarting under the savage lash . . . besides the miseries of hunger, thirst, imprisonment, naked-ness, and even tortures. . . . I myself have witnessed such scenes in different parts of my own country, and the bare recollection now chills my blood with horror. . . . I have now learned to look with compassion on my enslaved and oppressed fellow creatures. I will exert all my remaining faculties in endeavors to redeem the enslaved, and to shiver in pieces the rod of oppression. . . . I am far from being of opinion that they should all be emancipated immediately, and at once. I am aware that such a measure would not only prove ruinous to great numbers of my fellow-citizens, who are at present slave holders, and to whom this species of property descended as an inheritance; but that it would also turn loose . . . a race of men incapable of exercising the necessary occupations of civilized life, in such a manner as to ensure themselves an honest and comfortable subsistence; yet it is my earnest desire that such a plan should be devised . . . as will gradually, but [no?] less effectually, wither and extirpate the accursed tree of slavery, that has been suffered to take such deep root [and] put it out of the power of either the bond or the released slaves, or their posterity, ever to endanger our present or future domestic peace or political tranquility.[13]

Lincoln's sensibility, his political attitudes, his vision of justice, and his philosophical worldview had many streams that fed the main river. One of the most instrumental was the poetry that he became enamored of and immersed himself in. Beginning in 1821, he became an eager reader of poetry. By 1825, at the age of sixteen, he began to read regularly Thomas Gray, Alexander Pope, John Milton, and Shakespeare. Thirty tightly printed pages of selections from Shakespeare's histories and tragedies were printed in William Scott's *Lessons in Elocution, Or, a Selection of Pieces, In Prose And Verse* that Lincoln's stepmother brought into the household. They revealed to him a world of literary brilliance and insight into human character of which he had been only vaguely aware. Scott's anthology and Lindley Murray's *The English Reader* introduced him to the British literary canon. Both anthologies assumed the basics of literacy had been mastered. Since their young readers had already been inculcated in Christian virtue, much of the moral pedagogy could be implicit. Scott placed emphasis on reading aloud, a practice that Lincoln had already adopted. From the start, reading seemed to him an aspect of oral performance, the words enunciated in the theater of his own head or aloud to himself or to family and schoolmates. Public recitation as a teaching device emphasized the connection. Such repetition facilitated comprehension and promoted memorization. Lincoln developed an anthology of the mind, whether or not he had the actual book in hand.

"My mind is like a piece of steel," he later remarked, "very hard to scratch anything on it and almost impossible after you get it there to rub it out."[14]

For the first time, he found combinations of language and meaning that provided support for the emergence of his own ideas on what were to be the major concerns of his adult life. Lord Mansfield's words to Parliament in 1770, "True liberty . . . can only exist when justice is equally administered," and the eighteenth-century poet William Cowper's "Indignant sentiments on . . . slavery" and race prejudice, decrying slavery in the British Empire and by implication in the United States, had to rivet an inquiring mind to the issues of his immediate world. Slavery, Cowper writes, is "most to be deplored, / human nature's broadest, foulest blot" in which "The nat'ral bond / of brotherhood is sever'd" by one "who finds his fellow guilty of a skin / Not colour'd like his own." Lincoln's reading of Demosthenes's speech to the Athenians, exhorting them to perform heroically like the men of the previous generation, became the anchor of Lincoln's emphasis on the difficulty of living up to the achievements of the heroes of the Revolutionary period. And what did he make of Scott's inclusion of Publius Scipio's speech to the Roman army and Hannibal's speech to the Carthaginian army as they are about to do battle, each spurring his soldiers on with the high rhetoric of noble purpose and the blessing of the gods? When each side believes God is on its side, how are we to ascertain whose side God is on?—that was a question Lincoln returned to in a more perilous time for himself and his country.[15]

In these anthologies he read Hugh Blair on moral philosophy, David Hume on history, Edward Gibbon on the Roman Empire, Samuel Johnson on Joseph Addison's style, Lawrence Sterne on benevolence, and Alexander Pope on the "Great Chain of Being." These authors provided the intellectual groundwork on which to advance his cautious and reasoning temperament. They were antidotes to Protestant emotionalism, which valued religious enthusiasm more than Enlightenment rationalism. "We ought to distrust our passions, even when they appear the most reasonable," one of Scott's authors declares. Such writers gave high value to intellect, language, and reason as a process of discovering and understanding the world, including human nature. Most of them denied the supernatural, within or outside scripture. Reason, logic, and evidence were the guides to truth. The widely held synthesis, shared by Lincoln, emphasized Christian ethics, classical style, and natural law. It assumed that the power that made the universe had placed in it certain "self-evident truths." There could be disagreement about some of the truths and about which to emphasize but not about their existence.[16]

Thomas Gray's most anthologized poem, "Elegy in a Country Church-yard," became one of the formative poems of Lincoln's sense of himself and his position in life. He discovered it at an age early enough to be deeply impressed. He was also old enough to feel how closely connected were its themes to his concerns about himself and what he might become. "Elegy" memorializes the failure of talent and ambition to overcome obscure birth in a society with little social mobility. It is a stoic affirmation of the likely fate of the lowborn. Lincoln saw in the country boy's obscure station and gloomy temperament a mirror image of himself. His own and his family's history was one of "homely joys and destiny obscure . . . the short and simple annals of the poor." He had reason to fear that the fate of the "rustic moralist," whom "melancholy" had marked "for her own," prophesied his own likely end. At some moments and moods, "Elegy" had to have been a haunting warning about where his ambition might lead, what its likely end might be. "The paths of glory lead but to the grave" is a finely expressed universal truism. Ambition is dangerous, all accomplishment temporary. At the same time, Lincoln believed that America provided an important variant on the universal birthright. He had no desire to avoid "the madding crowd's ignoble strife," and he strongly desired to escape the constraints of country poverty. British class rigidity underlay Gray's sense of human limitation. America offered more, Lincoln came to believe. While he embraced "Elegy's" melancholy, he did not share, as a young man, its dark stoicism. Like his young country, he had an alternative vision of class mobility and the opportunity to rise in the world.

But the writer he most fully absorbed was Shakespeare. Though some years later he apparently owned his own edition of Shakespeare, at the start he had only what Scott's selections provided. As a result, he had little familiarity with the plays themselves other than what these selections conveyed. This was likely to be an advantage to someone who read slowly and repeatedly, gifted at getting the most quality out of the least quantity. Here was a master of language, of the human situation, and of human nature to learn from. Later, when he took the opportunity to become a regular theatergoer in Washington, he rarely missed a Shakespeare production. But he readily confessed that he preferred his own readings in the theater of his mind to those of professional actors. What Shakespeare's lines sounded like, and the best way to recite them, became settled in his mind from his first exposure.

Scott's fifteen Shakespearean dialogues and soliloquies from eight plays were uniquely fitted to Lincoln's concerns. Some of them taught the pitfalls of ambition-driven pride. On that subject Cardinal Wolsey in *Henry VIII* speaks eloquently: "I charge thee, fling away ambition . . . Farewell, a long farewell to all my greatness!" The cardinal warns against ambition because "the paths of glory lead but to the grave" but also because high ambition often distorts values and endangers the well-being of society. How much ambition is appropriate and to what end was the riveting topic for an introspective, ambitious young man like Lincoln, eager to rise in the world. Shakespeare assured him that overweening ambition leads to an inevitable fall. The cardinal's fall is from the king's grace. Compliant in a system in which the king can do no wrong, he inevitably blames himself, not the king. Scott's selections on the subject, including King Henry's soliloquy from *Henry IV, Part 1*—"Uneasy lies the head that wears a crown"—and King Richard's before his final battle in *Richard III,* provided dramatic examples of what Lincoln had absorbed in his earlier textbooks, that ambition is a two-edged sword. It could be used in Christian humility, serving virtue and the larger good, or it could be a manifestation of the sin of self-glorification. And he could not have missed the point of Hotspur's boastful, incendiary speech in *Henry IV* in support of conspiratorial rebellion and honor as self-glorification. Two decades later Lincoln might have heard Hotspur in the voices of the secessionists.[17]

Another Shakespearean monologue in Scott's anthology, Falstaff's "Soliloquy on Honor," expressed one of Lincoln's later preoccupations. It's a witty exposure of the uses and misuses of honor as a rationale for action. The portly knight, concluding that honor cannot preserve what he most values, his physical life, represents an aspect of human nature that Lincoln came to understand well. Later he made reference to and joked about his own lack of physical courage. In contrast, Henry V's exhortations at Agincourt and Othello's "Apology for his Marriage" offered examples of the Renaissance view of honor as virtue, requiring bravery, truthfulness, and self-sacrifice. By family and culture, and now by self-education, Lincoln was developing an image of himself as honorable. He had taken Washington as his most revered American historical model. Scott's selection from Joseph Addison's *Tragedy of Cato,* one of Washington's favorite plays, added a Roman hero to Lincoln's pantheon. Cato was a widely admired eighteenth-century exemplification of civic virtue. Two speeches in Addison's play, "Sempronius' Speech for War" and "Lucius' Speech for Peace," were echoed by Lincoln years later. Addison's Lucius pleads for peace: "Already have our quarrels fill'd the world / With widows and with orphans." In similar language, Lincoln proposed to "bind up the nation's wounds . . . for his widow, and his orphan."[18]

Scott provided Lincoln with three of *Hamlet*'s most trenchant soliloquies, which he memorized. They became a permanent part of his consciousness. Hamlet advises the "players" to "o'erstep not the modesty of nature" and states his criteria for effective public performance: balance, temperance, and restraint, even in the expression of passion, and a naturalistic performance style, holding "the mirror up to nature." That became Lincoln's view of how lines should be read and a play acted. Lincoln set similar standards for his own speeches. Some of them, like his Second Inaugural Address, were to be Shakespearean soliloquies of a sort. In an age when histrionic performance was the norm, his development of a naturalistic style occurred under the influence of Scott's and Murray's Shakespeare selections.

Hamlet's other two soliloquies in Scott became leitmotifs for an aspect of Lincoln's suffering: "To be or not to be" and Claudius on the murder of his brother, "Oh! My offence is rank; it smells to heaven." In two personal crises, Ann Rutledge's death and his courtship of Mary Todd, suicide had verbal presence for Lincoln in Hamlet's lines. During his presidency, Claudius's soliloquy came frequently to mind in reference to his own "offences," especially at those moments when he thought it possible the war might not be worth so much Southern and Northern blood. Was the war not also a form of self-murder, brother against brother, which, as a Southerner by birth, Lincoln could especially feel? "What if this cursed hand / Were thicker than itself with brother's blood— / Is there not rain enough . . . ?" Like Claudius, he hoped that despite the bloodshed "All may be well." And that the war continued so long seemed to Lincoln an affirmation of his tragic sense. In general, things in life tended to go badly, and Shakespearean tragedy taught acceptance and stoicism.

As a grand finale, Scott provided examples of how to use language economically and effectively by drawing from his preferred models— especially Shakespeare, Pope, Johnson, Hugh Blair, Demosthenes, and Michel de Montaigne. They stress eighteenth-century rhetorical devices such as antitheses, enumeration, interrogation, and climax. These became important elements in Lincoln's style. But his schooling in the relationship between language and human nature went much beyond such rhetorical devices. And though he never became an eloquent speaker mechanically, he did become a self-taught intellectual who could speak well and write brilliantly. No matter how powerful the appeal of bombast, moodiness, and melancholy, Lincoln found in his Enlightenment models and in Shakespeare the affirmation of his tested but enduring faith in man's reasoning as his highest faculty and in reason's power to advance good works. Two of the poetic maxims from Pope that Scott includes express the basics of Lincoln's art and mind: "True ease in writing comes from art, not chance" and "Two principles in human nature reign, / Self-love to urge, and reason to restrain." Scott included as his premier example of "the Principle Emotions and Passions" Hamlet's soliloquy, "What a piece of work is man! How noble in reason. . . ."[19]

Lincoln's little-known passion for the poetry of Robert Burns began about 1832. Widely available in Illinois by the 1830s, single-volume editions had been published in Philadelphia and New York in 1788, and multiple-volume editions began appearing in 1801. Burns's poems of love and sentiment, many of which had been set to music, were cherished by America's large Scots-Irish population. His folkloristic, storytelling poems, especially those of character and ideas, had a special appeal to Lincoln. With a New Salem friend with whom he briefly boarded, "an Educated as well as a well read man—deeply and thoroughly read in Burns and Shakespeare," he discussed Burns's humanistic genius, especially his comic and satiric sharpness, his identification with the common man, his skepticism about religion and theology, and his affirmation of personal and political liberty. In early 1865, as president, unable to attend a celebration honoring the 196th anniversary of the poet's birth, Lincoln expressed himself eloquently about how much Burns had meant to him. "I can not frame a toast to Burns. I can say nothing worthy of his generous heart and transcending genius. Thinking of what he has said, I can not say anything which seems worth saying." The tired president had the consolation not only of Shakespeare but of Burns as an inner resource, but he also appreciated how much Burns had meant to him as a young man.[20]

With his own gift for mimicry and dialect storytelling, Lincoln found Burns's language especially appealing. He recited the Scots dialect in an imi-

tative lilt that embodied its distinctiveness, delighting in both its economy
and exotic expressiveness. It was familiar to his ear: he had heard the burr
and the vocabulary in the speech of Scots-Irish immigrants in Indiana
and Illinois. So familiar was the Scots dialect in Lincoln's Illinois world
that the young Lincoln, in a letter in the *Sangamo Journal* in 1837, quoted
Burns's description of the devil, "For prey, a' holes and corners tryin'," on
the assumption that it would be understood.[21] Influenced by Burns and by
Wordsworthian currents in the general air, dialect speech appealed to him
for political reasons. Giving value to common speech affirmed the primacy
of the common man. At the same time it affirmed a communal bond, a way
for people to unite as a group. Burns's was the voice of the people, and the
Scots found in Burns their national poet. Overall, the Romantic movement
highlighted the language of ordinary people as the language of poetry, a
linguistic affirmation of the democratic values with which Lincoln identified.

The Burns that Lincoln enjoyed and identified with combined political
idealism with humanistic realism. Lincoln found a soul mate whose patriotism, his love of Scotland and the Scots people, especially their long-
standing struggle for independence, provided a corollary for Americans.
Like Americans the Scots had fought against English domination. And
Burns's emphasis on the inherent value if not the moral superiority of the
common man, whose poverty did not prevent him from being equal to a
king, seemed to Lincoln a powerful representation of his own valorization
of humanistic democracy. In Burns's poetry, political legitimacy and moral
authority arise from the consent of the governed, and those in power are
not superior as human beings to the humblest dweller in a cottage, the Scots
equivalent of the log cabin. Among Lincoln's favorites were "Tam o'Shanter,"
"The Cotter's Saturday Night," "Holy Willie's Prayer," "Willie's Wife," and
"Epistle to a Young Friend." A New Salem contemporary remembered that
when Lincoln "got possession of a Copy of Burns," he "repeated with great
Glee 'Sic a wife as willy had I wudna Gie a button for her.'" He most likely
read every poem in the volume he had in hand, including "For A' That And A'
That," with its emphasis on "honest poverty," "the man of independent mind,"
and the worldwide democratic brotherhood. And also "Here's a Health to
Them That's Awa," with its toast to the connection between literacy, free
speech, and liberty. In Burns's political rhetoric, Lincoln found a stirring
and memorable expression of his own belief in literacy, upward mobility,
respect for the common man, and democratic governance. Burns's poetry,

like all the literature Lincoln admired, did even more than that: it affirmed the connection between language and moral vision. That connection was to become Lincoln's most distinctive characteristic as a writer and as president.[22]

Despite the strength of Lincoln's commitment to Enlightenment values and its emphasis on rational analysis, Byron, the archetype of Romantic poetry, became one of his three favorite poets. Byron's elegiac Romanticism deeply moved him. When Lincoln met Ann Rutledge, he was in the process of developing his passion for Byron's poetry.[23] When, in 1835, Ann died, Lincoln's despair had Byronic resonance. For a man noted for emotional restraint, his intense misery at Ann's death reveals a sensibility immersed in Byron's poetry. Numbers of Byron's poems that express loss and despair are in language similar to descriptions by Lincoln's contemporaries of the state of his feelings at Ann's graveside. Lincoln's favorites among Byron's poems were "The Devil's Drive," "The Destruction of Sennacherib," "Darkness," *Childe Harold's Pilgrimage, The Bride of Abydos, Lara, The Corsair, Mazeppa,* and *Don Juan.* And those reported to be his favorites had to be the tip of the iceberg: editions containing these also would have had the lyric poems of *Hours of Idleness, Occasional Pieces, Hebrew Melodies, Domestic Pieces,* and probably *Satires,* including *The Vision of Judgment.* Numbers of multivolume editions, published in England and America, had been widely disseminated, even to the Western frontier, since Byron's death in 1824. The single-volume edition published in New York in 1832, edited by the Byron enthusiast Fitz-Greene Halleck, whose humorous poems also became favorites of Lincoln's and whose "beautiful lines on Burns" he praised in 1860, could have been in New Salem by autumn 1832. Joshua Speed, whom Lincoln met in 1837, told Herndon that "I do not think he had ever read much of Byron previous to my acquaintance with him."[24] He was wrong by about five years. Lincoln's attraction to Byron had little to do with Speed's influence. Byron was in the air. Byron was everyplace. And Byron provided the young Lincoln with a moral and a political touchstone for emotions and values that were already a part of his sensibility.[25]

Inevitably Lincoln found the Byron who focused attention on cultural and political issues, particularly slavery, revolution, and democracy, an ideological soul mate. These were matters he had a deep interest in. And they engaged personal and cultural concerns simultaneously. The potential for overly ambitious leaders, such as Napoleon, to become dictators frightened Lincoln, as it did Byron. Gray's depiction of the conflict between ambition and limitation in "Elegy in a Country Churchyard" reverberated anew in Byron's "The Adieu." The poet's inflection of the theme paralleled Lincoln's concern about the price to be paid for fame and its potential for good and evil. In 1860, still preoccupied with the theme, he echoed Byron and quoted Gray in reference to his "obscure" origins to one of his first biographers. And he publicly recited on at least one occasion his favorite lines about the dangers of ambition from *Childe Harold's Pilgrimage.* A colleague recalled that "in my office in 1854," when he was reentering public life, "he picked up Byron and read aloud . . . as impressively as it ever was read in the world." The passage was Byron's description of the ambition that drives "Conquerers and Kings, / Founders of sects and systems, to whom add / Sophists, Bards, Statesmen." Even the leader who leads in the name of liberation from oppression, Byron warns, cannot readily control his own impulse to command. And the ideals that inspire the overthrow of thrones and the establishment of republics have not the strength to maintain themselves against human nature's attraction to materialism, dependency, and corruption. Gore Vidal's depiction of Lincoln as a power-mad authoritarian determined to coerce into existence a strong central state has little relation to political reality and to Lincoln's political values.[26] On the contrary, Lincoln, with Byron as one of his touchstones, worried about the danger of his and any other leader's ambition. But Lincoln's awareness that his own ambition needed to be controlled by his political values was testimony to the existence of that ambition and its potential dangers. In this regard, Byron helped Lincoln with self-examination in the ongoing dialogue within himself and the ongoing tension in American history between democratic and authoritarian leadership.[27]

The exception to ambition's corrupting temptations that Byron cites was already dear to Lincoln's heart. Byron's depiction in *Childe Harold's Pilgrimage* of George Washington, "the Cincinnatus of the West," provided Lincoln with another touchstone text for his hero worship. It provided language and a model for his peroration of Washington in 1838. Byron's Washington is the poet's exception to the maxim that power corrupts. When Lincoln spoke to the Young Men's Lyceum of Springfield in January 1838, his first memorable speech, he had in mind not Byron's hope that Europe would find a Washington of its own but America's hope to preserve what Washington and his contemporaries had achieved. In the struggle that Lincoln saw in progress in the late 1830s, affirming Washington and what he stood for—reason, prudence, calmness, and dedication to liberty—would provide a guideline and a secure future for the nation: "That we improved to the last; that we remained free to the last; that, during his long sleep, we permitted no hostile foot to pass over or desecrate his resting place; shall be that which to learn the last trump shall awaken our WASHINGTON."[28]

Inevitably, as it was for Weems and Byron, the idealization of Washington was for Lincoln thematically empowering and rhetorically awkward. Byron of course is the better writer, and Lincoln's fall into the occasional strained sentences of his 1838 essay is a lapse in a learning process that later would bring such flourishes under the control of a tighter, more natural style. And Thomas Gray was to be a more important model for Lincoln in the few poems of his that survive. The Lyceum Address gave him the opportunity to hone his thoughts on the state of the nation, with Washington as the model of ultimate patriotism and wisdom. The audience was small, the occasion obscure, and the speaker irrelevant to the national debate, though Lincoln gives no sense that he thinks himself or his ideas peripheral, let alone irrelevant. The language positions itself in the first person voice of authorial self-confidence: he speaks from himself, for himself, with the voice of someone whose literary style creates the impression that he has earned the right to speak. What he says is credible because he has thought deeply, carefully, impartially, and with noble intentions, because he believes he has something important to contribute to the national discussion and because his argument is based on a combination of evidence, reason, and analysis. Lincoln's political message and his apotheosis of "the Cincinnatus of the West" in the Lyceum Address occasionally flares with the same passion with which Byron championed individual liberty and national self-determination.

But though the themes and political values are Byronic, the message is not. Byron argued for the primacy of passion in political life, especially love of liberty and hatred of tyranny. Lincoln argued for the rational expression and prudent application of the law. Context partly made the difference. Byron preached revolutionary change in Europe; Lincoln preached reinvigoration of a revolution in America that had already occurred. And Lincoln, in regard to this aspect of Byron, can be readily identified with the statement of another nineteenth-century English writer, Thomas Carlyle: "Close thy Byron, Open thy Goethe." Carlyle advised mature wisdom, not Romantic passion. Lincoln had only a modest measure of Romantic passion in him from the start, and much of it was channeled into darker currents, into melancholy and loss as a frame of mind. He expressed it in his behavior after Anne Rutledge's death.

And he was to have at least two more opportunities to express himself on the subject of Romantic love. By the mid-1840s, that aspect of Byron was behind him. Perhaps his friend Joshua Speed meant exactly that when he remarked that Lincoln "[f]orsook Byron—never Shakespear [*sic*]—& Burns." What bound him to Byron was his identification with the poet's Romantic Republicanism.[29]

To that Byron, Lincoln retained a life-long loyalty. The most widely read poet championing freedom from national oppression, Byron gave expression to Lincoln's developing political and philosophical beliefs. It was with Byron's political republicanism that Lincoln identified, and Byron's eloquent evocation of those republics that had failed had to have impressed him. Byron's warning that "religion—freedom—vengeance—what you will, / A word's enough to raise mankind to kill" surely registered in Lincoln's concerns. "I have a love for freedom too," the main character of *The Bride of Abydos* proclaims. In *Lara,* "slavery half forgets her feudal chain." The poem's hero frees "the soil-bound slaves, / Who dig no land for tyrants but their graves!" The itinerary of *Childe Harold's Pilgrimage* led Lincoln through Europe. The past and present of Venice had special meaning for Americans concerned about the fate of the American republic. In Spain, Byron dramatizes the nationalistic struggle against Napoleonic invasion and oppression. In Venice, Florence, and Rome, he valorizes centuries of republican self-rule and laments the fall of ancient city-states into decadence and tyranny. His depiction of the current state of Greece under Turkish tyranny highlighted its fall from ancient republican glory. In *Don Juan,* Byron championed the struggle to liberate Greece. What would be the American fate? Lincoln wondered. Would it go the way of the republics of the past? That possibility had struck fear into the hearts of the founding fathers. Lincoln read Byron, the champion of republics and liberty, much as John Adams and James Madison studied the history of Greece, Rome, and Europe. Why had the republics of the past failed, and how could the American experiment succeed? In that now famous Lyceum Address, Lincoln spoke in terms that made it clear that he recognized that the survival of the American republic was not a sure thing. He would bet in its favor, he assured his audience, as long as we remembered what Lincoln's Washington and Byron's Washington represented.

Lincoln found in the literature he absorbed not only ideas but experiences, not only inspiration but a measure of self-creation. The Lincoln who wrote the Gettysburg Address and his Second Inaugural Address had available to him resources of language and style that originated in the dynamic interaction between his reading and his personality. Shakespeare, Byron, Burns, the Bible, and the range of authors available to him in the anthologies of his early education helped shape his values and his vision. Personal values, political values, and cultural values were for Lincoln a continuum, as they are for most of us. These writers became his frame of reference, inseparable from his daily consciousness and his existential awareness of himself. When he told his audience at Illinois College in February 1859 that "*writing*—the art of communicating thoughts to the mind, through the eye—is the great invention of the world," he was also talking about the world within himself.[30]

Notes

1. Abraham Lincoln, "Second Lecture on Discoveries and Inventions" (February 11, 1859), in *Collected Works of Abraham Lincoln,* ed. Roy P. Basler, 8 vols. plus index (New Brunswick, NJ: Rutgers University Press, 1953), 3:356–63. Hereinafter cited as *CW;* emphases in original unless otherwise noted.

2. Abraham Lincoln, "First Lecture on Discoveries and Inventions" (April 6, 1858), in *CW,* 2:437–42.

3. Lincoln's nontheological uses of the Bible should be contrasted with Mark A. Noll's account of the importance of biblical theology during the period in *The Civil War as a Theological Crisis* (Chapel Hill: University of North Carolina Press, 2006).

4. See Daniel Walker Howe, *What Hath God Wrought: The Transformation of America, 1815–1848* (New York: Oxford University Press, 2007).

5. For the most recent account of the "debates," see Allen C. Guelzo, *Lincoln and Douglas: The Debates That Defined America* (New York: Simon & Schuster, 2008).

6. Lincoln, "Second Lecture on Discoveries and Inventions," 3:360, 361.

7. See Fred Kaplan, *Lincoln: The Biography of a Writer* (New York: Harper, 2008).

8. Thomas Dilworth, *A New Guide to the English Tongue* (Philadelphia: 1747).

9. Ibid., 129–32.

10. Ibid.

11. Louis Austin Warren, *Lincoln's Youth: Indiana Years, Seven to Twenty-One, 1816–1830* (Indianapolis: Appleton, Century, Crofts, 1959), 68–69.

12. William Grimshaw, *History of the United States from Their First Settlement as Colonies to the Cession of Florida, in Eighteen Hundred and Twenty-one*, rev. ed. (Philadelphia: John Grigg, 1826), 34–35, 300–301.

13. James Riley, *An Authentic Narrative of the Loss of the American Brig Commerce, Wrecked on the Western Coast of Africa, In the Month of August, 1816, with an Account of the Sufferings of the Surviving Officers and Crew, Who Were Enslaved by the Wandering Arabs, On the African Desert; and Observations Historical, Geographical, and Made During the Travels of the Author, While a Slave to the Arabs, and in the Empire of Morocco* (Hartford, CT: 1817), 260–61.

14. Don E. Fehrenbacher and Virginia Fehrenbacher, eds., *Recollected Words of Abraham Lincoln* (Stanford, CA: Stanford University Press, 1996), 413; Lindley Murray, *The English Reader: Or, Pieces in Prose and Poetry, Selected from the Best Writers, Designed to Assist Young Persons to Read with Propriety and Effect*, 11th Philadelphia ed. (Philadelphia: 1814); and William Scott, *Lessons in Elocution: Or, A Selection of Pieces, in Prose and Verse, for the Improvement of Youth in Reading and Speaking and Writing* (Leicester, MA: H. Brown, 1820).

15. Murray, *English Reader*, 206, 327.

16. Scott, *Lessons in Elocution*, 57.

17. Ibid., 359–77.

18. Abraham Lincoln, "Second Inaugural Address" (March 4, 1865), in *CW*, 8:333.

19. Ibid., 404.

20. Abraham Lincoln, "Memoranda on Robert Burns" (January 25, 1865), in *CW*, 8:237.

21. Abraham Lincoln, "Second Reply to James Adams" (October 18, 1837), in *CW*, 1:106.

22. Douglas L. Wilson and Rodney O. Davis, eds., *Herndon's Informants: Letters, Interviews, and Statements about Abraham Lincoln* (Urbana: University of Illinois Press, 1998), 66, 141, 145, 354–55, 420, 429.

23. Lewis Gannett, "The Ann Rutledge Story: Case Closed?," *Journal of the Abraham Lincoln Association* 31, no. 2 (Summer 2010), 21–60, provides a thorough and impressive review of the long-standing disagreement about the nature of the Rutledge-Lincoln relationship. He argues that the recent consensus (see, for example, Douglas L. Wilson, *Honor's Voice: The Transformation of Abraham Lincoln* [New York: Knopf, 1998], 118–24; Barry Schwartz, "Ann Rutledge in American Memory: Social Change and the Erosion of a Romantic Drama," *Journal of the Abraham Lincoln Association* 26 [Winter 2005], 1–27; and Michael Burlingame, *Abraham Lincoln: A Life*, 2 vols. [Baltimore: Johns Hopkins University Press, 2008], 1:97–101) is based on an overreliance on unreliable

oral evidence: "[T]he extraction of conclusions from ambiguous reminiscent material is a tricky business for storytellers of all stripes, including historians. One should be wary of the stories that oneself wants to hear." Gannett, "Ann Rutledge Story," 60.

24. Wilson and Davis, *Herndon's Informants*, 156.

25. Ibid., 21, 30, 141, 156, 383, 404, 497.

26. See Gore Vidal, *Lincoln* (New York: Random House, 1984).

27. Wilson and Davis, *Herndon's Informants*, 632.

28. Abraham Lincoln, "Address before the Young Men's Lyceum of Springfield, Illinois" (January 27, 1838), in *CW*, 1:115.

29. Wilson and Davis, *Herndon's Informants*, 30.

30. Abraham Lincoln, "Second Lecture on Discoveries and Inventions" (February 11, 1859), in *CW*, 3:360.

2

Lincoln, Shakespeare, and Tyranny

John Channing Briggs

What did Abraham Lincoln learn from William Shakespeare? The brief and still surprising answer is that he learned a good deal about tyranny. There is no readily adaptable pattern of emancipation in Shakespeare's plays. *Emancipate, emancipation, liberate,* and *liberation* are absent from his vocabulary. *Slave* appears five times, and *slavery* 135, but those instances almost never carry a meaning directly related to what became American slavery. The free Othello tells of being taken into slavery as a war captive, not as chattel. He has been liberated by a means he does not disclose. In *The Tempest,* the nobleman Ferdinand, not the servant Caliban, names his temporary servitude under Prospero's rule as slavery. Ariel is promised freedom from a contractual servitude. There is no similar liberation for that spirit or for Caliban, yet his status on the island is a blend of penal servitude, prior claims of precedence, and the possibility of freedom in his resumption of rule over the island once Prospero leaves for Milan.

For Lincoln, contrary to our expectations, Shakespeare seems to be attractive because he animates and plays out an intriguing variety of tyrannies in political and psychological spheres. The result, for Lincoln, is not a denial of the fact of slavery but a reimagination of what slavery is. The dramatist enlarges the range and meaning of tyranny so that, in Lincoln's terms, the tyrannical causes and consequences of slavery are more evident, more available to thought. In a speech in Chicago in 1858, Lincoln made the connection between slavery and tyranny adamant: slavery is "a state of oppression and tyranny unequaled in the world."[1] What Shakespeare did for Lincoln was to scatter and recollect that fact in ways that brought its truer meaning into the light.

Shakespeare's dramatic presentations of tyranny are didactic in some ways, but in others they are powerfully complex. They draw us into wondering how such tyrannies arise, what they entail, how they might be resisted or allayed, and how these processes reflect upon the human condition. Judging by Lincoln's few direct comments on the plays, it seems that his lifelong fascination with Shakespearean drama derived not so much from their didactic impact as their more subtle and probing effects, especially their power to hold the mirror up to tyranny in the human heart as well as in the political world.

Some historians have gone so far as to argue that Lincoln's interest in Shakespearean tyranny was a subconscious disclosure of a repressed inner tendency to commit tyrannical acts. His admiration for *Macbeth* and his warning in his 1838 address to the Young Men's Lyceum of Springfield against incipient tyranny in a mob-torn democracy have been taken as signs that he identified himself, unconsciously if not by design, with the lion and the eagle who would (by Lincoln's cautionary account) rise to liberate all the slaves or enslave all free men without constitutional compunction.[2] We can hypothesize with greater confidence that Lincoln's immersion in Shakespearean tragedy allowed him—through a lifetime of rereading and the witnessing of many performances—to experience and reflect upon the temptations of tyranny through the inoculating prism of great drama. Lincoln seems to have been able and willing to put himself repeatedly into the minds, characters, and psychologies of different kinds of tyrants and thereby to undergo—by sympathetic proximity and the repose of distance—the intriguing rigors of those bound up in tyranny's rigors and temptations.

Lincoln's interest in this Shakespearean experience, and the subjects it presents for contemplation, does us a continuing service as citizens of a self-governing republic in a new land. We remain vulnerable to a false optimism about our ability to keep tyranny in exile. It is part of being American to assume, against the sober opinions of the founders, that the dangers of tyranny have been defeated by our vigor and the newness of our experience, as well as our new methods—governmental, psychological, and technological—of keeping tyranny at a distance. In our commotion of activities, which amazed Alexis de Tocqueville as early as the 1840s, we are not likely to look for tyranny within. When we find tyranny anywhere, we consider it to be something external that oppresses us. We think we can identify and confine it, exorcise it, or move away from it. The spaciousness of our imagined frontier of personal and political action continues to make such tactics plausible. We have an Elba ready to imprison any home-grown Caesars and Napoleons who might arise. If that island off the coast of our normal experience is not sufficient, we think we have a remoter prison-island of isolation, a St. Helena shunned by the media.[3] If physical distance is not enough, then there is the power of the mind's willful or high-minded refusal to entertain the possibility that tyranny threatens our new order of the ages. But such thoughts and sentiments create a lethal blindness to the facts, a strange forgetfulness about the potential for tyranny in our personal and political affairs and—for us today—a tendency to stop remembering the insidious and formidable demonstrations of tyranny's power in the recent past—for example, in the history of the two totalitarian systems that almost dominated the twentieth century.

Lincoln's particular love of Shakespeare should provoke new generations to consider, as Lincoln asked his audience to consider, how the very triumph of American democracy might diminish our power to recognize tyranny, even though the prospect of tyranny haunts the American experiment. Insofar as we are successful, self-determining sovereign subjects—free persons who are in a sense kings and queens over ourselves rather than subjects of royal earthly power—the Shakespearean precedents suggest that we might *become* kingly tyrants over ourselves and others or, conversely, turn into slaves who for the sake of safety accept or even welcome tyranny's distortion of our free human natures.

Lincoln was not alone in suspecting that self-government was, and would always be, vulnerable to internal as well as external tyranny and slavery. In his Lyceum Address (1838), he focused on the idea that in a republic without vigilance, tyrants could rise without or within, regardless of region or level of enlightenment. Long before the Civil War, of course, many Americans believed that the institution of slavery contributed to this double bind. Free yet imperfect human beings in the North, including those whites who had fled the slave culture of the South, were in Lincoln's unusual view as susceptible to tyranny as those whose ways they rejected and condemned. The ruinous temptations of tyrannous rule over human beings owned as property were part of the lore of the age. Yet in the antebellum era, the prospect of acquiring good farming land in the new territories was also a great and subtly tantalizing invitation to tyranny. It presented millions of free farmers who had no interest in owning slaves with a temptation far beyond ordinary experience: would they exercise their acquisitive desires in a manner that was indifferent as to whether the land around their new farms became slave or free?

One does not have to rely upon Tocqueville's insights and observations to see such temptations at work in America's new order of the ages. Ordinary citizens, as Lincoln argued in his 1858 debates with Douglas, needed to be vigilant over themselves. The temptations for tyrannical domination were *deceptively* powerful. Douglas's effort to resolve the slavery issue by means of holding seemingly innocuous and respectable local votes—justified by the "great doctrine of popular sovereignty"—threatened, by Lincoln's lights, the soul and fabric of the republic because it ignored that power. An indiscriminate belief in popular sovereignty, he argued, would encourage the adherents of that doctrine to rationalize, in the name of free and equal suffrage for the new territories, a careless hunger for new land. As he subtly reminded farmers in his Milwaukee Speech of 1859, the availability of land at home and especially in the territories encouraged wasteful farming unless farmers adopted wise self-government as they plowed. With the advent of steam plows and other means of planting far more ground, careless farmers were especially prone to ignoring and distorting, as slave-holders did, principles of the Declaration that had informed the birth and development of the American republic.[4]

What Lincoln found most compelling in Shakespeare, then, was the *personal* side of the tyrant as well as the tyrant's insidious influence over others. Lincoln's opposition to dueling, which was partly the product of his own close call as a young politician in a matter of dubious stakes, is an interesting case in point. In a region that had declared such altercations illegal, he had answered the challenge thrown down by James Shields, who had demanded satisfaction for having endured Lincoln's anonymously published satires on Shields's ambitions for office. Although the fight never took place, and indeed became the humorous subject of one of Lincoln's letters to Joshua Speed, it was for Lincoln a painful memory.[5] The temptation to ignore the laws and settle a personal score with deadly weapons—that is, tyrannically, with absolute yet petty finality, as though one's personal honor were the center of all—was to Lincoln, in retrospect, a dangerous farce. Years later, when he wrote to a Union officer charged with preparing for a duel, he invoked Shakespeare's Polonius speaking to his son Laertes—with a twist. Quarrels there will be, and once begun they might have to be pursued with rigor.

But the dueling impulse, once indulged by a high-minded man, distorts the duelist's nature, reducing his pursuit of honor to a rivalry with an angry dog:

> The advice of a father to his son "Beware of entrance to a quarrel, but being in, bear it that the opposed may beware of thee," is good, and yet not the best. Quarrel not at all. No man resolved to make the most of himself, can spare time for personal contention. Still less can he afford to take all the consequences, including the vitiating of his temper, and the loss of self-control. . . . Better give your path to a dog, than be bitten by him in contesting for the right. Even killing the dog would not cure the bite.[6]

Written three days after Lincoln had seen Shakespeare's greatest tyrant in *Macbeth* on a Washington stage, the letter directs the young man to contemplate the limitless scope and pettiness of vengeful anger.[7] Macbeth's temper is vitiated by a desire for vindication that is doubly insidious because it seems not at first to depend upon anger. As he indulges the witches' promise of absolute power, Macbeth fights with all his rivals. In the tormented conviction that he is entitled to rule over all, his anger defends his entitlement, crushing those who stand in his way.

The capacity to respond to injustice in matters great or small is necessary for the perpetuation of a free republic. But the history of revolutions (in Lincoln's time, most notably the French Revolution, which had ended with Napoleon's dictatorial rule) had shown that rebellion did not guarantee freedom. It often had a way of creating greater tyranny. Concerning this reversal of expectations, Shakespeare offers magnificent and disturbing precedents. We see that the wish to be absolutely free is the tyrant's wish too.

Tyrant-tempting moments of apparent victory over tyranny were plentiful in Lincoln's political history, though the decisions those moments generated now often seem relatively inconsequential or self-evident. They arose, for instance, immediately after the Republican political victory in 1860; in the deliberations before the war over defending Fort Sumter; in the military administrations of zealous Union victors (John C. Frémont and others); in the deliberations over whether, when, and how to issue the Emancipation Proclamation; and in the temptation to act vengefully at the time of the delivery of the Second Inaugural Address. In all these, it could be argued, a free people faced the danger of overreaching, of fatally injuring the prospects of the free republic in the act of preserving it. Debate persists over the degree of Lincoln's success at these moments of vertiginous suspense (his measured suspension of habeas corpus being a prime topic of debate), but there is less disagreement over the general tenor of his responses. His oratorical and political wisdom joined justice and temperance, aspiration and restraint.[8]

In this, Lincoln's achievement was arguably Shakespearean because of what it anticipated and avoided. He seems to have been capable of identifying with and yet separating himself from the mind of the tyrant. In his last days, when he read to his cabinet Macbeth's "Sleep no more" speech in Act 2, Scene 2, about the embattled victor's tormented sleep, he was speaking in harmony with that pattern.[9] When he performed and meditated upon the words of that repellent, weirdly attractive exemplar of a king made sleepless by his inner and outer civil broils, what better literary precedent could there have been for raising and purging the nightmares of his office, acknowledging and distancing himself from the nightmare of Macbeth's tyranny? And what better place in early 1865 to read the country's nightmarish recognition of the mutual horrors of the Civil War and the growing temptation to suppress that knowledge with violence in the name of vengeance?

Do these claims really matter? Can one seriously entertain the possibility—so far from those days and in the light of the magnitude of the Union's victory—that Lincoln sympathized with and yet overcame such temptations, and with Shakespearean assistance? Even if one grants that Lincoln thought a great deal about tyranny and read his Shakespeare, why must one connect the one to the other? Lincoln had grown up in a republic where monarchy was assumed to be despotism and tyranny. With some exceptions, the revolutionary generation and their successors were habitually suspicious of all forms of domination. A failure of the American rebellion against royal rule, it was widely assumed in North and South, would have been an abandonment of the greatest experiment in self-government, a failure that would have damaged the prospects for self-government for all of mankind. We don't need to look to Shakespeare to take in what Lincoln means when he alludes to tyranny in this generalizing light. He was speaking in large measure from within the heritage of the founders. For him, chattel slavery was the embodiment of a tyranny menacing all, especially those who do not see the possibility of their own enslavement. For others, of course, the founders' legacy led to different conclusions. Slave-holders and their sympathizers and enablers—and most notoriously John Wilkes Booth—resisted what they believed was federal dictatorship over the states' institutions, which they identified with the tyranny Cato fought against when he resisted the rule of Julius Caesar.[10] Lincoln had himself invoked Caesar's name in his warning about tyranny in the Lyceum Address. Whichever side one was on in the Civil War era, who needed Shakespeare to tell him these things?

Lincoln's writings about tyranny send us back to Shakespeare because Lincoln's lifelong preoccupation with crucial plays gave him ways to experience and contemplate the causes and consequences of tyranny. Most notably they open ways of understanding tyranny as a profoundly human phenomenon as well as a manifestation of monstrous potentialities. Shakespeare's plays were the places Lincoln would have been most likely to undergo and study that phenomenon. Thus by his own testimony he was more interested in the tormented brother-murderer Claudius than in Hamlet, more concerned with the conscience-stricken usurper Macbeth than with Romeo, more intrigued with the devilishly devious and ruthless dream-haunted climber Richard III than with the honest Brutus who fights against Caesar. In his letter to the actor James Hackett, Lincoln singled out his interest in "Lear, Richard Third, Henry Eighth, Hamlet, and especially Macbeth." "I think nothing equals Macbeth," he wrote. "It is wonderful."[11] As playgoer and reader, he preferred to immerse himself in these tyrants' fascinating, repellent mixtures of virtue and viciousness.

The plays Lincoln mentioned in his list for Hackett are all works about deposition and usurpation within the human soul as well as within kingdoms. They take place in political and psychological settings distant from us, but their treatments of the complexities of tyranny seem to have been much of the reason for their anachronistic popularity in antebellum America: an ardently democratic polity haunted by its predemocratic, hierarchical heritage. The famous family of the Booths, some of them named after Roman heroes, were popular actors of Shakespeare's dramas of power.

Performances that manifested and probed the grand and baleful possibilities of inner and outer experience would have been especially attractive in a society that had enthusiastically yet defectively adopted the ideals of democratic life. Antebellum audiences would have been more than casually familiar with realms of tyrannical experience in the King James Bible and Milton's *Paradise Lost*. They would have had a good chance of undergoing, by imaginative displacement, the deeper currents in Shakespeare's playing out of tyrannical impulses. In other words, they would have been more likely than modern audiences to recoil from and yet identify with Macbeth himself.[12]

Would exposure to Shakespeare's powerful dramas of tyranny have been enough to remind democratic citizens of its dangers? Lincoln's Lyceum Address argued that the dangerous potentialities of tyranny were going unrecognized. Something more than artful drama was clearly needed. Only a rejuvenated "reverence for the law," he argued, could draw together political friends capable of resisting tyranny and saving the mob-torn republic from the false belief that liberty was enough. But could reverence for the law alone be enough to resist tyranny's threat?

If Lincoln looked to Shakespeare's plays to find encouragement for revering the law, he would have found discouragement at least as much as inspiration. Shakespearean kings rule by a kind of law, but they are frequently notorious and impressive rulers by fiat. In the history plays, their legitimacy is repeatedly and unavoidably muddied by substantial rival claims to the throne. In *Macbeth, Lear,* and *Hamlet,* claims to power are clouded by legitimate rivalry, usurpation, or madness. The Roman plays all involve civil war that undermines the political legitimacy of rulers, insurgents, and settled law. The rule of law in the comedies and problem plays is at best a transient premise for extralegal maneuvering; playmaker characters frequently scheme in secret to turn events toward their own ends. Empowered by poetic license, friars interfere with law and politics (as in *Romeo and Juliet, Much Ado about Nothing,* and *Measure for Measure*), a woman disguised as a lawyer alters the course of a trial (*The Merchant of Venice*), a duke uses magical trances to reconcile warring cities (*The Tempest*), and a prince in the garb of a highwayman (Prince Hal)—to our great satisfaction—robs the robber Falstaff and by extension his own crown-robbing father (*Henry IV, Part I*). In the very construction of almost all the plays, we see law poetically defied, subverted, or suspended for the sake of autocratic and artistic ends. If there is Providence at work, it would seem to serve ends above or below the law. From this evidence of transgression, Lincoln and his audiences would seem to have found no basis for reverence of the law.

Yet it seems presumptuous to assume that Shakespeare's portraits of tyrants did not speak to Americans and their concerns for self-government and the rule of law, as they pushed further into the New World, taking possession of lands as far as they could reach. The temptation to become tyrannous, if it were not already acted upon, would not have been far from a settler's heart. Shakespeare's plays, at least the ones Lincoln mentions, would have been especially valuable manifestations of the enlargement, destruction, and tempering of tyrannical aspirations.

Shakespeare offered more than cathartic indulgence: the plays about tyranny fostered speculation about the human origins of tyranny and hence how it might be averted rather than merely feared or repressed, by being feelingly understood. In that function, Shakespeare's tyrants would have been object lessons of intriguing complexity, manifestations of the range of human possibilities of salvation and perdition. In their grand and problematic dimensions, two things stand out with particular relevance to Lincoln's world. First, the plays present characters in richly layered dramas of *choosing*. Freedom of choice matters. We see the potential for self-rule and for wayward courses, and for the playing out of forces that overwhelm or transform human character. Amid forces beyond its control, that character's royal choosing amply displays a capacity for purposeful governing. Conversely it is capable of amplifying baleful forces.

Shakespeare's tyrannical protagonists exercise and entrap themselves in their choices. Richard III sees with amazing clarity into the weaknesses of his brother's decadent court. His sardonic wit limps artfully and self-knowingly across the stage. He hacks his way against all odds, often with ingenious persuasion, to the throne. He continually exercises a breathtaking if perverse freedom to reflect upon and justify his embittered self as he pursues his horrifying ends. As he loses the last of his control over events, his dream before the ultimate battle opens him momentarily to something like sympathy for his most innocent victims, the two princes—a sympathy he ponders and rejects before rushing into battle and his confrontation with death. We see, beyond expectation, Richard's capacity to choose good and ill in the rank flourishing of his malevolence.[13]

A variation of this pattern is of course Lincoln's favorite play, *Macbeth*, whose strangely active conscience keeps reminding Macbeth (and us) of his deeper human dimensions even as he permits it to drive him to worse crimes. The display repels us but not without drawing us into the tormented soul of a man who is caught up in a horror at his own deeds, a man who is recurrently overcome by the temptation to end that horror by eliminating those who remind him of what he has done.

Claudius, the murderer of King Hamlet, is perhaps the greatest of these examples of tyrants capable of self-knowledge and choice, and the one who comes closest to embodying the body politic of the American antebellum republic. He is the one who comes closest, in the speech Lincoln identified as superior to Hamlet's famous "To be or not to be," to using his powers to see his way to redemption from a crime that resembles the enslavement of one's fellow man:

> O my offense is rank, it smells to heaven!
> It hath the primal eldest curse upon't;
> A brother's murther. Pray can I not.[14]

In the following lines Claudius sees that he is torn between two positions: his conviction that he cannot pray because his crime is too terrible to be forgiven and his belief that divine forgiveness is capable of overcoming any degree of guilt if he can persist in his prayer. His soliloquy is a profound inner debate, a deliberation over what he should do in good conscience:

> Whereto serves mercy
> But to confront the visage of offense?[15]

Such a prayer, he says, can keep him from falling and even pardon him if he falls. But he knows his guilt is too deep for such a simple resolution. He retains the rewards of his crime, much as a slave-owner—or an antebellum Northern legislator, for that matter—benefits from the labor of millions of enslaved persons according to law. Claudius knows his desire for mercy is deeply hypocritical, a desire for something seemingly beyond his power to ask for free and clear. How can he give up what seems to make him what he is?

> I am still possess'd
> Of those effects for which I did the murther,
> My crown, mine own ambition, and my queen.[16]

But in Shakespeare's remarkable presentation of Claudius's aspiring guilt, this is not the full dilemma or the entire range of choice. Claudius's probing vacillations hold some promise. He keeps probing for merciful openings, and when they close he probes again, finally kneeling in prayer. He describes himself as a "limed soul, that struggling to be free / Art more engaged" with guilt, *and yet* to the speech's end he remains capable of calling on the help of angels and his own effort to repent. It is an important fact that in the logic of the drama his speech does not end. He persists on his knees as we begin to listen to Hamlet. Hamlet observes, as we do, that in the king's prayer is some "relish of salvation."[17] Hamlet will not kill him at a time when judgment might be persuaded.

Lincoln's explicit preference for Claudius's speech suggests that for him it spoke beyond itself, touching his imagination with its evocation of the self-binding, contradictory condition of the slave-holding republic. Most interestingly, in Claudius's seeming paralysis are clues to help us understand Lincoln's antebellum conception of what slavery truly was and how it could be curtailed.

As the South held to its peculiar institution, Lincoln did not directly seek—before and during most of the war—to cut the Gordian knot of the slavery dilemma. It is worth hypothesizing that he saw it more as Claudius's *dilemma*. That did not mean it was insoluble. On the one hand, it seemed irresolvable short of war, except by indirect and incomplete means. Lincoln had long worked to prohibit the expansion of slavery into the territories so that slavery would be put on a course of extinction. But that method relied largely upon the pressure of circumstances, not persuasion of hearts and minds on the basis of principle. Deprived of new lands, the slave-possessors would eventually have to give up their effects. On the other hand, the rich and problematic reasoning of Claudius's prayer suggests that all those materially benefiting from slavery, in the North as well as the South, were *persuadable* upon a matter of principle. The guilty king's meditation not only reveals his dilemma in a way that elicits our sympathy—it brings him to the verge of an inward change. It at least raises the possibility of willing dispossession, for the Southern slave-holder as well as for the Western farmer. Hope and despair vie for precedence in Claudius's prayer because each has foundation there. He feelingly identifies, though he cannot bear, the moral necessity for dispossession. In his private prayer made known to us (notably not to the unsympathetic Hamlet, the avenger), he momentarily opens the entire question. What does it mean to be a slave society, North and South? If slavery is at bottom a fratricidal crime, what acknowledgment of that fact is sufficient for mercy and justice? What can be done, if anything, to rid the country of the slavery—the possession of the effects of slavery—persisting in its midst? Why should a Western farmer, or any farmer, or any American, take on that burden when a little forgetfulness is all that is needed to keep possession of those effects? In the Western farmer's case, all that was needed under Douglas's Kansas-Nebraska Act was to take possession of free land in the territories and vote those lands free or slave without regard for the framing ideas of the American republic.

It is tempting to speculate that Claudius's prayer—failing in its original intent and yet continuing throughout the scene—was for Lincoln a compelling suggestion of the persistence of the Declaration's promise and spirit in the hearts of his countrymen, despite their denial. If so, it would also have suggested that the realization of that promise and spirit would require something more, probably something other, than force. In Hamlet's speech beginning "To be or not to be," which Lincoln contrasts with the prayer of Claudius, the question is not about persuasion of any kind. It is only about taking revenge or choosing suicide. In his letter to Hackett, Lincoln indicated that his view was profoundly different. We can speculate that he detected in Claudius's words the wavering prospect of mercy and indeed the "relish of salvation," which the vengeful, self-loathing, glittering Hamlet explicitly plotted to deny to the murdering king.[18]

Given that Shakespeare's *Macbeth,* more than any other of his plays, is preoccupied with the relation between free will and fate, it makes sense that Lincoln would have considered that play his favorite. *Macbeth* is not only Shakespeare's archetypal play about tyranny—it is his drama most preoccupied with prophetic knowledge, necessity, and the role of human choice. Somehow the witches' prophecies invade and haunt the heroic general's mind in such a way that his humanity disintegrates when they begin to come true.

We know from his writings that Lincoln was more than casually interested in the nature and action of Providence and its relation to human activities. In his early adulthood, he was preoccupied, by his own account, with what he called a doctrine of necessity's power over human actions.[19] He laid it aside (or at least kept it out of his writings) in his later prepresidential years, then during his presidency wrote several now-famous passages, most notably in the Second Inaugural and the Meditation on the Divine Will, about the possible relation between Providence and human effort. *Macbeth* would have offered Lincoln an extraordinarily rich point of focus for his meditations upon the attractions and hazards of providential speculation.

In *Macbeth* prophecy is deceptively absolute. It destroys the man who chooses to follow it—whether more by necessity than by Macbeth's actions it is not easy to tell. It comes from the Weird Sisters, from whom one would not expect to hear anything like a divine revelation. But Macbeth soon lets it haunt him, and he repeatedly chooses what he thinks is (and might be) a preordained path. In Shakespeare's rendering, Macbeth makes those choices with a conscience that conspires against itself, violating the humanity we see in him in almost every speech.

The witches' prophecy that Macbeth will be king seems concrete, but it is in many ways obscure and complex. It gives the impression of inevitability while tantalizing the desire for certainty. It sets out several conditions for its fulfillment: the promised kingship will come to a man of a certain station; it will last as long as the forest of Dunsinane does not move; it will be invulnerable except to the claim of a man not born of a woman. The curiously skeptical Macbeth at first avoids the idea that the prediction is about him at all, but when the witches' prediction is soon partially fulfilled, his ambition awakens, and he begins to accept the prophecy in its entirety, seeking out more news from the witches to overcome his lingering doubts. His crimes become all the more terrible as his own horror at his actions drives him to obliterate all reminders of his transgressions. The witches' occult prophecy, combined with his "milk of human kindness" and ambition, wreck his world.

One of Lincoln's most remarkable pieces of writing, discovered after his death and now called the "Meditation on the Divine Will," can be read as a reply to Macbeth, as an edifying transformation of Macbeth's falsely inspired ambition. Without praying (at least not directly praying) for God's guidance, Lincoln asks a particular question about the divine will. What is its meaning with regard to the war? When will the contest end? Macbeth would be obsessed with the outcome: Who will win? Lincoln's inquiry eschews the flattery of his ambition:

The will of God prevails. In great contests each party claims to act in accordance with the will of God. Both *may* be, and one *must* be wrong. God can not be *for*, and *against* the same thing at the same time. In the present civil war it is quite possible that God's purpose is something different from the purpose of either party— and yet the human instrumentalities, working just as they do, are of the best adaptation to effect His purpose. I am almost ready to say this is probably true—that God wills this contest, and wills that it shall not end yet. By his mere quiet power, on the minds of the now contestants, He could have either *saved* or *destroyed* the Union without a human contest. Yet the contest began. And having begun He could give the final victory to either side any day. Yet the contest proceeds.[20]

Lincoln's distancing of himself from Macbeth's fall to temptation can be instructively compared to the age's righteous millennial longings, which were sometimes supported by religious language in the Bible and in song, that could easily have been taken to suggest that Lincoln was the agent of destiny. There was the prominent association of the biblical Abraham with the Apostle Paul's proclamation in Galatians 3–4 that the blessing of Abraham, with the advent of the Savior, was coming into the world to end "bondage" to the law in "the fulness of the time."[21] In that vein, the apocalyptic spirit of "The Battle Hymn of the Republic" and a popular association of Lincoln with Father Abraham could easily have taken hold of a war president prone to imagine himself a political savior whose time had come.

In contrast with these prophecies, Lincoln's meditation expresses a desire to know God's purposes without exceeding the inquirer's human limitations. His deference to the unknown tempers his wondering. He puts everything into a single paragraph and does not publish. Granting that the will of God prevails, he puts everything under a higher authority he cannot know or control. At the same time, he leaves more than a little room for human action and human choice. The human "instrumentalities" seem best suited to carrying out God's unknowable intentions, and it would seem that as human instrumentalities they would therefore involve their ability to choose and act in certain ways. As instrumentalities they are apparently gifts of a creator, and yet in being human they are mindful participants in the conflict, capable of thought and choice. It seems that "working as they do," they would exhibit a characteristic power of choice.

The meditation's logic therefore draws conclusions from the ruling power of divine necessity that make room for human agency in the fulfillment of divine will. God's intervention by means of a "mere quiet power" would appropriately be felt through those instrumentalities, which in keeping with that power would act under its influence rather than as the result of coercion. Lincoln's language does not anticipate an apocalypse. He does not look for a day of judgment. The war will be won or lost, and the will of God will prevail, through the human instrumentalities. By these means Lincoln turns away from identifying himself with the biblical Abraham.

It might seem strange to end a discussion of Lincoln and Shakespearean tragedy with Falstaff, but there is a reason why Lincoln drew upon Falstaff's resources at the center of his pivotal Peoria Speech in 1854, just as he was appealing to uncertain voters to remember the wellsprings of their heritage amid dangerous distractions and to act upon self-interest rightly understood. The Peoria Speech was Lincoln's answer to Stephen Douglas's new legislation to end the slavery controversy by relying upon local territorial votes rather than national legislation prohibiting the spread of slavery into the territories. At that crucial moment, Lincoln found embodied in Falstaff sentiments that would frequently appear in his later antebellum speeches, as in his 1858 effort in Edwardsville, Illinois: "Our defense is in the preservation of the spirit which prizes liberty as the heritage of all men, in all lands, every where. Destroy this spirit, and you have planted the seeds of despotism around your own doors."[22]

In the Peoria Speech, Lincoln emphasized his point by evoking lines and sentiments particularly associated with Falstaff and his comical, insistent claim that his liberty is essential to human nature and the world: "Slavery is founded in the selfishness of man's nature—opposition to it, is [in?] his love of justice. These principles are an eternal antagonism; and when brought into collision so fiercely, as slavery extension brings them, shocks, and throes, and convulsions must ceaselessly follow. Repeal the Missouri compromise—repeal all compromises—repeal the declaration of independence—repeal all past history, you still can not repeal human nature. It still will be the abundance of man's heart, that slavery extension is wrong; and out of the abundance of his heart, his mouth will continue to speak."[23]

Concluding with Lincoln's appropriation of phrasing from Matthew 12:34 and Luke 6:45 about the power of the overflowing heart to speak what is good, this passage also calls up and refracts lines from *Henry IV, Part 1* in which Falstaff begs outlandishly and memorably for Hal's favor by arguing poetically that he is the spirit of the world's liberty: "No, my good lord, banish Peto, banish Bardolph, banish Poins; but for sweet Jack Falstaff, kind Jack Falstaff, true Jack Falstaff, valiant Jack Falstaff, and therefore more valiant being as he is old Jack Falstaff, banish not him thy Harry's company, banish not him thy Harry's company—banish plump Jack, and banish all the world."[24]

Falstaff is of course a thief and drunkard—a scalawag. In those things he embodies "the selfishness of man's nature" that Lincoln has just identified with the human condition. But in our appreciation of the humor of this scene, we see that Shakespeare (and Lincoln!) also make him an embodiment of the free wit and liberty that make us human, including the liberty of the comic spirit. Falstaff is in this sense a genius of the free spirit's persistence, its refusal to be enslaved. In his own words in *Henry IV, Part 2,* that spirit invents "anything that intends to laughter" and "the cause that wit is in other men."[25] In the Peoria Speech, Falstaff appears again, thinly disguised. Like him, the spirit of liberty in men's hearts will not be quelled. The death-defying persistence of Falstaff's free energy embodies the prevailing principle that "out of the abundance of his heart," man's "mouth will continue to speak" that slavery is wrong.

The president who once saw three history plays by Shakespeare in one week, who befriended Falstaff in the person of the actor Hackett, and who had reason to identify Falstaff's irreverent vein of humor with his own would have been likely to know these deep roots of the Falstaffian character in Shakespeare's play texts. It is not inappropriate to assume that many audience members in that era of reading and witnessing whole or partial Shakespearean dramas would have heard the Falstaffian echo and appreciated Lincoln's adaptation of Falstaff's appeal for his own purposes. The more important point for our purposes is that Lincoln uses Falstaff's larger-than-life spirit of liberty to meet the extrahuman demon of tyranny that haunts antebellum America's democratic life. With the help of Shakespeare, Lincoln invites his audiences to participate in a cure that would restore themselves and their polity to their better natures, thereby awakening their powers to resist tyrannous slavery without and within. For Lincoln, Shakespeare was a test and tonic for the spirit of liberty and, by extension, for the freedom-loving soul.

Notes

1. Abraham Lincoln, "Speech at Chicago" (July 10, 1858), *Collected Works of Abraham Lincoln,* ed. Roy P. Basler, 8 vols. plus index (New Brunswick, NJ: Rutgers University Press, 1953), 2:494. Hereinafter cited as *CW;* emphases in original unless otherwise noted.

2. For a compact review of commentary on Lincoln's ambition and the

locus classicus in the Lyceum Address, see Michael Burlingame, *The Inner World of Abraham Lincoln* (Urbana: University of Illinois Press, 1994), 236–67. The best-known argument that Lincoln revealed a tyrannical ambition in the Lyceum Address is in Edmund Wilson's *Patriotic Gore: Studies in the Literature of the Civil War* (New York: Oxford University Press, 1962), 99–130.

3. Both islands were places in which Napoleon was imprisoned by those who had stopped his conquests. Defeated in his battles to make France the governing power of Europe, Napoleon was first exiled to Elba, an island off the western Italian coast. After his escape in 1815, he raised another French army in a hundred days and fought Britain and its allies at Waterloo. After his defeat there in an immensely costly battle, the victors exiled him to the British island of Saint Helena, off the coast of Angola, where he had to be guarded with extraordinary military precautions. He died there in 1821.

4. See John Channing Briggs, *Lincoln's Speeches Reconsidered* (Cambridge, MA: Harvard University Press, 2005), 221–36.

5. In his early Springfield days, Lincoln published several anonymous satirical attacks on James Shields, who, upon discovering that Lincoln was the author, challenged him to a duel. For Lincoln's ingenious acceptance note, which attempted to deflect the challenge without backing down, see "To James Shields" (September 17, 1842) and "Memorandum of Duel Instructions to Elias H. Merryman" (September 19, 1842), in *CW*, 1:299–302. Negotiations for a suitable site were never completed, and Lincoln is said to have asked a friend, much later in life, not to remind him of the episode. Detailed discussions of these events can be found in Douglas L. Wilson, *Honor's Voice: The Transformation of Abraham Lincoln* (New York: Knopf, 1998), 265–83. Another source is James E. Myers, *The Astonishing Saber Duel of Abraham Lincoln* (Springfield, IL: Lincoln-Herndon Building Publishers, 1968). For Lincoln's humorous letter to Speed, see "To Joshua F. Speed" (October 5, 1842), in *CW*, 1:302–3.

6. Abraham Lincoln, "To James M. Cutts, Jr." (October 26, 1863), in *CW*, 6:538.

7. See an account of the relation of the October 23, 1863, production to events of the day in Alexander Nemerov's new study, *Acting in the Night*: Macbeth *and the Places of the Civil War* (Berkeley: University of California Press, 2010).

8. A popular saying attributed to Lincoln, one that is now ubiquitous on the Internet, focuses on the idea that power—in itself the license to exercise freedom without restraint—is the greatest test of character: "*Nearly all men can stand adversity, but if you want to test a man's character, give him power.*" The traditional association of these words with Lincoln, even though they are not found in the *Collected Works*, registers a common awareness of Lincoln's

interest in the potential for tyrannical ambition in those who find themselves given the power to do great things.

9. See David Herbert Donald, *Lincoln* (New York: Simon & Schuster, 1995), 580.

10. Accounts of Lincoln's assassination at the hands of John Wilkes Booth have traditionally claimed that after he fired he spoke words proverbially attributed to Brutus after the assassination of Caesar, though absent from Shakespeare's play: "Sic semper tyrannis" (Thus always to tyrants). The antebellum preoccupation with resisting tyranny was evident in the name of the Booth family patriarch: John's father's name was Junius Brutus Booth, named after the leader of those who killed Caesar, claiming they were freeing the Senate and the people of Rome from dictatorial rule.

11. Abraham Lincoln, "To James H. Hackett" (August 17, 1863), in *CW*, 6:392.

12. See John Channing Briggs, "Steeped in Shakespeare," *Claremont Review of Books* 9, no. 1 (Winter 2008–2009): 63–66.

13. Lincoln's simultaneous identification with and criticism of Richard III's character is famously described by the artist Francis Carpenter, who heard him recite Richard's opening soliloquy and supply commentary with uncanny skill and insight into Richard's character. For a compact and enlightening summary of this incident and many other evidences of Lincoln's understanding of Shakespeare, see Douglas L. Wilson, "His Hour upon the Stage," *The American Scholar* (Winter 2012), available at http://theamericanscholar .org/his-hour-upon-the-stage/#.Ugg74Hy9KSM. Another helpful source is Stephen Dickey's Folger lecture "Lincoln and Shakespeare," at http://www .shakespeareinamericanlife.org/identity/politicians/presidents/pick/lincoln/ lincoln_shakespeare_6.cfm. The freedom of maneuver Shakespeare gives to his tyrants, despite their susceptibility to larger forces, differs markedly from the treatment given protagonists by his rival Christopher Marlowe, who repeatedly presents his audiences with examples of absolute, cosmic rebellion paired with unmovable fate.

14. *Hamlet*, III.iii.36–38. All citations of Shakespeare are taken from *The Riverside Shakespeare*, ed. G. Blakemore Evans and J. J. M. Tobin (Boston: Houghton Mifflin, 1997).

15. Ibid., III.iii.46–47.

16. Ibid., III.iii.53–55.

17. Ibid., III.iv.92.

18. For the scope of Hamlet's reasoning, see his entire speech: III.iv.73–96. For evidence that such wavering between possession and dispossession was not

an isolated literary phenomenon, see Lincoln's serious though ultimately unsuccessful proposal for compensated emancipation, which he directed especially toward the Union-supporting but wavering border state of Kentucky: "Appeal to Border State Representatives to Favor Compensated Emancipation" (July 12, 1862), in *CW*, 5:317–19.

19. Abraham Lincoln, "Handbill Replying to Charges of Infidelity" (July 31, 1846), in *CW*, 1:382.

20. Abraham Lincoln, "Meditation on the Divine Will" (September 2, 1862), in *CW*, 5:403–4.

21. The King James Version, Galatians 3–4.

22. Abraham Lincoln, "Speech at Edwardsville, Illinois" (September 11, 1858), in *CW*, 3:95.

23. Abraham Lincoln, "Speech at Peoria, Illinois" (October 16, 1854), in *CW*, 2:271.

24. *Henry IV, Part 1*, II.iv.474–480.

25. *Henry IV, Part 2*, I.ii.8–10.

3

Lincoln and Race

Michael Burlingame

The subject of Lincoln and race is complicated and cannot be fully addressed in this chapter. I will therefore focus on only three considerations that critics of Lincoln cite regularly: the allegation that he was a "reluctant emancipator," his endorsement of colonization, and Frederick Douglass's characterization of him as "preeminently the white man's president."

Reluctant Emancipator?

It is fashionable in some circles to assert that Lincoln issued the Emancipation Proclamation only because of political and diplomatic pressure, not because he himself hated slavery and wished to abolish it. In fact, Lincoln loathed and despised slavery from his early years. "I have always hated slavery, I think as much as any Abolitionist," he said in 1858.[1] Six years later, he reiterated his strong opinion on the subject: "I am naturally anti-slavery. If slavery is not wrong, nothing is wrong. I cannot remember when I did not so think, and feel."[2]

There is good reason to take Lincoln at his word. At the age of twenty-seven, as a second-term member of the Illinois House of Representatives, he boldly denounced slavery. On March 3, 1837, he and another member of the legislature, Dan Stone, filed a protest against antiabolitionist resolutions that the legislature had adopted six weeks earlier by the lopsided vote of 77–6 in the House and 18–0 in the Senate. Lincoln and Stone were part of the tiny minority of six who opposed the resolutions—less than 7 percent of the entire General Assembly. The overwhelmingly popular resolutions were introduced at the behest of Southern state legislatures, which were outraged by the American Anti-Slavery Society's pamphlets depicting slave-owners as cruel brutes. Equally objectionable was the society's massive petition drive calling for the abolition of slavery in the District of Columbia. The resolutions declared that Illinois legislators "highly disapprove of the formation of abolition societies, and of the doctrines promulgated by them," that "the right of property in slaves is sacred to the slave-holding States by the Federal Government, and that they cannot be deprived of that right without their consent," and that "the General Government cannot abolish slavery in the District of Columbia, against the will of the citizens of said District."[3]

Lincoln wrote a protest against these resolutions and circulated it among his colleagues. None would sign except for Stone, a Vermont native who was not seeking reelection, for he was soon to become a judge. Lincoln declared in the document, which he and Stone entered into the journal of the House of Representatives, "that the institution of slavery is founded on both injustice and bad policy," a precursor of his landmark 1854 Peoria Speech attacking the "monstrous injustice of slavery." In 1860 a newspaper that was widely regarded as his organ explained that "Lincoln could not, and did not vote in favor of the resolutions . . . because the old Calhoun doctrine embraced in the second of the series ['that the right of property in slaves is sacred to the slave-holding states by the Federal Government'] was abhorrent to his ideas of the true meaning of the Constitution."[4]

To proclaim that "slavery is founded on both injustice and bad policy" was a remarkably bold gesture for 1837, when antislavery views enjoyed little popularity in central Illinois. Seven months after the Lincoln-Stone protest appeared, Springfielders publicly condemned abolitionism. While the Presbyterian synod was meeting there, citizens disrupted plans to have an antislavery sermon delivered. Violence was avoided, but some townspeople met and resolved that "as citizens of a free State and a peaceable community, we deprecate any attempt to sow discord among us, or to create an excitement as to abolition which can be productive of no good result . . . . [T]he doctrine of immediate emancipation in this country, (although promulgated by those who profess to be christians,) is at variance with christianity, and its tendency is to breed contention, broils and mobs, and the leaders of those calling themselves abolitionists are designing, ambitious men, and dangerous members of society, and should be shunned by all good citizens."[5] The Whig newspaper in Springfield rejoiced "that public opinion in the frontier states is likely to check at once the perfidy of these fanatical men [i.e., the abolitionists]." Westerners "could not be induced to visit upon the South such an accumulation of horrors as is embraced in the meaning of those two words—'universal emancipation.'"[6]

The newspaper was right: the antislavery movement had gained little traction in Illinois. Between 1817 and 1824, opponents of slavery had successfully defeated attempts to introduce the peculiar institution into their state constitution, but antislavery enthusiasm waned thereafter. Before 1837 the American Antislavery Society was able to establish an auxiliary in only one Illinois county. In 1837 attempts to circulate antislavery petitions proved futile. In 1841 Springfield authorities forbade an agent of the Illinois Antislavery Society to speak in public. Three years later, more than a hundred Springfielders thwarted the abolitionist Ichabod Codding when he sought to deliver a lecture. In 1854 the editor of Springfield's Whig paper noted that the term *abolitionist* "is an odious epithet among us; and we do not believe that there are a dozen men to be found in Sangamon county to whom it can be properly applied."[7]

In such a region in 1837, Lincoln could not reasonably expect that criticism of slavery, even if it stopped short of outright abolitionism, would endear him to the electorate. Yet by 1837 he had come to loathe slavery. In 1858 he said, "The slavery question often bothered me as far back as 1836–1840. I was troubled and grieved over it."[8] His friend Samuel C. Parks asserted that "Lincoln told the truth when he said he had 'always hated slavery as much as any Abolitionist' but I do not know that he deserved a great deal of credit for that for his hatred of oppression & wrong in all its forms was constitutional—he could not help it."[9] In 1860 Lincoln wrote in a third-person autobiographical sketch that the protest that he and Stone had issued in 1837 "briefly defined his position on the slavery question; and so far as it goes, it was then the same that it is now."[10]

In 1849 as a freshman congressman, Lincoln framed a bill to abolish slavery in the District of Columbia. The House of Representatives had been considering legislation to outlaw slave trading in the capital, but Lincoln's measure went much further, abolishing slavery there altogether. He evidently agreed with the eminent abolitionist William Lloyd Garrison that the "abolition of the slave traffic . . . is impractical while slavery exists. There is no reason why slave-trading should be prohibited if slave-holding is justified and allowed."[11] Lincoln's proposal stipulated that, starting in 1850, all children born to slave mothers in the District were to be free; that their mothers' owners would be responsible for supporting and educating those children; that the children in return "would owe reasonable service, as apprentices, to such owners . . . until they respectively arrive at the age of _____ years when they shall be entirely free"; that if owners emancipated slaves in the District, Congress would compensate them at full market value (to be determined by a board consisting of the president and his secretaries of state and the treasury); and that fugitive slaves reaching the District would be extradited by municipal authorities. The bill would take effect only after a majority of the voters of the District approved it. Lincoln announced "that he was authorized to say, that among fifteen of the leading citizens of the District of Columbia to whom this proposition had been submitted, there was not one but who approved of the adoption of such a measure."[12]

Two of those leading citizens were the coeditors of the *National Intelligencer,* Joseph Gales and William S. Seaton. A day earlier, Lincoln and the most prominent foe of slavery in Congress, Joshua R. Giddings, had called on Seaton. Years later Lincoln recalled:

> I visited [the] Mayor, Seaton, and others whom I thought best acquainted with the sentiment of the people, to ascertain if a bill such as I proposed would be endorsed by them. . . . Being informed that it would meet with their hearty approbation I gave notice in Congress that I should introduce a bill. Subsequently I learned that many leading southern members of Congress, had been to see the Mayor and the others who favored my bill and had drawn them over to their way of thinking. Finding that I was abandoned by my former backers and having little personal influence, I *dropped* the matter knowing it was useless to prosecute the business at that time.[13]

Like all other such measures introduced between 1805 and 1862, Lincoln's never reached a vote.

Some contemporaries sneered at Lincoln's proposed legislation. In 1860 the radical abolitionist Wendell Phillips denounced Lincoln as "the slave hound of Illinois" because his 1849 emancipation bill contained a fugitive slave clause.[14] Giddings published a letter defending Lincoln: "his conversing with the people of the District, the preparation of his bill, the avowal of his intention to present it, were important." Such actions placed him among "those who were laboring in the cause of humanity. He avowed his intention to strike down slavery and the slave trade in the District; to strike from our statute book the act by which freemen were transformed into slaves; to speak, and act, and vote for the right," and "cast aside the shackles of party, and took his stand upon principle." Chiding Phillips, Giddings added: "You speak of that act with great severity of condemnation. I view it as one of high moral excellence, marking the heroism of the man. He was the only member among the Whigs proper [as opposed to the handful of antislavery Whigs] of that session, who broke the silence on the subject of those crimes."[15]

The managing editor of the *New York Tribune,* Sydney Howard Gay, an outspoken opponent of slavery, also criticized his old friend Phillips. In August 1860 Lincoln's law partner, William Herndon, probably speaking for Lincoln, told Gay: "Your reply to Wendell Phillips's article in the Liberator was correct." Gay, Herndon said, was "familiar—too familiar—with legislative business not to know that . . . no one man can possibly get his own ideas put into any statute—any law, or any Constitution." Passing bills involved "concession—compromise." When "Lincoln was in Congress this State of affairs Existed: he was then a strong Anti-Slavery man and is now the same. This I know, though he wishes and will act under the Constitution: he is radical in heart, but in action he must Conform to Law & Constitution as Construed in good old times." Herndon, who admired Phillips extravagantly, concluded: "Lincoln, in reference to the Bill about which Mr. Phillips wrote his articles, was actuated by Anti-Slavery sentiments alone. . . . In doing this he had to consult his friends' feelings and ideas or he could do nothing; and so his bill was drawn up with a reference to all the aforesaid Conditions—conflicting sentiments & ideas." Lincoln "wanted the slave trade in the District of Columbia cut up by the roots and slavery gradually abolished."[16]

Similarly, in September 1849 a correspondent for the antislavery *New York Tribune* depicted Lincoln as "conspicuous in the last Congress— especially during the last session, when he attempted to frame and put through a bill for the gradual Abolition of Slavery in the District of Columbia. He is a strong but judicious enemy to Slavery, and his efforts are usually very practical, if not always successful."[17] In 1860 Joshua Giddings told a crowd that while he and Lincoln served in the House of Representatives, "they became intimately acquainted—boarding at the same house, and sitting opposite each other at meals; that he thought he knew the heart of Abraham Lincoln as well as any living man, and speaking from that knowledge, he believed that every beat of 'honest Abe's' heart was a throb of sincerity and truth—in a word, that he is that noblest work of God—an honest man. He believed Lincoln's loyalty to republican principles, and to the cause of freedom and humanity, was unquestionable and beyond suspicion."[18]

A document frequently cited to show that Lincoln did not much care about slavery is a letter he wrote in August 1862 to Horace Greeley offering a response to that journalist's editorial "The Prayer of Twenty Millions," in which Greeley demanded that the president enforce the Confiscation Acts, ignore the counsels of "fossil politicians hailing from the Border States," stop deferring to slaveholders, adopt some consistent policy with regard to slavery, and employ runaway bondsmen as "scouts, guides, spies, cooks, teamsters, diggers and choppers."[19]

Lincoln had been awaiting an opportunity to explain his thinking about emancipation and thus smooth the way for the Proclamation, which he had introduced to his cabinet a month earlier. (At the urging of Secretary of State William Henry Seward, he decided to delay issuing the fateful document until the Union army won a victory.) And so he wrote a public reply to Greeley that was widely copied in the press. Responding to the charge that he only *seemed* to have a policy regarding slavery, the president succinctly recounted the course he had been following:

> I would save the Union. I would save it the shortest way under the Constitution. The sooner the national authority can be restored; the nearer the Union will be 'the Union as it was.' If there be those who would not save the Union, unless they could at the same time *save* slavery, I do not agree with them. If there be those who would not save the Union unless they could at the same time *destroy* slavery, I do not agree with them. My paramount object in this struggle *is* to save the Union, and is *not* either to save or to destroy slavery. If I could save the Union without freeing *any* slave I would do it, and if I could save it by freeing *all* the slaves I would do it; and if I could save it by freeing some and leaving others alone I would also do that. What I do about slavery, and the colored race, I do because I believe it helps to save the Union; and what I forbear, I forbear because I do *not* believe it would help to save the Union. I shall do *less* whenever I shall believe what I am doing hurts the cause, and I shall do *more* whenever I shall believe doing more will help the cause. I shall try to correct errors when shown to be errors; and I

shall adopt new views so fast as they shall appear to be true views. I have here stated my purpose according to my view of *official* duty; and I intend no modification of my oft-expressed *personal* wish that all men every where could be free.[20]

By stating that he might liberate some slaves but not others, Lincoln paraphrased the proclamation that he had already written. In the last sentence, he underscored what he had been saying for several years: that he loathed slavery. But he stressed that as a public official bound by an oath, he must respect constitutional and political constraints.

Those who regard Lincoln's letter to Greeley as a definitive statement of his innermost feelings about the war's aims have misunderstood the document. Some commentators lamented the author's apparent failure to acknowledge the moral significance of emancipation. But in fact, the letter was a political statement that aimed to pave the way for the Proclamation, which he intended to issue soon. He realized that many Northerners, as well as denizens of the border states, would denounce the transformation of the war into an abolitionist endeavor. They were fully prepared to fight to save the Union but not to liberate the slaves. Lincoln felt obliged somehow to make emancipation acceptable to them. By stressing that emancipation was only a means to help save the Union, Lincoln sought to reduce the strength of the inevitable white backlash that the Proclamation would generate.[21]

Colonization

The same holds true for Lincoln's proposal to colonize freedmen abroad. In the annual message to Congress in December 1861, Lincoln recommended colonization, outraging many abolitionists. They claimed that the message "is thoroughly tinged with that colorphobia which has so long prevailed in Illinois" and denounced Lincoln for "so laboring under colorphobia, as to make emancipation dependent on colonization."[22] The leading critic of colonization, William Lloyd Garrison, deemed the president "a man of very small caliber." The colonization scheme, Garrison thundered, was "absurd and preposterous," and he sneered that "Lincoln may colonize himself if he choose, but it is an impertinent act, on his part, to propose the getting rid of those who are as good as himself."[23]

Many blacks echoed Garrison. The New York *Anglo-African* said that

Lincoln's message "does not contain one word of generous trust, generous cheer or cordial sympathy with the 'great uprising' of the nation" and recommended ironically that "any surplus change Congress may have can be appropriated 'with our consent' to expatriate and settle elsewhere the surviving slaveholders."[24] Eminent Boston blacks declared that "when we wish to leave the United States we can find and pay for that territory which shall suit us best," that "when we are ready to leave, we shall be able to pay our own expenses of travel," that "we don't want to go now," and that "if anybody else wants us to go, they must compel us."[25] Frederick Douglass, who said he was "bewildered by the spectacle of moral blindness, infatuation and helpless imbecility which the Government of Lincoln presents," denounced the president for showing himself to be "about as destitute of any anti-slavery principle or feeling" as his predecessor, James Buchanan.[26]

Ironically, a few months earlier Douglass had suggested that fellow blacks leave the United States for Haiti, "this modern land of Canaan," where "our oppressors do not want us to go, and where our influence and example can still be of service to those whose tears will find their way to us by the waters of the Gulf washing all our shores. Let us be there to help beat back the filibustering invaders from the cotton States, who only await an opportunity to extinguish that island asylum of the deeply-wronged colored race." Back in 1853 Douglass gave a speech describing Caribbean islands and British Guiana as fit locations where American blacks could resettle.[27]

In the 1850s black enthusiasm for colonization had increased. Henry Highland Garnet, Lewis Woodson, and Martin R. Delany, as well as other black leaders, supported emigration.[28] In 1854 blacks held a convention in Cleveland to consider a large-scale exodus from the United States. Delany visited the Niger River valley looking for sites where American blacks might relocate, James Whitefield conducted similar explorations in Central America, and James Theodore Holly examined the West Indies.[29] In 1858 Garnet founded the African Civilization Society, which encouraged American blacks to emigrate to part of present-day Nigeria and Benin. In 1862, 250 California blacks petitioned Congress expressing the desire to be colonized "in some country in which their color will not be a badge of degradation," and blacks in the District of Columbia asked Congress to send them to Central America.[30] A few years earlier, the abolitionist preacher Owen Lovejoy had introduced into the Illinois General Assembly "a remonstrance from the colored people of the State against their colonization in Africa, until they are all able to read and write, and unless separate colonies be assigned to those of different shades of color. The reason assigned for the latter objection is, that blacks and mulattoes cannot live in harmony together."[31]

Lincoln supported colonization not because he suffered from "color-phobia" but because he faced intractable political realities. Southerners would not emancipate their slaves unless the freedmen were colonized.[32] Kentucky senator Garrett Davis told Lincoln that Unionist slave owners in his state "would not resist his gradual emancipation scheme if he would only conjoin with it his colonization plan." (Lincoln quoted this statement when justifying his colonization proposal.)[33] Wisconsin senator James R. Doolittle similarly observed that "every man, woman, and child who comes from these [slave] States, tells me that it is utterly impossible for them to talk of emancipation within any slave State without connecting it with the idea of colonization."[34] In June 1862 Democratic congressman Charles John Biddle of Pennsylvania told the House that alarm about emancipation "would spread to every man of my constituents who loves his country and his race if the public mind was not lulled and put to sleep with the word 'colonization.' I say the word, not the thing; for no practicable and adequate scheme for it has ever been presented or devised. The word is sung to us as a sort of 'lullaby.'"[35] Lincoln was singing that essential lullaby. A Pennsylvania Democrat wrote his congressman: "If you can only send the whole race out of the country, I think all loyal democrats would be willing to see slavery abolished at once, regardless of any other consideration. . . . If the black race is once removed, we will have repose—not sooner."[36] New York Democrats asserted that they were "opposed to emancipating negro slaves, unless on some plan of colonization."[37] A gentleman who had resided in the South insisted to Ohio senator John Sherman "that colonization should be held out in order to win the nonslaveholding and especially the poor whites of the South, and these are the men who must uphold the United States rule in the slave states." Ninety percent of them "when they once understand it will hail manumission and colonization as God's blessing. The slaveholders rule them by creating a horror of what the Negroes would do if freed among them, but with all this there is a strong though secret hatred of slavery."[38]

Assistant Secretary of the Interior John Palmer Usher of Indiana (the most negrophobic of the free states) assured Lincoln that a colonization plan "will, if adopted, relieve the free states of the apprehension now prevailing, and fostered by the disloyal, that they are to be overrun by negroes made free by the war, [and] it will alarm those in rebellion, for they will see that their cherished property is departing from them forever and incline them to peace."[39] A supporter of colonization, Orestes Brownson, guessed that 75 percent of Northern voters were antislavery and 90 percent of them were antiblack.[40]

In December 1861, when Lincoln made his colonization proposal, the Union army had custody of thousands of slaves in Virginia, South Carolina, and elsewhere. The War Department did not wish to feed and house them, nor did Northern and border states want to admit them. Public opinion was opposed to allowing them to enlist in the armed forces. Colonization therefore seemed to be the only viable option.

Before 1861 Radical Republicans such as Salmon P. Chase and many others had supported colonization, and during the war some Radicals, among them James Redpath, promoted it. Frederick Douglass called Redpath "a sincere friend of the colored race."[41] In 1862 the ultra-Radical Moncure D. Conway, who would later become one of Lincoln's most bitter critics, published an influential book, *The Rejected Stone,* which contained a letter to the president urging him to colonize Haiti as part of a general plan of emancipation. "If," Conway wrote,

> under the formidable circumstances which now surround our na-
> tion, we should fear the expense, or the labors attending such a step
> [as emancipation], mark how Haiti stands ready to bear a hand to the
> holy work. The Queen of the Antilles sits there with her ungathered
> wealth about her, her spices and fruits gilding every wave around
> her shores, awaiting the ten millions of gatherers to whom she can
> yet give a hospitable home. One word from you, sir, and she is a rec-
> ognized sister Republic. Another word, and, whilst African troops
> march on to see that your decree is executed, the aged, the women
> and children, which we can scarcely sustain, are borne away to the
> happy clime where no fevers nor lashes await them.[42]

Some colonization enthusiasts insisted that American whites would never treat blacks decently and that blacks would do better in other lands. From St. Louis, William Davis Gallagher wrote his close friend Treasury secretary Chase, describing slaves who had escaped from the interior of Missouri but could find no employment in St. Louis and could not get passes allowing them to enter Illinois. Demoralized, they returned to their masters. Gallagher exclaimed "in this manner the *disability of color* in the Border States . . . is operating to strengthen the hands of the very rebels who have brought upon the country its grievous troubles! If these poor people were out of the State, employment could be found for most if not all of them in neighboring parts of Illinois," but the Prairie State's "Black Laws" prevented them from settling there. Gallagher deplored the hypocrisy of many Northerners: "The very people that at one moment denounce slave-holders as tyrants and sinners, the next moment turn their backs and shut their doors against the poor slaves whom accident or repentance has set free. Before we have Emancipation . . . I hope we shall have matured a system of *Colonization:* for if we have not, God pity the poor Negro!"[43]

On July 16, 1862, a congressional committee recommended that $20 million be appropriated to facilitate the voluntary emigration of American blacks. The committee noted that much

> of the objection to emancipation arises from the opposition of a large portion of our people to the intermixture of the races, and from the association of white and black labor. The committee would do nothing to favor such a policy; apart from the antipathy which nature has ordained, the presence of a race among us who cannot, and ought not to, be admitted to our social and political privileges, will be a perpetual source of injury and inquietude to both. This is a question of color, and is unaffected by the relation of master and slave. . . . the most formidable difficulty which lies in the way of emancipation . . . is the belief, which obtains especially among those who own no slaves, that if the negroes shall become free, they must still continue in our midst, and, so remaining after their liberation, they may in some measure be made equal to the Anglo-Saxon race.[44]

The "Anglo-American will never give his consent that the negro, no matter how free, shall be elevated to such equality. It matters not how wealthy, how intelligent, or how morally meritorious the negro may become, so long as he remains among us the recollection of the former relation of master and slave will be perpetuated by the changeless color of the Ethiop's skin, and that color will alike be perpetuated by the degrading tradition of his former bondage." The "highest interests of the white race, whether Anglo-Saxon,

Celt, or Scandinavian, require that the whole country should be held and occupied by those races alone." Therefore, a home "must be sought for the African beyond our own limits and in those warmer regions to which his constitution is better adapted than to our own climate, and which doubtless the Almighty intended the colored race should inhabit and cultivate."[45]

It is hard to know if Lincoln thought that colonization was either feasible or desirable. Harriet Martineau, a British abolitionist who famously toured and then wrote about American society, thought that he was not sincere: his "absurd" and "impracticable" plan, she wrote, "is so wrong and foolish that we might safely assume that Mr. Lincoln proposed something that would not do, in order to throw upon others the responsibility of whatever will have to be done."[46] Indeed, Lincoln was protecting himself against attacks that he knew would attend emancipation. Suggesting that blacks be colonized was one way to sugarcoat what was, for conservatives, the bitter pill of emancipation. Lincoln recommended colonization not because he thought it was practicable or just, but because he wanted to render emancipation more acceptable to Northern conservatives, to the border states, and to Southern unionists.[47] Lincoln's support for colonization was an attempt, as one observer noted, "to throw dust into the eyes of the Kentucky slaveholders."[48]

Frederick Douglass on Lincoln

Almost all commentators on Lincoln and race quote a speech Frederick Douglass delivered in 1876 in which he called Lincoln "preeminently the white man's president."[49] But most of those commentators ignore a speech that Douglass delivered at Manhattan's Cooper Union on June 1, 1865. Douglass told his large audience: "No people or class of people in the country have a better reason for lamenting the death of Abraham Lincoln, and for desiring to honor and perpetuate his memory, than have the colored people." The record of the martyred president, when compared "with the long line of his predecessors, many of whom were merely the facile and servile instruments of the slave power," was impressive. Douglass acknowledged that Lincoln was "unsurpassed in his devotion to the welfare of the white race" and that "he sometimes smote" blacks "and wounded them severely"; nevertheless he was also "in a sense hitherto without example, emphatically the black man's President: the first to show any respect for their rights as men. . . . He was the first American President who . . . rose above the prejudice of his times, and country." If during the early stages of the Civil War the president had favored colonizing the freedmen abroad, Douglass asserted, "Lincoln soon outgrew his colonization ideas and schemes and came to look upon the Black man as an American citizen." To illustrate this point, Douglass cited his personal experience: "It was my privilege to know Abraham Lincoln and to know him well. I saw and conversed with him at different times during his administration." Douglass found Lincoln's willingness to receive him remarkable in itself: "He knew that he could do nothing which would call down upon him more fiercely the ribaldry of the vulgar than by showing any respect to a colored man." (In a draft of this speech, Douglass said: "Some men there are who can face death and dangers, but have not the moral courage to contradict a prejudice or face ridicule. In daring to admit, nay in daring to invite a Negro to an audience at the White House, Mr. Lincoln did that which he knew would be offensive to the crowd and excite their ribaldry. It was saying to the country, I am President of the black people as well as the white, and I mean to respect their rights and feelings as men and as citizens.")

When Douglass was admitted to the president's office, he found him easy to talk with: "He set me at perfect liberty to state where I differed from him as freely as where I agreed with him. From the first five minutes I seemed to myself to have been acquainted with [him] during all my life. . . . [H]e was one of the very few white Americans who could converse with a negro without anything like condescension, and without in anywise reminding him of the unpopularity of his color."

Douglass recalled one episode in particular that demonstrated Lincoln's "kindly disposition towards colored people." While Douglass was talking with the president, a White House aide on two occasions announced that the governor of Connecticut sat in an adjacent room, eager for an interview. "Tell the Governor to wait," said the President. "I want to have a long talk with my friend Douglass." Their conversation continued for another hour. Douglass later speculated that "[t]his was probably the first time in the history of the country when the Governor of a State was required to wait for an interview, because the President of the United States was engaged in conversation with a negro."

Douglass did not rely solely on his own experience to explain why Lincoln should be considered "emphatically the black man's President." He told the Cooper Union audience about "[o]ne of the most touching scenes connected with the funeral of our lamented President," which "occurred at the gate of the Presidential Mansion: A colored woman standing at the gate weeping, was asked the cause of her tears. 'Oh! Sir,' she said, 'we have lost our Moses.' 'But,' said the gentleman, 'the Lord will send you another[']; [']That may be,' said the weeping woman, 'but Ah! we had him.'"

This woman, according to Douglass, represented millions of blacks who "from first to last, and through all, whether through good or through evil report, fully believed in Abraham Lincoln." Despite his initial tardiness in attacking slavery, Douglass said, they "firmly trusted in him" with a faith that constituted "no blind trust unsupported by reason." Blacks had "early caught a glimpse of the man, and from the evidence of their senses, they believed in him. They viewed him not in the light of separate individual acts, but in the light of his mission, in his manifest relation to events and in the philosophy of his statesmanship. Viewing him thus they trusted him as men are seldom trusted. They did not care what forms of expression the President adopted, whether it were justice, expedience, or military necessity, so that they see slavery abolished and liberty established in the country."

Black people, Douglass maintained, could observe with their own eyes astounding progress: "Under Abraham Lincoln's beneficent rule, they saw themselves being gradually lifted to the broad plain of equal manhood; under his rule, and by measures approved by him, they saw gradually fading the handwriting of ages which was against them. Under his rule, they saw millions of their brethren defend their freedom. Under his rule they saw the Confederate states . . . broken to pieces, overpowered, conquered, shattered to fragments, ground to powder, and swept from the face of existence. They saw the Independence of Hayti and Liberia recognized and the whole colored race steadily rising into the friendly consideration of the American people. In this broad practical common sense, they took no captious exceptions to the unpleasant incidents of their transition from slavery to freedom. All they wanted to know was that those incidents were only transitional not permanent."[50]

Several months later, in another address widely ignored by historians (James Oakes being a notable exception),[51] Douglass said that Lincoln's speech of April 11, 1865, in which he called for limited black suffrage, "seemed to mean but little," but it actually "meant a great deal. It was just like Abraham Lincoln. He never shocked prejudices unnecessarily. Having learned statesmanship while splitting rails, he always used the thin edge of the wedge first—and the fact that he used it at all meant that he would if need be, use the thick as well as the thin."[52] In dealing with slavery, he had inserted the thin edge of the wedge in March 1862 (with the recommendation to help compensate border states that adopted gradual emancipation), drove it in deeper in 1863 (with the Emancipation Proclamation), and fully drove home the thick part in 1865 (with the Thirteenth Amendment). Even before March 1862, Lincoln had worked behind the scenes to persuade Delaware to emancipate its slaves. So it was with black suffrage. In 1864 Lincoln privately urged Governor Michael Hahn to enfranchise at least some blacks in Louisiana:

> I congratulate you on having fixed your name in history as the first-free-state Governor of Louisiana. Now you are about to have a Convention which, among other things, will probably define the elective franchise. I barely suggest for your private consideration, whether some of the colored people may not be let in—as, for instance, the very intelligent, and especially those who have fought gallantly in our ranks. They would probably help, in some trying time to come, to keep the jewel of liberty within the family of freedom. But this is only a suggestion, not to the public, but to you alone.[53]

In 1865 he publicly endorsed the same policy. To be sure, Louisiana was a special case, for a number of educated blacks lived in New Orleans. Possibly Lincoln did not mean to extend suffrage to uneducated blacks in other states, but that seems unlikely, for if he wanted to enfranchise only educated blacks, he would not have suggested that black soldiers, regardless of educational background, be granted voting rights.

One member of Lincoln's audience did not underestimate the importance of Lincoln's call for limited black suffrage. Upon hearing the president's words, a handsome, popular, impulsive, twenty-six-year-old actor named John Wilkes Booth turned to two friends and declared: "That means nigger citizenship. Now by God I'll put him through!"[54] He added: "That is the last speech he will ever make."[55]

Three days later, Booth murdered Lincoln not because the president had issued the Emancipation Proclamation nor because he had endorsed the Thirteenth Amendment but because he had called for black voting rights. Thus Lincoln should be considered as much a martyr to black civil rights as Martin Luther King, Medgar Evers, Viola Liuzzo, James Reeb, Michael

Schwerner, James Chaney, Andrew Goodman, or any of the others who were slain while championing the civil rights revolution of the 1960s.

Notes

1. Abraham Lincoln, "Speech at Chicago, Illinois" (July 10, 1858), *Collected Works of Abraham Lincoln,* ed. Roy P. Basler, 8 vols. plus index (New Brunswick, NJ: Rutgers University Press, 1953), 2:492. Hereinafter cited as *CW;* emphases in original unless otherwise noted.

2. Abraham Lincoln, "To Albert G. Hodges" (April 4, 1864), in *CW,* 7:281.

3. *House Journal,* 1836–1837, 241–44.

4. *Illinois State Journal* (Springfield), August 25, 1860.

5. *Sangamo Journal,* October 28, 1837.

6. Andy Van Meter, *Always My Friend: A History of the* State Journal-Register *and Springfield* (Springfield, IL: Copley Press, 1981), 30.

7. *Illinois State Journal* (Springfield), October 19, 1854.

8. Robert H. Browne, *Abraham Lincoln and the Men of His Time,* 2 vols. (Cincinnati: Jennings and Pye, 1901), 1:285.

9. Samuel C. Parks to William H. Herndon, Lincoln, IL (March 25, 1866), in *Herndon's Informants: Letters, Interviews, and Statements about Abraham Lincoln,* ed. Douglas L. Wilson and Rodney O. Davis (Urbana: University of Illinois Press, 1998), 239.

10. Abraham Lincoln, "Autobiography Written for John L. Scripps" (ca. June 1860), in *CW,* 4:65.

11. *The Liberator* (Boston), February 9, 1849.

12. Abraham Lincoln, "Remarks and Resolution Introduced in United States House of Representatives Concerning Abolition of Slavery in the District of Columbia" (January 10, 1849), in *CW,* 2:20–22.

13. James Quay Howard's notes of an interview with Lincoln, May 1860, Lincoln Papers, Library of Congress.

14. *The Liberator* (Boston), June 30, 1860.

15. Joshua Giddings to Wendell Phillips, Jefferson, OH (July 30, 1860), *Sentinel* (Ashtabula, OH), n.d., copied in *The Liberator* (Boston), August 24, 1860.

16. William Herndon to Sydney Howard Gay, Springfield, IL (August 10, 1860), Gay Papers, Columbia University.

17. Washington correspondence by C. B. A., September 20, 1849, *New York Tribune,* September 22, 1849.

18. Speech of May 22, 1860, at Oberlin, OH, *Republican* (Springfield, MA), May 28, 1860.

19. *New York Tribune* (August 20, 1862).

20. Abraham Lincoln, "To Horace Greeley" (August 22, 1862), in *CW,* 5:388–89.

21. Don E. Fehrenbacher, *Lincoln in Text and Context: Collected Essays* (Stanford, CA: Stanford University Press, 1987), 284.

22. *New York Independent,* n.d., copied in *New York World,* December 7, 1861; Worthington G. Snethen to Lyman Trumbull, Baltimore (December 8, 1861), Trumbull Papers, Library of Congress; and Worthington G. Snethen to George W. Julian, Baltimore (January 20, 1862), Giddings-Julian Papers, Library of Congress.

23. William Lloyd Garrison to Oliver Johnson, Boston (December 6, 1861), in *The Letters of William Lloyd Garrison,* 6 vols., ed. Walter M. Merrill (Cambridge, MA: Harvard University Press, 1971–1981), 5:47; Garrison to Sumner, Boston (December 20, 1861), ibid., 5:53; and *The Liberator* (Boston), December 6, 1861.

24. *Weekly-Anglo African* (New York), December 7, 1861.

25. James M. McPherson, "Abolitionist and Negro Opposition to Colonization," *Phylon* 26 (1965), 393.

26. Frederick Douglass to Gerrit Smith, Rochester, NY (December 22, 1861), Smith Papers, Syracuse University, and *Douglass's Monthly,* January 1862, 577.

27. "Emigration to Hayti," *Douglass's Monthly,* January and May 1861, 386, 450, and John W. Blassingame et al., eds., *The Frederick Douglass Papers, Series 1: Speeches, Debates, and Interviews,* 5 vols. (New Haven, CT: Yale University Press, 1979–91), 4:437–38 (speech of May 11, 1853). Cf. *Douglass's Monthly,* March 1861, 420.

28. Floyd J. Miller, *The Search for a Black Nationality: Black Emigration and Colonization, 1787–1863* (Urbana: University of Illinois Press, 1975).

29. Richard Blackett, "Martin R. Delany and Robert Campbell: Black Americans in Search of an African Colony," *Journal of Negro History* 62 (1977): 1–25; Martin R. Delany et al., "Political Destiny of the Colored Race on the American Continent," appendix 3 of *Report of the Select Committee on Emancipation and Colonization,* House Report no. 148, 37th Cong., 2nd sess., 37–59; and David M. Dean, *Defender of the Race: James Theodore Holly, Black Nationalist Bishop* (Boston: Lambeth Press, 1979).

30. Washington correspondence, January 18, 1862, *New York Times,* January 19, 1862, and Joseph Enoch Williams et al. to the Honorable Senate and House of Representatives, April 1862, 37A-G21.4, Select Committee on Emancipation, Petitions and Memorials, ser. 467, 37th Cong., RG 233 [D-83], in Ira Berlin et al., eds., *The Wartime Genesis of Free Labor: The Upper South* (New York: Cambridge University Press, 1993), 263–65.

31. *Telegraph* (Alton, IL), January 15, 1855.

32. Robert H. Zoellner, "Negro Colonization: The Climate of Opinion surrounding Lincoln, 1860–65," *Mid-America* 42 (1960): 131–50, and "Emancipation and Colonization," *New York World,* March 29, 1862.

33. Abraham Lincoln quoted Senator Davis's remark to Kansas senator Samuel C. Pomeroy. Adams S. Hill to Sydney Howard Gay, Washington (August 25, 1862), Gay Papers, Columbia University.

34. *Congressional Globe,* 37th Cong., 2nd sess., 1633 (April 11, 1862).

35. Ibid., 2504–5 (June 2, 1862).

36. Charles N. Schaeffer to Edward McPherson, Gettysburg (December 16, 1861), McPherson Papers, Library of Congress.

37. James M. McPherson, ed., *The Negro's Civil War: How American Negroes Felt and Acted during the War for the Union* (New York: Pantheon Books, 1965), 77.

38. Eli Nichols to John Sherman, New Castle, OH (January 20, 1862), John Sherman Papers, Library of Congress.

39. John Palmer Usher to Abraham Lincoln, Washington (August 2, 1862), Lincoln Papers, Library of Congress.

40. Speech by Orestes Brownson, August 26, 1862, *Evening Star* (Washington), August 27, 1862.

41. *Douglass's Monthly,* March 1861, 420; Willis D. Boyd, "James Redpath and American Negro Colonization in Haiti, 1860–1862," *The Americas* 12 (1955): 169–82; John R. McKivigan, "James Redpath and Black Reaction to the Haitian Emigration Bureau," *Mid-America* 69 (1987): 139–53; and Christopher Dixon, "Nineteenth Century African American Emigrationism: The Failure of the Haitian Alternative," *Western Journal of Black Studies* 18 (1994): 77–88.

42. Moncure D. Conway, *The Rejected Stone; or, Insurrection vs. Resurrection in America,* 2nd ed. (Boston: Walker, Wise, 1862), 101.

43. W. D. Gallagher to Salmon P. Chase, St. Louis (February 12, 1862), Chase Papers, Historical Society of Pennsylvania.

44. "Report of the Select House Committee on Emancipation and Colonization," House Report no. 148, 37th Cong., 2nd sess., issued July 16, 1862 (Washington, DC: Government Printing Office, 1862), 15, 14, 16.

45. Ibid.

46. *National Anti-Slavery Standard* (New York), February 1862, and *Once a Week: An Illustrated Miscellany of Art, Science, and Popular Information,* February 1, 1862, in *Harriet Martineau: Writings on Slavery and the American Civil War,* ed. Deborah Anna Logan (DeKalb: Northern Illinois University Press, 2002), 161, 183–84.

47. Michael Vorenberg, "Abraham Lincoln and the Politics of Black Colonization," *Journal of the Abraham Lincoln Association* 14, no. 2 (Summer 1993), http://jala.press.uiuc.edu/14.2/vorenberg.html. Recent attempts to prove that Lincoln enthusiastically supported colonization, even after 1862, are unconvincing. See Allen C. Guelzo, "Review: Phillip W. Magness and Sebastian N. Page, *Colonization after Emancipation: Lincoln and the Movement for Black Resettlement*," *Journal of the Abraham Lincoln Association* 34, no. 1 (Winter 2013): 78–87.

48. An American told this to the English professor F. W. Newman. Newman to the editor of *The Leader* (London) September 1, 1864, copied in the *National Antislavery Standard* (New York), October 8, 1864.

49. Frederick Douglass, *The Life and Times of Frederick Douglass* (Hartford, CT: Park, 1881), 354.

50. Frederick Douglass Papers, Library of Congress.

51. James Oakes, *The Radical and the Republican: Frederick Douglass, Abraham Lincoln, and the Triumph of Antislavery Politics* (New York: Norton, 2006). Oakes's more recent study of emancipation credits Lincoln and his Republican colleagues with genuine antislavery zeal. James Oakes, *Freedom National: The Destruction of Slavery in the United States, 1861–1865* (New York: Norton, 2012).

52. Manuscript of a speech, ca. December 1865, Frederick Douglass Papers, Library of Congress.

53. Abraham Lincoln, "To Michael Hahn" (March 13, 1864), in *CW*, 7:243.

54. Lewis J. Weichman reported that Booth uttered these words to him and a friend in response to Lincoln's remarks. Michael W. Kauffman, *American Brutus: John Wilkes Booth and the Lincoln Conspiracies* (New York: Random House, 2004), 210.

55. Lewis Powell told this to Thomas T. Eckert. "Impeachment of the President," House Report no. 7, 40th Cong., 1st sess. (1867), 674.

4

Learning to Love Lincoln

Frederick Douglass's Journey from Grievance to Gratitude

Diana J. Schaub

"Any man can say things that are true of Abraham Lincoln, but no man can say anything that is new of Abraham Lincoln." That observation was made by Frederick Douglass in his great oration in memory of Lincoln, delivered in 1876 upon the occasion of the dedication of the Freedmen's Memorial Monument to Abraham Lincoln, in Washington, DC. It's still the case today. Not even by resorting to lies and untruths can one find anything new to say about Abraham Lincoln. The truths and untruths—and maybe most common, the half-truths—have all been around a long time. The task is thus not to be original in one's appreciation but to be just.

Proper appreciation of Lincoln's statesmanship, particularly during his lifetime, was rare. The contrast with George Washington is instructive. Although both experts and ordinary citizens now routinely consider Washington and Lincoln the greatest of American presidents, Washington's rank as a statesman was clear and uncontested from the first—so uncontested that his election to the presidency was unanimous, while the election of Lincoln was so contentious as to provoke civil war. In addition to the seditious opposition of the South, Lincoln encountered plenty of loyal opposition in the North, not only from Democrats, but also from those more radical than he both within the Republican Party and outside it (among the various strands of abolitionism). Radicals, then and now, have been particularly stinting in their praise of Lincoln. Some today suggest that credit for emancipation belongs more to those, like Frederick Douglass, who pressured Lincoln to take that decisive step. At the extreme, this position asserts that Lincoln was antiblack, that the Proclamation was basically a fraud, and that Lincoln does not deserve any credit for emancipation since he was "forced into glory."[1]

Before signing on to the contemporary radical critique, we might want to examine what the greatest of the abolitionists himself had to say about Lincoln. From his newspaper editorials before and during the war to his speeches and personal reminiscences after the war, the trajectory of Frederick Douglass's thinking about Lincoln is one of increasing and deepening appreciation, often revising his own earlier negative assessments. Perhaps because Douglass was self-educated, he remained a lifelong learner, capable of open-minded and rigorous reconsiderations. The way in which the exercise of his critical faculties could lead him to substantive re-evaluations was evident early in his career when he dramatically changed his opinion about the status of slavery under the Constitution. Repudiating the Garrisonian view of the proslavery character of the Constitution, Douglass embraced an antislavery reading of the document, thereby transforming himself from a revolutionary, intent on annulling the Constitution, to a reformer, still fiercely critical of American practice but ever after a staunch defender of America's founding principles.[2] A parallel, but more subtle, shift occurred as a result of Douglass's encounter with Lincoln—an encounter that taught him to appreciate the statesman (which is to say the prudent politician) as well as the John Browns of the world. Douglass learned to love Lincoln, and in his 1876 "Oration in Memory of Lincoln" he recapitulated that intellectual and emotional journey for the benefit of all Americans.[3]

First Things

As befitted the ceremonial nature of the occasion, Douglass's speech expressed gratitude toward Lincoln, but more intriguingly it reflected on the political significance of gratitude. It is a speech both of gratitude and about gratitude. Douglass says that "the sentiment of gratitude" that "perpetuate[s] the memories of great public men" is "one of the noblest that can stir and thrill the human heart." Further, he points out that with the dedication of the Freedmen's Monument, a monument funded by donations raised among the newly emancipated race, black Americans now "[f]or the first time in the history of our people, . . . join in this high worship." Douglass wants the world to notice what "we, the colored people" are doing in honoring Abraham Lincoln. As he explains, "First things are always interesting, and this is one of our first things."

While Douglass throughout his life was a, if not *the,* spokesman of his race, this is especially true in this speech, where he employs the collective pronoun "we" much more frequently than the singular "I." Most strikingly, he makes no reference at all to his personal acquaintance with Lincoln. In his other postassassination eulogies and accounts of Lincoln, Douglass regularly (and charmingly) retold the stories of his three meetings with Lincoln.[4] While the "Oration" retraces Douglass's journey toward Lincoln, it does so in a generalized form, purged of the purely personal or adventitious. Learning to love Lincoln must not depend on having had the privilege of sitting across from him in the Oval Office.

The story of how the Freedmen's Monument took the shape it did, and Douglass's role in ensuring that his people's first "national act" came off well, is fascinating. Douglass was approached by W. J. Wilson in 1865 to lend his name to the Educational Monument Association, which proposed to raise money from blacks and whites alike to build a black college in honor of Lincoln's memory. Douglass writes a letter in response, declining to associate himself with the project and strongly discountenancing the association's plans. Always civil, Douglass is at the same time emphatic. He states that he regards "this whole monument business, in its present shape, . . . as an offence against good taste, and as calculated to place the colored people in an undesirable and discreditable position before the country."[5] His reasoning is worth quoting and exploring at length, in part because our own philanthropic instincts and practices have become so much less scrupulous than those articulated by Douglass. Here is the key passage:

> For a monument, by itself, and upon its own merits, I say *good.* For a college by itself . . . and upon its own merits, I say good. But for a college-monument, or for a monument-college, I do not say good; . . . . the whole scheme is derogatory to the character of the colored people of the United States. It carries on its front a distasteful implication. *It looks to me like an attempt to wash the black man's face in the nation's tears for Abraham Lincoln!* It places the paddle-wheels of the colored man's boat in the tide of the popular grief, with a view to his special advantage. I am for washing the black man's face (that is, educating his mind), for that is a good thing to be done, and I

appreciate the nation's tears for Abraham Lincoln; but I am not so enterprising as to think of turning the nation's veneration for our martyred President into a means of advantage to the colored people, and, of sending around the hat to a mourning public.[6]

Douglass doesn't want gratitude—which he calls "one of the holiest sentiments of the human heart"—to be contaminated with blatant self-interest, for gratitude isn't even gratitude then.[7] Being a rigorous bookkeeper when it comes to credits and debits in the economy of the soul, Douglass wants to keep the generous outpourings of the heart distinct from the fiscal inflows.[8] In the proposed monument scheme, the problem of impure motives would have been even worse, since there would not just be a mixture of motives but actually a division of motives along racial lines. Whites would be doing the creditable giving and blacks the self-interested taking. Douglass does not want blacks to enter upon citizenship by feeding at the trough of white solicitude. Instead of an ennobling display of black gratitude, which would elevate the givers and, moreover, elevate the givers in the minds of white observers, this college-monument idea would reduce blacks primarily to the role of recipients.

Douglass was not, in principle, opposed to white philanthropy on behalf of blacks. Years earlier he had sketched a plan for an industrial college in answer to an inquiry from Harriet Beecher Stowe about what she could do to contribute to black advancement.[9] However, Douglass was always sensitive to the dangers of ill-timed and overly intrusive assistance, which could have the perverse effect of sapping black initiative, thereby impeding the long-term prospects of the race. Douglass worried that there was always more of benevolence and pity rather than straightforward justice in white America's dealings with the Negro. His preference was for justice—sternly and blindly equal, with no special pleadings or privileges.[10]

This leads to what at first might seem a contradiction in Douglass's reaction to the monument-college project. As is well-known, Douglass's vision of America is fundamentally integrationist. Nonetheless, he wants the monument to be exclusively a black effort; however humble, it should be, he says, "our own act and deed."[11] On the other hand, when it comes to the idea of a college, Douglass speaks against not only the self-serving hybrid of a monument-college, but also against the idea of any college being built for the permanent and exclusive use of blacks. Given the discrimination of the day, Douglass admitted the need for temporary recourse to complexional institutions, but he did not want to see the founding of any institution that made its peace with the perpetuity of segregation. As he says, "the American people must stand each for all and all for each, without respect to color or race."

So, he is in favor of a separately erected monument but opposed to an avowedly separate college. Why a Freedmen's Monument but not a Freedmen's College? What accounts for the different, and seemingly contradictory, judgments on these two endeavors? The explanation, I think, hinges on the nature of the two undertakings and their potential contribution to either ameliorating or prolonging racial prejudice. A display of gratitude by black Americans, reflecting the special sentiments they bear toward Lincoln, would undercut white prejudice, by showing blacks capable of "the holiest sentiments of the human heart."[12] Conversely a college explicitly and exclusively reserved to blacks (whoever foots the bill for it), by accommodating race prejudice, in effect bolsters it. Thus Douglass accepts all-black institutions only with great reluctance and always with the proviso that, as soon as circumstances permit, blacks must make their way into the parallel majority institutions, whether they be educational, fraternal, residential, commercial, or political.[13] Douglass is consistent in that he judges instances of racial solidarity and group action by their effects on friendship between the races. His guiding question is always, does the doing of this deed point us toward the overcoming of race prejudice and contribute to an ethos of common citizenship? Acts of black self-reliance, both individual and group-based, can create the conditions for nonracial brotherhood. Douglass understood that before the black man could be recognized as a brother, he must be recognized as a man. Manliness precedes fraternity.

As Douglass had hoped, the monument-college plan was abandoned and, in the end, the memorial took the pure form he had recommended, with Douglass himself delivering the dedicatory address. Not surprisingly, his first paragraph refers to the "manly pride" with which blacks should view the occasion, while the final paragraph sets forth the black man's claim to "human brotherhood." More especially it pointedly informs those whites who seek to "scourge [blacks] beyond the range of human brotherhood" that the Freedmen's Monument stands as a refutation of their "blighting slander." In between the opening invocation of manliness and the closing invocation of fraternity, the speech itself demonstrates, with deep and wonderful sophistication, how a still divided nation could develop a shared perspective on the achievements of Abraham Lincoln. We might hazard the following comparison: What Lincoln's "Gettysburg Address" did for the Union, Douglass's "Oration on Lincoln" did—or sought to do—for racial union.

Any analysis of the speech must take into account not only the uniqueness of the occasion but the rhetorical dilemma posed by the larger historical moment. The speech was given in 1876, as the Reconstruction period was coming to an end. With the federal government increasingly reluctant to enforce the Fourteenth and Fifteenth Amendments, Douglass was rightly worried about the resurgent spirit of the Old South. Douglass attempts to turn the memory of Lincoln into a bulwark against the tendency toward appeasement and accommodation. He did this much more blatantly in two speeches he gave in the first months after Lincoln's death, at the start of Reconstruction.[14] In an unpublished speech from June 1865, Douglass forcefully argued that the assassin John Wilkes Booth was an agent and emblem of the South:

> We have here the concentrated *virus,* the moral poison, accumulated by more than two centuries of human slavery, pouring itself out upon the nation as a vial of wrath in one dreadful and shocking crime the first of its kind in the annals of the country.
>
> The accursed theory, so long defended in the name of the Bible and religion—defended thus while known to live upon blood and tears—the hateful crime, so long defended in the name of law and order, properly celebrates its own death by a crime that sends a shudder around the world.
>
> England, France, Germany, all European nations have been literally struck dumb by this appropriate exhibition of slaveholding hate. It is well that slavery should give this mean and bloody sign at its death. Cradled in theft, and living by robbery, it is meet that it should go to its grave under a storm of execration from every quarter of the globe.
>
> Hereafter when men think of slavery, they will think of murder. Hereafter when men think of slaveholders, they will think of assassins. Hereafter when men think of Southern chivalry they will think of our starving prisoners at Andersonville. Hereafter when

men think of Southern honor, they will think of the assassination of Abraham Lincoln.[15]

Similarly, in a December 1865 speech, Douglass spoke approvingly of the check that the assassination delivered to the "sickly sentimental" spirit of Northern clemency.[16] He notes how, at the close of the war, "men seemed as thankful to General Lee for surrendering as to General Grant for making him surrender. The South was no longer our deadly foe but our erring Brother."[17] The assassination, however, restored men to moral realism. Douglass acknowledges that for him it serves as "an instructive and convenient meadium [*sic*] through which we may survey to some extent the dangers, and learn the solemn duties of this hour."[18] Interestingly, Douglass, who believed in the ultimate justice of the cosmic order, often saw evil as the spur to good and didn't shy from giving credit, and a kind of thanks, to evildoers. It is an odd twist on gratitude.[19] Accordingly Douglass says: "We are indebted to our enemies here as elsewhere. They have given us in this, as in many other instances during the last thirty years the events which have been most efficient in the overthrow of slavery and the slave power."[20] Douglass specifically mentions the annexation of Texas, the repeal of the Missouri Compromise, the attempt to subvert Kansas, the Fugitive Slave Bill, and the hanging of John Brown—all culminating in the assassination of Lincoln:

> Dying thus, his name becomes a text from which to preach that Liberty, and that human Equality, to strike down which he was ruthlessly murdered.
>
> The name of Abraham Lincoln pleads to day with all the eloquence of martyrdom, for the utter extinction of every root and fibre, not merely of slavery, but of the insolent, aggressive, and malignant oligarchy—or privileged class founded upon it.[21]

While Douglass refuses to tap the nation's grief and sorrow for financial gain, he is quite willing to do so for political gain. In these 1865 speeches, he seeks to muster patriotism against racial prejudice and proscription.

By 1876 Douglass is facing a more difficult persuasive task, in response to which his treatment of the meaning of Abraham Lincoln becomes more nuanced (and less exclusively focused upon the assassination). One sign of the changed environment is that he does not repeat the striking claim from the June 1865 speech that Lincoln was "emphatically the black man's President."[22] Indeed he seems to reverse tack in 1876, insisting that Lincoln "was preeminently the white man's President." Can both labels be accurate? Why highlight one rather than the other?

From Grievance to Gratitude

The "Oration" has a careful structure, comprising eight distinct sections, each of which begins with what grammarians call a "vocative expression": in the first two sections Douglass addresses "Friends and Fellow Citizens," in the subsequent six, simply "Fellow Citizens." Politicians, of course, often rely on direct address of this sort. Sometimes it even becomes a kind of verbal tic, like John McCain's repeated use of "my friends" or Lyndon Johnson's overreliance on "my fellow Americans." Douglass's iterations, however, are more deliberate. They signal new phases of an argument that delineates the different (but not irreconcilable) claims of whites and blacks to the memory of Lincoln.

Douglass begins by addressing his immediate audience: those who assembled that day in Lincoln Park due east of the Capitol on the eleventh anniversary of Lincoln's assassination. The audience was a large and racially mixed one, composed of twenty-five thousand ordinary citizens along with numerous representatives of official Washington. Douglass mentions the presence of members of the House of Representatives and the Senate, the chief justice and Supreme Court, and the president himself. In the 1893 edition of his autobiography, Douglass singled out this event for having "brought me into mental communication with a greater number of the influential and distinguished men of the country than any I had before known."[23] The elite audience influenced his aim for the speech: "Occasions like this have done wonders in the removal of popular prejudice and lifting into consideration the colored race."[24] Those present deserved to be called not just "Fellow Citizens," but "Friends," whose attendance gave evidence of their sympathies. Interestingly, this first section of the speech makes no mention at all of Lincoln but instead congratulates "you," a pronoun that seems to refer, at least initially, only to Douglass's fellow blacks. Thus he speaks of "our condition as a people" and the remarkable progress in that condition. The evidence of progress, which Douglass says is a "credit to American civilization," provides the occasion for a shift to congratulating "all." Douglass notes that the "new dispensation of freedom"—"the gratifying and glorious change . . . has come both to our white fellow-citizens and ourselves."

The second section of the speech acknowledges especially the federal government and its friendly role in this new dispensation. The official program for the inaugural ceremonies points out that the erection of the memorial received congressional approval, that the pedestal for the statue was paid for by a $3,000 congressional appropriation, and that the day itself had been declared a federal holiday.[25] Douglass, however, highlights the awful sacrifice that lies behind this federal friendship. This section contains Douglass's first mention of Lincoln, whom he calls "the first martyr President of the United States." Moreover, Lincoln's martyrdom is presented as the climax of the larger national sacrifice to which Douglass alludes with his reference to "yonder heights of Arlington," visible from Lincoln Park, where sixteen thousand Civil War soldiers had been buried, including fifteen hundred black troops.[26]

Five years before, on Decoration Day 1871, Douglass had delivered an address at Arlington National Cemetery, near the monument to the "Unknown Loyal Dead."[27] Douglass inserts the full text of this short speech into his autobiography, drawing attention to his departure from his usual practice of avoiding "copious quotations from my letters, speeches, or other writings" and explaining that this speech, also delivered before an impressive audience including President Ulysses S. Grant and his cabinet, "expresses, as I think, the true view which should be taken of the great conflict between slavery and freedom."[28] In the speech he scouts the growing tendency to gloss over the difference between the parties to the conflict: "We are sometimes asked, in the name of patriotism, to forget the merits of this fearful struggle, and to remember with equal admiration those who struck at the nation's life and those who struck to save it, those who fought for slavery and those who fought for liberty and justice."[29] Douglass admits that "unflinching courage marked the rebel not less than the loyal soldier," but he insists that "we are not here to applaud manly courage, save as it has been displayed in a noble cause."

Douglass is increasingly worried that reconciliation between North and South could take the wrong form, thereby excluding the freedmen and eliding the meaning of the conflict. In his "Oration," he alludes to this earlier Decoration Day address when he approves "the sentiment which from year to year adorns with fragrant and beautiful flowers the graves of our loyal, brave, and patriotic soldiers." Within a few years, Douglass delivered another Decoration Day Address, this time in Rochester, New York, in which he argued for the continued observance of Decoration Day, countering those who now sought to scale back or discontinue the holiday out of a fear that it stoked sectional animosity. Douglass's defense takes a curious twist. He is not by nature a conservative, attached to tradition. Once customs become empty, they should fade: "Let not the smoke survive the candle."[30] However, Douglass is not prepared to part with Decoration Day just yet. In fact, he argues for its preservation on progressive grounds: "[Man] is a progressive being, and memory, reason, and reflection are the resources of his improvement."[31] Douglass wants to remember the past for the sake of the future. Although it is certainly true that, in the three decades after the war, Douglass was an activist, campaigning for a variety of new and expanded causes (such as women's rights and labor reform), it is also the case that a goodly portion of his public speaking was dedicated to commemorating the past. On the eleventh anniversary of Lincoln's death, what Douglass wanted to remind his audience of was "blood-bought freedom"—"our blood-bought freedom"—in which "we, the colored people" rejoice.

Gratitude is the bridge between heroic deeds and their commemoration, from the perishable flowers upon the graves at Arlington to the "most enduring works of art, designed to . . . perpetuate the memories of great public men." While Douglass emphasizes the sentiment of appreciation that gives rise to the monuments of civilization, curiously he says next to nothing about the statue before him, just unveiled. It is known that he was not altogether pleased with the design, which shows Lincoln, Emancipation Proclamation in one hand, standing over the crouching figure of a slave. Indeed, there is an eyewitness report that Douglass departed from his written text to criticize the submissive posture of the slave. Dissatisfaction with the sculpture was apparently not limited to Douglass, but was shared by other African Americans. The official program for the festivities, prepared by the Western Sanitary Commission, which had overseen the fundraising and commissioning, attempts to blunt possible objections by explaining certain dignifying changes that were made:

> In the original the kneeling slave is represented as perfectly passive, receiving the boon of freedom from the hand of the great liberator.

But the artist justly changed this, to bring the presentation nearer to the historical fact, by making the emancipated slave an agent in his own deliverance.

He is accordingly represented as exerting his own strength with strained muscles in breaking the chain which had bound him.[32]

The official history also mentions that there was an alternative design by the female sculptor Harriet Hosmer, which was rejected as too costly. It would have depicted Lincoln atop a central pillar, flanked by smaller pillars showing, among other figures, black Union soldiers. Douglass would certainly have preferred this design, embodying as it did his favorite aphorism: "Hereditary bondsmen! know ye not / Who would be free themselves must strike the blow?"[33] Even the program expresses the hope that one day "the gratitude of the freed people will prompt them to execute this grand design."[34] In the years since, decorously concealed chagrin and embarrassment have turned into outright hostility toward the perceived paternalism and racism of the existing statue.[35] Perhaps the time has come to return to the original conception. Avoiding overt insult, Douglass alludes to the alternative Hosmer design by the way he acknowledges both "our loyal, brave, and patriotic soldiers who fell in defense of the Union and liberty" and "the vast, high, and preeminent services rendered to ourselves, to our race, to our country, and to the whole world by Abraham Lincoln."

Having spent the opening two sections proclaiming the generous deed of the moment and commending it to the notice of "men of all parties and opinions," including "those who despise us," Douglass in the third section begins to speak to the larger, nationwide audience—an audience of "Fellow-citizens" not all of whom are necessarily "Friends." Douglass now treads very carefully. He does not want the black embrace of Lincoln to trigger a white flight from Lincoln. And so, he quite dramatically backs away from the Great Emancipator, insisting that

Abraham Lincoln was not, in the fullest sense of the word, either our man or our model. In his interests, in his associations, in his habits of thought, and in his prejudices, he was a white man.

He was preeminently the white man's President, entirely devoted to the welfare of white men. He was ready and willing at any time during the last years of his administration to deny, postpone and sacrifice the rights of humanity in the colored people, to promote the welfare of the white people of his country.

. . . The race to which we belong were not the special objects of his consideration. Knowing this, I concede to you, my white fellow-citizens, a pre-eminence in this worship at once full and supreme.

. . . You are the children of Abraham Lincoln.

Douglass devotes the whole of section 3 to reassuring nervous whites—whites who are patriotic but probably prejudiced. Basically he tells them, "Look, don't worry. Lincoln always loved you best. Take it from me, a Negro: Lincoln was not a Negro-lover." It's a rather startling rhetorical gambit, but it allowed Douglass to exhort white Americans to heap high their hosannas of Lincoln. He tells them: "To you it especially belongs to sound his praises, to preserve and perpetuate his memory, to multiply his statues, to hang his pictures on your walls, and commend his example, for to you he was a great and glorious friend and benefactor."

By the close of this section of the speech, which we might dub the white supremacist section, one might wonder why blacks are bothering to honor Lincoln at all? Douglass's answer, set forth in the last paragraph of this section, is that while whites are Lincoln's children, blacks are "his step-children, children by adoption, children by force of circumstances and necessity." Moreover, what Lincoln did for his stepchildren, whether it was part of his original intention or not, was deliver them from bondage. Accordingly Douglass entreats whites "to despise not the humble offering" of former slaves. The separate claims of whites and blacks upon the memory of Lincoln can coexist. This, by the way, had been the message of the June 1865 speech as well. There Douglass acknowledged the "unsurpassed" devotion of Lincoln to "the welfare of the white race," while declaring him at the same time "emphatically the black man's President." Shared homage, if it is ever to develop, must begin with toleration for racially specific homage.

Frederick Douglass had a gift for metaphor, and this image of blacks as Lincoln's stepchildren is one of his finest. It accords nicely with Lincoln's own account of the relation between the cause of union and the cause of emancipation, as expressed in his famous letter to Horace Greeley. Here is how Lincoln himself explained his duty as president:

My paramount object in this struggle *is* to save the Union, and is *not* either to save or to destroy slavery. If I could save the Union without freeing *any* slave I would do it, and if I could save it by freeing *all* the slaves I would do it; and if I could save it by freeing some and leaving others alone I would also do that. What I do about slavery and the colored race, I do because I believe it helps to save the Union; and what I forbear, I forbear because I do *not* believe it would help to save the Union.[36]

Douglass reminds his listeners that Lincoln was a Unionist first and foremost and that he became the Great Emancipator only "by force of circumstances and necessity." Whites ought to revere Lincoln as the savior of the nation. And indeed, the inscription on the Lincoln Memorial, built on the National Mall half a century after the Freedmen's Monument, reads: "In this temple, as in the hearts of the people for whom he saved the Union, the memory of Abraham Lincoln is enshrined forever."[37]

Of course, the Union to which Lincoln was devoted had at its foundation the principle of human equality. The Union was itself a moral project. That was why Lincoln set himself resolutely against the extension of slavery into the territories. If that point were lost, the Union would have decisively jettisoned its moral content. In another famous letter, Lincoln indicated that if the nation chose to fatally compromise its own founding creed, then he "should prefer emigrating to some country where they make no pretence [*sic*] of loving liberty—to Russia, for instance, where despotism can be taken pure, and without the base alloy of hypocracy [*sic*]."[38]

Because the bond of genuine union is a teaching about natural right, American patriotism ought to produce citizens who are, as Douglass says, "friendly to the freedom of all men." In the fourth section of the speech, Douglass shifts to presenting the stepchildren's view of Lincoln, the essential feature of which was faith in Lincoln's "living and earnest sympathy" with their fate. Again, Douglass doesn't paper over the disagreements and disappointments that blacks experienced during the war years. "We were," he admits, "at times stunned, grieved and greatly bewildered." Douglass provides a litany of reasons why blacks might have doubted Lincoln's good will: he supported colonization schemes; he refused to enlist black troops; after finally allowing black recruitment, he refused to retaliate when the Confederates violated the rules of warfare by massacring black prisoners; and he revoked early emancipation decrees by Union generals in the field.

Nonetheless, Douglass asserts that "we were able to take a comprehensive view of Abraham Lincoln"—a view that took the measure of the man and, after factoring in the "logic" of events and even "that divinity that shapes our ends," Douglass says, "we came to the conclusion that the hour and the man of our redemption had met in the person of Abraham Lincoln." Douglass then gives a counterlitany of the liberationist and racially transformative policies that transpired under Lincoln's rule. As he lists nine achievements, culminating in the Emancipation Proclamation, Douglass each time repeats a version of the phrase "under his rule we saw. . . ." The phrase is crucial for both whites and blacks. Blacks—who longed for liberty but who might understandably be suspicious of rule and law, having suffered under generations of misrule—are reminded that their liberty came to them through law and through "wise and beneficent rule." Conversely whites are reminded that the actions of Lincoln, which struck not only at slavery but at "prejudice and proscription" as well, were the actions of a dedicated constitutionalist. The closing paragraph of section 4 celebrates emancipation and, moreover, shows that the celebration can be shared by all. Douglass asks, "Can any colored man, or any white man friendly to the freedom of all men, ever forget the night which followed the first day of January, 1863?" Whites can appreciate black liberation, and blacks can appreciate white "statesmanship"—a word that Douglass now uses for the first but not the last time in the address.

On this new biracial basis of union and liberty, Douglass goes on to a reconsideration of Lincoln in sections 5, 6, and 7. He argues that Lincoln's "great and good" character was transparent to those "who saw him and heard him." Indeed, direct contact wasn't even necessary. In a passage with tremendous import for us today, Douglass says that "the image of the man went out with his words, and those who read him knew him." We are indebted to biographers and historians who have scoured and scavenged for all the bits and pieces of eyewitness testimony and hearsay evidence and who have laboriously contextualized and hypothesized and speculated, to such a degree that, with the exception of Jesus, there is now no one who ever walked the earth more written about than Abraham Lincoln. Nonetheless, it is reassuring to know that Lincoln's words alone are enough. In light of this fundamentalist insight, Douglass now revises his earlier "white supremacist" account of Lincoln. He reconsiders Lincoln's deference to popular prejudice in the appropriate context, that of the requirements of democratic statesmanship. Here's what he says at the close of section 5:

I have said that President Lincoln was a white man, and shared the prejudices common to his countrymen towards the colored race. Looking back to his times and to the condition of the country, this unfriendly feeling on his part may be safely set down as one element of his wonderful success in organizing the loyal American people for the tremendous conflict before them, and bringing them safely through that conflict. His great mission was to accomplish two things; first, to save his country from dismemberment and ruin, and second, to free his country from the great crime of slavery. To do one or the other, or both, he must have the earnest sympathy and the powerful cooperation of his loyal fellow-countrymen. Without this primary and essential condition to success, his efforts must have been vain and utterly fruitless. Had he put the abolition of slavery before the salvation of the Union, he would have inevitably driven from him a powerful class of the American people, and rendered resistance to rebellion impossible. Viewed from the genuine abolition ground, Mr. Lincoln seemed tardy, cold, dull, and indifferent; but measuring him by the sentiment of his country, a sentiment he was bound as a statesman to consult, he was swift, zealous, radical, and determined.

Frederick Douglass himself always occupied "the genuine abolition ground," and his editorials, from the early years of the war especially, often manifested great frustration with Lincoln's caution. Douglass was prominent among those who, "from opposite quarters," assailed Lincoln, until he was "covered and blistered with reproaches." In retrospect, however, Douglass generously acknowledges the partiality of his own abolitionist stance and credits Lincoln as the "comprehensive statesman."

The final paragraph of this section carefully distinguishes Lincoln's views on race from his views on slavery. Douglass iterates (for the third time) that Lincoln was prejudiced or more precisely that he "*shared* the prejudices of his white fellow-countrymen against the Negro [italics added]." According to Douglass, racial prejudice is a social construct, rather than an innate or invincible sentiment. It seems that Douglass does not regard Lincoln as particularly progressive on the question of race; he was a follower or a sharer. However, in this very same section in which Douglass refers to Lincoln's prejudices, he explicitly says that "the humblest could approach him and feel at home in his presence." This statement echoes the account that Douglass gave in other speeches and writings of the experience of being in Lincoln's personal presence. Speaking of his second meeting with Lincoln, Douglass in his autobiography says: "Mr. Lincoln was not only a great President, but a GREAT MAN—too great to be small in anything. In his company I was never in any way reminded of my humble origin, or of my unpopular color."[39]

One wonders whether the presentation of Lincoln's racial prejudice is compatible with the presentation of his capacious humanity. Of course, it might be possible for someone to regard a particular class of people as inferior in certain respects, while still treating individual members of that class with consideration. Lincoln could have been both prejudiced and polite (even solicitous or magnanimous). If so, it would still be necessary to explain why Douglass in the "Oration" chooses to draw attention to one quality more than the other. Perhaps he wishes to indicate to both blacks and whites that racial prejudice is not an insuperable obstacle to black advancement or bettered race relations. Alternatively, I believe it is possible to interpret Douglass's remarks in a way consistent with the view that Lincoln deferred to popular prejudice without fully subscribing to popular prejudice. The issue might be elucidated by asking "what was the nature of Lincoln's 'sharing' in white prejudice?" When he describes the relation between Lincoln and "the sentiment of his country," Douglass credits Lincoln with being in advance of popular opinion (measured against which he was "swift, zealous, radical, and determined"). Douglass introduces the key verb "consult," claiming that "the sentiment of his country" was something Lincoln "was bound as a statesman to consult." To the extent that popular sentiment was unfriendly to blacks, Lincoln's sharing in it may have been political rather than personal—deliberately affected rather than deeply held. Douglass conveys a crucial lesson about the limits within which democratic statesmen operate. More than others perhaps, black citizens must incorporate this insight into their assessment of political figures. In taking the measure of Lincoln, Douglass shows how granting this latitude of maneuver is compatible with respect for the burdens of statesmanship as well as the self-respect of citizens. As Douglass had indicated in section 4, a "comprehensive view" must "make reasonable allowance for the circumstances" and not judge on the basis of "stray utterances" or "isolated facts."

However one might come down on the question of Lincoln's views on race, Douglass is emphatic that Lincoln's attitude toward slavery was above reproach. Douglass quotes from the atonement passage of the Second Inaugural, in which Lincoln interpreted the Civil War as the blood price exacted by a just God for the nation's sins toward the slave. These are lines that Douglass quoted (at varying length and with varying accuracy) in nearly every postwar speech about Lincoln.[40] The Second Inaugural's solemn invocation of divine reparations, Douglass says, "gives all needed proof of [Lincoln's] feeling on the subject of slavery."

Douglass now revisits an issue he had highlighted earlier. In section 3, when he mentioned Lincoln's policy of "opposition to the extension of slavery," he had stressed Lincoln's willingness to "protect, defend, and perpetuate slavery in the states where it existed." This (objectionable) tolerance of slavery was cited as evidence of Lincoln's prowhite views. Now, however, in section 5, Douglass explains that Lincoln acted as he did not because he was indifferent to the fate of black slaves, but "because he thought that it was so nominated in the bond." In other words, he acted out of fidelity to the Constitution. Lincoln's antebellum stance toward the South does not in any way disprove or lessen his antislavery convictions. Of course, Douglass himself disagreed with Lincoln about what precisely was "nominated in the bond." Most notably Douglass argued that the so-called "fugitive slave" clause did not, in truth, refer to slaves but rather to indentured servants. Moreover, Douglass adhered to a version of natural law jurisprudence that would invalidate any bond demanding "its pound of flesh."[41] Nonetheless, even though he is not fully in accord with Lincoln's reading of the document, Douglass moves his audience toward an appreciation of constitutional devotion. He is acutely aware that racial progress in the future will depend upon the fidelity of both blacks and whites to the Constitution as purified and completed by the Thirteenth, Fourteenth, and Fifteenth Amendments.

Fittingly, sections 6 and 7 transcend race altogether. These are the only sections that make no reference to either whites or blacks. Section 6 describes Lincoln's early years and his preparation, through plain speaking and plain dealing, for the great crisis of civil war. Douglass emphasizes Lincoln's humble origins: "A son of toil himself he was linked in brotherly sympathy with the sons of toil in every loyal part of the Republic." In this section, racial division is overcome and replaced by the class division between the patrician, James Buchanan, who was willing to allow "national dismemberment," and the plebeian, Abraham Lincoln, who had "an oath in heaven" to preserve, protect, and defend the Constitution of the United States. The division we ought to dwell on, Douglass implies, is that between patriotism and treason.

This theme reaches its apotheosis in section 7, which describes the assassination of Abraham Lincoln. Despite the "hell-black spirit of revenge" that motivated the crime, Douglass argues, once again, that good has arisen from evil. Dying as a martyr to "union and liberty"—these twin aims now conjoined and equal—Lincoln has become "doubly dear to us."[42]

In the final section, just one paragraph in length, Douglass comes full circle, speaking once more to his largely black audience: "In doing honor to the memory of *our friend* and liberator we have been doing highest honor to ourselves and those who come after us [emphasis added]." Note that despite the "unfriendly feeling" ascribed to Lincoln in sections 3 and 5, Lincoln by the end has become "our friend."[43] Through his interpretation and masterful presentation of Lincoln's statesmanship, Douglass has knit together the American polity in mutual understanding and appreciation of Lincoln. Douglass has acted as a statesman himself by demonstrating how memory and memorialization, done well, might shape a postracial future. Despite his own brilliant oratory, Douglass is aware that there will continue to be whites who reject the black claim to human brotherhood. This monument, he says, stands as their reproof. And to that I would add: this speech too, for it is a manly and magnanimous act.

WWDD (What Would Douglass Do?)

The bicentennial of Lincoln's birth was also the year that saw the inauguration of the nation's first black president. Were Frederick Douglass to reappear among us, what would he say about these two events? About the forty-fourth president, Douglass would, I imagine, have shared the pride of the moment. However, it is worth remembering that in an address titled "The Present and Future of the Colored Race in America," Douglass indicates that a black president is not the proper litmus test for race relations in America: "The question is not whether colored men will be likely to reach the Presidential chair. I have no trouble here: for a man may live quite a tolerable life without ever breathing the air of Washington." The real question is "Can the white and colored people of this country be blended into a common nationality, and enjoy together, in the same country, under the same flag, the inestimable blessings of life, liberty and the pursuit of happiness, as neighborly citizens of a common country?"[44] So, according to Douglass, we could achieve "a common nationality" without ever electing a black president. Presumably, we could also elect a black president before having fully achieved "a common nationality."

The test of common nationality that Douglass proposes in the "Oration" involves gratitude. How we honor the sixteenth president is as much a test of our joint citizenship as the election of the forty-fourth. Knowing Lincoln as he did, Douglass would be intensely interested in whether what is said today about Lincoln is true. He might especially care to know whether the descendants of Lincoln's stepchildren still honor him. Clearly, some do. We all know of Barack Obama's invocations and emulation of Lincoln, much of it highly symbolic, such as opening his campaign in Springfield, Illinois, and taking the oath of office upon Lincoln's Bible. In this, Obama has gone against the grain of the black establishment and, indeed, black opinion generally, for it seems the prevailing view among African Americans, gathering force over the last few decades, is that Lincoln was a white supremacist and ought not to be the favored recipient of black thanks or tribute. In a Library of America volume called *The Lincoln Anthology,* Harold Holzer cites a 1991 poll that found "only 35 percent of the black respondents named Lincoln as one of the three greatest presidents."[45] That is an astonishing defection and one that would have appalled Frederick Douglass. One might also note that the National Association for the Advancement of Colored People (NAACP) was founded in 1909 on the centennial of Lincoln's birthday; however, there was no commemoration of the Lincoln bicentennial as part of the NAACP's own centennial in 2009.

I suspect that this turn away from Lincoln began with W. E. B. Du Bois. At least his is the first public disparagement of Lincoln from a prominent postbellum black leader. In May 1922, coinciding with the dedication of the national Lincoln Memorial, Du Bois penned a glib paragraph demeaning Lincoln in *The Crisis,* the magazine he edited for the NAACP. The debunking approach that Du Bois pioneered reached its apogee in a very influential article (and subsequent book) by Lerone Bennett Jr., the longtime editor of *Ebony* magazine, in 1968. The article was titled "Was Abe Lincoln a White Supremacist?" To that leading question, Bennett replied with a most tendentious "yes." While Du Bois's remarks were still an appreciation of sorts, Bennett found nothing worthy of praise in Lincoln's career or character.[46] "In the final analysis," he said, "Lincoln must be seen as the embodiment, not the transcendence, of the American tradition, which is, as we all know, a racist tradition." Adding insult to injury, Bennett attempted to enlist Douglass on the Lincoln-bashing side, crediting him with having "punctured the myths and looked frankly at the man."[47] Not surprisingly, he quotes solely from the "white supremacist" paragraph of the Douglass address, thereby seriously distorting Douglass's message—his "comprehensive view" of a "comprehensive statesman." Bennett manages to traduce not only Abraham Lincoln and the American tradition, but Frederick Douglass too. Bennett invokes Douglass only to unsay what Douglass said and undo what Douglass did.[48]

The contemporary alienation of affection on the part of African Americans from both the founders and Lincoln is damaging. Aristotle spoke of the civic good of *homonoia,* or like-mindedness. Echoing Aristotle, Douglass admonished his people not to "adopt for ourselves a political creed apart from the rest of our fellow citizens."[49] Barack Obama could contribute much to both historical memory and racial accord by restoring the founders and Lincoln to their rightful place in a unified national consciousness. For a model of how to do it, there is none better than Frederick Douglass.

Notes

1. Lerone Bennett Jr., *Forced into Glory: Abraham Lincoln's White Dream* (Chicago: Johnson, 2000).

2. Diana J. Schaub, "Frederick Douglass's Constitution," in *The American Experiment: Essays on the Theory and Practice of Liberty,* ed. Peter Augustine Lawler and Robert Martin Schaefer (Lanham, MD: Rowman & Littlefield, 1994), 459–74.

3. The editor of this volume, Lucas Morel, has spoken and written insightfully on the "Oration." See "America's First Black President? Lincoln's Legacy of Political Transcendence," in *Lincoln Reshapes the Presidency,* ed. Charles M. Hubbard (Macon, GA: Mercer University Press, 2001), 120–52, and "Frederick Douglass's Emancipation of Abraham Lincoln," Lincoln Studies Center Lecture, Knox College, Galesburg, IL, September 16, 2005. See also the excellent article by Peter C. Myers, "'A Good Work for Our Race To-Day': Interests, Virtues, and the Achievement of Justice in Frederick Douglass' Freedmen's Monument Speech," *American Political Science Review* 104, no. 2 (May 2010): 209–25.

4. *Life and Times of Frederick Douglass,* in Frederick Douglass, *Autobiographies* (New York: Library of America, 1994), 785–87, 795–98, 802–805. See also "The Assassination and Its Lessons: An Address Delivered in Washington, D.C., on 13 February 1866," "The Black Man's Debt to Abraham Lincoln: An Address

Delivered in Washington, D.C., on 12 February 1888," and "Abraham Lincoln, the Great Man of Our Century: An Address Delivered in Brooklyn, New York, on 13 February 1893," in *Frederick Douglass Papers,* ed. John W. Blassingame and John R. McKivigan, 5 vols. (New Haven, CT: Yale University Press, 1992), 4:106–18, 5:338–44, 5:535–45.

5. Frederick Douglass to W. J. Wilson (August 8, 1865), *Life and Writings of Frederick Douglass,* ed. Philip S. Foner, 5 vols. (New York: International Publishers, 1975), 4:171.

6. Ibid., 4:173.

7. Ibid., 4:172.

8. One can only imagine the anathemas he would heap on our modern-day tax write-off for charitable giving. In thus "incentivizing" charity, we indicate that we care more for the gifts than the giver, more for quantity than quality.

9. Frederick Douglass to Harriet Beecher Stowe (March 8, 1853), in Foner, *Life and Writings,* 2:229–36.

10. See especially Frederick Douglass, "What the Black Man Wants," Speech at the Annual Meeting of the Massachusetts Anti-Slavery Society at Boston (April 1865), in Foner, *Life and Writings,* 4:157–65.

11. Frederick Douglass to W. J. Wilson (August 8, 1865), in Foner, *Life and Writings,* 4:172.

12. Ibid.

13. See especially Frederick Douglass, "The Nation's Problem: An Address Delivered in Washington, D.C., on 16 April 1889," in Blassingame and Mc-Kivigan, *Frederick Douglass Papers,* 5:414–16.

14. Untitled speech from June 1865 and "Abraham Lincoln: A Speech" from December 1865. Both speeches can be found online as part of the Frederick Douglass Papers at the Library of Congress. Scholars owe a debt to Michael Burlingame for having discovered them in the course of his research for *Abraham Lincoln: A Life,* 2 vols. (Baltimore: Johns Hopkins University Press, 2008). Some of the material from these two unpublished speeches does appear in "The Assassination and Its Lessons: An Address Delivered in Washington, D.C., on 13 February 1866," in Blassingame and McKivigan, *Frederick Douglass Papers,* 4:106–18. A few key passages also reappear in the "Oration."

15. "[Lincoln, Abraham] Folder 3 of 3," available online through the Frederick Douglass Papers at the Library of Congress, http://hdl.loc.gov/loc.mss/mfd.31017, 20–21.

16. "Abraham Lincoln: A Speech," available online through the Frederick Douglass Papers at the Library of Congress, http://hdl.loc.gov/loc.mss/mfd.22015, 3.

17. Ibid.

18. Ibid., 7.

19. In his autobiography, Douglass tells the wonderful story of how he taught himself to read, virtually uninstructed, once the generous guidance offered by his mistress was curtailed by his master, who railed that "learning would spoil the best nigger in the world. . . . [I]t would forever unfit him for the duties of a slave." Douglass described this tirade as "the first decidedly anti-slavery lecture" he had heard, for it sketched out "the direct pathway from slavery to freedom." Douglass's unorthodox conclusion: "In learning to read, therefore, I am not sure that I do not owe quite as much to the opposition of my master, as to the kindly assistance of my amiable mistress." *My Bondage and My Freedom*, in Douglass, *Autobiographies*, 217–18.

20. "Abraham Lincoln: A Speech," 7.

21. Ibid., 9.

22. The passage reads: "But what was A. Lincoln to the colored people or they to him? As compared with the long line of his predecessors, many of whom were merely the facile and servile instruments of the slave power, Abraham Lincoln, while unsurpassed in his devotion to the welfare of the white race, was also in a sense hitherto without example, emphatically the black man's President: the first to show any respect for their rights as men." The specific trigger for these remarks is worth noting: Douglass was responding to the attempt in New York to prevent black mourners from joining Lincoln's funeral procession. That disgraceful act of exclusion led Douglass to state the obvious (the special claim of blacks to the memory of Lincoln) but in a nonobvious way. Douglass's formulation blends natural rights ("their rights as men") and civic status (for the first time, blacks could be said to have a president).

23. Douglass, *Autobiographies*, 855.

24. Ibid.

25. "Inaugural Ceremonies of the Freedmen's Memorial Monument to Abraham Lincoln, Washington City, April 14th, 1876," available online through the Frederick Douglass Papers at the Library of Congress, http://hdl.loc.gov/loc.mss/mfd.

26. "Facts about Section 27," Official Website of Arlington National Cemetery, http://www.arlingtoncemetery.mil/History/Facts/AncSec27.aspx.

27. Decoration Day was begun in 1868 by order of the Grand Army of the Republic to honor the Union dead. Later renamed Memorial Day, it was expanded after World War I to commemorate all servicemen who gave their lives in the nation's wars.

28. Douglass, *Autobiographies*, 850.

29. Ibid., 851.

30. Frederick Douglass, "We Must Not Abandon the Observance of Decora-

tion Day: An Address Delivered in Rochester, New York, on 30 May 1882," in Blassingame and McKivigan, *Frederick Douglass Papers,* 5:42.

31. Ibid., 5:45.

32. "Inaugural Ceremonies of the Freedmen's Memorial Monument."

33. Douglass cited these lines from Byron's *Childe Harold's Pilgrimage* (canto II, stanza LXXVI) often, including in "What Are the Colored People Doing for Themselves?," *The North Star* (July 14, 1848), in Foner, *Life and Writings,* 1:315.

34. "Inaugural Ceremonies of the Freedmen's Memorial Monument."

35. Aaron Lloyd, "Statue of Limitations: Why Does D.C. Celebrate Emancipation in Front of a Statue That Celebrates 19th-Century Racism?," *Washington City Paper,* April 28, 2000, http://www.washingtoncitypaper.com/articles/19522/statue-of-limitations.

36. Abraham Lincoln to Horace Greeley (August 22, 1862), in Abraham Lincoln, *Speeches and Writings, 1859–1865* (New York: Library of America, 1989), 358.

37. At the dedication of the Lincoln Memorial in 1922, the keynote address was given by Dr. Robert Moton, Booker T. Washington's successor as president of Tuskegee Institute. Douglass might have been intrigued to learn that Moton spoke not of union, but of liberty, fixing Lincoln's claim to greatness in "the word that gave freedom to a race." In the draft of his speech, Moton proceeded to transform the Negro's debt to Lincoln into the nation's (unpaid) debt to the Negro, a rhetorical move that displeased the organizers and forced Moton to tone down his talk of a "great unfinished work" of "equal opportunity." Even with the edits, however, the focus of the speech was emancipation. Almost a half-century later, Dr. Martin Luther King Jr. would sound a very similar theme in his "I Have a Dream" speech on the steps of the Lincoln Memorial.

38. Abraham Lincoln to Joshua F. Speed (August 24, 1855), in Lincoln, *Speeches and Writings, 1832–1858* (New York: Library of America, 1989), 363.

39. Douglass, *Autobiographies,* 797.

40. See especially Douglass, "The Black Man's Debt to Abraham Lincoln" and "Abraham Lincoln, the Great Man of Our Century."

41. Like Portia in *The Merchant of Venice,* who granted Shylock his pound of flesh but not one drop of blood, Douglass believed that the strictest of strict construction might serve the cause of liberty.

42. Walt Whitman's lecture, "Death of Abraham Lincoln," first delivered April 14, 1879, further develops the meaning of Lincoln's martyrdom. See Walt Whitman, *Prose Works 1892,* ed. Floyd Stovall, 2 vols. (New York: New York University Press, 1963–1964), 2:497–509.

43. Douglass's eulogy of his fellow abolitionist Wendell Phillips provides an interesting point of comparison. Douglass asserts that "none have a better

right" to honor the memory of Phillips than "the colored people of the United States." Although he was active for a variety of causes, Phillips "was primarily and pre-eminently the colored man's friend. . . . The cause of the slave was his first love; and from it he never wavered, but was true and steadfast through life." "Wendell Phillips Cast His Lot with the Slave: An Address Delivered in Washington, D.C., on 22 February 1884," in Blassingame and McKivigan, *Frederick Douglass Papers,* 5:151–52.

44. Frederick Douglass, "The Present and Future of the Colored Race in America" (June 1863), in Foner, *Life and Writings,* 3:352.

45. Harold Holzer, ed., *The Lincoln Anthology: Great Writers on His Life and Legacy from 1860 to Now* (New York: Library of America, 2009), 737.

46. That Du Bois's remarks were an appreciation was especially evident in the rejoinder he made to his outraged readers where he said, "I glory in that crucified humanity that can push itself up out of the mud of a miserable, dirty ancestry; who despite the clinging smirch of low tastes and shifty political methods, rose to be a great and good man and the noblest friend of the slave." W. E. B. Du Bois, *Writings* (New York: Library of America, 1986), 1198.

47. Lerone Bennett Jr., "Was Abe Lincoln a White Supremacist?," in Holzer, *Lincoln Anthology,* 752.

48. At the close of his Cooper Union Address, Lincoln calls on the carpet those who employ "invocations to Washington, imploring men to unsay what Washington said, and undo what Washington did." "Address at Cooper Institute, New York City" (February 27, 1860), in Lincoln, *Speeches and Writings, 1859–1865,* 130.

49. Frederick Douglass, "The United States Cannot Remain Half-Slave and Half-Free," Speech on the Occasion of the Twenty-First Anniversary of Emancipation in the District of Columbia (April 1883), in Foner, *Life and Writings,* 4:370.

Part II

Lincoln's Politics

5

Lincoln and Political Principles

Thomas L. Krannawitter

Commenting on the meaning of the Fourth of July in an 1858 speech in Chicago, Abraham Lincoln argued that America's founding political principle, the self-evident truth that all men are created equal, is "the father of all moral principle."[1] For Lincoln, individual freedom under republican self-government is a moral no less than a political cause. And Lincoln understood that moral and political right spring from the sound ground—nature, or natural right—by which the human mind can discern rational principles for human action, principles that cut through time and across space and are therefore universal, principles that are not the reserve of one people or one historical epoch or one place.

Thus, in the same speech, Lincoln pointed out that while some men and women in the audience could trace their ancestry back to the families of the American founding, many could not. "If they look back through this history to trace their connection with those [founding] days by blood," Lincoln remarked, "they find they have none, they cannot carry themselves back into that glorious epoch and make themselves feel that they are part of us." "But," Lincoln was quick to add, "when they look through that old Declaration of Independence, they find that those old men say that 'We hold these truths to be self-evident, that all men are created equal,' and then they feel that that moral sentiment taught in that day evidences their relation to those men."[2] *All* Americans, Lincoln argued, including those whose ancestors came to America after the founding and were not direct descendants of the founding families, were nonetheless "blood of the blood, and flesh of the flesh of the men who wrote that Declaration" precisely because the timeless principle of natural human equality, within the American political order, replaced accidents of birth or race or tribal membership or religious dogma as the ground of political legitimacy.[3]

At a time when prominent American thinkers rejected the natural right principles of the founding in favor of European historicism or evolutionary right and others either ridiculed the principle of equality or were blinded to it by their appetite for slavery, it was Lincoln above all others who not only studied and mastered American political principles, but also worked tirelessly to craft his rhetoric so that he could better articulate and better teach the meaning of those principles, allowing his audience to be better students of them. All the while, Lincoln prudently navigated the tumultuous waters of mid-nineteenth-century American politics, winning the highest political office in the land, a position he would use to remind Americans, through public speeches and public policies, of their own good principles. In this way Lincoln was eminently conservative—it was his purpose to conserve, to preserve, what he called on one occasion the "sheet anchor" of free, republican government: the natural right principles of the American founding, foremost the principle of equality, upon which rested the entire experiment in self-government.[4]

Lincoln never understood himself as possessing political principles different than those of the founders, though he did understand that in his own day, unlike during the founding, those principles were under serious attack and therefore in need of serious political and philosophic defense. Providing that defense formed the core of Lincoln's statesmanship. This chapter will focus on three important lessons we can learn from Lincoln regarding the political principles for which he ultimately gave the last full measure of devotion. The first is that the egalitarian natural right principles of the founding are the only foundation for free society and limited, constitutional government. Second, the political principles of the American founding are timeless, not confined to the eighteenth or nineteenth centuries, and therefore may be of no less interest to us today than they were to Lincoln in his day or to the founders in their day. And third, America's political principles are universal, rooted in a human nature shared by all human beings everywhere and therefore apply to all human beings of all colors and varieties.

American Political Principles: Foundation for Free Society

If one considers Lincoln to be the founder of the Republican Party, in the qualified sense that he was the first to win a national election on the Republican ticket and thereby legitimize the party as a contending force in American politics, and if one considers Thomas Jefferson to be the effective founder of what would become the Democratic Party, in the qualified sense that Jefferson's legacy of a minimal and fiscally restrained national government, opposition to Hamiltonian-style economics, and an emphasis on states' rights informed what became the Democratic Party throughout much of the nineteenth century, then it becomes all the more remarkable to hear the founder of the Republican Party praise the founder of the Democratic Party. "All honor to Jefferson," Lincoln wrote glowingly in an 1859 letter. "The principles of Jefferson are the definitions and axioms of free society."[5]

Lincoln was a careful student of Euclidean geometry—he mastered the first six books of Euclid's *Geometry* while serving his lone term in Congress—and he understood that a man might "start with great confidence that he could convince any sane child that the simpler propositions of Euclid are true." Nevertheless, Lincoln continued, he "would fail, utterly, with one who should deny the definitions and axioms." This was important because the principles of Jefferson—the "definitions and axioms of free society"—were being "denied, and evaded, with no small show of success" in Lincoln's day, as "[o]ne dashingly calls them 'glittering generalities,' another bluntly calls them 'self evident lies,' and still others insidiously argue that they apply only to 'superior races.'"[6]

For Lincoln it was impossible to deny the self-evident truth of human equality without denying the very ground of free society and constitutional self-government. The various rejections of the founding principle of equality, while "differing in form, are identical in object and effect—the supplanting the principles of free government, and restoring those of classification, caste, and legitimacy." The various rejections of the founding principle of equality "would delight a convocation of crowned heads, plotting against the people," argued Lincoln, because "they are the van-guard—the miners, and sappers—of returning despotism." "We must repulse them, or they will subjugate us. This is a world of compensations; and he who would *be* no slave, must consent to *have* no slave. Those who deny freedom to others, deserve it not for themselves; and, under a just God, cannot long retain it."[7]

Lincoln understood that "popular sovereignty," or the right of self-government, is right so long as it is understood to refer to what James Madison called the "social compact"—that is, free people voluntarily governing themselves in recognition of, and for the protection of, their equal natural rights.[8] This is precisely why Lincoln opposed the "popular sovereignty" argument of Stephen A. Douglas, because Douglas tried to divorce "popular sovereignty" from the principle of human equality and the purpose of protecting equal natural rights. "When the white man governs himself, that is self-government," Lincoln said, "but when he governs himself and also governs another man . . . that is despotism." Drawing upon the principles of the Declaration of Independence, Lincoln argued, "[M]y ancient faith teaches me that 'all men are created equal,' and that there can be no moral right in connection with one man's making a slave of another."[9]

The founders, Madison especially, repeatedly argued that all free government rests on "compact." The founders formed a government, or a "social compact," the end or purpose of which was to protect the equal natural rights of those who consented to live under that compact. But the compact itself was a necessary moral and political inference from the principle of equality: if no man is the natural ruler of another, then the only legitimate political rule is consensual rule, and a body politic formed by voluntary consent is a social compact. Government by consent is foremost a moral principle. It is *wrong* for one man to rule another without the other's consent. And just as no person who does not wish to be a slave should enslave another, so governments should not rule without the consent of the governed. "As I would not be a *slave*, so I would not be a *master*," Lincoln wrote in a surviving fragment. "This expresses my idea of democracy. Whatever differs from this, to the extent of the difference, is no democracy."[10] Lincoln's definition of "democracy" is nothing less than the moral conditions required by the social compact theory of the founders.

From the point of view of the founders no less than of Lincoln, the social compact framework of government is best suited for achieving man's highest political ends. Consider, for example, some of the leading public documents from the founding period:

- The Declaration of Independence, proclaiming that all human beings naturally possess certain "unalienable rights," including the rights to "life, liberty, and the pursuit of happiness" among others, asserts "that to secure these rights, governments are instituted among men."
- Later the Declaration states that the end or goal of government is "to effect" the "safety and happiness" of the people.
- James Madison echoes the Declaration in *Federalist* No. 43, writing

"that the safety and happiness of society are the objects at which all political institutions aim."[11]

- The Constitution's preamble states the following ends of American government: "We the people of the United States, in order to form a more perfect union, establish justice, insure domestic tranquility, provide for the common defense, promote the general welfare, and secure the blessings of liberty to ourselves and our posterity, do ordain and establish this Constitution for the United States of America."

- In *Federalist* No. 51, Madison writes, "Justice is the end of government. It is the end of civil society. It ever has been, and ever will be pursued, until it be obtained, or until liberty be lost in the pursuit."[12]

There is a logic to these different ends; they are aspects of one sovereign purpose. The first and most basic purpose of government is to secure the "safety" of the citizens. This means securing their rights to life and liberty. Government must protect citizens from foreign enemies, as well as from fellow citizens who threaten their rights. The first instance requires strong national defense and a prudent foreign policy; the second requires effective criminal laws that justly punish those citizens who violate the rights of others and police who help to enforce those laws. Securing the safety of the people is a necessary condition to fulfill the other purposes of government. Only when the lives, liberties, and properties of citizens are secure against foreign and domestic dangers will the people enjoy the "domestic tranquility" needed to "establish justice."

The founders also understood not only justice but all the moral virtues to be essential ingredients of the citizenry's "general welfare." As Jefferson once remarked, man is "inherently independent of all but moral law."[13] The "moral law" is the source of the rights, duties, and happiness of man. The founders understood the principles of free government within this framework of moral law. As the Virginia Declaration of Rights proclaims, the blessings of liberty depend on "a firm adherence to justice, moderation, temperance, frugality, and virtue."[14] In the founders' view, a government that succeeds in securing a safe, free, tranquil, and moral society will have succeeded in establishing, as far as human design is capable, the conditions for achieving the ultimate purpose of government, the "happiness of society." This is precisely why Lincoln, in his Second Annual Message to Congress, referred to the American social compact form of government as "the last best, hope of earth."[15]

When the ends of government and the purpose of the American social compact are understood, the connection between the Declaration of
Independence and the Constitution becomes intelligible as the means (the
Constitution) relates to the ends (the Declaration). Consider, for example,
how the Constitution points to the Declaration: the Constitution is established in order to "secure the blessings of liberty," and what is a blessing
other than a gift from God? The liberty that the Constitution is designed to
protect is not government-granted, but rather God-given. Thus the Constitution implicitly recognizes that human beings have been "endowed by their
Creator with certain unalienable rights," as the Declaration states, among
which is the right to liberty.

In the heated political disputes prior to the eruption of civil war, the
leading political lights both Northern and Southern claimed adherence to
the Constitution. The dispute was not *whether* to obey the Constitution but
over what the Constitution *means*. In particular, Southerners who argued for
"states' rights" and defended slavery as a "positive good" tended to interpret
the Constitution without reference to the principles of the Declaration. The
Republican Party was founded for the immediate purpose of organizing
resistance to the Kansas-Nebraska Act, but its larger purpose was to restore
the connection between the principles of the Declaration and the Constitution in public opinion as well as public policy. Thus the first "resolve" of the
first Republican Party platform of 1856 asserted, "That the maintenance
of the principles promulgated in the Declaration of Independence, *and
embodied in the Federal Constitution*, are essential to the preservation of
our Republican institutions, and that the Federal Constitution, the rights
of the States, and the union of the States, must and shall be preserved."[16]
The second Republican Party platform—the one upon which Lincoln was
elected president in 1860—repeated the Constitution's embodiment of the
Declaration's principles, but this time the Republicans quoted from the
Declaration just to make sure they were clear about the principles to which
they were referring: "That the maintenance of the principles promulgated
in the Declaration of Independence and embodied in the Federal Constitution, 'That all men are created equal; that they are endowed by their Creator
with certain inalienable rights; that among these are life, liberty and the
pursuit of happiness; that to secure these rights, governments are instituted
among men, deriving their just powers from the consent of the governed,'
is essential to the preservation of our Republican institutions; and that the

Federal Constitution, the Rights of the States, and the Union of the States must and shall be preserved."[17]

Lincoln and the Republicans were in agreement on the question of principle. Lincoln believed the Constitution was good precisely because he believed it embodied the principles of the Declaration. In a draft speech, he employed a familiar biblical metaphor to explain the relationship between the Declaration and Constitution: "The assertion of that principle [that all men are created equal and possess equal natural rights], at that time, was the word, 'fitly spoken' which has proved an 'apple of gold' to us. The Union, and the Constitution, are the picture of silver, subsequently framed around it. The picture was made, not to conceal or destroy the apple, but to adorn and preserve it. The picture was made for the apple—not the apple for the picture."[18]

The growing chorus of "states' rights" echoing from the South and used to justify the perpetuation of slavery was based on a constitutionalism divorced from the principles of the Declaration. The "slave power" in the South talked endlessly about the constitutional rights of states, while ignoring or ridiculing the natural rights of individuals, especially individuals with black skin. Thus Lincoln responded with the constitutionalism of the founding, which viewed the Constitution as a means of protecting the natural rights acknowledged in the Declaration of Independence.

The most powerful defense of freedom, as well as the most devastating critique of slavery, derives from the immutable principle of human equality. Lincoln understood that the American regime of 1776, the first nation founded upon that principle, is uniquely good and therefore especially worthy of preservation and protection. In his 1854 Peoria Speech, for example, Lincoln said:

> Our republican robe is soiled, and trailed in the dust. Let us repurify it. Let us turn and wash it white, in the spirit, if not the blood, of the Revolution. Let us turn slavery from its claims of "moral right," back upon its existing legal rights, and its arguments of "necessity." Let us return it to the position our fathers gave it; and there let it rest in peace. Let us re-adopt the Declaration of Independence, and with it, the practices, and policy, which harmonize with it.... If we do this, we shall not only have saved the Union; but we shall have so saved it, as to make, and to keep it, *forever worthy of the saving.*[19]

When Lincoln spoke of saving the Union during the secession crisis and the Civil War, it was a *good* union he wanted to save. Saving the Union and placing slavery in the "course of ultimate extinction" were two sides of the same coin: the union Lincoln wanted to save was one in which slavery was in jeopardy because it was a union dedicated to the principle of human equality. But the American mind was becoming corrupted; Americans were abandoning the good principle with which they had started their experiment in freedom in 1776. Few American patriots in 1776 questioned the natural rights argument for equality used to justify their own revolution against the British Crown.[20] But it had become highly questionable by the middle of the nineteenth century whether the American union remained a union of citizens united by their belief in the natural right principles of the founding. If Americans could return to those principles—if they could once again stand united in their conviction that all men are created equal and that slavery, which might be tolerated out of necessity for a period, was nonetheless an evil that needed to be eliminated as soon as possible—then America would be "worthy of the saving."

But if America degenerated to the point at which its citizens no longer viewed slavery as an evil because they no longer believed in the principle of equality, Lincoln probably would have believed the nation was no longer worth saving. In an 1855 letter to his friend Joshua Speed, Lincoln commented: "Our progress in degeneracy appears to me to be pretty rapid. As a nation, we began by declaring that '*all men are created equal.*' We now practically read it 'all men are created equal, *except negroes.*' When the Know-Nothings get control, it will read, 'all men are created equal, except negroes, *and foreigners, and catholics.*' When it comes to this I should prefer emigrating to some country where they make no pretence [*sic*] of loving liberty—to Russia, for instance, where despotism can be taken pure, and without the base alloy of hypocracy [*sic*]."[21]

Lincoln, however, would not give up. Instead, he would use every opportunity afforded him to remind Americans of the noble principles of their own founding, producing some of the most memorable utterances now etched in marble and bronze, the Gettysburg Address and Second Inaugural Address chief among them, as well as policies such as the Emancipation Proclamation and the Thirteenth Amendment that steered American practice in the direction of American principle.

America's Political Principles Are Timeless

In an 1859 letter in which he was celebrating the birthday of Thomas Jefferson, Lincoln described the self-evident truth that all men are created equal as "an abstract truth, applicable to all men and all times."[22] Lincoln believed that the political principles of the American founding were both good and true—yesterday, today, and tomorrow. He believed the principles of Jefferson's Declaration of Independence to be timeless because those principles were rooted in and emanated from human nature, and on the question of human nature Lincoln joined the founders in holding a very old, classical view. Contrary to philosophical arguments offered by Jean-Jacques Rousseau, Georg W. F. Hegel, Karl Marx, and other modern thinkers who hold that human nature is malleable, changeable, and therefore evolutionary, Lincoln argued repeatedly that the natural right principles of right and wrong do not change or evolve, because human nature does not change or evolve. In his seventh and last debate with Douglas, for example, Lincoln argued with especial poignancy that natural right and wrong are eternal and unchanging:

> That is the real issue. That is the issue that will continue in this country when these poor tongues of Judge Douglas and myself shall be silent. It is the eternal struggle between these two principles—right and wrong—throughout the world. They are the two principles that have stood face to face from the beginning of time; and will ever continue to struggle. The one is the common right of humanity and the other the divine right of kings. It is the same principle in whatever shape it develops itself. It is the same spirit that says, "You work and toil and earn bread, and I'll eat it."[23]

In his Peoria Speech, Lincoln defended the idea of an unchanging human nature in light of Stephen Douglas's Kansas-Nebraska Act, which repealed the Missouri Compromise: "Repeal the Missouri compromise," Lincoln said, go ahead and "repeal all compromises—repeal the Declaration of Independence—repeal all past history, *you still cannot repeal human nature.*"[24] And in his 1860 address at New York's Cooper Institute, Lincoln admitted that "human action can be modified to some extent, but *human nature cannot be changed.*"[25] Echoing classical political philosophy, Lincoln consistently maintained that history does not alter human nature in any fundamental way.

But many academics assume that we cannot know whether Lincoln's principles are true because they assume that historical research does not extend beyond stating what Lincoln (and others of his day) said and did. The reason is that the question of whether Lincoln's principles are true—not *what* Lincoln believed but *whether* his beliefs are true—is not a historical but rather a philosophical question. Is there some unchanging realm within which historical change takes place? In particular, is human nature unchanging, and can the human mind discern unchanging truths about unchanging human nature? Historians and other scholars often do not bother to give these questions much thought. Instead, they tend to exclude these thorny philosophical issues from their historical research and confine their historical verdicts to the historical context they happen to be studying. Many Lincoln scholars are good at describing what Lincoln and others around him did and said, and the best scholars explain what those things meant in their time, but they fail to indicate whether they agree with Lincoln or provide an argument explaining why. According to most mainstream academic scholarship on Lincoln, we can know what Lincoln said and did, and we might even know if he had the better argument *of his time,* but we cannot know if his ideas or principles are true, simply.

At least since the German theorist Hegel published his *Philosophy of History* in the early nineteenth century, it has been common for intellectuals to describe thinkers from the past as "children of their age" or "men of their time" and to attribute their (allegedly) antiquated ideas to the historical and cultural forces that preceded and surrounded them.[26] The premise of this view, rightly called *historicism,* is a widely held conviction that human nature is evolutionary and therefore human thought is more or less bound to the historical context in which it appears. When writing about American political principles, historicist academics often refuse to believe that any truth—including the self-evident truth of human equality announced in the Declaration of Independence and enshrined in Lincoln's Gettysburg Address—remains true as time marches on.

In his 2004 book *Rights from Wrongs,* for example, the prominent law professor at Harvard University Alan Dershowitz asserts "that a set of specific rights based on natural law (as announced in the Declaration) simply does not exist" because "natural law is a human invention."[27] Contrast Dershowitz with Lincoln, who argued in an 1857 speech that while a black woman may not be his equal "in some respects," in her "*natural right*" to eat the bread she earns with her own hands without asking leave of anyone else, she is my equal, and the equal of all others."[28]

Dershowitz, however, was merely restating what Richard Hofstadter had argued more than fifty years earlier. In his influential 1948 book *The American Political Tradition and the Men Who Made It,* Hofstadter easily dismissed the natural right principles of the Declaration as relics of a bygone age: "But no man who is as well abreast of modern science as the Fathers were of eighteenth-century science believes any longer in unchanging human nature."[29] Hofstadter assumed that no sophisticated person could doubt the basic Hegelian premise that human nature is evolutionary; he assumed, without offering any proof, that there is no permanent human nature and therefore no permanent truths or principles that apply to human beings throughout time.

But this historicist position hardly originated with Hofstadter. A generation earlier, in 1922, Carl Becker produced what perhaps is still the most comprehensive theoretical and literary analysis of the Declaration, in *The Declaration of Independence: A Study in the History of Ideas.* Near the end, Becker argued that "to ask whether the natural rights philosophy of the Declaration of Independence is true or false is essentially a meaningless question" because the Declaration was "founded upon a superficial knowledge of history," as well as "a naïve faith in the instinctive virtues of human nature." "This faith," Becker almost seemed to lament, "could not survive the harsh realities of the modern world" as increasing "scientific criticism steadily dissolv[ed] its own 'universal and eternal laws' into a multiplicity of incomplete and temporary hypotheses."[30] For Lincoln, no moral or political question was more important or more meaningful than the question of whether it is true that all men are created equal. If the Declaration's principle of equality is true, Lincoln understood, then slavery must be wrong; if that principle is wrong, then slavery might not be wrong. "If slavery is not wrong," Lincoln correctly concluded, then "nothing is wrong."[31] Yet the very question that Lincoln believed of vital importance in determining the rightness and wrongness of freedom versus slavery Becker believes is "meaningless."

From 1922 to 1948 to 2004, from Becker to Hofstadter to Dershowitz, three distinguished scholars of American political history rejected the idea that there are timeless truths or principles rooted in an unchanging human nature. Without question, there have been many changes in historical research paradigms over the past century of scholarship; in Lincoln and Civil

War historiography in particular, historians now pay far more attention to slavery and race as major causes for the sectional conflicts preceding the war than earlier generations of historians did. Yet the basic premise of historicism—that the ideas of Lincoln and his contemporaries were decisively nineteenth-century ideas that are of little relevance to us today and therefore cannot be judged as right or wrong by modern standards—has not much changed. Hofstadter's insistence that no one "believes any longer in unchanging human nature" fairly describes the intellectual framework within which many scholars understand and describe Lincoln. Few academics today who write about Lincoln would agree with Lincoln that there is "an abstract truth applicable to all men and all times." Few academics, therefore, understand Lincoln as Lincoln might have understood himself.

This leads to some rather odd interpretations on the part of academics who do not believe in timeless truths regarding an unchanging human nature, as they try to understand Lincoln, who did believe there are timeless truths and that human nature is immutable. Consider David Donald's award-winning 1995 biography titled simply *Lincoln*. When Donald writes about the Lincoln-Douglas Debates, he seems almost baffled over why Lincoln and Douglas spent so much time debating the morality of slavery. He writes, for example: "The controversy over whether the framers of the Declaration of Independence intended to include blacks in announcing that all men are created equal dealt with an interesting, if ultimately unresolvable, historiographical problem, but it was not easy to see just what it had to do with the choice of a senator for Illinois in 1858."[32]

When Donald characterizes the question of whether the Declaration's proposition of human equality included blacks as an "unresolvable historiographical problem," he denies the very ground of Lincoln's politics. If we cannot know whether blacks are "men" as the word is used in the Declaration, after all, and if we cannot know whether the founders included all human beings of all colors when they wrote and ratified the Declaration, then Lincoln's critique of slavery rests on nothing. At best, Lincoln appears as a radical agitator unnecessarily whipping up public emotion over the problem of slavery, a problem that is "unresolvable" according to Donald. If modern academics cannot know, in principle, whether blacks are men or not, then they cannot know, in principle, whether slavery is truly right or wrong. On this unprincipled historicist ground, the very academics who write about Lincoln cannot know, in principle, if Lincoln deserves praise or contempt.

Lincoln, of course, did not believe the question of whether blacks were men to be unresolvable—he emphatically and repeatedly defended the humanity and the equal natural rights of blacks and all persons of all colors—and he did not believe that the principles of the Declaration were confined to the eighteenth century. In his speech on *Dred Scott v. Sandford*, Lincoln pointed out that the principle that all men are created equal was of no practical use in effecting our separation from Great Britain: "[I]t was placed in the Declaration, not for that, *but for future use*. Its authors meant it to be, thank God, it is now proving itself, a stumbling block to those who in after times might seek to turn a free people back into the hateful paths of despotism. They knew the proneness of prosperity to breed tyrants, and they meant when such should re-appear in this fair land and commence their vocation they should find left for them at least one hard nut to crack."[33]

Lincoln is undoubtedly correct on this point: the founders did not need to announce the principle of equality in order to separate themselves from British rule and gain their independence. They only needed military victory. More precisely, the Americans needed only for the British to grow tired of fighting and go home, thus leaving the Americans to rule themselves as they desired. More important, Lincoln argues that the principle of equality, rather than being an idea confined to the eighteenth century, remained true and was actually more useful for later generations. In this way, Lincoln might suggest to us that anyone who teaches the principles of the founders, or the principles of Lincoln himself, as relics of the eighteenth or nineteenth centuries has missed entirely what those principles mean, because those principles are timeless, not time-bound.

America's Political Principles Are Universal

Many scholars argue that Lincoln was a typical nineteenth-century racist or white supremacist, that he did not believe that blacks were included in the principle that all men are created equal, or that perhaps he believed in some primitive equality of certain rights, but he did not believe blacks deserving of equal civil rights or equal social status with whites. In *Why Lincoln Matters*, former Democratic governor of New York Mario Cuomo, for example, quotes from scholars who defend Lincoln as a champion of color-blind principles and others who scorn him as a racist, but Cuomo himself never says which view he believes is correct. Instead, he laments that "there are not many respected scholars or authors who would deny Lincoln held . . . unsavory racial views before he assumed the presidency."[34] In a 2005 feature essay in *Time* magazine, then-senator Barack Obama wrote, "I cannot swallow whole the view of Lincoln as the Great Emancipator. As a law professor and civil rights lawyer and as an African American, I am fully aware of his limited views on race."[35] According to journalist and author Michael Lind, Lincoln was simply a "white supremacist" whose "racial policies, intended to produce a homogenous, all-white America, seem repugnant in a post-racist United States where not only racial integration but also racial intermarriage increase with each generation." Thankfully, Lind concludes, Lincoln-the-racist "is a figure of the past" whose beliefs have become "obsolete."[36] According to historian Clyde Wilson, "Lincoln . . . like ninety-eight percent of his voters and most Americans of several succeeding generations, was also a white supremacist."[37] Or as libertarian Charles Adams sums it up, "Lincoln believed in white supremacy."[38]

While no one can peer into Lincoln's soul and know for certain what he believed about matters related to race and equality or any other subject, I think the evidence suggests that Lincoln most likely understood American political and moral principles to be universal and to include all men and women of all colors everywhere. Perhaps the most frequently quoted lines from Lincoln presented as evidence that he was a white supremacist are the following from the opening of the fourth debate with Douglas in 1858:

> I will say then that I am not, nor ever have been, in favor of bringing about in any way the social and political equality of the white and black races—that I am not nor ever have been in favor of making voters or jurors of negroes, nor of qualifying them to hold office, nor to intermarry with white people; and I will say in addition to this that there is a physical difference between the white and black races which I believe will forever forbid the two races living together on terms of social and political equality. And inasmuch as they cannot so live, while they do remain together there must be the position of superior and inferior, and I as much as any other man am in favor of having the superior position assigned to the white race.[39]

When reading statements such as the above from Lincoln, it is useful to remember the degree to which white supremacist, racist views had penetrated the American mind that Lincoln was trying to influence in the 1850s. Anyone seeking to advance the principle of equality through electoral politics had to speak carefully to the American people. As historian Phillip Paludan writes, "Most white people disliked blacks as a group, as a race that was inferior and corrosive of ideals they cherished. They did not want blacks to live, shop, play, learn, celebrate, worship, or even be buried anywhere near them."[40] Ever the careful student of the rhetorical art of persuasion, Lincoln spoke cautiously and measured his words so that he might introduce the principle of equality into the public discussion without overtly offending the racial prejudices of his white audience, an audience whose votes he was attempting to attract.

When Lincoln said, "I am not nor ever have been in favor" of certain policies for blacks, it was true: he had never endorsed policies to make jurors or voters or officeholders of blacks or to make them eligible for marriage with whites, and he was proposing no such policies in 1858, but he maintained a prudent silence on what he might "favor" or support in the future. In the context of his many other statements insisting on the equality of whites and blacks, it seems likely that his refusal to advocate such policies was more a matter of strategy than principle on his part. Lincoln knew that there was no possibility at all of getting such policies enacted into law, so why destroy his political career by proposing those policies to an audience that wanted nothing to do with them? Contrary to Douglas—who opened the first of the joint debates by announcing, "I believe this government was made on the white basis" and "I believe it was made by white men, for the benefit of white men and their posterity forever, and I am in favor of confining citizenship to white men, men of European birth and descent, instead of conferring it upon negroes, Indians and other inferior races"—nowhere did Lincoln suggest that policies allowing for equal citizenship and civil rights for blacks would be wrong.[41] Nor did he deny that he might support such policies in the future, perhaps when the American mind had cleansed itself of some of its racial prejudice and was better prepared to entertain the full implications of human equality.

In light of the argument above, consider Lincoln's comments on the Declaration in his speech on the *Dred Scott* case:

> I think the authors of that notable instrument intended to include all men, but they did not intend to declare all men equal in all respects. They did not mean to say all were equal in color, size, in-

tellect, moral developments, or social capacity. They defined with tolerable distinctness, in what respects they did consider all men created equal—equal in "certain inalienable rights, among which are life, liberty, and the pursuit of happiness." This they said, and this they meant. . . . [The founders] meant simply to declare the *right*, so that the *enforcement* of it might follow as fast as circumstances should permit. They meant to set up a standard maxim for free society, which should be familiar to all, and revered by all; constantly looked to, constantly labored for, and even though never perfectly attained, constantly approximated, and thereby constantly spreading and deepening its influence, and augmenting the happiness and value of life to all people of all colors everywhere.[42]

And in an 1858 speech in Chicago, Lincoln reinforced this view by arguing: "[L]et us discard all this quibbling about this man and the other man—this race and that race and the other race being inferior, and therefore they must be placed in an inferior position. . . . Let us discard all these things, and unite as one people throughout this land, until we shall once more stand up declaring that all men are created equal."[43]

Thus Lincoln believed that blacks were included in the Declaration's principle of equality and therefore it was both wrong and unjust to deny the equal humanity and the equal natural rights of blacks as well as the equal civil rights that mirrored and were meant to secure equal natural rights. But Lincoln also understood, as few others of his time did, that as white Americans accepted arguments defending black slavery, to the degree these arguments shaped the minds of white Americans, whites were accepting the principle of their own enslavement. In a surviving fragment of a speech from 1854, Lincoln demonstrated the alternatives between universal freedom and universal slavery this way:

If A. can prove, however conclusively, that he may, of right, enslave B.—why may not B. snatch the same argument, and prove equally, that he may enslave A?—

You say A. is white, and B. is black. It is *color*, then; the lighter, having the right to enslave the darker? Take care. By this rule, you are to be slave to the first man you meet, with a fairer skin than your own.

You do not mean *color* exactly?—You mean the whites are *intellectually* the superiors of the blacks, and, therefore, have the right to enslave them? Take care again. By this rule, you are to be slave to the first man you meet, with an intellect superior to your own.

But, say you, it is a question of *interest*; and, if you can make it your *interest*, you have the right to enslave another. Very well. And if he can make it his interest, he has the right to enslave you.[44]

Here we see that Lincoln understood that any argument justifying the enslavement of black men equally justified the enslavement of white men and men of all different colors.

Throughout his speeches and writings, Lincoln demonstrated repeatedly why chattel slavery was unjust and injurious to black slaves. But he also tried to teach his audience of free whites that the argument for slavery was harmful not only to blacks but to whites as well because it undermined the ground of freedom that whites claimed for themselves. In an 1858 speech in Edwardsville, Illinois, which Lincoln delivered between his debates with Douglas, Lincoln explained in stark terms how proslavery principles threatened the freedom of white people no less than that of black people:

Now, when by all these means you [whites] have succeeded in dehumanizing the negro; when you have put him down, and made it forever impossible for him to be but as the beasts of the field; when you have extinguished his soul, and placed him where the ray of hope is blown out in darkness like that which broods over the spirits of the damned; are you quite sure the demon which you have roused *will not turn and rend you*? What constitutes the bulwark of our own liberty and independence? . . . Our reliance is in the *love of liberty* which God has planted in our bosoms. Our defense is in the preservation of the spirit which prizes liberty as the heritage of all men, in all lands, every where. Destroy this spirit, and you have planted the seeds of despotism around your own doors. Familiarize yourselves with the chains of bondage, and you are preparing your own limbs to wear them. Accustomed to trample on the rights of those around you, you have lost the genius of your own independence, and become the fit subjects of the first cunning tyrant who rises.[45]

In his 1858 speech in Chicago, Lincoln explained how any argument denying the equal rights of mankind, any argument that attempted to exempt certain groups or races of men from the principle that all men are created equal, was the same argument that had been employed to justify the divine right of some men to rule other men as a king:

> Those arguments that are made, that the inferior race are to be treated with as much allowance as they are capable of enjoying; that as much is to be done for them as their condition will allow. . . . They are the arguments that kings have made for enslaving the people in all ages of the world. You will find that all the arguments in favor of king-craft were of this class; they always bestrode the necks of the people, not that they wanted to do it, but because the people were better off for being ridden. That is their argument, and this argument of [Stephen Douglas's] is the same old serpent that says you work and I eat, you toil and I will enjoy the fruits of it. Turn it whatever way you will—whether it comes from the mouth of a King, an excuse for enslaving the people of his country, or from the mouth of men of one race as a reason for enslaving the men of another race, it is all the same old serpent.[46]

Criticism surrounded Lincoln for his defense of equality. Southerners and "popular sovereignty" Northerners, on the one hand, thought Lincoln was too radical, that he was carrying the principle of equality too far by including blacks in any way. Abolitionists, on the other hand, thought Lincoln was too timid, that he should have stood up in public and demanded full social and political equality for blacks immediately. But Lincoln knew better. While never disavowing the universal reach of the principle of equality— Lincoln never denied that blacks possess the same, equal natural rights as whites—he avoided both extremes as he tried to keep alive in the American mind, during America's darkest hours, the understanding of natural right that had informed the founders' politics. His reward was a bullet blasted through his skull.

There was no better student, and therefore no better teacher, of American political principles than Abraham Lincoln. The natural right principles of the founding, especially the self-evident truth that all men are created equal, were Lincoln's political guiding star. From Lincoln, Americans can learn that the principles of the Declaration of Independence are the only solid foundation for a free society and just government. Absent the principle of equality, any teaching of moral or political right can be turned on its head, turned into a teaching of moral wrong or political injustice, by exempting some members of the human race from the scope of moral and political right.

Lincoln also believed the natural right principles of the founding to be timeless, not time-bound. He argued that the principles of the founding were as relevant in his own days as they were to the days of the founders. By implication, we might conclude that those principles are as relevant today for us as they were for Lincoln and for the founders before him.

Finally, Lincoln believed the natural right principles of the founding to be universal, applicable to all men of all colors everywhere. Lincoln believed there is one fundamental self-evident moral and political truth—human equality—upon which all other moral and political truths rest. So long as America remains dedicated to the proposition that all men are created equal, as Lincoln said at Gettysburg, America remains uniquely good. Lincoln certainly believed that America was the crown jewel of Western civilization—a model for the rest of mankind, the last best hope of the earth—precisely because America was the first to be founded upon that universal truth.

Notes

1. Abraham Lincoln, "Speech at Chicago" (July 10, 1858), *Collected Works of Abraham Lincoln,* ed. Roy P. Basler, 8 vols. plus index (New Brunswick, NJ: Rutgers University Press, 1953), 2:499. Hereinafter cited as *CW;* emphases in original unless otherwise noted.

2. Ibid.

3. Consider that the US Constitution prohibits "the United States" from granting to anyone a "title of nobility" (Article I, Section 9). Consider also the prohibition against religious tests as a qualification "to any office or public trust" (Article VI), as well as the fact that the original Constitution contained no reference to race or skin color or ethnicity.

4. Abraham Lincoln, "Speech at Peoria, Illinois" (October 16, 1854), in *CW,* 2:266.

5. Abraham Lincoln, "To Henry L. Pierce and Others" (April 6, 1859), in *CW,* 3:376.

6. Ibid.

7. Ibid.

8. James Madison, "Sovereignty," in *Writings of James Madison*, ed. Gaillard Hunt, 9 vols. (New York: Putnam, 1900–1910), 9:570.

9. Lincoln, "Speech at Peoria, Illinois," 2:265–66.

10. Abraham Lincoln, "Definition of Democracy" [August 1, 1858?], in *CW*, 2:532.

11. James Madison, *Federalist* No. 43, in *The Federalist Papers*, ed. Charles R. Kesler and Clinton Rossiter (New York: Signet Classics, 2003), 276.

12. James Madison, *Federalist* No. 51, in Kesler and Rossiter, *The Federalist Papers*, 321.

13. Thomas Jefferson, "Letter to Judge Spencer Roane" (September 6, 1819), in Thomas Jefferson, *Writings*, ed. Merrill D. Peterson (New York: Library of America, 1984), 1426.

14. Virginia Declaration of Rights, June 12, 1776, Avalon Project, http://avalon.law.yale.edu/18th_century/virginia.asp (accessed June 27, 2014).

15. Abraham Lincoln, "Annual Message to Congress" (December 1, 1862), in *CW*, 5:537.

16. Republican Party Platform of 1856 (June 18, 1856), American Presidency Project, http://www.presidency.ucsb.edu/ws/index.php?pid=29619 (accessed June 27, 2014); emphasis added.

17. Republican Party Platform of 1860 (May 17, 1860), American Presidency Project, http://www.presidency.ucsb.edu/ws/index.php?pid=29620 (accessed June 27, 2014).

18. Abraham Lincoln, "Fragment on the Constitution and the Union" [ca. January, 1861], in *CW*, 4:169

19. Lincoln, "Speech at Peoria, Illinois," 2:276.

20. On July 6, 1776, John Hancock, in his capacity as president of the Continental Congress, ordered the transmission of the newly ratified Declaration of Independence to the American people. Accompanying the Declaration was a letter by Hancock in which he announced to all Americans: "The important Consequences to the American States from this Declaration of Independence, considered as the Ground & Foundation of a future Government, will naturally suggest the Propriety of proclaiming it in such a Manner, that the People may be universally informed of it." See "John Hancock to Certain States," Letters of Delegates to Congress: Vol. 4, May 16, 1776–August 15, 1776, available on the website of the American Memory project of the Library of Congress, http://memory.loc.gov/cgi-bin/query/r?ammem/hlaw:@field(DOCID+@lit(dg004313)) (accessed June 27, 2014).

21. Abraham Lincoln, "To Joshua F. Speed" (August 24, 1855), in *CW*, 2:323.

22. Lincoln, "To Henry L. Pierce and Others," 3:376.

23. Abraham Lincoln, "Seventh and Last Debate with Stephen A. Douglas at Alton, Illinois" (October 15, 1858), in *CW,* 3:315.

24. Lincoln, "Speech at Peoria, Illinois," 2:271; emphasis added.

25. Abraham Lincoln, "Address at Cooper Institute, New York City" (February 27, 1860), in *CW,* 3:541; emphasis added.

26. Georg W. F. Hegel, *The Philosophy of History* (New York: Prometheus Books, 1991 [1837]).

27. Alan Dershowitz, *Rights from Wrongs: A Secular Theory of the Origins of Rights* (New York: Basic Books, 2004), 62.

28. Abraham Lincoln, "Speech at Springfield, Illinois" (June 26, 1857), in *CW,* 2:405; emphasis added.

29. Richard Hofstadter, *The American Political Tradition and the Men Who Made It* (New York: Vintage Books, 1974 [1948]), 20–21.

30. Carl Becker, *The Declaration of Independence: A Study in the History of Ideas* (New York: Vintage Books, 1958 [1922]), 277–79.

31. Abraham Lincoln, "To Albert G. Hodges" (April 4, 1864), in *CW,* 7:281.

32. David Herbert Donald, *Lincoln* (New York: Simon & Schuster, 1995), 226.

33. Lincoln, "Speech at Springfield, Illinois," 2:406.

34. Mario M. Cuomo, *Why Lincoln Matters: Today More Than Ever* (New York: Harcourt Press, 2004), 157.

35. Barack Obama, "What I See in Lincoln's Eyes," *Time* (July 4, 2005), 74.

36. Michael Lind, *What Lincoln Believed: The Values and Convictions of America's Greatest President* (New York: Doubleday, 2004), 264.

37. Clyde Wilson, "DiLorenzo and His Critics" (June 18, 2002), LewRockwell.com, www.lewrockwell.com/orig/wilson7.html (accessed September 26, 2013).

38. Charles Adams, *When in the Course of Human Events: Arguing the Case for Southern Secession* (Lanham, MD: Rowman & Littlefield, 2000), 159.

39. Abraham Lincoln, "Fourth Debate with Stephen A. Douglas at Charleston, Illinois" (September 18, 1858), in *CW,* 3:145.

40. Phillip Shaw Paludan, *The Presidency of Abraham Lincoln* (Lawrence: University Press of Kansas, 1994), 221. See also Phillip Shaw Paludan, *"A People's Contest": The Union and Civil War, 1861–1865* (Lawrence: University Press of Kansas, 1996), 209.

41. Abraham Lincoln, "First Debate with Stephen A. Douglas at Ottawa, Illinois" (August 21, 1858), in *CW,* 3:9.

42. Lincoln, "Speech at Springfield, Illinois," 2:406.

43. Lincoln, "Speech at Chicago, Illinois," 2:501.

44. Abraham Lincoln, "Fragment on Slavery" [July 1, 1854?], in *CW,* 2:222–23.

45. Abraham Lincoln, "Speech at Edwardsville, Illinois" (September 11, 1858), in *CW,* 3:95.

46. Lincoln, "Speech at Chicago, Illinois," 2:500.

6

Lincoln, Liberty, and the American Constitutional Union

Lucas E. Morel

A perennial question regarding Abraham Lincoln's understanding of the federal constitution is whether preserving the American union was more important to him than promoting liberty for all. Lincoln took up the question of liberty when he addressed a sanitary fair (the Women's Central Association of Relief) in Baltimore, Maryland, on April 18, 1864:

> The world has never had a good definition of the word liberty, and the American people, just now, are much in want of one. We all declare for liberty; but in using the same *word* we do not all mean the same *thing*. With some the word liberty may mean for each man to do as he pleases with himself, and the product of his labor; while with others the same word may mean for some men to do as they please with other men, and the product of other men's labor. Here are two, not only different, but incompatable [*sic*] things, called by the same name—liberty. And it follows that each of the things is, by the respective parties, called by two different and incompatable [*sic*] names—liberty and tyranny.[1]

So what does it mean to be for liberty? For Southerners who rejected Lincoln as president and attempted to form a government separate from the American union, liberty meant the right of a white slaveholder to deprive a black man of his freedom simply on the basis of race.[2] Lincoln reminded

Americans that this policy of whites doing just what they please with black slaves, "being responsible to God alone," bore a "strong resemblance to the old argument for the 'Divine right of Kings.'" "Freedom for me at the expense of thee" does not sound like the proper application of the Declaration of Independence, but this was how slaveholders translated the fundamental charter of American liberty. This definition could only be found in what Lincoln called at Baltimore "the wolf's dictionary." Needless to say, Lincoln rejected this definition of liberty.[3]

But he would also reject the practical definition of liberty offered by many abolitionists. Folks such as William Lloyd Garrison, publisher of the premier abolitionist newspaper in America, *The Liberator,* defined liberty as the equal possession of rights by all human beings, regardless of race. So far Lincoln would agree. However, Lincoln found their definition untenable as a political matter because Garrison and his ilk dismissed the federal constitution because it represented a union with slaveholders and therefore an unconscionable compromise with God's endowing all men with the same rights. In addition, so long as the national government could be enlisted in the protection of slavery—through the notorious Fugitive Slave Law of 1850, for example—it was not a government morally binding on any decent American citizen.[4]

Garrison's rhetoric also created difficulties for civic discussion and resolution regarding the future of slavery and freedom in America. In 1832 Garrison called the US Constitution "the most bloody and heaven-daring arrangement ever made by men" and "an unblushing and monstrous coalition to do evil that good might come." In 1838 he helped establish the Non-Resistance Society, which proclaimed, "We cannot acknowledge allegiance to any human government." In 1845 he said the United States "was conceived in sin, and brought forth in iniquity." In his most infamous formulation, Garrison called the Constitution a "covenant with death" and an "agreement with hell" and concluded that it was "a mighty obstacle in the way of universal freedom and equality."[5] Clearly Garrison was no constitutionalist! Beholden only to his conscience, he gave short shrift to the consent of the governed that makes government legitimate and, in America's case, brought the Union, the *United* States, into existence. This was unacceptable to Lincoln, as it championed one principle of the Declaration of Independence—equality—while giving short shrift to that other key principle of the Declaration—consent, which Lincoln called "the leading principle—the sheet anchor of American republicanism."[6]

Lincoln's nemesis, Illinois senator Stephen A. Douglas, proposed an alternative to the immediatist abolition folks. His doctrine of "popular sovereignty" made consent the prime directive and eclipsed liberty as the *summum bonum* of American politics. He applied it to the Kansas and Nebraska Territories in 1854, and would simply "let the people rule" on the question of slavery in those territories. The "doctrine of non-interference by Congress" would be the rule, allowing only the settlers of the territories to decide the fate of slavery there. What could be more American than letting majority rule determine the outcome?[7]

But where Garrison sought equality for all at the expense of government by the consent of the governed, Douglas enshrined majority rule at the expense of human equality. Douglas's professed indifference regarding the future of slavery in the federal territories—a position Lincoln referred to as the "don't care" policy because it taught Americans not to care about slavery as long as it was black slavery—would actually result in the spread of slavery and its eventual legality in every state of the Union.[8] As Lincoln noted in his 1854 speech at Peoria, Illinois:

> This *declared* indifference, but as I must think, covert *real* zeal for the spread of slavery, I can not but hate. I hate it because of the monstrous injustice of slavery itself. I hate it because it deprives our republican example of its just influence in the world—enables the enemies of free institutions, with plausibility, to taunt us as hypocrites—causes the real friends of freedom to doubt our sincerity, and especially because it forces so many really good men amongst ourselves into an open war with the very fundamental principles of civil liberty—criticising [*sic*] the Declaration of Independence, and insisting that there is no right principle of action but *self-interest.*[9]

Applying popular sovereignty to the slavery question taught white Americans that as long as they voted on the issue, white majority rule could determine whether black slavery was right or wrong.

Lincoln believed justice required both human equality and government by consent of the governed and therefore was devoted to the principles of the Declaration of Independence as well as the practice of self-government as manifested in the Constitution and the rule of law. Replying to a committee of German Republicans, Lincoln wrote: "Ever true to *Liberty,* the *Union,* and the Constitution—true to Liberty, not *selfishly,* but upon *principle*—not for special *classes* of men, but for *all* men; true to the Union and the Constitution, as the best means to advance that liberty." He exhorted the committee to be true to three things: liberty, union, and the Constitution. First on the list is liberty. Lincoln explained that the way to be true to liberty is to do so "not *selfishly,* but upon *principle,*" which means universally: to wit, "not for special *classes* of men, but for *all* men." This was his restatement of the human equality principle of the Declaration of Independence, what he once called *"that immortal emblem of Humanity."*[10]

After liberty, Lincoln said that true devotion to union and the Constitution was "the best means to advance that liberty."[11] Because the liberties each person possesses by nature are not self-enforcing, the mechanism by which these liberties were to be protected becomes especially important. In other words, to speak of liberty as a priority without also explaining how one believed liberty ought to be secured in practice was to engage in mere moral grandstanding.

At a Republican banquet in Chicago after the fall election of 1856, a reporter noted the connection Lincoln made between liberty as an end and union as its means: "He maintained that the Liberty for which we contended could best be obtained by a firm, a steady adherence to the Union. As Webster said, 'Not Union without liberty, nor liberty without Union; but Union and liberty, now and forever, one and inseparable.'"[12] Note the extremes Webster seeks to avoid: union without liberty is a union of American states indifferent to the spread of black slavery, while liberty without union is a call to free American slaves without concern for the rule of law and the Constitution—the principal political mechanisms that secure liberty in a civil society. Lincoln makes clear that union and liberty in America needed to be "one and inseparable" in order for self-government to survive.

After the Civil War, the former vice president of the Confederate States of America, Alexander H. Stephens, denigrated Lincoln's devotion to union: "I do not think he intended to overthrow the Institutions of the country. I do not think he understood them or the tendencies of his acts upon them. The Union, with him, in sentiment rose to the sublimity of a religious mysticism, while his ideas of its structure and formation, in logic, rested upon nothing but the subtleties of a sophism!"[13] Did Lincoln have only an emotional attachment to union, as Stephens suggests, with no principled understanding of what it was or how it operated, or did he explain what he believed the American union consisted of, how it operated, and what its ends were? Lincoln did not want citizens to favor just any union of the American states, but a particular kind of union: one he believed was established by the American founders but in the mid-nineteenth century appeared to be losing its hold on the public mind.

Lincoln's reverence for the American union reflected his awareness of the fragility of self-government. This explains his willingness to support the Constitution, despite its protections for slavery as it then existed, for the good it already achieved and was yet capable of achieving. The peace of the union, vital to the rights that the American experiment in free government aimed to secure, was something Lincoln never took for granted. In fact, as he pointed out at length in his 1838 speech on "the perpetuation of our political institutions," the public peace was no simple matter to achieve. It was the product of the orderly processes of law and courts, and conducive of the justice that is the hallmark of self-government. But it also required the orderly processes of thought in public discourse.[14]

Much is made about Lincoln's focus on preserving the Union as the aim of his presidential administration. Why not pursue the obviously noble end of emancipation? Lincoln believed that the executive department's primary responsibility was to enforce the laws. As he put it at his first inauguration, "I shall take care, as the Constitution itself expressly enjoins upon me, that the laws of the Union be faithfully executed in all the States." Almost eight months into the Civil War, in his first state of the union address, Lincoln discussed the main objective of the war—as far as the federal government was concerned: "In considering the policy to be adopted for suppressing the insurrection, I have been anxious and careful that the inevitable conflict for this purpose shall not degenerate into a violent and remorseless revolutionary struggle. I have, therefore, in every case, thought it proper to keep the integrity of the Union prominent as the primary object of the contest on our part, leaving all questions which are not of vital military importance to the more deliberate action of the legislature."[15]

The following year, in a famous letter responding to *New York Tribune* editor Horace Greeley, Lincoln described his purpose in a statement still debated to this day: "My paramount object in this struggle *is* to save the Union, and is *not* either to save or to destroy slavery. If I could save the Union without freeing *any* slave I would do it, and if I could save it by freeing *all* the slaves, I would do it; and if I could save it by freeing some and leaving others alone I would also do that."[16] Why is "the Union" so important to Lincoln that he would make emancipation a secondary priority in the war effort?

For Lincoln, not any union, but a union of a certain character, is essential. One hears so much about Lincoln's devotion to the Union that one should not overlook what union signified for Lincoln: a national, common devotion to certain principles of self-government that Lincoln believed "gave promise that in due time the weight would be lifted from the shoulders of all men." In preserving the American union, Lincoln believed he was defending self-government, which was the key to securing individual liberty. As Lincoln put it in his 1854 speech at Peoria: "Let us re-adopt the Declaration of Independence, and with it, the practices, and policy, which harmonize with it. . . . If we do this, we shall not only have saved the Union; but we shall have so saved it, as to make, and to keep it, forever worthy of the saving." He believed that rejecting the universal principles of American self-government, especially "the sentiment of liberty in the country," would lead people "to transform this government into a government of some other form." Only by restoring liberty as the end served by the Constitution would the American union be worth saving. Two years later, he would argue that "we have an interest in the maintenance of the principles of the Government, and without this interest, it is worth nothing. . . . I think we have an ever growing interest in maintaining the free institutions of our country."[17]

As the nation grew increasingly divided over the future of slavery, Lincoln repeatedly cited the Declaration of Independence to remind Americans of the goal to which their federal union and governmental structures should be devoted. To lose sight of the goal of "Liberty to all" was to subvert American self-government. It would turn republican government into a form of majority rule that allowed mere numerical might to determine which individuals would receive the protection of their rights. If this were to happen, Lincoln once remarked, he would "prefer emigrating to some country where they make no pretence [sic] of loving liberty—to Russia, for instance, where despotism can be taken pure, and without the base alloy of hypocracy [sic]."[18]

This particular union, therefore, requires a particular constitution—namely, one devoted to liberty. Lincoln understood this liberty to be the birthright of all men and women, the equal entitlement of every human being, regardless of race. For Lincoln, "the Union, the Constitution, and the freedom of mankind" were always inextricably linked.[19] Again, the Constitution and the Union do not exist for their own sake, but to secure liberty. As the Declaration of Independence states, "That to secure these rights, governments are instituted among men, deriving their just powers from the consent of the governed." One could say that the Constitution channels the consent of the governed, and if it is a prudently designed constitution, it directs that consent toward protecting the natural rights of all.

The consent of the governed found its political expression in the rule of law and the Constitution. In contrast with vigilante justice or mob rule, laws and courts operate to secure the public's pursuit of justice in an orderly, deliberative fashion. What some interpret as Lincoln's "inaction" toward slavery is simply his profound awareness that any good he tried to achieve politically must derive from the powers of office vested in him by the American people, whom he called "my rightful masters." Lincoln explained this in his now famous 1864 letter to Albert Hodges: "I am naturally anti-slavery. If slavery is not wrong, nothing is wrong. I can not remember when I did not so think, and feel. And yet I have never understood that the Presidency conferred upon me an unrestricted right to act officially upon this judgment and feeling."[20] He could not exercise power or authority that was not first delegated to him by the American people.

Now, the constraint of consent sets the context for any progress in securing the rights of individuals in a free society. True statesmanship in a self-governing society displays a clear grasp of this just and necessary connection between republican means and ends. Simply put, political prudence in a government "of the people, by the people, for the people" recognizes that to achieve justice, moral posturing is not enough; one has the duty to *persuade* one's fellow citizens, which involves an appeal to both their hearts as well as their heads.[21] Persuasion, not platitudes, is the democratic order of the day. And Lincoln thought the best way to persuade people to pursue justice in the political arena was to show them how it was in their best interest to do so. This meant he had to inform their opinions while he accommodated their prejudices.

What form did this persuasion take for Lincoln? It took a constitutional form. Simply stated, a "constitutionalist" is someone who understands the Constitution as a *limiting* delegation of political power, as well as an *aspiring* instrument of liberty. In fact, without the principled aspirations of the Constitution, there would be no limitations on government's authority. To focus on the Constitution as a limiting document, important as that is, without due attention to the Constitution as an aspiring document, is to forget that the Constitution is a means to an end and not an end in itself. That said, Lincoln thought the Constitution deserved to be revered as the best means of securing civil and religious liberty.

As early as 1838, at the Young Men's Lyceum of Springfield, Illinois, Lincoln addressed a problem the United States faced as Revolutionary War veterans passed this earth, leaving no living memory of the sacrifices that helped secure the grand American experiment in self-government. Lincoln saw this as a major weakening of the republic and believed only a "political religion" of reverence for the laws and the Constitution could prevent mob rule from giving rise to a "towering genius" who sought to gratify his thirst for fame "at the expense of emancipating slaves, or enslaving freemen." Lincoln proclaims:

> Let reverence for the laws, be breathed by every American mother, to the lisping babe, that prattles on her lap—let it be taught in schools, in seminaries, and in colleges;—let it be written in Primmers, spelling books, and in Almanacs;—let it be preached from the pulpit, proclaimed in legislative halls, and enforced in courts of justice. And, in short, let it become the *political religion* of the nation; and let the old and the young, the rich and the poor, the grave and the gay, of all sexes and tongues, and colors and conditions, sacrifice unceasingly upon its altars.[22]

Only a respect for the laws and Constitution bordering on sacred obedience could prevail against what Lincoln saw as the only real threat to American self-government—namely, a condition of political laxity whereby the people were corrupted by their own freedom, unmindful of the true ground of their rights, and unaware of the threat posed by mob violence that sought justice but subverted the rule of law in the process. This political religion needs a political preacher. By alerting his audience to the danger that lurks in vigilante justice, Lincoln fulfills the role.

This early concern about lawlessness in a self-governing regime turns out to be quite prescient, as Lincoln will have to deal with the most extensive lawlessness in the nation's history almost a quarter century later when he becomes president of a divided country. In his First Inaugural Address, we find one of several proof texts for establishing Lincoln's *bona fides* as a constitutionalist. After equating secession with anarchy, a lawless social condition, Lincoln presents the only truly American alternative: "A majority, held in restraint by constitutional checks and limitations, and always changing easily with deliberate changes of popular opinions and sentiments is the only true sovereign of a free people. Whoever rejects it, does, of necessity, fly to anarchy or to despotism."[23]

A month before the 1864 presidential election, Lincoln said of the citizenry: "Their will, constitutionally expressed, is the ultimate law for all." Note the phrase "constitutionally expressed." For Lincoln, a written constitution, with suitable "checks and limitations," enables the people to secure their individual rights and pursue the common good in a deliberate, thoughtful manner—what *The Federalist Papers* called "the cool and deliberate sense of the community."[24]

Lincoln's constitutionalism reminded citizens that the Constitution, laws, and courts should be used by the people to secure the rights of all and not just the self-interest of the majority. To forget this is to undermine the basis of the majority's right to rule. This would lead to tyrannical abuses of power and hence the subversion of constitutional self-government. In particular, just as Lincoln limited his presidential authority to his powers and role stipulated in the Constitution, American citizens should limit their political objectives to those consistent with the ideals of the American republic. Lincoln located these in the Declaration of Independence, what he called "the father of all moral principle" in the American people. Contrary to Stephen Douglas's popular sovereignty, which turned majority rule into crude majoritarianism by divorcing it from the natural equality of human beings, Lincoln taught the nation to resist the temptation to become tyrants themselves: he exhorted them to resist using their freedom to enslave others or permit their enslavement. In a note to himself, Lincoln wrote, "As I would not be a *slave,* so I would not be a *master.*" In a public letter this became "he who would *be* no slave, must consent to *have* no slave. Those who deny freedom to others, deserve it not for themselves; and, under a just God, can not long retain it." In the heat of the Kansas-Nebraska crisis, Lincoln summed up everyone's justifiable fear of unaccountable power when he said that "no man is good enough to govern another man, *without that other's consent.*"[25]

On December 30, 1860, president-elect Lincoln received a letter from his former Whig friend Alexander H. Stephens, who had spoken against secession (to no avail) in his home state of Georgia and would nevertheless be elected vice president of the Confederate States of America. He asked Lincoln to "do what you can to save our common country" and quoted from Proverbs 25:11: "A word fitly spoken by you now would be like 'apples of gold in pictures of silver.'" A student of the Bible in his own right, Lincoln reflected on Stephens's biblical reference and, in a note to himself, used the "apples of gold" reference to clarify the connection between America's constitutional union and the principle of "Liberty to all."[26]

This note offers a telling description of the principle of equality that informed Lincoln's political philosophy. Lincoln wrote that "the principle of 'Liberty to all,'" expressed in the self-evident truth of the Declaration of Independence that "all men are created equal," was "the primary cause of our great prosperity." He thought that the American colonists could have declared independence from England without that principle, "but *without it*, we could not, I think, have secured our free government, and consequent prosperity." Lincoln distinguishes "independence" from "our free government, and consequent prosperity" to point out that mere separation from Great Britain would not have prospered the American people unless they had established their new government on the principle of liberty. Without freedom as the goal, "our fathers" would not have fought for "a mere change of masters." What Lincoln called "a philosophical cause" was the very heart of American self-government.[27]

Alluding to Proverbs 25:11 himself, Lincoln added: "The assertion of that *principle*, at *that time*, was *the* word, '*fitly spoken*' which has proved an 'apple of gold' to us. The *Union*, and the *Constitution*, are the *picture* of *silver*, subsequently framed around it. The picture was made, not to *conceal*, or *destroy* the apple; but to *adorn*, and *preserve* it. The *picture* was made *for* the apple—*not* the apple for the picture." Lincoln's repeated emphases of words and phrases in his note on constitutional union and liberty, especially in reference to Proverbs 25:11, show that he believed the word fitly spoken had already been uttered—in the Declaration of Independence, a document Stephens rejected in his infamous "Corner Stone Speech" of March 21, 1861.[28] All Lincoln could do was to point the nation back to it as a way of moving forward so that "neither *picture*, or *apple* shall ever be blurred, or bruised or broken."[29]

Lincoln's illustration suggests how means could be mistaken for ends in themselves. "Pictures" or settings made of silver could be mistaken as the main object of beauty, thereby obscuring the real object to be noticed—the apples of gold. Similarly, without human liberty as the aim of the Constitution and the Union, the republican forms of government could become instruments of oppression, as when one group of people (e.g., whites) uses their numerical might to deprive another class of people (e.g., blacks) of their natural rights.

To the extent Americans began thinking that slavery could be made compatible with liberty—for example, by making slaves of some men according to race—to that extent Lincoln believed the ground of liberty was eroding. In his first state of the union address, he warned "against this approach of returning despotism." He said that he always hated slavery but that he kept "quiet about it" in the knowledge that "the great mass of the nation . . . rested in the belief that slavery was in course of ultimate extinction." Back in his Peoria Address of 1854, he cleverly equated the founders' approach to the peculiar institution with its eventual demise: "Let us turn slavery from its claims of 'moral right,' back upon its existing legal rights, and its arguments of 'necessity.' Let us return it to the position our fathers gave it; and there let it *rest in peace.*" With the send-off "rest in peace," Lincoln employs the proverbial tombstone epitaph to suggest the restoration of the founders' intention that slavery be eliminated gradually, so as not to disturb the civil peace that would be necessary for self-government to take hold in the nascent American republic. But the pun "rest in peace," *requiescat in pace,* makes clear that Lincoln joins the founders in expecting the American people to put slavery into its grave as soon as practicable. Alas, the peace of the nation was disturbed by the notion of the compatibility of freedom and slavery, as long as the enslavement was of Africans and what Douglas called "other inferior races."[30]

Lincoln once wrote that the passage of the Kansas-Nebraska Act in 1854 "aroused him as he had never been before." This law repealed the 1820 Missouri Compromise by treating slavery not as an evil to be tolerated where it already existed but as a good for those who would seek its use in the territory hitherto held by the federal government as free. Lincoln called American slavery "a state of oppression and tyranny unequalled in the world." Contrast this with Stephen Douglas, whom Lincoln said had "no very vivid impression that the negro is a human" and therefore viewed slavery, in Lincoln's words, as "an exceedingly little thing" and "something having no moral question in it."[31]

Lincoln's public statements and policy proposals indicate that his concern for the survival of self-government meant that the key priority in the 1850s was preventing slavery's spread into the federal territories. This required that he remind white Americans in free states such as Illinois that their rights derived not from their race or ethnicity but from their humanity, a nature they shared with the black man on American soil. If he could not get whites in the North to acknowledge the *natural* rights of blacks, it was pointless even to raise the question of equal *civil and political* rights with that same prejudiced citizenry. Put differently, we know how much Lincoln was devoted to liberty by the seriousness with which he took the greatest threat to liberty—namely, the spread of slavery into the federal territories. He feared the American union was becoming a nation he did not recognize: "On the question of liberty, as a principle, we are not what we have been."[32] During the 1856 presidential campaign, he stated the issue directly: "This government is sought to be put on a new track. Slavery is to be made a ruling element in our government."[33]

Lincoln argued that during the founding era, ownership of black slaves was viewed by white citizens as a necessary evil; however, by the 1850s, slavery was increasingly defended in the South as good for both the master and the slave and as a state institution that could not be interfered with by the federal government. This view of the Constitution meant that "the Blessings of Liberty" promised in its preamble would apply only to white Americans. Lincoln believed the Constitution was being reinterpreted to establish a race-based, federal system of government that would eventually extend slavery into every territory and state of the American union. This "blurred" the meaning of the Constitution, as it became a tool of despotism rather than liberation.

By 1860 Lincoln would exhort the nation to "HAVE FAITH THAT RIGHT MAKES MIGHT, AND IN THAT FAITH, LET US, TO THE END, DARE TO DO OUR DUTY AS WE UNDERSTAND IT."[34] He believed that matters of right and wrong were not the mere product of majority vote, but derived from moral standards that transcended nations and reached across time. Lincoln believed the American founders declared their independence by appealing to these standards of right and that the nation now faced a crisis that could best be resolved by a return to the founders' approach to the issue.

So why did Lincoln want to save a constitutional union that permitted the enslavement of men on the basis of race and hence violated "the original idea" of equality that formed its basis? He replied, "We had slavery among us, we could not get our Constitution unless we permitted them to remain in slavery, we could not secure the good we did secure if we grasped for more, and having by necessity submitted to that much, it does not destroy the principle that is the charter of our liberties." He added, "If we cannot give freedom to every creature, let us do nothing that will impose slavery upon any other creature."[35] Lincoln pointed out that this holds true only if the people rest in the conviction that slavery is in course of ultimate extinction. With the "don't care" rhetoric of an incumbent US senator gaining credence, the American people began to think they could continue to "secure" the good of self-government while maintaining slavery in their midst. The security of self-government required, therefore, not only the right political institutions, but the right political convictions for their long-term preservation.

But this requires a certain understanding of the American regime, a devotion to the equal rights of humanity. Keep sight of this, and Americans will be able, in the words of Lincoln, to "rise up to the height of a generation of men worthy of a free Government." In Lincoln's devotion to both "the cause of the union and liberties of the country," one finds a statesmanship of the highest order and an abiding invitation to rise to the challenge of American self-government. Lincoln's legacy is his repeated appeals to "the better angels of our nature" in his political rhetoric.[36] He was concerned that the lesser angels of American politics and society—the democratic demons, if you will—would sabotage the nation's experiment in self-government.

Abraham Lincoln loved union—the American union—because of what it could accomplish on behalf of liberty, and when he saw it being corrupted for the sake of slavery or disrupted to that same end, he made it his political goal to defend the United States with words and deeds that stand as the greatest political legacy of any American president.

Notes

1. Abraham Lincoln, "Address at Sanitary Fair, Baltimore, Maryland" (April 18, 1864), *Collected Works of Abraham Lincoln,* ed. Roy P. Basler, 8 vols. plus index (New Brunswick, NJ: Rutgers University Press, 1953), 7:301–2. Hereinafter cited as *CW*; emphases in original unless otherwise noted.

2. For examples of arguments made by whites of the lower South to whites of the upper South to secede as a means of preserving white supremacy in general and white enslavement of blacks in particular, see Charles B. Dew, *Apostles*

of Disunion: Southern Secession Commissioners and the Causes of the Civil War (Charlottesville: University of Virginia Press, 2001). A recent account of the travails of Northern Democrat Stephen A. Douglas as he solicited Southern votes for his presidency also affirms "how prominent in the election of 1860 the theme of property rights in slavery was in Southern oratory." See James L. Huston, "The 1860 Southern Sojourns of Stephen A. Douglas and the Irrepressible Separation," in *The Election of 1860 Reconsidered*, ed. A. James Fuller (Kent, OH: Kent State University Press, 2013), 29–67, esp. 30–31, 45–46, 54–55.

3. Abraham Lincoln, "Speech at Peoria, Illinois" (October 16, 1854), in *CW*, 2:278. Lewis E. Lehrman argues persuasively for the centrality of the Peoria Address to Lincoln's political thought in *Lincoln at Peoria: The Turning Point* (Mechanicsburg, PA: Stackpole Books, 2008).

4. For Garrison's praise of the Declaration of Independence and condemnation of the Constitution, see "On the Constitution and Union" (December 29, 1832), in *William Lloyd Garrison and the Fight against Slavery: Selections from* The Liberator, ed. William E. Cain (Boston: Bedford / St. Martin's, 1994), 87–89. For an account of Garrison's opposition to the Fugitive Slave Act, which was part of the Compromise Measures of 1850, see the excellent biography by Henry Mayer, *All on Fire: William Lloyd Garrison and the Abolition of Slavery* (New York: St. Martin's, 1998), 392–416.

5. William E. Cain, ed., *William Lloyd Garrison and the Fight against Slavery: Selections from* The Liberator (Boston: Bedford / St. Martin's, 1994), 87, 101, 113–14, 115.

6. Lincoln, "Speech at Peoria, Illinois," 2:266.

7. Stephen A. Douglas, "'Let the People Rule': Speech of Hon. Stephen A. Douglas, at Concord, New Hampshire" (July 31, 1860), 3, 1, and 5, available at https://archive.org/details/letpeoplerulespe00doug, last accessed June 6, 2014 (see the Johns Hopkins University Sheridan Libraries, James Birney Collection of Anti-Slavery Pamphlets, at archive.org).

8. Abraham Lincoln, "Speech at Dover, New Hampshire" (March 2, 1860), in *CW*, 3:554.

9. Lincoln, "Speech at Peoria, Illinois," 2:255.

10. Abraham Lincoln, "To Anton C. Hesing, Henry Wendt, Alexander Fisher, Committee" (June 30, 1858), in *CW*, 2:475, and Abraham Lincoln, "Speech at Lewistown, Illinois" (August 17, 1858), in *CW*, 2:547.

11. Lincoln, "To Anton C. Hesing, Henry Wendt, Alexander Fisher, Committee," 2:475.

12. Abraham Lincoln, "Speech at a Republican Banquet, Chicago, Illinois" (December 10, 1856), in *CW*, 2:383.

13. Alexander H. Stephens, *Recollections of Alexander H. Stephens: His Diary Kept When a Prisoner at Fort Warren, Boston Harbour, 1865,* ed. Myrta Lockett Avary (New York: Doubleday, Page, 1910), 61–62.

14. Abraham Lincoln, "Address before the Young Men's Lyceum of Springfield, Illinois" (January 27, 1838), in *CW,* 1:114. The best exposition of this speech remains Harry V. Jaffa, *Crisis of the House Divided: An Interpretation of the Issues in the Lincoln-Douglas Debates* (Seattle: University of Washington Press, 1973; reprint ed., Chicago: University of Chicago Press, 1982 [1959]), supplemented by Harry V. Jaffa, *A New Birth of Freedom: Abraham Lincoln and the Coming of the Civil War* (Lanham, MD: Rowman & Littlefield, 2000).

15. Abraham Lincoln, "First Inaugural Address: Final Text" (March 4, 1861), in *CW,* 4:265, and Abraham Lincoln, "Annual Message to Congress" (December 3, 1861), in *CW,* 5:48–49.

16. Abraham Lincoln, "To Horace Greeley" (August 22, 1862), in *CW,* 5:388. Lincoln actually paced the country through all three of these options: First Inaugural Address objective (save the Union without freeing any slave), Emancipation Proclamation (save the Union by freeing some slaves while leaving others alone), and the Thirteenth Amendment (save the Union by freeing all the slaves). Cf. James Oakes, *Freedom National: The Destruction of Slavery in the United States, 1861–1865* (New York: Norton, 2012), which argues that Lincoln and the Republican Party intended slavery's demise from the outset of Lincoln's election to the presidency.

17. Abraham Lincoln, "Speech in Independence Hall, Philadelphia, Pennsylvania" (February 22, 1861), in *CW,* 4:240; Lincoln, "Speech at Peoria, Illinois," 2:276; Abraham Lincoln, "Speech at Chicago, Illinois" (July 10, 1858), in *CW,* 2:500; and Abraham Lincoln, "Speech at Kalamazoo, Michigan" (August 27, 1856), in *CW,* 2:364.

18. Abraham Lincoln, "To Joshua F. Speed" (August 24, 1855), in *CW,* 2:323.

19. Abraham Lincoln, "To John M. Clay" (August 9, 1862), in *CW,* 5:364.

20. Lincoln, "Speech at Peoria, Illinois," 2:266; Lincoln, "First Inaugural Address," 4:265, and Abraham Lincoln, "To Albert Hodges" (April 4, 1864), in *CW,* 7:281. Lincoln's literal bottom line regarding the politics of American slavery came at the conclusion of his long-debated public letter to *New York Tribune* editor Horace Greeley: "I have here stated my purpose according to my view of *official* duty; and I intend no modification of my oft-expressed *personal* wish that all men every where could be free." Lincoln, "To Horace Greeley," 5:389.

21. Abraham Lincoln, "Address Delivered at the Dedication of the Cemetery at Gettysburg" (November 19, 1863), in *CW,* 7:23. For a sophisticated reflection on responsible rhetoric and public opinion, see Abraham Lincoln, "Temperance

Address" (February 22, 1842), in *CW*, 1:271–79. Its true subject is less about temperance with respect to alcohol consumption and more about temperance or moderation in speech. See Lucas E. Morel, *Lincoln's Sacred Effort: Defining Religion's Role in American Self-Government* (Lanham, MD: Lexington Books, 2000), chap. 4, 124–62.

22. Lincoln, "Address before the Young Men's Lyceum," 1:112.

23. Lincoln, "First Inaugural Address," 4:268. For an analysis of Lincoln's understanding of secession as tantamount to the destruction of self-government, see William Lee Miller, *President Lincoln: The Duty of a Statesman* (New York: Knopf, 2008), chap. 6, 140–54.

24. Abraham Lincoln, "Response to a Serenade" (October 19, 1864), in *CW*, 8:52, and James Madison, *The Federalist Papers* (New York: Penguin, 1999), essay no. 63, 382.

25. Lincoln, "Speech at Chicago, Illinois," 2:499; Abraham Lincoln, "Definition of Democracy" [August 1, 1858?], in *CW*, 2:532; Abraham Lincoln, "To Henry L. Pierce and Others" (April 6, 1859), in *CW*, 3:376; and Lincoln, "Speech at Peoria, Illinois," 2:266.

26. Alexander H. Stephens cited in Abraham Lincoln, "To Alexander H. Stephens" (December 22, 1860), in *CW*, 4:161n1. When Lincoln was elected the first Republican president of the United States on November 6, 1860, he received almost no votes from nine Southern states; what Lincoln called in 1858 the "crisis" of the American "house divided" had come to a head. On December 22, 1860, the president-elect wrote Stephens, a former Whig ally in Congress, to assuage his fears about the incoming administration: "Do the people of the South really entertain fears that a Republican administration would, *directly*, or *indirectly*, interfere with their slaves, or with them, about their slaves? If they do, I wish to assure you, as once a friend, and still, I hope, not an enemy, that there is no cause for such fears." Ibid., 4:160. Stephens, who in February 1861 would be elected vice president of the Confederate States of America, replied with his December 30 letter, which led Lincoln to jot down his "Fragment on the Constitution and Union" [ca. January 1861], in *CW*, 4:168–69.

27. Lincoln, "Fragment on the Constitution and Union," 4:169.

28. What follows is the relevant passage from Stephens's speech regarding the improvement of the Confederate Constitution upon the original United States Constitution with respect to slavery:

> The prevailing ideas entertained by him [Thomas Jefferson] and most of the leading statesmen at the time of the formation of the old constitution, were that the enslavement of the African was in violation of the laws of nature; that it was wrong in *principle*, socially, morally, and politically. It

was an evil they knew not well how to deal with, but the general opinion of the men of that day was that, somehow or other in the order of Providence, the institution would be evanescent and pass away. This idea, though not incorporated in the constitution, was the prevailing idea at that time. The constitution, it is true, secured every essential guarantee to the institution while it should last, and hence no argument can be justly urged against the constitutional guarantees thus secured, because of the common sentiment of the day. Those ideas, however, were fundamentally wrong. They rested upon the assumption of the equality of races. This was an error. It was a sandy foundation, and the government built upon it fell when the "storm came and the wind blew."

Our new government is founded upon exactly the opposite idea; its foundations are laid, its corner-stone rests upon the great truth, that the negro is not equal to the white man; that slavery—subordination to the superior race—is his natural and normal condition.

This, our new government, is the first, in the history of the world, based upon this great physical, philosophical, and moral truth. . . .

With us, all of the white race, however high or low, rich or poor, are equal in the eye of the law. Not so with the negro. Subordination is his place. He, by nature, or by the curse against Canaan, is fitted for that condition which he occupies in our system. . . . [B]y experience we know that it is best, not only for the superior, but for the inferior race, that it should be so. It is, indeed, in conformity with the ordinance of the Creator. It is not for us to inquire into the wisdom of his ordinances, or to question them. For his own purposes, he has made one race to differ from another, as he has made "one star to differ from another star in glory."

Henry Cleveland, *Alexander H. Stephens, in Public and Private: With Letters and Speeches, Before, During, and Since the War* (Philadelphia: National Publishing Company, 1866), 721, 722, 723.

29. Lincoln, "Fragment on the Constitution and Union," 4:169.

30. Lincoln, "Annual Message to Congress," 5:51; Lincoln, "Speech at Chicago, Illinois," 2:492; Lincoln, "Speech at Peoria, Illinois," 2:276 (emphasis added); and Stephen A. Douglas cited in Abraham Lincoln, "First Debate with Stephen A. Douglas at Ottawa, Illinois" (August 21, 1858), in *CW*, 3:9.

31. Abraham Lincoln, "Autobiography Written for John L. Scripps" [ca. June 1860], in *CW*, 4:67; Lincoln, "Speech at Peoria, Illinois," 2:281; Lincoln, "Speech at Chicago, Illinois," 2:494.

32. Abraham Lincoln, "To George Robertson" (August 15, 1855), in *CW*, 2:318. He made a similar statement a year earlier: "I particularly object to the NEW position which the avowed principle of this Nebraska law gives to slavery

in the body politic. I object to it because it assumes that there CAN be MORAL RIGHT in the enslaving of one man by another. I object to it as a dangerous dalliance for a few [free?] people—a sad evidence that, feeling prosperity we forget right—that liberty, as a principle, we have ceased to revere." "Speech at Peoria, Illinois," 2:274.

33. Lincoln, "Speech at Kalamazoo, Michigan," 2:365.

34. Abraham Lincoln, "Address at Cooper Institute, New York City" (February 27, 1860), in *CW*, 3:550.

35. Lincoln, "Speech at Chicago, Illinois," 2:501.

36. Abraham Lincoln, "Speech to the One Hundred Sixty-Fourth Ohio Regiment" (August 18, 1864), in *CW*, 7:505; Abraham Lincoln, "Response to a Serenade" (July 7, 1861), in *CW*, 6:320; and Lincoln, "First Inaugural Address," 4:271.

7

The Democratic Statesmanship of Abraham Lincoln

Steven Kautz

Democracy is self-government. Statesmanship can often *diminish* self-government: when we think of George Washington or James Madison, we say "founding father," often with capital Fs—not "fellow citizen." We are governed by such men; we do not govern ourselves. And yet the statesmanship of a Winston Churchill or an Abraham Lincoln can also *ennoble* democracy, enabling "We the People" to be worthy of self-government. How should we understand this paradox of democratic statesmanship?

Lincoln's task in the 1850s was to restore slavery to a "course of ultimate extinction," upon which (as he often said, perhaps with some exaggeration) the founders had placed it—and thereby to make our republic "worthy of the saving." From his 1854 Peoria Speech to the December 1862 Annual Message to Congress, Lincoln sought to ensure that slavery would sooner or later be extinguished but also that the end of slavery would be achieved as far as possible by democratic means, by the consent of a people who had somehow nobly achieved a victory over its wicked past. The price of democracy was endurance of a terrible injustice. But for how long could that price, in justice, be paid? And when he *failed,* first when war was forced upon him and upon the North, and then when that war became, as he described his fear, a "remorseless revolutionary struggle," he was compelled to do more than to guide his people to discover the better angels of our nature. He was compelled to act ahead of his people and to achieve as a commander of armies what in the event could not be achieved by democratic means: he would himself free the slaves, in an extraordinary proclamation, as "an act of justice, warranted by the Constitution, upon military necessity." To do justice to the democratic statesmanship of Abraham Lincoln, we must come to grips both with the extraordinary patience with the people that led him to resist abolitionism (in the name of republicanism) for so long and in such trying circumstances, and with the limits of that patience, when the demands of justice finally required first a course of policy that would take the nation to the brink of war and then a course of policy that would transform that war into a revolutionary struggle.

Douglass's Measure

Begin with the testimony of the abolitionist Frederick Douglass, himself once a slave and then in his own right a rather extraordinary statesman. These words were delivered to a distinguished audience of the good and great of Washington, DC, on the occasion of the unveiling of the Freedmen's Memorial Monument to Abraham Lincoln, on April 14, 1876, eleven years after Lincoln's assassination. Here is the story of the monument: it was wholly paid for by funds contributed by those made free by the Emancipation Proclamation themselves, including many who had served in the Union army; it is the only such memorial to Lincoln; and it was for several decades the principal memorial to Lincoln in Washington. It is a disquieting monument, a worthy counterpoise to the majestic Lincoln Memorial. Douglass said, in dedicating the monument:

> Abraham Lincoln was not, in the fullest sense of the word, either our man or our model. In his interests, in his associations, in his habits of thought, and in his prejudices, he was a white man.
>
> He was preeminently the white man's President, entirely devoted to the welfare of white men. He was ready and willing at any time during the first years of his administration to deny, postpone, and sacrifice the rights of humanity in the colored people to promote the welfare of the white people of this country. In all his education and feeling he was an American of the Americans. . . . First, midst, and last, you and yours were the objects of his deepest affection and his most earnest solicitude. You are the children of Abraham Lincoln. We are at best only his step-children; children by adoption,

children by forces of circumstances and necessity. . . . But . . . we entreat you to despise not the humble offering we this day unveil to view; for while Abraham Lincoln saved for you a country, he delivered us from a bondage, according to Jefferson, one hour of which was worse than ages of the oppression your fathers rose in rebellion to oppose.[1]

Douglass's words are powerful and disquieting. His "Oration in Memory of Abraham Lincoln" is, still today, among the finest appreciations of Lincoln's statesmanship, a masterly study of statesmanship by a master. And Douglass's considered judgment, as he says, is that Lincoln was "the greatest statesman that ever presided over the destinies of this Republic."[2] And yet Lincoln was also "the white man's President"—or, more precisely, he was "preeminently the white man's President." Can a comprehensive view of Lincoln, which Douglass claimed for himself, accommodate both of these truths?

Douglass was himself a great statesman, who had earned the right to sit in judgment of Lincoln. On this point, it is even possible to offer some modest testimony from Lincoln himself. He is reported to have said to Douglass, at a reception at the White House on the night of his Second Inaugural Address, "there is no man in the country whose opinion I value more than yours. I want to know what you think of it." It is pleasing to report that Douglass greatly admired the speech: "Mr. Lincoln," he said, "that was a sacred effort."[3]

The tasks of a statesman of course depend on the character and the circumstances of the people he would lead. Certainly Douglass would not have been a great statesman had he *not* been an abolitionist, but perhaps Lincoln would not have been a great statesman had he been an abolitionist. For all his frustration, from time to time, with Lincoln, Douglass somehow—to his great credit—knew this:

His great mission was to accomplish two things: first, to save his country from dismemberment and ruin; and, second, to free his country from the great crime of slavery. To do one or the other, or both, he must have the earnest sympathy and the powerful cooperation of his loyal fellow-countrymen. Without this primary and essential condition to success his efforts must have been vain and utterly fruitless. Had he put the abolition of slavery before the salvation of the Union, he would have inevitably driven from him a powerful class of the American people and rendered resistance to rebellion impossible. Viewed from the genuine abolition ground, Mr. Lincoln seemed tardy, cold, dull, and indifferent; but measuring him by the sentiment of his country, a sentiment he was bound as a statesman to consult, he was swift, zealous, radical, and determined.[4]

A judicious and "comprehensive" understanding of Lincoln's statesmanship requires us to come to grips with the truths that are contained in Douglass's disquieting words. Here, I will argue, is what we might learn from Douglass. We do not do justice to Lincoln's statesmanship unless we see the truth in Douglass's remark that Lincoln "was preeminently the white man's President" and unless we recognize that fact as one of those "honorable device[s] that statesmanship might require."[5]

Lincoln, Common Man?

Lincoln was a *democratic* statesman, and his *demos,* his people, was constituted by the mostly white free citizens of the United States of America. He was therefore "preeminently the white man's President." What does it mean to say that Lincoln was a democratic statesman?

Lincoln had the democratic advantage of actually being, in one sense, a common man.[6] He did not hesitate to cultivate that reputation, and it served him well. He would one day be able to say to a regiment of Northern soldiers: "I happen temporarily to occupy this big White House. I am a living witness that any one of your children may look to come here as my father's child has."[7] In this respect and others, Lincoln was the first author of the Lincoln story. But in writing this myth, he had good material to work with. "It is a great folly to attempt to make anything out of me or my early life," Lincoln once said. "It can all be condensed into a single sentence; and that sentence you will find in Gray's 'Elegy':—'The short and simple annals of the poor.'—That's my life, and that's all you or anyone else can make out of it."[8] His short autobiography, published for the 1860 campaign, makes for somewhat discomfiting reading, so great is its emphasis on his youthful poverty and commonness—although he does not hesitate to report in that campaign autobiography that he had "studied and nearly mastered the Six-books of Euclid, since he was a member of Congress."[9] But to all external appearances—that is, if we take no notice of the inner life of this extraordinary youth, who mastered Euclid and perhaps imagined himself a Napoleon[10]—the simple truth is that Lincoln "appeared in every sense of the word like one of the plain people among whom he loved to be counted."

That last remark appears in a fine speech delivered by Joseph Choate (ambassador to Great Britain under President McKinley and a notable Republican from New York), during his service in England, on that "most American of all Americans." "It is now forty years since I first saw and heard Abraham Lincoln," said Choate, "but the impression which he left on my mind is ineffaceable."

> He appeared in every sense of the word like one of the plain people among whom he loved to be counted. At first sight there was nothing impressive or imposing about him—except that his great stature singled him out from the crowd; his clothes hung awkwardly on his giant frame, his face was of a dark pallor, without the slightest tinge of color; his seamed and rugged features bore the furrows of hardship and struggle; his deep-set eyes looked sad and anxious. His fame as a powerful speaker had preceded him, and exaggerated rumor of his wit—the worst forerunner of an orator—had reached the East. A vast sea of eager upturned faces greeted him, full of intense curiosity to see what this rude child of the people was like.

So far we see the Lincoln of story: the awkward child of a plain and rude people. But "he was equal to the occasion," reports Choate:

> When he spoke he was transformed; his eye kindled, his voice rang, his face shone and seemed to light up the whole assembly. For an hour and a half he held his audience in the hollow of his hand. . . . "The grand simplicities of the Bible," with which he was so familiar, were reflected in his discourse. With no attempt at ornament or rhetoric, without parade or pretence [sic], he spoke straight to the point. If any came expecting the turgid eloquence or the ribaldry of the frontier, they must have been startled at the earnest and sincere purity of his utterances. It was marvellous to see how this untutored . . . man found his own way to the grandeur and strength of absolute simplicity.[11]

The contrast between Abraham Lincoln and George Washington is instructive on the present point, I think. "What is the highest ambition that is suitably republican?" asks the political philosopher Harvey Mansfield. "To be father of one's country," Mansfield answers, in praise of Washington, the father of our republic.[12] We are even now in the habit of speaking of the framers of the Constitution of the United States as the "founding fathers." But is this habit quite republican? Is there no higher ambition, or no more suitably republican ambition, than to be the father of one's country?

Begin with this observation: Washington was a gentleman; Lincoln was not. Washington was a far more aristocratic man than Lincoln, and it is hard for a gentleman to be a democrat. There are many stories about Washington's gentlemanly dignity. It is said, for example, that at the outset of the Constitutional Convention, Alexander Hamilton and Gouverneur Morris and a few other delegates were discussing Washington's character. Morris, we are told, objected that their portrait of Washington's impenetrable reserve was an exaggeration. Hamilton offered a wager: a dinner if Morris would dare to approach Washington, slap him on the back, and offer his good wishes. In the event, Morris was not quite so impertinent as that. But he did approach Washington; he bowed and placed his hand on Washington's shoulder, offering as he did so his good wishes. Washington, we are told, stiffened, removed the offending hand, and scowled at Morris, to the embarrassment of Morris and doubtless the quiet amusement of those who witnessed the incident. In Max Farrand's version: "Hamilton lost the bet, but Morris in recounting his experience said that he had never won a bet which cost him so dearly, and Washington had only 'looked at' him."[13]

Lincoln was somehow a man of the people in a way that Washington was not. Certainly these differences reflect a change in the nature of our democracy from the time of Washington to the time of Lincoln. But perhaps too they reflect an important difference between the statesmanship of Washington and that of Lincoln. Lincoln would learn to make himself the "sincere friend" of a democratic people who had begun to lose, or perhaps never quite possessed, the habits and virtues of self-government. This is Lincoln's greatest contribution to the emergence of a democratic ethos in America: his statesmanship was designed to welcome the people into our democratic politics, by educating and ennobling the people, as Washington (and even Jefferson) had not quite done or had not done in the same democratic spirit. Lincoln's aspiration was to make statesmanship safe for democracy or to be the statesman who was also a "sincere friend" of democracy. That aspiration is quite different, and perhaps higher, than the republican statesmanship of Washington, the father of his country.

And the War Came

"There is no peaceful extinction of slavery in prospect for us," writes Lincoln in August 1855, in a private letter to George Robertson, a Kentucky lawyer and Whig politician.[14] All things considered, perhaps 1855 is surprisingly early for such pessimism. It is after the Kansas-Nebraska Act (1854) but during a period of heady anticipation of better days for the ascendant anti-Nebraska cause (and the emerging Republican Party). It is also before the demoralizing victory of the Democrats in 1856 and the *Dred Scott* decision (1857), which would together arouse Lincoln to speak during the Lincoln-Douglas Debates of a Democratic Party "conspiracy" to "make slavery perpetual and universal in this nation."[15] Here is the core of the letter to Robertson:

> You are not a friend of slavery in the abstract. . . . [Y]ou spoke of *"the peaceful extinction of slavery"* and used other expressions indicating your belief that the thing was, at some time, to have an end. . . . Since then we have had thirty six years of experience; and this experience has demonstrated, I think, that there is no peaceful extinction of slavery in prospect for us. The signal failure of Henry Clay, and other good and great men, in 1849, to effect any thing in favor of gradual emancipation in Kentucky, together with a thousand other signs, extinguishes that hope utterly. On the question of liberty, as a principle, we are not what we have been. When we were the political slaves of King George, and wanted to be free, we called the maxim that "all men are created equal" a self evident truth; but now when we have grown fat, and have lost all dread of being slaves ourselves, we have become so greedy to be *masters* that we call the same maxim "a self-evident lie." . . . The fourth of July has not quite dwindled away; it is still a great day—*for burning fire-crackers!!!*
>
> That spirit which desired the peaceful extinction of slavery, has itself become extinct, with the *occasion,* and the *men* of the Revolution. Under the impulse of that occasion, nearly half the states

adopted systems of emancipation at once; and it is a significant fact, that not a single state has done the like since. So far as peaceful, voluntary emancipation is concerned, the condition of the negro slave in America, scarcely less terrible to the contemplation of a free mind, is now as fixed, and hopeless of change for the better, as that of the lost souls of the finally impenitent. The Autocrat of all the Russias will resign his crown, and proclaim his subjects free republicans sooner than will our American masters voluntarily give up their slaves.

Our political problem now is "Can we, as a nation, continue together *permanently—forever*—half slave, and half free?" The problem is too mighty for me.[16]

The founders, Lincoln often says, had placed slavery on a "course of ulti-mate extinction." But by 1857, no honest observer of the American political scene could believe that slavery was *still* on a course of ultimate extinction. The founders had somehow been betrayed, between 1787 and 1857, first in 1820 (the Missouri Compromise), then again in 1850 (the Compromises of 1850), and again in 1854 (the Kansas-Nebraska Act), and above all in 1857 (*Dred Scott*). By the middle of the 1850s, the purpose of the "ultimate extinction" argument, for Lincoln, is less to vindicate the wisdom of the founders, whose slavery policies had by then largely been abandoned, than it is to inspire the citizens of his America to undertake a "restoration" of the policies and principles of the founders.

In order to see the betrayal, it is necessary to consider briefly the found-ers' policy—without for present purposes considering too deeply whether or not Lincoln was right to say that the founders believed, or assumed, that they had placed slavery on a "course of ultimate extinction." How had they attempted to do so? The *principle* of the founding was that slavery was wrong, a "monstrous injustice," and contrary to the principles of the American republic.[17] The *policy* of the founders was "the policy of prohibiting slavery in new territory," as most clearly manifested in the Northwest Ordinance of 1787. "Thus, with the author of the declaration of Independence, the policy of prohibiting slavery in new territory originated. Thus, away back of the constitution, in the pure fresh, free breath of the revolution, the State of Virginia, and the National congress put that policy in practice. Thus through sixty odd of the best years of the republic did that policy steadily work to its great and beneficent end."[18] Lincoln argued that this policy (no extension of slavery) would in time vindicate the principle by bringing an end to the monstrous injustice of slavery. Partly for this reason it was permissible, morally and politically, for the founders to compromise with slavery, as a necessity and only for a time—so Lincoln argued. It was also permissible, morally and politically, for the emerging Republican Party to rest on a platform of "no extension." At the beginning of the Peoria speech of 1854, Lincoln announces: "I wish to MAKE and to KEEP the distinction between the EXISTING institution, and the EXTENSION of it, so broad, and so clear, that no honest man can misunderstand me, and no dishonest one, successfully misrepresent me."[19] He consistently maintained this distinction until it was overtaken by events.[20]

We need not here consider further the adequacy of this argument, either as an interpretation of the designs of the founders or as a defense of the necessity of compromise with slavery at the time of the founding. For present purposes, it is enough to note the ground of Lincoln's confidence that the *principle* and the *policy,* consistently maintained, would one day bring the peaceful extinction of slavery.[21] As long as "the great mass of mankind . . . consider slavery a great moral wrong," says Lincoln, "no statesman can safely disregard it."[22] Those who would perpetuate slavery cannot abide the endurance of the moral opinion that "all men are created equal." On this point, Lincoln cites Henry Clay: "They must blow out the moral lights around us, and extinguish that greatest torch of all which America presents to a benighted world—pointing the way to their rights, their liberties, and their happiness. . . . They must penetrate the human soul, and eradicate the light of reason, and the love of liberty. Then, and not till then, when universal darkness and despair prevail, can you perpetuate slavery, and repress all sympathy, and all humane, and benevolent efforts among free men, in behalf of the unhappy portion of our race doomed to bondage."[23]

It is noteworthy that not only enemies but also friends of slavery doubted that the institution could long survive in the face of a universal democratic moral opinion condemning it as unjust. The growing intransigence of the South during this period might be taken for evidence that many in the South feared, what Lincoln and others hoped, that the deepest contest regarding the future of slavery was the contest over public opinion. The principal task of Lincoln's statesmanship in the 1850s was to preserve and to cultivate, and if necessary to restore, the democratic moral opinion that would one day, sooner than later, lead the people themselves to choose to free the slaves.

Recall the Robertson letter, quoted earlier: thirty-six years of experience since the Missouri Compromise had demonstrated "that there is no peaceful extinction of slavery in prospect for us."[24] That private sentiment of 1855 is reaffirmed in the House Divided Speech of 1858: "Either the *opponents* of slavery, will arrest the further spread of it, and place it where the public mind shall rest in the belief that it is in course of ultimate extinction; or its *advocates* will push it forward, till it shall become alike lawful in *all* the States, *old* as well as *new*—*North* as well as *South*. Have we no *tendency* to the latter condition?"[25]

In both the Robertson and the Joshua Speed letters of August 1855, Lincoln attributes this tendency to a "degeneracy" of public opinion: "On the question of liberty, as a principle, we are not what we have been."

What is the ground of Lincoln's pessimism "on the question of liberty"? The first part of Lincoln's 1854 Peoria Speech, on "the repeal of the Missouri Compromise, and the propriety of its restoration," offers an answer.[26] Lincoln argues that the founders' policy of prohibiting expansion of slavery into new territories had been defeated over time, gradually but undeniably, and that this victory had been achieved on the basis of a new principle (the "spirit of Nebraska") inconsistent with the principle of the Declaration of Independence (the "spirit of seventy-six").[27] That defeat might in time be reversed, Lincoln at that time hoped. Thus the immediate political aim of the Peoria Speech is to make the case for the "propriety" of the restoration of the Missouri Compromise. But by 1854, certainly by 1857, the "tendency" was clear.[28]

Begin with Missouri. The occasion of the Peoria Speech is the Kansas-Nebraska Act, which repeals the Missouri Compromise. The purpose of the speech is to call for the "restoration" of the Missouri Compromise prohibition on slavery extension into the territory north of 36° 30'. For this reason, we might expect that the speech must present a robust defense of the Missouri Compromise or that Lincoln must argue that the Missouri Compromise is faithful to the founders' intention. That first impression is misleading. The first great slavery struggle in the nation concerned Missouri, an acquisition of the 1803 Louisiana Purchase into which slavery had already extended. When Missouri sought admission as a slave state, the North honorably resisted. That resistance is perhaps the strongest evidence that, for at least a time, Northern public opinion embraced something like Lincoln's view of the founders' intention to prohibit slavery extension. In his account of the controversy, Lincoln emphasizes this Northern resistance.[29] Here was the first great test of the policy prohibiting slavery extension, and the antislavery party lost. Missouri was admitted as a slave state in clear contravention of the founders' policy. In exchange, slavery was prohibited in the territory north of 36° 30' (including Kansas and Nebraska), but it would be permitted in Missouri (and in smaller territories south of that latitude).

Missouri was thus a defeat for the North and for the founders' policy. Looking back from the vantage of the 1850s, Lincoln was prepared to excuse this settlement. Indeed, he is able to skewer Douglas by quoting an 1849 speech: "'[T]his Compromise had been canonized in the hearts of the American people, as a sacred thing which no ruthless hand would ever be reckless enough to disturb.'"[30] Lincoln himself, unlike Douglas and his partisan friends, accepts the Missouri Compromise *only* as a *compromise:* the concession seemed modest (Missouri) and the reward great (peaceful preservation of the Union). As he puts the point in his Peoria Speech, "Much as I hate slavery, I would consent to the extension of it rather than see the Union dissolved, just as I would consent to any GREAT evil, to avoid a GREATER one."[31] But this is a troubling argument, for Lincoln here expresses a willingness to accept a retreat from the policy of the founders—on the basis of which slavery had supposedly been placed on a course of ultimate extinction—for the sake of preserving the Union. The concession of Missouri, however modest on the ground, was great in principle: at what time do such concessions undermine one's reasonable confidence that slavery will one day be extinguished, since that confidence had been founded on unwillingness to compromise on precisely this point—that is, the unwillingness to permit any extension of slavery into new territory? As Lincoln came to recognize, at some point (probably not in the Missouri case, perhaps in the 1850 compromise respecting New Mexico, certainly in the Nebraska case) compromise on territorial extension is no longer a (temporary) compromise with a necessary evil but a (permanent) compromise on the basis of a new principle that recognizes the moral parity of the claims of freedom and of slavery in the Union.

The case is even clearer, as Lincoln indicates, with the Compromises of 1850. "And there California stood, kept *out* of the Union, because she would not let slavery *into* her borders. Under all the circumstances perhaps this was not wrong. There were other points of dispute, connected with the general question of slavery, which needed adjustment."[32] It is noteworthy that Lincoln's defense of the Compromises of 1850 is far less robust than his defense of the Missouri Compromise.[33] Charnwood reproaches Lincoln for this judgment, however tepid, in support of the Compromises of 1850:

> Zachary Taylor . . . was no politician at all, but placed in the position of President, for which fairness and firmness were really the greatest qualifications, he was man enough to rely on his own good sense. . . . When, as we shall shortly see, the great men of the Senate thought the case demanded conciliation and a great scheme of compromise, he resolutely disagreed; he used the whole of his influence against their compromise. . . . The greatest minds in American politics . . . viewed the occasion otherwise, but, in light of what followed, it seems a signal and irreparable error that, when the spirit of aggression rising in the South had taken definite shape in a demand which was manifestly wrongful, it was bought off and not met with a straightforward refusal.[34]

However that might be, by 1855 the point of no return had surely been reached and passed, and thus Lincoln thought that "there is no peaceful extinction of slavery in prospect for us." No reasonable observer could still believe that slavery was on a "course of ultimate extinction." The great Democratic folly of the Kansas-Nebraska Act of 1854, repealing the Missouri Compromise prohibition on slavery extension, constituted a decisive repudiation of the founders' policy.

Here, then, is the root of Lincoln's growing intransigence: "an increasing number of men" during this period, says Lincoln—including John Calhoun, among others—"for the sake of perpetuating slavery, are beginning to assail and to ridicule the white man's charter of freedom—the declaration that 'all men are created equal.'" This gradual but fundamental transformation of democratic moral opinion in the nation was not isolated within Southern elites. Douglas himself, Lincoln argues, had practically repudiated the Declaration of Independence. According to Douglas, the founders did not mean that *all* men were created equal: rather, they "were speaking of British subjects on this continent being equal to British subjects born and residing in Great Britain." Lincoln mocks Douglas's Declaration: "We hold these truths to be self-evident that all British subjects who were on this continent eighty-one years ago, were created equal to all British subjects born and *then* residing in Great Britain."[35]

The most dangerous feature of the Kansas-Nebraska Act, then, was not that it opened Kansas and Nebraska to slavery (troubling though that was), but rather that Douglas and his partisan friends defended the act on the basis of principles—the doctrine of popular sovereignty and Douglas's "care not" posture toward slavery—that were incompatible with *the* fundamental principle of American republicanism, the "white man's" own charter of freedom, that "all men are created equal." According to Lincoln, this is precisely Douglas's role in the program of the Democratic political dynasty ("a conspiracy to make slavery perpetual and national," he goes so far as to call it): "to *educate* and *mould* public opinion, at least *Northern* public opinion, to not *care* whether slavery is voted *down* or voted *up*."[36] Lincoln might have been prepared to accept another slave territory or slave state for the sake of peace with the slave power, as he quietly admitted. But he could not abide this retreat from the *principles* of the Declaration in the moral opinion of *his* people. It now began to appear that the Union would, one way or another, be destroyed in the ensuing struggle—probably by abandoning its fundamental moral principle, perhaps by dissolution. In the face of this prospect, Lincoln's strategy was to advance a party platform that would open a third possibility: the victory of the *principle* of the North, a victory that could only be achieved by Southern capitulation on the question of political right and so, *almost certainly,* by war.[37]

That last remark bears repeating and further discussion. Lincoln's strategy was to advance a Republican Party platform that would open a third possibility: the victory of the *principle* of the North, a victory that could only be achieved by Southern capitulation on the question of political right and so, *almost certainly,* by war. I do not say that Lincoln anticipated the likelihood of the Civil War as early as 1855. But I do say that the position he advances in the 1850s is a pessimistic one. Perhaps the most likely future is the victory of Douglas Democracy in the North and thus the transformation of the American republic into a slave republic—the nationalization and perpetuation of slavery that Lincoln argued was the tendency of the course of policy, from the Kansas-Nebraska Act through *Dred Scott*, of the governing Democratic dynasty. Even if that catastrophe could be averted, and a Republican Congress and president elected, the new Republicans would be more likely to blink than their Southern adversaries to avert war. But if those more likely results could be avoided and the moderate but intransigent Republican Party could somehow prevail, then only Southern capitulation would avert war. One might hope for such a capitulation, but in light of the consistent course of the Southern Democratic

Party in the 1850s, there could be little reason to expect it. "There is no peaceful extinction of slavery in prospect for us."

The fundamental quarrel between Stephen Douglas and Abraham Lincoln, then, concerned their irreconcilable efforts to educate public opinion, and especially public opinion in the North, regarding the fundamental principles of the American regime: either the "spirit of seventy-six" or the "spirit of Nebraska" must prevail. The core of democratic statesmanship, then, is the education of democratic moral opinion. That task requires patience and moderation, but it also requires a readiness to challenge the people to earn self-government and to accept necessary burdens in its defense.

An Act of Justice, Warranted by Military Necessity

Let us turn next to the second moment of Lincoln's democratic statesmanship, the decision to issue the Emancipation Proclamation in 1862. This decision is usually taken as a triumph of Lincoln's statesmanship, and so it was. But its necessity was also, in one important respect, his greatest failure. What a tragedy for our country that emancipation was thus achieved by force of arms, by the edict of a commander of armies, and not by more democratic means.

In a letter to Horace Greeley in August 1862, Lincoln wrote:

> I would save the Union. I would save it the shortest way under the Constitution. . . . My paramount object in this struggle *is* to save the Union, and is *not* either to save or to destroy slavery. If I could save the Union without freeing *any* slave, I would do it, and if I could save it by freeing *all* the slaves, I would do it; and if I could do it by freeing some and leaving others alone I would also do that. What I do about slavery, and the colored race, I do because I believe it helps to save the Union.[38]

Lincoln is called the Great Emancipator. But we know that he resisted emancipation as a war aim for many months; he finally accepted the necessity of emancipation somewhat reluctantly, and only as a "military necessity." The letter to Greeley was published on August 22, 1862. Picking up the relevant story in the middle, in July 1862 Lincoln was pressing border state representatives to accept his proposal for a program of gradual and compensated emancipation in the border states, about which more presently. Congress too was acting in July 1862 to adopt measures that were transforming the war into a war for emancipation—what Lincoln called "a remorseless revolutionary struggle." Time was running out for "moderation." In mid-July 1862, the border state representatives decisively rejected Lincoln's proposals for a program of gradual and compensated emancipation. Only days later, on July 22, 1862, Lincoln informed his cabinet of his intention to issue the Emancipation Proclamation. It was agreed to postpone the proclamation until a military victory so that it would not seem, as in the event it nevertheless did seem, to be an act of desperation. That victory, such as it was, came at Antietam on September 17, 1862, and the Preliminary Emancipation Proclamation was then issued on September 22, 1862. The Final Emancipation Proclamation was issued on January 1, 1863.

The famous letter to Greeley clearly takes on a new meaning in this light. The letter is written and published *after* Lincoln had already taken the decision to issue the Emancipation Proclamation as soon as a military victory made it possible, which he in the event did. The letter to Greeley is therefore not the conservative, Unionist statement that it is often taken to be. What is new in that letter is this: "if I could save [the Union] by freeing *all* the slaves, I would do it." That is, the letter is partly designed to prepare the people of the North for emancipation *as a Union-saving measure.*

Lincoln would be accused of acting the tyrant in thus freeing the slaves. His response to the charge of dictatorship is contained in a famous 1864 letter to Albert Hodges: "I am naturally anti-slavery. If slavery is not wrong, nothing is wrong. I can not remember when I did not so think, and feel. And yet I have never understood that the Presidency conferred upon me an unrestricted right to act officially upon this judgment and feeling. . . . And I aver that, to this day, I have done no official act in mere deference to my abstract judgment and feeling on slavery."[39]

The final proclamation itself describes emancipation as "an act of justice, warranted by the Constitution upon military necessity"—and in the Hodges letter Lincoln hints, with tolerable clarity, that this coincidence of moral sentiment and constitutional authority was for him, by that time, a happy one.

But *why* did Lincoln seek to limit the war aims of the North to preservation of the Union only? He had good reasons, and we today must, I think, lament his failure.

Here again I begin with an appeal to the authority of Frederick Douglass:

> Can any colored man, or any white man friendly to the freedom of
> all men, ever forget the night which followed the first day of January,
> 1863, when the world was to see if Abraham Lincoln would prove to
> be as good as his word? I shall never forget that memorable night,
> when in a distant city I waited and watched at a public meeting, with
> three thousand others not less anxious than myself, for the word
> of deliverance which we have heard read today. . . . In that happy
> hour we forgot all delay, and forgot all tardiness, . . . and we were
> thenceforward willing to allow the President all the latitude of time,
> phraseology, and *every honorable device* that statesmanship might
> require for the achievement of a great and beneficent measure of
> liberty and progress.[40]

Why did Lincoln so long postpone this great consummation, to which he must have been profoundly tempted on grounds of justice?

He had many reasons, some less to the present point than others. First, at the outset of the war, Lincoln hoped to preserve the *political* unity of the North. Initially the war enjoyed the support of a more or less united Democratic Party, led until he died by Stephen Douglas. Moreover, the Union in early 1861 included a number of slave states, at first including even Virginia—and always including the key states of Missouri, Maryland, and Kentucky. A hasty move toward emancipation would threaten the unity of the North on both dimensions, since many in the Democratic Party and in the border states would support a war to restore the Union but not a war to emancipate the slaves. As the war continued, a substantial part of the Democratic Party abandoned the war party (and the border states were made secure by the presence of the Union army in them), and so the political reasons for restraint quickly faded. As the war became a Republican war, it became more reasonable to fight the war for Republican purposes.

Second, for more narrowly *military* reasons, it was necessary for the North to keep Maryland and especially Kentucky in the Union—for control of the District of Columbia and the Ohio River, respectively. A hasty move toward emancipation would likely drive these states out of the Union. "I hope to have God on my side," Lincoln reportedly once quipped, "but I must have Kentucky."[41] Again, as the war continued, Kentucky and Maryland and even Missouri were forcefully secured to the Union, and so this ground of restraint in war aims also faded.

Third, as the letter to Hodges indicates, Lincoln doubted whether he had, as president, the *constitutional* authority to abolish slavery. Thus he overruled John C. Frémont's early emancipation edict partly on the grounds that it was a usurpation of powers properly belonging either to Congress or more probably to the people in their sovereign or constitutional capacity. Lincoln evidently changed his mind about the authority of the *president* to emancipate the slaves as an act of "military necessity." In any case, as early as May 1862 in overturning Maj. Gen. David Hunter's emancipation order and again in July 1862 in the letter to Horace Greeley already discussed, Lincoln clearly indicated that he was reconsidering the question of the power of the *president* to free the slaves as an act of military necessity. Having said that, it is also clear that Lincoln *never* abandoned the ground that it was *only* as an act of military necessity that he had the power to free the slaves, however much he might have wished to do so as an "act of justice."

Fourth, Lincoln understood that the *moral* costs of war required him to avoid, as far and as long as possible, any policy that would transform the war into a "violent and remorseless revolutionary struggle."[42] He had, so he thought, a duty to win this war, which was after all a war among friends and brothers, in such a way as to make possible a restoration of the Union on terms of friendship and shared citizenship. At the outset of the war, that aim required a willingness to seek peace on terms that would not require an immediate revolution in the South—that is, on terms that would not require immediate abolition but would restore slavery to that "course of ultimate extinction" on which the founders placed it and that it was the stated aim of the Republican party to restore. Conversely, when the war became more terrible and so much blood and treasure of the North had been spent, Lincoln argued that the moral imperatives were transformed. Lincoln then insisted that by "the friction and abrasion of war"—"broken eggs can never be mended"—no return to the antebellum compromises would be just or even imaginable.[43] We might in retrospect wish that Lincoln had found a wiser audience in the border state representatives to whom he made this argument in July 1862, in the context of urging upon them a program of gradual and compensated emancipation:

> Discarding *punctillio* [sic], and maxims adapted to more manage-able times, and looking only to the unprecedentedly stern facts of our case, can you do better in any possible event? You prefer that

the constitutional relation of the states to the nation shall be practically restored, without disturbance of the institution. . . . But it is not done, and we are trying to accomplish it by war. The incidents of the war cannot be avoided. If the war continue long, as it must, if the object be not sooner attained, the institution in your states will be extinguished by mere friction and abrasion—by the mere incidents of the war.[44]

Too much blood and treasure had been spent, and it had been spent because the citizens of the South would not otherwise submit to the authority of the Union. The moral equation had thereby been transformed, and the reasons for moral restraint (that a war among friends and brothers should not be permitted to become a "remorseless revolutionary struggle") would soon pale before the reasons for insistence on something approaching revolution as the just deserts of a gravely wounded people. It would be transformed even more radically after the Emancipation Proclamation: "If they [the emancipated slaves] stake their lives for us, they must be prompted by the strongest motive—even the promise of freedom. And the promise being made, must be kept."[45]

But fifth and above all, there is the tragedy of the necessity of the Emancipation Proclamation. Lincoln hoped to achieve emancipation, if possible, by *democratic* means, by *consent,* which explains his eagerness, as late as the end of 1862 in his December Annual Message to Congress, less than a month before the Emancipation Proclamation was issued, to secure the agreement of border state representatives to a policy of gradual and compensated emancipation. Among other reasons, Lincoln understood himself to be bound as a democratic statesman to refrain from doing for the people what in the better case the people would choose to do for themselves. This is the deepest meaning of Douglass's observation that "Lincoln was preeminently the white man's President." Lincoln's people were the democratic people of the United States; his task was to lead that people to choose to abandon its practice of slavery. Who can doubt that the future relations between the former masters and the former slaves would have been a happier one had Lincoln's course of policy in early 1862 not been a failure—that is, had the Emancipation Proclamation, Lincoln's greatest achievement, not been necessary?

Lincoln's progress toward his decision to issue the Emancipation Proclamation illustrates both his moderation and patience—his eagerness, in the name of democracy, to avoid the unhappy necessity of the Proclamation—and the limits of that patience, manifested in his decision finally to act to achieve by force of arms, given the constitutional opportunity, what could not be achieved by more democratic means.

The Freedmen

As the war came to an end, Lincoln was compelled to reflect on a new set of tasks associated with the reconstruction of a democratic Union. How would the now crushed and conquered citizens of the South be welcomed back into the new Union? And how might the enormous challenges of achieving a new birth of freedom for the freedmen be met?

The thought of reunion with the South had long been on Lincoln's mind, at least as far back as the First Inaugural in 1861, where he had said: "I am loth to close. We are not enemies, but friends. We must not be enemies."[46] And we know of course that the task of reconstruction proved to be unmanageable after Lincoln's death; the enduring difficulties of that task are a vindication of Lincoln's worry and his warning. And yet the Civil War to some extent transformed Lincoln into a qualified and tentative and uncertain partisan of social and political equality of the races—as a project to be realized over generations, not immediately, but also as the just deserts of the freedmen. In an 1863 letter to James Conkling, who represented a group of Democratic opponents of the war, Lincoln writes: "Peace does not appear so distant as it did. I hope it will come soon, and come to stay; and so come as to be worth the keeping in all future time. . . . And then, there will be some black men who can remember that, with silent tongue, and clenched teeth, and steady eye, and well-poised bayonet, they have helped mankind on to this great consummation; while, I fear, there will be some white ones, unable to forget that, with malignant heart, and deceitful speech, they have strove to hinder it."[47]

For Lincoln, the question of social and political equality could not be settled on the abstract ground of natural rights, the ground upon which the slavery question must be settled. The question of social and political equality had to be settled on the ground of the capacity of the former slaves and the freedmen to live together as fellow citizens. And that is a question of many dimensions—the malignant hearts of "some white" men had to be cured, and the capacity of the freedmen to enter into full citizenship had to be demonstrated. For Lincoln, the black soldier in the Civil War had begun to make a powerful case for social and political equality—a presumptive argument, though perhaps not quite dispositive, that the nation now had an obligation to offer the freedmen social and political equality, over time and with suitable efforts to lift the freedmen from a degraded condition the responsibility for which rested on their former masters. Like Douglass, Lincoln seems to have judged that the "new birth of freedom" would include measures designed to achieve social and political equality of the races: "If they stake their lives for us, they must be prompted by the strongest motive—even the promise of freedom. And the promise being made, must be kept." It is tolerably clear, for example, that Lincoln supported a limited extension of suffrage to the newly freed slaves at the end of the war, especially for those who had fought for the Union.

Lincoln's late rhetoric is often directed at chastening his white fellow citizens, including those of the North, by urging them—sometimes gently, as in the Second Inaugural, sometimes fiercely, as in the Conkling letter ("with malignant heart, and deceitful speech")—not to claim a premature triumph, not to think that the work of defeating the legacy of slavery is complete with the emancipation and the end of the war, and not to forget the "offence" of *both* North and South (so he says in the Second Inaugural) that gave rise to "this terrible war."

The unfinished work of the nation's "new birth of freedom" would have two dimensions: the transformation of the freedmen into free men and fellow citizens and the defeat of those former masters who "with malignant heart, and deceitful speech, . . . strove to hinder" emancipation and whose prejudice and enmity would endure as obstacles to the new birth of freedom that emancipation promised, but only promised. The fact that emancipation was an incomplete work sheds light, I think, on Lincoln's extraordinary patience in the choice of means to bring it about. Since emancipation was the beginning, not the end, of a great work, it mattered how it was achieved: it might be achieved in such a way as to ease, or in such a way as to obstruct, the unfinished work. Lincoln resisted the temptation to seek emancipation by means of what he once called a "remorseless, revolutionary struggle," not only because of his understanding of the limits on his constitutional powers, not only because of his prudential fears about the prospect of losing the Unionist border states and Unionist Democrats in the fight to defeat secession, but above all because emancipation achieved by war, and not by some form of consent, would make "reconstruction," broadly conceived to include both of the tasks just mentioned, very nearly impossible. The "new birth of freedom" would remain an "unfinished work."

The Freedmen's Monument in memory of Abraham Lincoln portrays two figures: Lincoln and a young freedman. Lincoln is standing; he holds the Emancipation Proclamation in one hand, which rests on a column that contains a figure of George Washington. Lincoln is gazing down at the kneeling freedman, his left hand extended over him in a kindly and vaguely paternal gesture of benefaction. He is hovering over the freedman, who is ill-clothed, his shackles newly broken (still fixed to one wrist), a number of symbols of slavery strewn about him. The freedman is looking away from Lincoln, and his face is barren, not sad or angry—just utterly empty. It is fitting that this should be the monument *of the freedmen* to Lincoln: one's eyes are inexorably drawn to the crouched figure of the young freedman, and to his face, rather than to the towering figure of the Great Emancipator. We are invited, I think, to reflect on the condition of that freedman, and this monument is for that reason a much more disquieting tribute to Lincoln than the majestic Lincoln Memorial. Or, put slightly differently, the monument is a powerful portrait of how *much* and how *little* Lincoln achieved.

How much? The monument reveals the truth in Jefferson's remark, cited by Douglass: "for while Abraham Lincoln saved for you a country, he delivered us from a bondage, according to Jefferson, one hour of which was worse than ages of the oppression your fathers rose in rebellion to oppose."[48] It reveals that truth through the unforgettable portrait of the young freedman, of a human being whose face contains so little of our common humanity, a face that reveals a soul so little capable of sadness, anger, or joy even at the moment of emancipation; it reminds us of the "monstrous injustice" of slavery by showing its effect in the expressionless face of a young man. Is there any doubt that the defeat of that monstrous injustice would justify, as Douglass said, "every honorable device that statesmanship might require" for its achievement?

But the monument also reveals, and this too is fitting, *how little* Lincoln achieved: the young freedman is not yet a free man; the "new birth of freedom" is an "unfinished work." The freedman depicted in the Freedmen's Monument is not yet a republican citizen; through no fault of his own, he is not yet the social and political equal of his former masters. Here is Douglass on that question, at about the same time as his "Oration in Memory of Abraham Lincoln":

> We all know what the Negro has been as a slave. In this relation we have his experience of two hundred and fifty years before us, and can easily know the character and qualities he has developed and exhibited during this long and severe ordeal. In his new relation to his environment, we see him only in the twilight of twenty years of semi-freedom; for he has scarcely been free long enough to outgrow the marks of the lash on his back and the fetters on his limbs.[49]

It is hard not to wince at that thought, but there is something manly too, dignified and proud, in it. The beauty of the Freedmen's Monument is that it impresses on us both the grandeur of the completed work of emancipation and the magnitude of the "unfinished work" of achieving social and political equality that had then only just begun (and that was, in only a few years, substantially abandoned for many decades). Just as Douglass's "Oration" is marked by manly ambivalence, so too is the Freedmen's Monument itself: all honor to Lincoln the Emancipator, but let us not celebrate, at least not too much, for there is work to be done.

Notes

Some parts of this chapter were previously published as "Abraham Lincoln: The Moderation of a Democratic Statesman," in *History of American Political Thought*, ed. Bryan-Paul Frost and Jeffrey Sikkenga (Lanham, MD: Rowman & Littlefield, 2003).

1. Frederick Douglass, "Oration in Memory of Abraham Lincoln," in *Life and Writings of Frederick Douglass*, ed. Philip S. Foner, 5 vols. (New York: International Publishers, 1955), 4:312–13.

2. Frederick Douglass, "The United States Cannot Remain Half-Slave and Half-Free" (April 1883), ibid., 4:368.

3. Frederick Douglass, *The Life and Times of Frederick Douglass*, in Frederick Douglass, *Autobiographies* (New York: Library of America, 1994), 804.

4. Douglass, "Oration," 316.

5. Ibid., 315. For an insightful account of the relationship between Douglass and Lincoln, see James Oakes, *The Radical and the Republican: Frederick*

Douglass, Abraham Lincoln, and the Triumph of Anti-Slavery Politics (New York: Norton, 2008).

6. This paragraph and the following paragraph are borrowed from my "Abraham Lincoln: The Moderation of a Democratic Statesman," in *History of American Political Thought*, ed. Bryan-Paul Frost and Jeffrey Sikkenga (Lanham, MD: Lexington Books, 2003), 401–2.

7. Abraham Lincoln, "Speech to One Hundred Sixty-Sixth Ohio Regiment" (August 22, 1864), *Collected Works of Abraham Lincoln*, ed. Roy P. Basler, 8 vols. plus index (New Brunswick, NJ: Rutgers University Press, 1953), 7:512. Hereinafter cited as *CW*; emphases in original unless otherwise noted.

8. Cited from Lord Charnwood, *Abraham Lincoln* (Lanham, MD: Madison Books, 1996 [1916]), 10. Throughout this essay, I rely on this fine, if dated, biography of Lincoln, because Charnwood's key insight—the theoretical core of his understanding of Lincoln's statesmanship—is his claim that Lincoln was "the greatest among those associated with the cause of popular government" (326). That is, as Charnwood reveals, Lincoln's statesmanship was a *democratic* statesmanship. For works that emphasize other aspects of Lincoln's statesmanship, see David Herbert Donald's authoritative biography *Lincoln* (New York: Simon & Schuster, 1995), whose epigraph is a quote from Lincoln's letter of April 5, 1864, to Albert G. Hodges ("I claim not to have controlled events, but confess plainly that events have controlled me"), 9 and 14; Doris Kearns Goodwin, *Team of Rivals: The Political Genius of Abraham Lincoln* (New York: Simon & Schuster, 2005), xvi ("Abraham Lincoln would emerge the undisputed captain of this most unusual cabinet, truly a team of rivals"); and the groundbreaking book that launched the modern study of Lincoln's political thought, Harry V. Jaffa, *Crisis of the House Divided: An Interpretation of the Lincoln-Douglas Debates* (Seattle: University of Washington Press, 1959), especially 22–23, 181–272, 308–29.

9. Abraham Lincoln, "Autobiography Written for John L. Scripps" [ca. June 1860], in *CW*, 4:62.

10. Abraham Lincoln, "Address before the Young Men's Lyceum of Springfield, Illinois" (January 27, 1838), in *CW*, 1:114.

11. Joseph H. Choate, *Abraham Lincoln and Other Addresses in England* (New York: Century, 1910), 23–24.

12. Harvey Mansfield, "Paterfamilias," *New Criterion*, March 1996.

13. Max Farrand, *The Framing of the Constitution of the United States* (New Haven, CT: Yale University Press, 1913), 22.

14. Abraham Lincoln, "To George Robertson" (August 15, 1855), in *CW*, 2:318.

15. Abraham Lincoln, "First Debate with Stephen A. Douglas at Ottawa, Illinois" (August 21, 1858), in *CW*, 3:20.

16. Lincoln, "To George Robertson," 2:318. The letter to George Robinson is dated August 15, 1855. A more famous letter, taking a similarly grim tone with an erstwhile friend, Joshua Speed, is dated a few days later (August 24): "Our progress in degeneracy appears to me to be pretty rapid. As a nation, we began by declaring that '*all men are created equal.*' We now practically read it 'all men are created equal, *except negroes.*' When the Know-Nothings get control, it will read 'all men are created equal, except negroes, *and foreigners, and catholics.*' When it comes to this I should prefer emigrating to some country where they make no pretence [*sic*] of loving liberty—to Russia, for instance, where despotism can be taken pure, and without the base alloy of hypocrisy [*sic*]." Abraham Lincoln, "To Joshua F. Speed" (August 24, 1855), in *CW,* 2:320–23, 323. Caution is required in evaluating the relation between privately expressed judgments of this kind and public arguments; the necessity of caution cuts both ways. The pessimism of these letters is, I argue, consistent with aspects of the arguments even of the Peoria Speech (1854); it is more evidently consistent with the arguments of the 1858 debates with Douglas.

17. Abraham Lincoln, "Speech at Peoria, Illinois" (October 16, 1854), in *CW,* 2:255.

18. Ibid., 2:249.

19. Ibid., 2:248.

20. See, for example, Abraham Lincoln, "First Inaugural Address" (March 4, 1861), in *CW,* 4:262–63.

21. For this framework of argument, see Don E. Fehrenbacher, *Prelude to Greatness: Lincoln in the 1850's* (Stanford, CA: Stanford University Press, 1962).

22. Lincoln, "Speech at Peoria, Illinois," 2:281–82.

23. Abraham Lincoln, "Eulogy on Henry Clay" (July 6, 1852), in *CW,* 2:131.

24. Lincoln, "To George Robertson," 2:318.

25. Abraham Lincoln, "'A House Divided': Speech at Springfield, Illinois" (June 16, 1858), in *CW,* 2:461–62.

26. Lincoln, "Speech at Peoria, Illinois," 2:248; see generally 2:248–61.

27. Ibid., 2:275: "the spirit of seventy-six and the spirit of Nebraska are utter antagonisms."

28. Compare the passage just cited from the House Divided Speech—"Have we no *tendency* to the latter condition?"—with this passage from the debates with Douglas: "My main object was to show, so far as my humble ability was capable of showing to the people of this country, what I believed was the truth—that there was a tendency, if not a conspiracy among those who have engineered this slavery question for the last four or five years, to make slavery perpetual and universal in this nation." Lincoln, "First Debate with Stephen A. Douglas at Ottawa, Illinois," 3:20.

29. Lincoln, "Speech at Peoria, Illinois," 2:250: "this was resisted by northern members of Congress; and thus began the first great slavery agitation in the nation." Lincoln argues that in every previous case, the extension of slavery into new states (e.g., Kentucky, Alabama) had not been a true extension in contravention of the founders' policy, since slavery had already been planted in the relevant territories at the time of the Constitution. That argument is in a few cases problematic, but something like it is necessary to explain the fact that Missouri provoked the first great slavery agitation in the nation.

30. Ibid., 2:252.

31. Ibid., 2:270. Lincoln is here speaking of the Nebraska measure. Compare ibid., 2:250–51.

32. Ibid., 2:253.

33. Compare the discussion of both the Missouri Compromise and the Compromises of 1850 in Lincoln's Clay eulogy, delivered in 1852, prior to the Kansas-Nebraska Act. See Lincoln, "Eulogy on Henry Clay," 2:129. But even in that earlier speech, the 1850 measures are treated as more dubious than the Missouri Compromise.

34. Charnwood, *Abraham Lincoln,* 76–77.

35. Lincoln, "'A House Divided,'" 2:406–7.

36. Abraham Lincoln, "Second Debate with Stephen A. Douglas at Freeport, Illinois" (August 27, 1858), in *CW,* 3:45. Cf. ibid., 3:48; Abraham Lincoln, "Sixth Debate with Stephen A. Douglas at Quincy, Illinois" (October 13, 1858), in *CW,* 3:282; Abraham Lincoln, "Seventh and Last Debate with Stephen A. Douglas at Alton, Illinois" (October 15, 1858), in *CW,* 3:299; and Lincoln, "'A House Divided,'" 2:465.

37. See my "Abraham Lincoln: The Moderation of a Democratic Statesman," in Frost and Sikkenga, *History of American Political Thought,* 406–11, from which this paragraph and a few other sentences in this section are borrowed.

38. Abraham Lincoln, "To Horace Greeley" (August 22, 1862), in *CW,* 5:388.

39. Abraham Lincoln, "To Albert G. Hodges" (April 4, 1864), in *CW,* 7:281.

40. Douglass, "Oration," 315; emphasis added.

41. Cited in William E. Gienapp, "Abraham Lincoln and the Border States," *Journal of the Abraham Lincoln Association* 13, no. 1 (1992), 13.

42. Abraham Lincoln, "Annual Message to Congress" (December 3, 1861), in *CW,* 5:49.

43. Abraham Lincoln, "Appeal to Border State Representatives to Favor Compensated Emancipation" (July 12, 1862), in *CW,* 5:318. Cf. Lincoln, "To Horace Greeley," 5:389; Abraham Lincoln, "To August Belmont" (July 31, 1862), in *CW,* 5:350; and Abraham Lincoln, "To John A. McClernand" (January 8, 1863), in *CW,* 6:48.

44. Lincoln, "Appeal to Border State Representatives," 5:318.

45. Abraham Lincoln, "To James C. Conkling" (August 26, 1863), in *CW,* 6:409.

46. Lincoln, "First Inaugural Address," 4:271.

47. Lincoln, "To James C. Conkling," 6:410.

48. Douglass, "Oration," 313.

49. Frederick Douglass, "The Future of the Colored Race" (May 1866), in Foner, *Life and Writings of Frederick Douglass,* 4:194. This is the beginning of an argument, not the end. Douglass's thought on this question is more complex than this passage alone reveals.

8

"Public Sentiment Is Everything"

Abraham Lincoln and the Power of Public Opinion

Allen C. Guelzo

"Our government rests in public opinion," Abraham Lincoln said in 1856. And how could it be otherwise (he explained in 1859), since "in a Government of the people, where the voice of all the men of the country, enter substantially into the execution,—or administration, rather—of the Government—in such a Government, what lies at the bottom of it all, is public opinion." "Public sentiment is everything," he replied to Stephen A. Douglas in 1858. "Whoever can change public opinion can change the government." It is "public opinion" that "settles every question here," he added in 1860, and in order for "any policy to be permanent," it "must have public opinion at the bottom." It was in homage to public opinion, Lincoln told Charles Halpine in 1862, that he committed large portions of his presidential schedule to the wearisome and taxing labor of interviews with any and all members of the public who had the patience to stand in a line in his outer office waiting to see him. "The office of the president is essentially a civil one," Lincoln said, and no matter that "many of the matters" in these interviews were "utterly frivolous," nevertheless "all serve to renew in me a clearer and more vivid image of that great popular assemblage, out of which I sprang, and which at the end of two years I must return." These "promiscuous receptions" served as his "public-opinion baths," and as much as they "may not be pleasant in all their particulars," they served to connect him to popular feeling, like some political Antaeus reconnecting with the earth that gave him strength. "The effect as a whole," Lincoln insisted, "is renovating and invigorating to my perceptions of responsibility and duty."[1]

John Hay wrote years later that Lincoln "disliked anything that kept people from him," and he was certain that "nobody ever wanted to see the President who did not. . . . There was never a man so accessible to all sorts of proper and improper persons." Although Sen. Henry Wilson warned him that "these swarms of visitors" would end up sapping his strength rather than "invigorating" it, Lincoln only replied, "They don't want much; they get but little, and I must see them." The Sacramento journalist Noah Brooks reported in the spring of 1863 that Lincoln was a man who looked past the machinations of "mere politicians to find his best friends . . . in the mass of the people," and a year later he still believed that Lincoln, in some mystical way, "always feels for his clients—the people." The prominent jurist George Curtis told the Philadelphian Sidney George Fisher in 1864 that whereas others in the Lincoln administration whom he knew had "lost faith in the intelligence of the people" and "the success of democracy," Lincoln "has faith in the vitality of the nation and the ability of the people to meet and dispose of all difficult questions as they arise." It is as much from this, as from any other feature of Lincoln's political life, that his reputation as "the Man of the People" springs, since it manifests a humble deference (rather than personal arrogance or overweening self-righteousness) to the ideas of ordinary citizens. "All the people came to him as to a father," Isaac Arnold wrote in 1866. "He believed in the people, and had faith in their good impulses" and "always treated the people in such a way, that they knew that he respected them, believed them honest, capable of judging correctly and disposed to do right." At the same time, he agonized over the impact of Union defeats on public opinion, groaning in distress over the disaster at Chancellorsville as he said, "My God! my God! What will the country say! What will the country say!"[2]

But deference of this sort, while it may be some evidence of humility, may not necessarily be a *willing* deference, and it is not clear, even from Lincoln's own statements, whether he regarded public opinion as a cause to be served or a beast to be appeased and tamed. He told Emil Preetorius, the St. Louis German-language newspaper editor, that he "would rather be a follower than a leader of public opinion," but John Nicolay thought that it was Lincoln who did the leading and that "the Archimedean lever whereby he moved the world was public opinion." He might, as William Henry Herndon wrote years later, insist that he was a fatalist and that yielding to public opinion was simply another application of that fatalism, but Herndon saw that he actually "believed firmly in the power of human effort to modify the environments which surround us" and "made efforts at all times to modify and change public opinion." Lincoln was, as Henry Clay Whitney remembered, "very sensitive to public opinion," but this was not because he worshipped at democracy's altar with the proletarian zeal of Walt Whitman but instead because he was personally thin-skinned "and dreaded the censure of the newspapers and politicians." Or perhaps it was that Lincoln neither led nor followed public opinion but instead manipulated it. George Boutwell was convinced that Lincoln's "opinions were in advance usually, of his acts as a public man," but he "possessed the faculty of foreseeing the course of public opinion" and positioned himself to meet it and thus control it.[3]

In some measure, any uncertainty about Lincoln's reverence toward public opinion grows out of the uncertainty that the nineteenth century itself manifested toward public opinion—something that extended even to how the term should be defined. "Public Opinion is the one omnipotent ruling principle" in the American democracy, declared the *Democratic Review* in 1838, and the venerable Robert Winthrop of Massachusetts simply described "that mighty current of Public Opinion" as "nothing less than Law in its first reading." And on the eve of civil war, it was James Buchanan's plea that "our Union rests upon public opinion and can never be cemented by the blood of its citizens shed in civil war," which persuaded him not to brandish the sword in response to Southern threats of secession. But what, exactly, was *public opinion?* Was it the sum of the opinions of the entire American democracy? But what guarantees that these opinions are exactly the same or are filled with informed content or amount to more than mere irritated responses? How was it to be measured, in an age that lacked the means to undertake more than the most limited and crude of polling samples? What was available to measure it—the numbers who turned out for political rallies? The sum of newspaper editorial commentary? The educated guesses of friendly advisers in key places? And did the context of war—and especially civil war—change the standing of public opinion? Did civil war make public opinion *more* important, as a necessary prop for waging fratricidal conflict, or *less,* since it was liable to tire easily in such a struggle? Still, in a representative democracy, who could deny that public opinion held the political whip handle or that it could snap back on unwary candidates who so much as uttered an incautious word? "No eye hath seen it," smirked another contributor to the *Democratic Review* in 1845. "No hand hath grasped it. It hath no shape, nor color, nor ponderable bulk. And yet, in thoughts, alike of the day and night, it passeth before the faces of men, and the hair of their flesh standeth up and fear cometh on them and trembling, which maketh all their bones to shake."[4]

Of course, it has become no easier over time to identify the meaning of "public opinion," even in an era of mass polling, focus groups, and town halls. "Public opinion deals with indirect, unseen, and puzzling facts," admitted Walter Lippmann in 1922, and Lippmann's best attempt at pinning this elusive quantity to the wall was to say that public opinion was an amalgam of "the pictures inside the heads of human beings . . . of their needs, purposes, and relationships . . . which are acted upon by groups of people, or by individuals acting in the name of groups," without much regard for logic, consistency, or even accuracy. A. Lawrence Lowell, writing in the same decade as Lippmann, tried to grasp how "public opinion" managed to bind even those who dissented from its explicit beliefs. "In order that it may be public," Lowell believed, "a majority is not enough. . . . The opinion must be such that while the minority may not share it, they feel bound, by conviction, not by fear, to accept it." More recently, Jürgen Habermas's history of the development of a "public sphere" (*Öffentlichkeit*) in which uncoerced dialogue over the political order supplanted the top-down, single voice of power and aristocracy has pictured "public opinion" as the product of public-minded rational consensus (a consensus that, it has to be said, Habermas feared that the capitalist mass culture and state bureaucracies have succeeded in shutting down once again). This "public sphere" became the nursery of public opinion, as "a forum in which the private people come together to form a public" and ready "themselves to compel public authority to legitimate itself before public opinion." But the most ambitious attempt to isolate a precise notion of "public opinion" in the American context was James Bryce's *The American Commonwealth* in 1908: "Government by public opinion exists where the wishes and views of the people prevail, even before they have been conveyed through the regular law-appointed organs." It was in the nature of "free government," Bryce wrote, to assume the form of either small-scale democratic assemblies or large-scale representative republics; public opinion afforded a middle way by which small-scale democracy could meet large-scale representation and "apply the principle of primary assemblies to large countries." Public opinion, by acting "directly and constantly upon its executive and legislative agents," ensured that those agents never dared stray too far from popular control, and Bryce believed that "government by public opinion" was the end "toward which the extension of the suffrage, the more rapid diffusion of news, and the practice of self-government" would inevitably and "necessarily lead free nations."[5]

On the other hand, it was precisely this unbounded potential of public opinion for control that drove Alexis de Tocqueville to wonder whether public opinion might become the worst enemy of democracy. "Democratic republics put the spirit of a court within reach of the many and let it penetrate all classes at once," with the result that an offender against public opinion "is the butt of mortifications of all kinds and persecutions every day" until "he finally bends under the effort of each day and returns to silence as if he felt remorse for having spoken the truth." John Stuart Mill (whose *Principles of Political Economy* Lincoln greatly admired) thought the principal weakness of liberal democracy was "the absolute dependence of each on all, and surveillance of each by all" imposed by public opinion. In that case, it was a serious question "whether public opinion would not be a tyrannical yoke." On the other hand, it was that same powerful potential that dazzled Charles Sumner into hailing "that invincible Public Opinion" as the means by which law, "without violence or noise, gently as the operations of nature," is made and unmade. In fact, public opinion alone was what held out the only hope of reforming what the laws could not touch. Gambling, for instance, was a vicious and immoral practice, but the Jacksonian editor William Leggett balked at the notion that "government" should make itself into a reform agency: "For gambling, public opinion is the great and only salutary corrective. If it cannot be suppressed by the force of the moral sense of the community, it cannot be suppressed by statutes and edicts." Even slavery, added Leggett, "cannot always exist against the constant attrition of public opinion."[6]

It is tempting to sort out these alternations of fear and praise for public opinion along party and ideological lines in Lincoln's America, especially since Sumner (at least until 1850) and Leggett were so closely identified with the genius of Jacksonian democracy, while the Whigs labored under the opprobrium of being the party of the silk-stockinged elite. And to a certain extent, political ideology did condition the value set on public opinion. Even before the Whig Party assumed formal organization in 1834, John Quincy Adams had already put the stamp of elitism on it by urging Congress not to be "palsied by the will of our constituents" into refusing to fund internal improvements. The Missourian Edward Bates (who would serve as Lincoln's attorney general) scorned the assumption that "the people" are "always WISE and VIRTUOUS" and hence their opinions always right and true. The truth was that "very few men have the information necessary to form distinct opinions upon political questions as they arise," and so the direction of political life was best left in the hands of the educated and talented. "This is," he admitted, "PUBLICLY, a very unpopular belief, but, PRIVATELY, it has the hearty concurrence of 99 in every 100 intelligent men." What was currently called "PUBLIC OPINION," snarled Bates in his diary, "is never spontaneous with the people" but instead is "a MANUFACTURED ARTICLE, made by parties, to suit their occasions." Henry Clay and John Minor Botts were hailed by their Whig brethren precisely because they refused to court "the shifting gales of popularity," while those politicians who did were adopting "the schemes, the arts, and the seductions of the demagogue." The "accredited organs and exponents" of these demagogues were "a host of paltry newspapers, which, like the army of locusts, darken the land, and threaten to destroy and devour every bud, shoot and germ of civilization amongst us," and "the unceasing efforts" of "the orator" to promote "political agitation." The true statesman, like the noble Roman, "does not watch for public opinion," and "in the face of the multitude he forms his opinions fearlessly." He speaks with authority, not as "restless and unprincipled men," and "must enter the lists as champion of social purity and uncorrupt republicanism." Why truckle to public opinion, argued the *American Whig Review* in 1846, when public opinion is merely "the average opinion of the mass" and "authority is the opinion of the more enlightened few"? On those terms, "we hesitate not to prefer authority to public opinion."[7]

But it was by no means a given that Democrats would always be the partisans of public opinion and Whigs its enemies. Much as the *Democratic Review* was opposed to "all self-styled wholesome restraints on the free action of the popular opinion and will" and lauded a political order in which "all should be dependent with equal directness and promptness on the influence of public opinion," any estimates of the legitimacy of popular opinion in shaping policy frequently depended on whose political ox was being gored at the time. When Democrats suspected that public opinion was being "manufactured by mad fanatics for a mad purpose and threatening to overthrow all law under the insidious disguise of love to man and his rights"—a long-winded way of describing abolitionists—the *Democratic Review* was just as horrified as the Whigs at "the tyranny of public opinion." Henry Tuckerman worried that the "cant of reverence applied to man in the abstract" would force his compatriots to "refer our actions, thoughts and feelings to the idolized standard of public opinion."[8] Elitist or democratic, Americans idolized public opinion as the last step before that ultimate democratic arbiter, the popular election, but they also strove to shape and manipulate it; they worshipped public opinion as the spirit of democracy and feared it as the coarsener of democratic culture; they invoked it as the handmaiden of the laws and despised it as the corrupter of them. And Abraham Lincoln would not differ significantly from them in any important particular.

Public opinion, Lincoln said in 1841 while still a state legislator in Illinois, is "the great moving principle of free government," and policy "uncalled for by public opinion, or public convenience" was "unjust and unwise." It was abhorrent, in his view, for "men, professing respect for public opinion" to betray their public responsibility "to make way for party interests" and aim at producing "political results favorable to their party & party friends." Public men ought to be willing to accommodate public opinion to such a degree that even their private beliefs should be subsumed to it. "I do not think I could myself, be brought to support a man for office, whom I knew to be an open enemy of, and scoffer at, religion," Lincoln declared. Even though the "eternal consequences between him and his Maker" were an affair for only those two parties to resolve, public contempt for an overwhelmingly Protestant and evangelical culture betrayed the possibility of public contempt for other, more political issues. Hence, "I . . . do not think any man has the right thus to insult the feelings, and injure the morals, of the community in which he may live." Fifteen years later, as he journeyed eastward by train for his inauguration as president, Lincoln was still promising deference and accommodation toward public opinion. "I deem it due to myself and the whole country," he said in Cincinnati, "in the present extraordinary condition of the country and of public opinion, that I should wait and see the last development of public opinion before I give my views or express myself at the time of the inauguration." And this dovetailed nicely with Lincoln's larger deterministic worldview in which he would "claim not to have controlled events but confess plainly that events have controlled [him]," like a piece of driftwood that had "drifted into the very apex of this great event."[9]

But determinism is often mistaken for passivity, and if there is one thing that Lincoln cannot be accused of, it is passivity. He might protest his preference to "wait and see the last development of public opinion" before expressing his own, but that did not mean that he was waiting and seeing before actually forming it—as, in fact, he had on the issue of secession and the maintenance of federal property in the seceding states. "Universal public opinion" was the wind that powered the ship of state in a democracy, and when public opinion "not only tolerated, but recognized and adopted" a policy, the prudent politician bows to that fact and steers accordingly. But public opinion was not only changeable but liable (unlike the wind) to *being* changed, and there were tides in public affairs, running under the wind, that were just as important to reckon with and quite enough of a question about who actually constituted the "public" to give a certain selectivity to the public whose opinion one served. Despite Lincoln's obeisances to public opinion, he did not intend to be its slave, nor did he put much faith in those who disarmingly claimed to be. There was, as Horace White, Jesse Weik, and William Herndon all discerned, "a certain degree of moral obtuseness in Abraham Lincoln" that "cared nothing for public opinion." And the degrees that *did* care about public opinion saw it alternately as a belle to be courted, an ignoramus to be educated, and an animal whose self-interest could be attracted by the right bait. And especially in the context of the Civil War, Lincoln turned out to be notoriously reluctant to being pushed or pulled by public opinion on issues that mattered deeply to him. When John Hay asked him whether he was irritated at hostile newspaper commentary on the Emancipation Proclamation, he merely replied that "he had studied the matter so long that he knew more about it than they did." And when Lincoln was warned that Congress "would absolutely refuse" to seat representatives elected by newly reconstructed districts in Louisiana, his comment was the very opposite of deference: "Then I am to be bullied by Congress am I? I'll be d—d if I will."[10]

The first question that lay before Lincoln in dealing with public opinion was to identify what the public was whose opinion was being solicited. And nowhere does Lincoln's tightly held Whiggery stand out more clearly. "Public opinion is formed relative to a property basis," Lincoln said in 1860. That had two corollaries for Lincoln. The first, he expressed in his 1836 campaign announcement for the Illinois legislature. "I go for all sharing the privileges of the government, who assist in bearing its burthens," he wrote for the *Sangamo Journal*. "Consequently I go for admitting all whites to the right of suffrage, who pay taxes or bear arms, (by no means excluding females)." This is frequently offered today as evidence of at least some forward thinking on Lincoln's part on the subject of gender; this misses the real point he was trying to make, which was the subordination of gender to property-owning, since the only taxpayers would be those assessed for taxes on the real estate they actually owned. The real public whose opinion he was offering to serve were its property-owners, irrespective of gender (but not of race). "While acting as their representative, I shall be governed by their will, on all subjects upon which I have the means of knowing what their will is; and upon all others, I shall do what my own judgment teaches me will best advance their interests." And those interests, if anyone actually needed an explanation, were entirely commercial ones: "I go for distributing the proceeds of the sales of the public lands to the several states, to enable our state, in common with others, to dig canals and construct rail roads." What Lincoln meant twenty-five years later by hitching public opinion to "a property basis" was to argue that public opinion on slavery varied in exact proportion to how much people had invested in it. "The plainest print cannot be read through a gold eagle," he quipped. "The slaveholders battle any policy which depreciates their slaves as property," and "whatever increases the value of this property, they favor." Denouncing them for perpetuating an immoral institution might be ethically correct but politically meaningless "because they do not like to be told that are interested in an institution which is not a moral one."[11] Public opinion was not a mystery or an expression of some form of mass democratic sentimentality; it was an environmental response to a threat—any threat—to property.

Precisely because public opinion was not a mystery but a response, it was capable of being formed and shaped, and so, far from bowing into a doglike passivity in the face of public opinion, Lincoln believed that it could be cultivated, persuaded, shaped, and molded by an appeal to self-interest. Lincoln, said Herndon, "contended that motives moved the man to every voluntary act of his life." But precisely because human judgment was so malleable, it was vital to educate it properly, since it was just as liable to be educated wrongly, and when that occurred, its power for evil—or at least for tolerating evil—could be irresistible. What aroused him in 1854 about the Kansas-Nebraska Act was not just the freedom that the bill gave to slavery to compete equally with freedom for the allegiance of the Western territories, but the skillful way in which Stephen A. Douglas, the bill's author, had set out "to educate and mold public opinion" by wrapping "the Nebraska doctrine" in the attractive guise of "popular sovereignty." Beginning with the apparently harmless premise that Americans in the territories had the right, as free-born citizens, to determine for themselves what—or what not—to legalize, "the miners and sappers" like Douglas were performing a "gradual and steady debauching of public opinion," to the point where he would tell a campaign audience in Ohio in 1859 that "popular sovereignty and squatter sovereignty have already wrought a change in the public mind" and that "there is no man in this crowd who can contradict it."[12]

Douglas's "popular sovereignty" doctrine actually became Lincoln's principal example of why public opinion was *not* the polestar of political navigation. No one, Lincoln insisted, placed a higher value on popular government than he did. "The doctrine of self government is right—absolutely and eternally right," Lincoln said. "My faith in the proposition that each man should do precisely as he pleases with all which is exclusively his own, lies at the foundation of the sense of justice there is in me." But the "absolute" right of self-government stopped outside the circle of one's own self and property. The moment it was arbitrarily extended to the control of another person and over-rode *their* "absolute" right to self-government, "it has no just application." So, simply on first principles, a decision by one part of a community to legalize the enslavement of another part of that community is not an example of self-government, but an outrage on it, no matter how thumping the majority of those who support legalization. Popular sovereignty cannot trump the natural rights every man has to life, liberty, and the pursuit of happiness. So, Lincoln asked, "If the negro is a man, is it not to that extent, a total destruction of self government, to say that he too shall not govern himself?" Hence, "there can be no moral right in connection with one man's making a slave of another," no matter how much a community, in the way of exercising "popular sovereignty," may vote for it. Genuine popular sovereignty, Lincoln countered, "would be about this: that each man shall do precisely as he pleases with himself, and with all those things which exclusively concern him." Anything that stepped beyond that private circle or invaded what "exclusively" concerned others required the consent of those *others,* and that boundary could not be violated without that consent in anything that wanted to call itself a free government. "No man is good enough to govern another man, without that other's consent. I say this is the leading principle—the sheet anchor of American republicanism."[13]

In that respect, public opinion was exactly what Lincoln did *not* propose to serve. Instead, he trimmed around it, placating it with calm assurances that he had no intention of converting the Civil War into a war for emancipation and especially treating opinion in the border states with kid gloves. He was actually incensed when public opinion soured in the wake of the Peninsula Campaign in 1862, since it seemed to him "unreasonable that a series of successes, extending through half-a-year, and clearing more than a hundred thousand square miles of country, should help us so little, while a single half-defeat should hurt us so much." When George McClellan proposed to embark the Army of the Potomac from Annapolis rather than Washington in the spring of 1862, Lincoln was at once alarmed that an "extremely sensitive and impatient public opinion" would see this as "a retreat from Washington. But his solution was to fool it: "Could not 50,000 men or even 10,000 men be moved in transports directly down the Potomac" so as to create the illusion of "a self-evident forward movement, which the public would comprehend without explanation"? He employed listening posts across the broad belt of the border and elsewhere—his old friend Joshua Speed in Lexington (Kentucky), Cuthbert Bullitt in Louisville, Frank Blair in St. Louis, John W. Schaeffer in New Orleans, Anson Henry on the West Coast, and Orville Hickman Browning in Illinois, while using Leonard Swett, Ward Hill Lamon, and his two principal White House staffers, John Nicolay and John Hay, on public-opinion missions. But he employed his remote listeners not so much for the purpose of molding his policies after public opinion, as in determining how to navigate through public opinion toward political goals that he never offered up for compromise. "He would listen to everybody; he would hear everybody, but he never asked for opinions," Leonard Swett said. "In dealing with men he was a trimmer," said Swett, "and such a trimmer the world has never seen." In the absence of polls, Lincoln "kept a kind of account book of how things were progressing for three, or four months," but his accounting only served "to show how everything on the great scale of action—the resolutions of Legislatures, the instructions of delegates, and things of that character, was going exactly—as he expected." It was folly to try "to hasten public opinion," but it was also folly to be ruled by it. Rather, he set out the motives before public opinion, and let the "great scale of action" bring "the ripening of the fruit" and thus "the ripe pear at length falls into his lap!"[14]

But Lincoln was not content even to take this advice at all times. Rather than waiting for public opinion to provide him with an opportune moment for issuing the Emancipation Proclamation, Lincoln bolted dangerously far ahead of it, something he justified by the sheer necessity of acting before all opportunity for emancipation had disappeared. "When I issued that proc-lamation," Lincoln told John McClintock, the Methodist newspaper editor and scholar, "I did not think the people had been quite educated up to it." Indeed, they hadn't. William O. Stoddard, who also served on Lincoln's White House staff beside Hay and Nicolay, remembered "how many editors and how many other penmen within these past few days rose in anger to remind Lincoln that this is a war for the Union only, and they never gave him any authority to run it as an Abolition war. . . . [T]hey tell him that the army will fight no more, and that the hosts of the Union will indignantly disband rather than be sacrificed upon the bloody altar of fanatical Abolitionism." In the White House, "dread of the army" and "fear of a revolution in the North" pervaded the administration. Six weeks after the issuance of the Preliminary Emancipation Proclamation in the fall of 1862, congressional by-elections dumped thirty-one Republicans from their seats in the House of Representatives and sliced the Republican vote by 16 percent from 1860. "Seldom has the personnel of a House been so completely changed with a change of parties," admitted Pennsylvania congressman Albert Gallatin Riddle. "Indeed there were well grounded apprehensions that in the un-certainty of party lines in some States and districts the House might not be organized by an unquestioned Republican majority." It is at this point that Lincoln's oft-quoted estimate of the importance of public opinion takes on the appearance of an obstacle to be surmounted rather than a monument to be reverenced. Nevertheless, Lincoln defiantly insisted that "he would rather die than take back a word of the Proclamation of Freedom." One truculent Southern sympathizer in Washington wrote in his diary that "the Presdt is grieved at the result of the elections, but if any believe that he will change his course or policy because of the result they are woefully mistaken. He will not retreat from the Proclamation . . . or anything else because of an election, State or Congressional."[15] The situation posed by the environment of civil war made Lincoln even less deferential to public opinion than otherwise. When complaints erupted over military arrests of civilian dissenters, Lincoln retorted, "I insist that in such cases, they are constitutional wherever the public safety does require them." He had no sympathy for expressions of public opinion about the war when they involved "getting a father, or brother, or friend, into a public meeting, and there working upon his feelings, till he is persuaded to write the soldier boy, that he is fighting in a bad cause, for a wicked administration of a contemptable [*sic*] government, too weak to arrest and punish him if he shall desert." In that context, neither public opinion nor the Constitution are "in all respects the same, in cases of Rebellion or invasion, involving the public Safety, as it is in times of profound peace and public security." It was as though the stress of war induced a sort of derangement in the public mind, which should not be heeded in quite the same way as it might be in times of peace and stability.[16]

Far from deferring to wartime opinion, Lincoln instead took up the task of molding and shaping it himself. From his earliest days in politics, Lincoln had been a regular contributor to the *Sangamo Journal* (which later became the *Illinois State Journal* and, along with the *Chicago Tribune,* one of Lincoln's strongest advocates in Illinois politics), writing "hundreds of such Editorials" under a variety of pseudonyms. Once elected to the presidency, the conventional rule that limited a president to his executive tasks and forbade his using the presidency as a bully pulpit to influence public opinion put an end to his modest career as a journalist. But it did nothing to stop him from prompting Hay, Nicolay, and Stoddard to place anonymous editorials in prominent newspapers. Not only did Hay, writing for the St. Louis *Missouri Democrat* in 1861, send material "direct from Lincoln's office," but the pieces were "inspired by Lincoln," and more than a few believed that "Lincoln wrote some of the political correspondence which Hay sent to St. Louis." Hay also wrote material for the *Providence Journal,* the *New York World,* the *Missouri Republican,* and John W. Forney's *Washington Daily Morning Chronicle,* all of it aggressively puffing administration policy and sometimes ironically congratulating Lincoln on "his wonderful intuitive knowledge of the feeling and wish of the people." But the violent backlash against the Proclamation finally prompted Lincoln to abandon even the restraint of convention and issue a series of public letters as president that turned out to have been some of the most persuasive documents he ever wrote. Beginning with his brief but trenchant reply to Horace Greeley on emancipation in August 1862 (which Lincoln published over his own signature in the *Washington National Intelligencer*), Lincoln went on to produce four more public letters in 1863, to be published in major Northern newspapers and distributed as offset pamphlets—a brief reply to a series of resolutions passed by a workingmen's convention in Manchester, England; a response to Erastus Corning and a convention of New York Democrats on war policy and military detentions; yet another response on military arrests, this time speaking to resolutions of the Ohio Democratic State Convention; and finally, a powerful argument in defense of emancipation for James Cook Conkling and a state-wide Union "mass meeting" in Springfield, Illinois. Whatever violation of presidential protocol these letters represented, New York politico Chauncey Depew thought that through them Lincoln had caught "the ear of the public; he commanded the front page of the press, and he defended his administration and its acts and replied to his enemies with skill, tact, and extreme moderation."[17]

Newspapers, as Herndon wrote, were Lincoln's "food," fully as much as politics was his "life" and his "heaven." But he did not hesitate to manipulate them to his own ends. Unlike previous presidents, he did not authorize the establishment (or adoption) of a Washington newspaper to be his administration's "house organ." Instead, he played off against each other the forty-odd Washington-based journalists who represented the Associated Press (Lawrence Gobright), the *Philadelphia Inquirer* (W. H. Painter), the *Cincinnati Times* (John Hickox), the *Boston Herald* (H. R. Tracy), the *New York Times* (Simon Hanscom), the *New York Herald* (A. S. Hill), the *New York Tribune* (E. F. Underhill), the *Chicago Tribune* (Horace White), and others, distributing inside scoops and inside information in proportion to the favorable press each was willing to give him. He courted newspaper editors, inviting Henry Raymond of the *New York Times* to the White House for a private interview and sending him away "full of admiration for the president, saying he had more clearly than anybody the issues of this matter in his mind"—all of which resulted in a series of what John Hay called "remarkable sensible articles which have appeared recently in the Times." James Gordon Bennett, the editor of the *New York Herald,* was a much more difficult project, and so the offer of a diplomatic post was dangled in his path; ensuring the loyalty of Horace Greeley and the *New York Tribune* may have even involved a promise of a cabinet post. Occasionally, when favorable press did *not* appear, Lincoln could be "worried a good deal by what had been said in the newspapers," especially "about my suspension of the writ of habeas corpus and the so-called arbitrary arrests that had followed," and it "caused me to examine and reexamine the subject." But it did not cause him to change his mind. To the contrary, on one occasion it cost editors their jobs. When the *New York World* and the *New York Journal of Commerce* were suckered into printing a bogus conscription proclamation in May 1864, Lincoln was so infuriated (because he really was contemplating a new draft call) that he ordered the commandant of the Department of the East, John A. Dix, to arrest the owners and editors of the papers and shut down their publication.[18]

Lincoln loved the newspapers in more or less the same way he loved public opinion in general—pleased when it aligned itself with his ideas of right but dismissive when it didn't. "For newspaper public opinion he cared but little," William O. Stoddard recalled, and Nicolay actually thought that, apart from the Washington dailies, "the President rarely ever looks at any papers." The bulk of the newspaper attacks on his policies Lincoln dismissed as unworthy of reply, much less notice: "If the end brings me out all right, what is said against me won't amount to anything. If the end brings me out wrong, ten angels swearing I was right would make no difference." As it was, he was convinced the end would bring him out right. When John Hay would call "his attention to an article on some special subject," Lincoln would hold up his hand and say as he had said before, "I know more about that than any of them." He had his own course to steer, his own internal compass to mind. "They have never been friendly to me & don't know that this will make any special difference as to that," Lincoln once said to Hay about his critics. But "at all events, I must keep some consciousness of being somewhere near right: I must keep some standard of principle fixed within myself." This sounds nothing like deference to public opinion; it is scarcely even what can be called humility. But then again, as Hay remarked, "It is absurd to call him a modest man. No great man was ever modest. It was his intellectual arrogance and unconscious assumption of superiority that men . . . never could forgive."[19]

Lincoln might have been a "fatalist," but his fatalism did more to arm him against the ebb-and-flow of public opinion than it did to make him passive before it. Behind the protestations of being more the guided than the guide, Hay discovered that Lincoln could also be a "backwoods Jupiter" who "sits here and wields . . . the bolts of war and the machinery of government with a hand equally steady & equally firm. . . . He is managing this war . . . foreign relations, and planning a reconstruction of the Union, all at once. I never knew with what tyrannous authority he rules the Cabinet, til now. The most important things he decides and there is no cavil." Lot Morrill, a US senator from Maine, sensed from his encounters with Lincoln in Washington that "it was his policy to hold the nation true to the general aim" of the war, rather than the other way round and "to disregard petty deviations and delays. . . . He moderated, guided, controlled or pushed ahead as he saw his opportunity" and "held the ship true to her course."[20]

His regard for public opinion was thus ambivalent—sometimes bowing to it, sometimes disregarding it, and occasionally arguing his point with it. One thing he never imagined himself as being, however, was its oracle. Even at the outer limits of presidential authority, said Noah Brooks, Lincoln "liked to feel that he was the attorney of the people, not their ruler." This stands in sharp contrast to post–Civil War progressivism's recasting of the presidency as a vehicle for circumventing a leaden-footed Congress and the anointed embodiment of the general will. "Some of our Presidents have deliberately held themselves off from using the full power they might legitimately have used," wrote Woodrow Wilson in *Constitutional Government in the United States* in 1908 (the same year James Bryce struggled to define "public opinion"). "They have held the strict literary theory of the Constitution, the Whig theory, the Newtonian theory" of checks and balances, of limited powers, of the paralysis of leadership. Wilson believed that "the President is at liberty, both in law and conscience, to be as big a man as he can," and "if Congress be overborne by him, it will be . . . because the President has the nation behind him, and Congress has not." Only by the forthright action of a president who saw himself as a walking plebiscite could the paralysis of federal action be cured and the true ills of the nation addressed. This may not be what the letter of the Constitution had in mind for the presidency. But "the Constitution of the United States is not a mere lawyers' document," Wilson argued, "it is a vehicle of life, and its spirit is always the spirit of the age." Lincoln's notion of the Constitution, however, was entirely that of a "lawyers' document," and the principles it was built upon (and articulated in the Declaration of Independence) were his responsibility to defend, even in the face of "the spirit of the age." He expected "to maintain" the war for the Union "until successful, or till I die, or am conquered, or my term expires, or Congress or the country forsakes me"—but not to surrender it to public opinion or make himself the means of overriding it.[21]

The irony that stands behind this contrast, however, is that Lincoln, who was so cautious in his handling of public opinion, was apotheosized by it after his death, while Wilson, in reaching to make himself the *vox populi*, found himself decisively and savagely rejected by it. In the end, it was Lincoln's cautious engagement with public opinion in a democracy, not the overweening progressive confidence of Wilson that he could speak for it, that has enshrined him in the hearts—and public opinion—of people everywhere.

Notes

1. Abraham Lincoln, "Speech at a Republican Banquet, Chicago, Illinois" (December 10, 1856), "First Debate with Stephen A. Douglas at Ottawa, Illinois" (August 21, 1858), "Speech at Cincinnati, Ohio" (September 17, 1859), and "Speech at Hartford, Connecticut" (March 5, 1860), in *Collected Works of Abraham Lincoln,* ed. Roy P. Basler, 8 vols. plus index (New Brunswick, NJ: Rutgers University Press, 1953), 2:385, 3:27, 442, and 4:9 (hereinafter cited as *CW*); Charles Halpine, in *Recollected Words of Abraham Lincoln,* ed. Don E. Fehrenbacher and Virginia Fehrenbacher (Stanford, CA: Stanford University Press, 1996), 194.

2. John Hay, "Life in the White House in the Time of Lincoln," in *At Lincoln's Side: John Hay's Civil War Correspondence and Selected Writings,* ed. Michael Burlingame (Carbondale: Southern Illinois University Press, 2000), 132; Michael Burlingame and J. R. T. Ettlinger, ed., *Inside Lincoln's White House: The Complete Civil War Diary of John Hay* (Carbondale: Southern Illinois University Press, 1997), 221; Noah Brooks, *Lincoln Observed: Civil War Dispatches of Noah Brooks,* ed. Michael Burlingame (Baltimore: Johns Hopkins University Press, 1998), 24, 110; Sidney George Fisher, diary entry for February 12, 1864, in Sidney George Fisher, *A Philadelphia Perspective: The Civil War Diary of Sidney George Fisher,* ed. Jonathan W. White (New York: Fordham University Press, 2007), 211; Isaac N. Arnold, *The History of Abraham Lincoln, and the Overthrow of Slavery* (Chicago: Clark & Co., 1866), 684, 687; and Noah Brooks, *Washington, D.C., in Lincoln's Time* (Chicago: Quadrangle, 1971), 60–61.

3. Helen Nicolay, *Personal Traits of Abraham Lincoln* (New York: Century, 1912), 350; William Herndon to Jesse Weik (February 26, 1891), in *The Hidden Lincoln: From the Letters and Papers of William H. Herndon,* ed. Emanuel Hertz (New York: Viking, 1938), 265–66; Henry Clay Whitney, *Life on the Circuit with Lincoln* (Caldwell, ID: Caxton, 1940), 423; and George S. Boutwell, "Lincoln in History," in *Reminiscences of Abraham Lincoln by Distinguished Men of His Time,* ed. Allen Thorndike Rice (New York: North American, 1886), 129.

4. "Political Portraits with Pen and Pencil, No. V: John Caldwell Calhoun," *United States Democratic Review* 2 (April 1838): 72; Robert C. Winthrop, "Free Schools and Free Government," in Robert C. Winthrop, *Addresses and Speeches on Various Occasions* (Boston: Little, Brown, 1852), 161; James Buchanan, "The

Annual Message of December 3, 1860," in George Ticknor Curtis, *Life of James Buchanan, Fifteenth President of the United States* (New York: Harper & Bros., 1883), 2:347; and "Our Times," *United States Democratic Review* 16 (March 1845): 238.

5. Walter Lippmann, *Public Opinion* (New York: Harcourt, Brace, 1922) 26–30; A. Lawrence Lowell, *Public Opinion and Popular Government* (New York: Longmans, Green, 1921), 14; Jürgen Habermas, *The Structural Transformation of the Public Sphere: An Inquiry into a Category of Bourgeois Society* (Cambridge, MA: Harvard University Press, 1989 [1962]), 25–26; and James Bryce, *The American Commonwealth*, 2 vols. (London: Macmillan, 1908), 2:279–81.

6. Alexis de Tocqueville, *Democracy in America*, ed. Harvey C. Mansfield and Delba Winthrop (Chicago: University of Chicago Press, 2000), 247, 244; John Stuart Mill, *The Collected Works of John Stuart Mill: The Principles of Political Economy with Some of Their Applications to Social Philosophy*, ed. J. M. Robson, 33 vols. (Toronto: Routledge & Kegan Paul, 1963 [1848]), 3:106; Charles Sumner, "Speech on our Present Anti-Slavery Duties, at the Free-Soil Convention in Boston, October 3, 1850," in Charles Sumner, *Orations and Speeches*, 2 vols. (Boston: Ticknor, Reed and Fields, 1850), 2:407; and William Leggett, "Stock Gambling" (1835) and "The Question of Slavery Narrowed to a Point" (1837), in *Democratick Editorials: Essays in Jacksonian Political Economy*, ed. Lawrence H. White (Indianapolis: Liberty Fund, 1984), 63.

7. John Quincy Adams, "State of the Union Message" (1825), in *The American Whigs: An Anthology*, ed. D. W. Howe (New York: John Wiley, 1973), 21; Edward Bates, diary entry for January 12, 1866, in *The Diary of Edward Bates, 1859–1866*, ed. Howard K. Beale (Washington, DC: Government Printing Office, 1933), 533; *Obituary Addresses on the Occasion of the Death of the Hon. Henry Clay* (Washington, DC: R. Armstrong, 1852), 100; "Hon. John Minor Botts, and the Politics of Virginia," *American Whig Review*, November 1847, 510; "The Mormons," *Harper's New Monthly Magazine*, April 1853, 621; "Civilization: American and European," *American Whig Review*, July 1846, 31; and "Monthly Record of Current Events," *Harper's New Monthly Magazine*, January 1851, 269.

8. "Introduction," *United States Democratic Review* 1 (October 1837): 2; "James Fenimore Cooper," *North American Review* 89 (October 1859): 301; Henry T. Tuckerman, "New England Philosophy," *United States Democratic Review* 16 (January 1845): 80; and "Atrocious Judges: Lives of Judges Infamous as Tools of Tyrants and Instruments of Oppression," *United States Democratic Review* 37 (March 1856): 244–45.

9. Abraham Lincoln, "Circular from Whig Committee against the Judiciary Bill" (February 8, 1841), "Handbill Replying to Charges of Infidelity" (July 31,

1846), and "To Albert G. Hodges" (April 4, 1864), in *CW,* 1:235, 236, 245, 246, 382, 7:281, and Josiah Blackburn, in Fehrenbacher and Fehrenbacher, *Recollected Words,* 31.

10. Abraham Lincoln, "An Address Delivered before the Springfield Washington Temperance Society" (February 22, 1842), in *CW,* 1:274; Jesse W. Weik, *The Real Lincoln: A Portrait* (Boston: Houghton Mifflin, 1922), 215–16; Hay, diary entry for September 24, 1862, in Burlingame and Ettlinger, *Inside Lincoln's White House,* 41; "Conversation with Hon. J. P. Usher" (October 8, 1878), in *An Oral History of Abraham Lincoln: John G. Nicolay's Interviews and Essays,* ed. Michael Burlingame (Carbondale: Southern Illinois University Press, 1996), 67.

11. Abraham Lincoln, "To the Editor of the *Sangamo Journal*" (June 13, 1836), "Speech at Springfield, Illinois" (June 26, 1857), and "Speech at Hartford, Connecticut" (March 5, 1860), in *CW,* 1:48, 2:409, 4:2.

12. Herndon to Weik (February 25, 1887), in Hertz, *Hidden Lincoln,* 179; William Herndon, "Analysis of the Character of Abraham Lincoln," in *Abraham Lincoln Quarterly* 1 (December 1941): 411; and Abraham Lincoln, "'A House Divided': Speech at Springfield, Illinois" (June 16, 1858) and "Speech at Columbus, Ohio" (September 16, 1859), in *CW,* 2:461, 3:423–24.

13. Abraham Lincoln, "Speech at Peoria, Illinois" (October 16, 1854) and "Speech at Columbus" (September 16, 1859), in *CW,* 2:265–66, 3:405; Lewis E. Lehrman, *Lincoln at Peoria: The Turning Point* (Mechanicsburg, PA: Stackpole Books, 2008), 133–35.

14. Brooks D. Simpson, "Great Expectations: Ulysses S. Grant, the Northern Press, and the Opening of the Wilderness Campaign," in *The Wilderness Campaign,* ed. Gary W. Gallagher (Chapel Hill: University of North Carolina Press, 1997), 4; Gustavus V. Fox, in Fehrenbacher and Fehrenbacher, *Recollected Words,* 163; Douglas L. Wilson and Rodney O. Davis, eds. *Herndon's Informants: Letters, Interviews, and Statements about Abraham Lincoln* (Urbana: University of Illinois Press, 1998), 165, 167; Francis B. Carpenter, *Six Months at the White House: The Story of a Picture* (New York: Hurd & Houghton, 1866), 77; and Nicolay, *Personal Traits of Abraham Lincoln,* 32.

15. McClintock, in Fehrenbacher and Fehrenbacher, *Recollected Words,* 314; William O. Stoddard, *Inside the White House in War Times: Memoirs and Reports of Lincoln's Secretary,* ed. Michael Burlingame (Lincoln: University of Nebraska Press, 2000), 97; Albert Gallatin Riddle, *Recollections of War Times: Reminiscences of Men and Events in Washington, 1860–1865* (New York: G. P. Putnam's Sons, 1895), 249; Allan Nevins, *War for the Union, 1862–1863: War Becomes Revolution* (New York: Konecky & Konecky, 1960), 325–34; Abraham Lincoln, "Remarks to Union Kentuckians" (November 21, 1862), in *CW,* 5:503;

and William Owner, diary entry for November 8, 1862, in William Owner manuscript diary, Library of Congress.

16. Abraham Lincoln, "To Erastus Corning and Others" (June 12, 1863), in *CW*, 6:266-67.

17. David H. Donald, *Lincoln* (New York: Simon & Schuster, 1995), 440; Michael Burlingame, *Abraham Lincoln: A Life*, 2 vols. (Baltimore: Johns Hopkins University Press, 2008), 1:95; Walter B. Stevens, *A Reporter's Lincoln*, ed. Michael Burlingame (Lincoln: University of Nebraska Press, 1998), 278; Introduction and "Washington Correspondence" (December 5, 1861), in *Lincoln's Journalist: John Hay's Anonymous Writings for the Press, 1860–1864*, ed. Michael Burlingame (Carbondale: Southern Illinois University Press, 1998), xi, 160; Abraham Lincoln, "To the Workingmen of Manchester, England" (January 19, 1863), "To Erastus Corning and Others" (May 28, 1863), "To Matthew Birchard and Others" (June 29, 1863), and "To James C. Conkling" (August 26, 1863), in *CW*, 6:53–54, 260–69, 300–306, and 406–11; and Chauncey M. Depew, *My Memories of Eighty Years* (New York: Charles Scribner's Sons, 1922), 30.

18. Herndon to Weik (December 29, 1885), in Hertz, *Hidden Lincoln*, 116; *Congressional Directory for the Second Session of the Thirty-Seventh Congress* (Washington, DC: 1861), 33; Hay, diary entry for early September 1863, in Burlingame and Ettlinger, *Inside Lincoln's White House*, 78; David H. Donald, *Lincoln Reconsidered: Essays on the Civil War Era* (New York: Vintage, 1956), 176; Harry J. Carman and Reinhard H. Luthin, *Lincoln and the Patronage* (New York: Columbia University Press, 1943), 286; James F. Wilson, in Fehrenbacher and Fehrenbacher, *Recollected Words*, 500; Menahem Blondheim, "'Public Sentiment Is Everything': The Union's Public Communications Strategy and the Bogus Proclamation of 1864," *Journal of American History* 89 (December 2002): 869–99; and Simpson, "Great Expectations," in Gallagher, *The Wilderness Campaign*, 28–29.

19. Stoddard, *Inside the White House in War Times*, 148; John G. Nicolay, "To the Chicago Tribune" (June 19, 1863), in *With Lincoln in the White House: Letters, Memoranda, and Other Writings of John G. Nicolay, 1861–1865*, ed. Michael Burlingame (Carbondale: Southern Illinois University Press, 2000), 116; Carpenter, *Six Months at the White House*, 258–59; Hay, diary entry for July 4, 1864, in Burlingame and Ettlinger, *Inside Lincoln's White House*, 219; and Hay to Herndon (September 5, 1866), in *Herndon's Informants*, 332.

20. Hay to John G. Nicolay (September 11, 1863), in Burlingame, *At Lincoln's Side*, 54, and "Conversation with Hon. Lot M. Morrill of M[aine]" (September 20, 1878), in Burlingame, *Oral History of Abraham Lincoln*, 55.

21. Brooks, *Lincoln Observed*, 216; Wilson, *Constitutional Government in the United States* (New York: Columbia University Press, 1917), 70; and Abraham Lincoln, "To William H. Seward" (June 29, 1862), in *CW*, 5:292.

9

Lincoln and the Lessons of Party Leadership

Matthew Pinsker

Even the most casual students of Abraham Lincoln are familiar with his greatest speeches. Literary achievements such as the Gettysburg Address, Second Inaugural, and sections of the Lincoln-Douglas Debates have become enshrined in American national memory. Lesser-known but still significant efforts such as the Peoria Speech (1854), the Cooper Union Address (1860), and the First Inaugural (1861) are also now part of the cultural literacy of any serious Lincoln devotee. But press Lincoln buffs on the content of his shrewdest confidential political statements, ask them to describe in detail his most significant partisan letters, memos, or documents, and even the best might stumble. Everyone acknowledges that Lincoln was an active partisan with deft political skills, but there is no canon for Lincoln's behind-the-scenes political career. To some, this might seem self-evident. Party organizing leaves behind little contemporary textual evidence, and nobody would claim that a missive fired off in the heat of a campaign—no matter how pivotal—deserves the kind of exegesis now routinely offered for Lincoln's public writings.

Yet it should also be clear that there are literally hundreds of documents in Lincoln's *Collected Works* that taken together might offer a kind of anthology for the best in nineteenth-century party leadership, or what Americans in those days ominously referred to as wire-pulling. We tend not to think of party management as a literary skill, but in an era before telephones or Twitter, the ability to command party legions through letters was an essential

191

component of effective party leadership. So, where might such a partisan anthology begin? This chapter proposes to start the collection-building process with what might arguably be considered the most significant confidential letter in Lincoln's entire political career, a report to Norman B. Judd (the Chicago politician then serving as chairman of the Republican state central committee) written near the end of the famous Lincoln-Douglas senatorial campaign that included what Lincoln termed "a bare suggestion."[1] This brief note from 1858 offers a window into much of what we've learned over the years about Lincoln's talents as a party leader, while also raising a profound and provocative question about his political ethics.

On Wednesday, October 20, 1858, nearly a week after the final Lincoln-Douglas Debate at the river town of Alton and with less than two weeks to go before Illinois election day, Lincoln shared some surprising political intelligence with Judd. Writing from Rushville, the seat of Schuyler County, the habitually circumspect senate candidate began by reporting that for once he had "a high degree of confidence that we shall succeed," though Lincoln quickly tempered this bullish prediction with a dark warning, adding "if we are not over-run with fraudulent votes to a greater extent than usual." He noted that on passing through nearby Naples on Monday, he had seen "about fifteen Celtic gentlemen with black carpet-sacks in their hands," associated with the railroad and busying themselves by hanging about the "doggeries," or saloons, of that small town in Scott County.

This was ominous news. Irish-born railroad workers appeared to be flooding into critical swing counties, especially in this western part of the state, presumably to help steal close legislative contests for the Democrats. Republican newspapers and correspondents had been reporting on such movements in various districts for weeks. In this case, Lincoln claimed that he had heard "about four hundred of the same sort were to be brought into Schuyler, before the election, to work on some new Railroad," though he acknowledged that the Republican chieftain of Rushville and state committee treasurer, John C. Bagby, had dismissed that particular concern out of hand.

Nonetheless, Lincoln was worried. "What I most dread," he wrote, "is that they will introduce into the doubtful districts numbers of men who are legal voters in all respects except residence and who will swear to residence and thus put it beyond our power to exclude them," adding, "They can & I fear will swear falsely on that point, because they know it is next to impossible to convict them of Perjury upon it."

Lincoln claimed that "finding a way to head this thing off" was "the great remaining part of the campaign." He then offered what he termed "a bare suggestion." "When there is a known body of these voters," he wrote, "could not a true man, of the 'detective' class, be introduced among them in disguise, who could, at the nick of time, control their votes?" Without specifying exactly how those votes would be controlled or what he meant by "a true man, of the 'detective' class," Lincoln urged Judd to "think this over." He observed, "It would be a great thing, when this trick is attempted upon us, to have the saddle come up on the other horse."

Clearly the suggestion was sensitive and meant to be kept secret. Lincoln explained, "I have talked, more fully than I can write," to "Mr. Scripps," or John Locke Scripps, an editor of the *Chicago Press & Tribune* and a former resident of Rushville who had been present earlier in the day for Lincoln's speech in the town square. At some point, either before or after the lengthy parade (which preceded the great Rushville rally and reportedly stretched a mile and a half according to local newspaper accounts), Lincoln and other party leaders such as Bagby and Scripps had quietly debated the growing rumors of impending election fraud. Lincoln's position on this issue was firm. He wanted the state committee to take immediate action. "If we can head off the fraudulent votes," he concluded in his letter to Judd, "we shall carry the day."

Lincoln's startling note from October 20, 1858, contains fifteen sentences and nearly 320 words—just a little longer than the Gettysburg Address. Yet despite the utter absence of any prose poetry, profound insights from the American civic faith, or even a shred of ideological appeal, it still might be considered a significant document in the annals of American political history. Historian Mark E. Neely goes so far as to claim that no serious collection of Lincoln's political writings should exclude the "bare suggestion" letter.[2] But why is such a tactical document so important? First, the letter illustrates Lincoln's often-underrated managerial talents. Lincoln the party leader was an exceptional listener and a sometimes Machiavellian boss. These were qualities that he developed in various antebellum political campaigns and then employed with even greater impact as a surprisingly capable commander in chief during the military campaigns of the Civil War. Second, the letter reveals Lincoln's competitive fire at its most intense. On the verge of winning his most important contest yet, Lincoln was pushing as hard as he had ever pushed for anything. Whether or not Honest Abe was also pushing through the ethical boundaries that had always guided his behavior in the past remains a question that biographers and historians still need to interpret. Or, to put it more bluntly, we still do not know if Lincoln's "bare suggestion" was an illegal one.

Listening was a key element of Lincoln's success from his youthful time in New Salem to the wartime period at the White House. He always seemed to understand the value of information and worked hard to obtain it from as many informed perspectives as possible. Consider the extent of the one-man intelligence-gathering effort that he revealed in his comments to Judd in 1858. After encountering those "fifteen Celtic gentlemen" at Naples, Lincoln apparently wasted no time in asking around about them. He reported, "I learned that they had crossed over from the Rail-road in Brown county, but where they were going no one could tell." He then claimed he "was told" in Brown County on Tuesday during his trip up to Rushville that about four hundred more Irish immigrant voters were coming to Schuyler on the pretext of working on the railroad. Lincoln obviously shared this concern with John Bagby by Wednesday, because he also reported to Judd that Bagby "thinks that is not so." In other words, over the course of three days while traveling through western Illinois, senate candidate Abraham Lincoln spent a significant amount of his time chasing after information regarding some disturbing local political rumors. He weighed competing testimonies, made critical judgments, and served his party as a principal investigator and correspondent all while he was also quite busy traveling up from Alton, preparing speeches, and glad-handing farmers.

This had always been Lincoln's style. In the very first extant political letter from Lincoln's pen, a short note sent in 1837 to Rushville attorney and state legislator William A. Minshall, the future president wrote on behalf of John Todd Stuart, his senior law partner and then a candidate for Congress. "On receipt of this," the twenty-eight-year-old legislator wrote firmly, "write me all you *know* and all you *think,* in regard to our prospects for the race."[3] After he entered Congress himself in the late 1840s, Lincoln quickly cast his eyes beyond the doubtful districts of western Illinois. He took it upon himself, for example, to contact former Whig legislator Thaddeus Stevens during the 1848 presidential campaign in an effort to obtain soundings from the state of Pennsylvania. "You may possibly remember seeing me at the Philadelphia convention," Lincoln began, reminding him that he was "the lone whig star of Illinois." Reporting that he was about to leave the nation's capital, Lincoln stated that he desired "the undisguised opinion of some experienced and sagacious Pennsylvania politician, as to how the vote of that state, for governor, and president, is likely to go," asking that Stevens send such opinions by mail to him in Springfield.[4]

During the 1854 elections, Lincoln encountered a last-minute campaign crisis with echoes to the situation he would face in Schuyler County four years later, and he dealt with it in much the same way. This time the problem involved reports that a small community of British immigrants previously aligned with Richard Yates, the Whig / Anti-Nebraska Party candidate for Congress, had become alienated from him by rumors that Yates was a closet nativist. Lincoln was so disturbed by this news that he fired off at least two nearly identical letters to Yates while he was traveling through the busy railroad junction at Naples. The notes contained both critical information and stern advice for his candidate. "I learned that the English in Morgan county have become dissatisfied about No-Nothingism," Lincoln reported, though he also observed that local allies "think they have got the difficulty arrested." The second note was somewhat more explicit: "I heard at Jacksonville a story which may harm you if not averted—namely, that you have been a Know-Nothing." Ever vigilant, Lincoln urged upon Yates an aggressive response, in this case enclosing in both letters a draft statement that he had prepared (and copied) denying the charge and suggesting that it be distributed in targeted precincts the day before the election. At that time, Lincoln was merely a candidate for state legislature from Sangamon County, yet he was traveling in Morgan (which was actually Yates's home turf) and attempting to coordinate an ambitious response on behalf of his vulnerable (and soon to be defeated) congressional candidate.[5]

The partisan battle over immigrant voters and their nativist opponents was a recurring one throughout the 1850s, and Lincoln habitually paid close attention to this complicated dynamic. In September 1856, for example, while traveling through Bloomington in central Illinois, he wrote to Charles H. Ray, the editor of the *Chicago Tribune,* that he "was scared a little by being told that the enemy are getting the german's [*sic*] away from us at Chicago," asking nervously, "Is there any truth in that?"[6] By the 1860 presidential campaign, however, his fears had shifted more in the other direction. Concerned about reports that he had once visited a Know-Nothing lodge in Quincy, Illinois, Lincoln wrote a confidential letter to Abraham Jonas asking him to obtain affidavits from "respectable men" who could deny the accusation but warning him to keep his name out of it. "Our adversaries think they can gain a point, if they could force me to openly deny this charge," Lincoln wrote, "by which some degree of offence would be given to the Americans. For this reason, it must not publicly appear that I am paying any attention to the charge."[7]

Yet by 1860 it was clear that Lincoln had learned to pay attention to practically everything that appeared on his political radar. He even wrote a "Private & Confidential" note to Maj. David Hunter in late October that described some anxious warnings he had received in the mail about officers at Fort Kearney who had reportedly pledged to "take themselves, and the arms at that point, South" if the Republicans won the election. Though Lincoln confessed that "there are many chances to one that this is a humbug," he still asked Hunter, then stationed at Fort Leavenworth in Kansas, to "apprize me of it" if such a movement did seem afoot.[8] Near the end of the 1864 campaign, Lincoln offered a credo for this type of vigilance. "One can not always safely disregard a report, even which one may not believe," he wrote to Maj. Gen. William Rosecrans while ordering him to allow Missouri soldiers to participate in the upcoming election.[9]

In this fashion, Lincoln seems to have prepared himself quite well for the challenges of his presidency. His aggressive attitude about gathering political intelligence was the perfect posture for navigating the fog of war. Those "public opinion baths" that he claimed to have received from his open-door White House policy provided invaluable outside input. And whenever he felt limited in his access to good information, Lincoln simply left what he derided as the "iron cage" of the executive mansion. He frequently obtained useful insights about the condition of Northern morale during his travels around Washington, whether to the city's theaters or the Navy Yard or when heading out to his wartime retreat, his summer cottage at the Soldiers' Home. The *New York Herald* reported that on July 4, 1862, for instance, President Lincoln had encountered a wagon train of wounded soldiers while riding out past Boundary Street (now Florida Avenue) toward his cottage. Yet instead of evading a potentially unpleasant moment, he waded in among the men, "seeming anxious to secure all the information possible with regard to the real condition of affairs."[10] Even more important, Lincoln's habit of insisting upon occasional face-to-face meetings with military commanders such as with George McClellan at Harrison's Landing and Antietam in 1862 and with Ulysses Grant at City Point near the end of the war was at least partly a by-product of a partisan career that had taught him the value of active listening.

Lincoln also learned quite effectively during his many years as an antebellum party boss how to move from listening to commanding. He developed different strategies for dealing with different types of subordinates and rivals. At times, Lincoln could be direct; at other moments, subtle. Sometimes he cajoled and persuaded. Other challenges required more full-throttle confrontation—even, on occasion, a little bullying. He became skilled at reading people and learned how to respond in kind to their signals. The nuances of the "bare suggestion" letter illustrate just how far along Lincoln had come in his self-education as a personnel manager.

Dissecting Lincoln's relationship with his correspondent in this critical letter offers a fine starting point for analysis. Judd was the party chairman in 1858, a longtime state senator serving from Cook County and a prototypical nineteenth-century Chicago political boss who, in the words of John Hay, always seemed to have "that inevitable unlighted cigar between his lips."[11] Yet here was Lincoln prodding him to action on a matter of party management, what should have properly been Judd's sole domain. The word "bare" here, which Lincoln used occasionally in his correspondence, meant "mere," as in a mere suggestion, but the implication of the letter as a whole was much more forceful. The note pulsated with urgency. "If we can head off the fraudulent votes," Lincoln had concluded, "we shall carry the day." The prodding quality of Lincoln's suggestion becomes even more apparent when one considers that he had written Judd on this topic before but to no apparent effect. On September 23, reporting from Danville on the other side of the state in eastern Illinois, Lincoln had predicted success for the party "unless they overcome us by fraudulent voting." He had warned, "We must be especially prepared for this. It must be taken into anxious consideration at once. How can it be done?" Then, perhaps to goad Judd who despised his Chicago rival "Long" John Wentworth, Lincoln asked innocently: "Is 'Long John' at hand? His genius should be employed on this question."[12]

The full force of Lincoln's communications with Judd cannot be understood unless the intricate web of their personal, political, and even financial relationships are taken into consideration. Judd and Lincoln had known each other for years on friendly terms, even though they had also been political enemies. Judd was originally a Democrat who had helped kill Lincoln's best chance to become a US senator in 1855. Judd and a handful of other so-called anti-Nebraska Democrats in the legislature had refused to support Lincoln, the former Whig congressman, over the incumbent

Democrat senator James Shields, even though Shields had been a notable supporter of Stephen Douglas's controversial Kansas-Nebraska Act. Lincoln had ultimately negotiated a last-minute and dramatic deal with the anti-Nebraska Democrats that made one of their own, Lyman Trumbull, a US senator but that also solidified Lincoln's reputation as a forward-thinking partisan.[13] The next year, Judd became chairman of the state's new Republican organization (though still calling itself the Anti-Nebraska Party), and he and Lincoln continued to solidify their new alliance through the 1858 election cycle. One of the ways they did this was with money. Railroad attorney Judd had helped bring Lincoln on board the *Effie Alton* case (1857), which proved to be one of the more significant in Lincoln's legal career and involved a contest between steamboat and railroad interests along the Mississippi (with Lincoln joining Judd on the side of the railroads). While they argued the case together in September 1857, Judd convinced Lincoln to loan him $2,500 (at 10 percent annual interest) for the purpose of speculating in lands near Council Bluffs, Iowa, that fell within the right of way for what would eventually become (with President Lincoln's signature) the Union Pacific railroad line.[14]

After the 1858 contest, Lincoln and Judd continued their complicated personal and political dance. Judd needed money to help cover expenses from the election contest, which Lincoln provided, albeit somewhat grudgingly. "I am willing to pay according to my ability," Lincoln wrote in response to the chairman's request to help raise funds, but he pledged only $250 to the committee and with a catch. "I will allow it," he wrote, "when you and I settle the private matter between us," presumably referring to the large loan from the previous year (and which was not settled until after Lincoln's death).[15] Then Judd, who wanted desperately to become governor, sought during the following year to obtain Lincoln's endorsement in order to overcome sniping orchestrated by his rival John Wentworth that suggested he had not only botched the 1858 campaign, but also had been disloyal to Lincoln all along. In December 1859 Judd sent a sharp note to Lincoln asking him to respond to the smear campaign with more vigor. "Does not your position in the party require you to right these things?" he demanded. Lincoln responded cautiously and somehow managed to navigate the treacherous feud between Judd and Wentworth throughout the rest of the 1860 campaign.[16] But he finally ran into the brick wall of resentment when as president-elect he decided to pass over Judd as a cabinet appointee. "He never had a truer friend than myself," Judd complained bitterly to Lyman Trumbull in January 1861, "and there was no one in whom he placed greater confidence till circumstances embarrassed him about a Cabinet appointment. Or in my own language he is trimming and wants to get rid of me."[17] Judd eventually settled for the continued extension of the loan repayment and an appointment as minister to Prussia.

If Lincoln's relationship with Judd suggests a Machiavellian talent for deft manipulation, he was also quite capable of invoking the Florentine philosopher's famously stern admonition that it was better to be feared than loved. This element of Lincoln's leadership style often gets overlooked, but it was a central component of both his rise to power and his greatness as commander in chief. In January 1841, not so long after the "Fatal First of January" when Lincoln was reportedly suicidal following his broken engagement with Mary Todd, he proved to be nonetheless quite commanding in rebuking a fellow Whig legislator who was bucking the party line. "I have just learned with utter astonishment, that you have some notion of voting for Walters [the Democratic candidate for official printer]," he wrote. "What! Support that *pet* of all those who continually slander and abuse you, and labour, day and night, for your destruction. All our friends are ready to cut our throats about it." The young legislator then wheeled into boss mode. "Stand by us this time," he promised, "and nothing in our power to confer, shall ever be denied you."[18] A recently discovered Lincoln letter from early in the 1858 campaign shows his partisan teeth bared even more sharply. "How in God's name do you let such paragraphs into the Tribune," he wrote to Charles H. Ray, complaining about an article from the previous day's *Chicago Tribune.* "Does *Sheahan* write them?" he added, sarcastically referring to James Sheahan, the Democratic editor of the *Chicago Times.* Continuing the assault and the gratuitous insults, Lincoln then asked, "How can you have failed to perceive that in this short paragraph you have completely answered all your own well put complaints of [Horace] Greely [*sic*] and Sister Burlingame?"[19] The slur against Massachusetts congressman Anson Burlingame's manhood might actually qualify this particular letter as the fiercest in the Lincoln partisan canon.

Late in the war, an astute visitor from Wisconsin who spent an evening at the Soldiers' Home discussing momentous political concerns with the embattled president commented in his diary on what he called Lincoln's remarkable "elasticity of spirits." Judge Joseph T. Mills was impressed by the president's graceful ability to switch tone and topics in the course of a single conversation.[20] Any review of Lincoln's wartime correspondence and encounters with his various generals or his ever-evolving tactics in managing his contentious cabinet certainly reveals this "elasticity" in full force. Though not always successful in his attempts to control subordinates or rivals, Lincoln was persistent in his efforts to adapt and manage them according to their own peculiar needs and personalities. And there can be little doubt that he developed much of this acute sense of audience and tight self-control during his many years of partisan leadership.

In some ways, what makes the "bare suggestion" letter so compelling are the questions it raises about Lincoln's legendary self-control. The stakes had never been higher for the Springfield attorney. He had already acknowledged to Judd that he believed they were on the verge of defeating Douglas. He had seen enough of the coverage of his debates with the Little Giant to realize what this victory would mean for himself and the Republican Party. And yet here was this nagging concern about illegal Irish voters. In his seminal study of the 1858 debates, Allen Guelzo largely dismisses the Republican concerns over fraudulent voting as "another rancid expression of nineteenth-century nativism" and "pure calculation by the state committee."[21] Yet neither characterization seems to account for Lincoln's concern. Instead, Lincoln appeared to agree wholeheartedly with the *Chicago Tribune,* which commented sharply just several days after his note to Judd that the state's election laws were "very lame and defective" and almost appeared to "have been purposely framed for the encouragement of rascality."[22] The translation for political leaders such as Lincoln and Judd was that there was little hope that the legal system could protect Republicans; they had to protect themselves. Thus Lincoln appeared very much in earnest as he suggested to Judd that they take matters into their own hands.

However, what exactly Lincoln meant by his "bare suggestion" cannot be so easily determined. "When there is a known body of these voters," he wrote, "could not a true man, of the 'detective' class, be introduced among them in disguise, who could, at the nick of time, control their votes?" There are perhaps three plausible ways to interpret this proposal. First, Lincoln might have been suggesting that Republicans find so-called detectives who could follow Irish voters to the polls and challenge their credentials. This would have been legal at the time and completely aboveboard but utterly ineffective, as Lincoln himself had noted in his previous lines to Judd about how he worried over voters who "will swear falsely" as to their legal residence "because they know it is next to impossible to convict them of Perjury upon it." Clearly, Lincoln intended more than this action by his suggestion.

A more obvious and effective solution would have been to suggest detectives who might "control" Irish voters by bribing them to vote Republican or suborning them with some other illicit means into not voting at all. Lincoln's exceptional caginess in this letter ("I have talked, more fully than I can write, to Mr. Scripps") coupled with his playful comment about having "the saddle come up on the other horse" when "this trick is attempted upon us," indicates that this option must be seriously considered despite all of his legendary integrity. Although few scholars have actually raised this prospect in their works on Lincoln, Pulitzer Prize–winning historian Mark Neely appears to have few doubts about the plausibility of this level of corruption. "Abraham Lincoln," he writes, "was thus a product of this party system and a master practitioner of politics under it." While analyzing Lincoln's "bare suggestion" letter, Neely concludes that Lincoln "knew" the "abuses" of antebellum politics and "could be provoked to instigate some of them himself," adding parenthetically that "suborning votes with private detectives was election fraud by any standard."[23] In his recent and exhaustive two-volume study of Lincoln, Michael Burlingame proceeds more cautiously than Neely but still leans toward condemnation. "It is not entirely clear what Lincoln intended," Burlingame writes, even as he acknowledges that the "detective" "was perhaps a distributor of bribes."[24]

One additional possibility that nobody seems to have seriously considered involves the possibility that Lincoln was proposing not to bribe the "Celtic gentlemen" but rather to redirect them toward some less important district through undercover trickery. In this fashion, Lincoln's comments about finding a "true man, of the 'detective' class," who could "be introduced among them in disguise" and "at the nick of time" makes more particular sense. The US Senate contest was not conducted by popular votes but rather by legislative balloting. As Lincoln himself had pointed out, the danger to Republicans from colonized Irish voters came only in those "doubtful districts" where they might affect the outcome. If those fraudulent voters were somehow directed toward nearby safe districts (for either party) by an undercover agent, then their impact would have been quietly mitigated. Thus, with his "bare suggestion," Lincoln was perhaps outlining merely a high-stakes political trick—something sensitive but certainly not a felony.

The key to deciphering Lincoln's elusive intentions revolves around de-fining what he meant by the term "a true man, of the 'detective' class." Were these detectives potential distributors of bribes, as Burlingame suggests, or less nefarious figures, more akin to modern-day poll watchers? The term "detective" was a new usage in Lincoln's era, but its meaning had become rather precisely defined, in Illinois at least, by the great American pioneer of the private detective industry, Allan Pinkerton. By the 1858 campaign, the *Tribune* was already labeling the thirty-nine-year-old Scottish immigrant "the celebrated detective of this city."[25] Pinkerton had become famous during the previous couple of years for his work as an undercover agent fighting a crime wave in Chicago and for his agency's role in helping to ferret out fraud and theft on the Illinois railroads. Lincoln was almost surely referring directly to Pinkerton & Co. when he invoked the term "detective class" in his letter to Judd. In fact, Judd was one of Pinkerton's most enthusiastic advo-cates, a connection that Lincoln may or may not have known at the time. It was Judd, for example, who endorsed Pinkerton's famous offer to President Lincoln for his services in April 1861 as the Civil War erupted. "You know my confidence in Pinkerton and his men," Judd wrote.[26] Judd may have been simply referring perhaps to conversations the two had conducted regarding the alleged Baltimore plot to assassinate the president-elect, or he may have been referencing discussions that dated all the way back to 1858. Regardless, however, Pinkerton was the type of detective whom Lincoln had in mind in October 1858, and he embodied neither the shady distributor of bribes nor any de facto poll watcher. A Pinkerton detective was an undercover agent, especially associated with the railroads, who was employed to enforce the law (or the interests of management) when the regular police or state's pros-ecutorial officials were unable or unwilling to do so.[27] This suggests support for—but does not prove—the third scenario involving trickery, not illegality, in Lincoln's plans for the "Celtic gentlemen."

Ultimately, however, there is no single correct interpretation for the "bare suggestion" letter, just as there is no one way to read the Gettysburg Address or Second Inaugural. However, the nuances, richness, and strategic significance of the 1858 letter to Judd should appear beyond much debate. This letter deserves more attention and a secure place in any anthology of Lincoln's partisan writings. Yet it remains obscure. Prominent historians such as David Herbert Donald and Doris Kearns Goodwin do not include an analysis of the letter in their important biographies of Lincoln. And those scholars who have done so in other recent studies have been surprisingly reticent about its wider ethical implications. Ronald White, for example, quotes from Lincoln's anxieties about "Celtic gentlemen" but offers nothing at all about the "bare suggestion." In his well-regarded study of the debates, Allen Guelzo provides the fullest context for Republican fears of "colonized" Irish voters, but he also ducks the issue of Lincoln's peculiar suggestion to Judd.[28] During the last generation of Lincoln scholarship, there has been a veritable explosion of works concerning his words and ideas. Yet there has not been a comparable proliferation of studies about his competitive behavior within the political arena. They are needed, because it is impossible to put Lincoln's aggressive actions as commander in chief into their full context without studying how he learned to bend, and perhaps even break, the rules of partisan life during the 1840s and 1850s. In the middle of the Civil War, President Lincoln vowed that he would leave no "available card unplayed" in his determination to save the nation. "What I *cannot* do, of course, I *will* not do," Lincoln assured Reverdy Johnson in the summer of 1862, but as his earlier proposal to Judd had revealed, Lincoln had learned during critical junctures of his career how to allow himself wide berth on the question of what was actually forbidden.[29] It was an ethical framework that some will celebrate, others will condemn, but that all of us need to consider more carefully.

Notes

1. Abraham Lincoln, "To Norman B. Judd" (October 20, 1858), in *Collected Works of Abraham Lincoln,* ed. Roy P. Basler, 8 vols. plus index (New Brunswick, NJ: Rutgers University Press, 1953), 3:329–30. Hereinafter cited as *CW;* emphases in original unless otherwise noted.

2. Mark E. Neely Jr., "Lincoln and the Politics of 1858," Lincoln-Douglas Debates 150th Anniversary Teacher Workshop, June 13, 2008, Dickinson College, Carlisle, PA.

3. Abraham Lincoln, "To William A. Minshall" (December 7, 1837), in *CW,* 1:107.

4. Abraham Lincoln, "To Thaddeus Stevens" (September 3, 1848), in *CW,* 2:1.

5. Abraham Lincoln, "To Richard Yates" (October 30, 1854) and "To Richard Yates" (October 31, 1854), in *CW,* 2:284–85.

6. Abraham Lincoln, "To Charles H. Ray" (September 13, 1856), in *Col-*

lected Works of Abraham Lincoln: First Supplement, 1832–1865, ed. Roy P. Basler (New Brunswick, NJ: Rutgers University Press, 1990 [1974]), 27–28.

7. Abraham Lincoln, "To Abraham Jonas" (July 21, 1860), in *CW,* 4:85–86.

8. Abraham Lincoln, "To David Hunter" (October 26, 1860), in *CW,* 4:132.

9. Abraham Lincoln, "To William Rosecrans" (September 26, 1864), in *CW,* 8:24.

10. Quoted in Matthew Pinsker, *Lincoln's Sanctuary: Abraham Lincoln and the Soldiers' Home* (New York: Oxford University Press, 2003), 37.

11. January 9, 1861, in *Lincoln's Journalist: John Hay's Anonymous Writings for the Press, 1860–1864,* Michael Burlingame, ed., (Carbondale: Southern Illinois University Press, 1998), 18.

12. Abraham Lincoln, "To Norman B. Judd" (September 23, 1858), in *CW,* 3:202.

13. For more detailed discussion of the 1855 Senate contest and its impact on Lincoln's partisan career, see Matthew Pinsker, "Senator Abraham Lincoln," *Journal of the Abraham Lincoln Association* 14 (Summer 1993): 1–22.

14. See details on this loan in Harry E. Pratt, *The Personal Finances of Abraham Lincoln* (Springfield, IL: Abraham Lincoln Association, 1943), 77–79.

15. Norman B. Judd to Abraham Lincoln, November 15, 1858, Abraham Lincoln Papers, Library of Congress, and Abraham Lincoln, "To Norman B. Judd" (November 16, 1858), in *CW,* 3:337.

16. Norman B. Judd to Abraham Lincoln (December 1, 1859), Abraham Lincoln Papers, Library of Congress. For the best analysis of this feud and its impact on Lincoln, see Don E. Fehrenbacher, *Prelude to Greatness: Lincoln in the 1850's* (Stanford, CA: Stanford University Press, 1962), 143–61.

17. Norman B. Judd to Lyman Trumbull (January 3, 1861), Lyman Trumbull Papers, Library of Congress. There is also a good analysis of the Lincoln-Judd relationship online at "Mr. Lincoln & Friends," Lehrman Institute, http://www.mrlincolnandfriends.org/inside.asp?pageID=68&subjectID=5.

18. Abraham Lincoln, "To Andrew McCormick" [January 1841?], in Basler, *Collected Works of Abraham Lincoln: First Supplement,* 5.

19. Abraham Lincoln to Charles H. Ray (June 27, 1858), Papers of Abraham Lincoln, Illinois State Historic Preservation Agency, http://www.papersofabrahamlincoln.org/New_Documents.htm. This letter was first made public in 2005 and has not yet been published as part of the *Collected Works* series.

20. See Pinsker, *Lincoln's Sanctuary,* 161.

21. Allen C. Guelzo, *Lincoln and Douglas: The Debates That Defined America* (New York: Simon & Schuster, 2008), 209.

22. "Illegal Voting: An Explanation," *Chicago Tribune,* October 29, 1858.

23. Mark E. Neely Jr., *The Last Best Hope of Earth: Abraham Lincoln and the Promise of America* (Cambridge, MA: Harvard University Press, 1993), 53.

24. Michael Burlingame, *Abraham Lincoln: A Life,* 2 vols. (Baltimore: Johns Hopkins University Press, 2008), 1:545.

25. *Chicago Daily Tribune,* April 10, 1858, 1:2.

26. Norman Judd to Abraham Lincoln (April 21, 1861), Abraham Lincoln Papers Library of Congress. Enclosed with Allan Pinkerton's letter to Lincoln from the same date.

27. See Frank Morn, *"The Eye That Never Sleeps": A History of the Pinkerton National Detective Agency* (Bloomington: Indiana University Press, 1982).

28. David Herbert Donald, *Lincoln* (New York: Simon & Schuster, 1995); Doris Kearns Goodwin, *Team of Rivals: The Political Genius of Abraham Lincoln* (New York: Simon & Schuster, 2005); Ronald C. White Jr., *A. Lincoln: A Biography* (New York: Random House, 2009), 286; and Guelzo, *Lincoln and Douglas,* 207–12.

29. Abraham Lincoln, "To Reverdy Johnson" (July 26, 1862), in *CW,* 5:343.

10

Lincoln's Theology of Labor

Joseph R. Fornieri

Near the end of the Civil War, Abraham Lincoln was reunited with his best friend and Springfield roommate Joshua Speed. Upon observing the president reading the Bible, Speed asked whether or not he had abandoned his youthful skepticism. Lincoln's reply is noteworthy in testifying to his understanding of a potential harmony between faith and reason. He explained, "[T]ake all of this book upon reason that you can, and the balance on faith, and you will live and die a happier and better man."[1]

Speed's reminiscence is credible because it accounts for the well-documented facts of Lincoln's youthful skepticism along with his mature understanding of the relationship between faith and reason. The youthful Lincoln of New Salem read the works of Thomas Paine and the comte de Volney, mimicked the gestures of frontier preachers, composed "a little Book on Infidelity" in 1834, and seemed to have denied the virgin birth and other miracles.[2] Roughly a decade later, Lincoln's heterodox views would almost cost him a seat in the House of Representatives during the 1846 election when his opponent, the fiery Methodist preacher Peter Cartwright, accused him of "infidelity" or lack of faith. It is possible that Lincoln's views remained heterodox, in some respects, his entire life. As is well documented, he never joined a church.

However, it would be wrong to cast Lincoln as an atheist who was dogmatically closed to transcendence and the belief in a providential God who oversees human affairs. William Herndon, Lincoln's law partner, who was outraged by the hagiographic qualities of Josiah Gilbert Holland's biography of the sixteenth president, published a series of lectures to prove that Lincoln was an "infidel." Yet in the same sentence where Herndon refers to

Lincoln as an infidel or unbeliever, he also refers to him as "a Universalist," a "Unitarian," and a "Theist." As David Herbert Donald has noted, these are three distinct propositions affirming belief in God.[3] In sum, the holding of unorthodox views does not necessarily make one an unbeliever. Though the precise character of Lincoln's early religious views cannot be fully known, we are perhaps best justified in describing the youthful Lincoln as a seeker whose heterodoxy was rooted in a more profound devotion to truth and whose reservations about religion had more to do with the crude emotionalism, hypocrisy, ignorance, and corruption of the fire-and-brimstone preachers he encountered in the religious environment of the frontier. This, at least, is William Barton's assessment in his important work on Lincoln's religious views, *The Soul of Abraham Lincoln,* an assessment affirmed by two recent biographers, Michael Burlingame and Ronald C. White.[4]

While the Calvinist beliefs of his early religious environment seemed to remain with Lincoln his entire life, even alongside his youthful skepticism, his religious beliefs also seemed to deepen with maturity, as measured by speech and deed during the presidency. One would have a difficult time dismissing the sincerity of the faith revealed in his correspondence with the Quaker woman Mrs. Eliza P. Gurney, his relationship with Presbyterian ministers James Smith and Phineas Gurley, his private prayer sessions on Thursday evenings at Gurley's Church, and his invocation of a solemn vow to God during the momentous decision to emancipate the slaves. Indeed, scholars have noted the remarkable consistency between Lincoln's private religious faith in works such as "Meditation on the Divine Will" and his public articulation of this faith in his Second Inaugural Address.[5] Reinhold Niebuhr correctly, in my view, described the religious rhetoric of the Second Inaugural as an expression of Lincoln's living faith.[6]

The complementary view of faith and reason found in Speed's reminiscence likewise informed the president's broader vision of politics. Indeed, Lincoln's political genius consisted not only in his ability to manage his cabinet, as Doris Kearns Goodwin has suggested, but also in his theoretical vision of politics, man, and society.[7] Most notably it consisted in his ability to provide an ultimate moral justification of American public life based on the traditions of Enlightenment rationalism, revelation in the Bible, and republican teachings of the American founders on equality, consent, and ordered liberty.

In vindicating self-government and the Union, Lincoln articulated a political faith that provided a comprehensive vision of politics based upon the "laws of nature and nature's God" in the Declaration of Independence. The precepts of equality and consent in the Declaration were discovered by unassisted reason, confirmed by revelation, and constituted a moral standard or rule and measure for judging political life. Elsewhere I refer to these traditions of reason, revelation, and republicanism as the three Rs of Lincoln's political faith.[8] John Adams conveyed the potential harmony between the teachings of reason and revelation in American republicanism when he noted in 1807 that "[t]he Bible contains the most perfect philosophy, the most perfect morality, and the most refined policy, that ever was conceived upon earth. It is the most republican book in the world."[9] In a similar vein, founder and legal theorist James Wilson, whom Lincoln had read, likewise explained that "The law of nature and the law of revelation are both divine: they flow, though in different channels, from the same adorable source. It is, indeed, preposterous to separate them from each other. The object of both is—to discover the will of God—and both are necessary for the accomplishment of that end."[10]

To be sure, Lincoln's comprehensive vision of politics included an economic dimension that combined these same sources of reason, revelation, and republicanism to vindicate free labor against rival interpretations of the Bible and political economy that sought to sanction slave labor. Contrary to the mudsill theory (the belief that every society rested upon some bottom rung of permanently fixed labor to perform menial work), Lincoln argued that free society was dynamic and defined by an improvement of condition. As extended to economics, the principle of equality in the Declaration also guarantees each human being a "right to rise." In sum, this meant an equal right to compete in the race of life, to enjoy the fruits of one's own labor, and to advance on the basis of merit. Lincoln's vindication of free labor provides one of the most enduring and cogent visions of the American Dream of equal opportunity.

In what follows, I will explore Lincoln's theology of labor as constituted by the mutual influence of American religious and democratic traditions. More specifically, I will consider the influence of William Paley's *Natural Theology* (1802). Natural theology may be defined as "the practice of inferring the existence and wisdom of God from the order and beauty of the world."[11] Despite many fine studies of Lincoln's political thought, the influence of Paley's work has not received the attention it deserves.[12] This essay seeks to remedy that gap.

Paley was an Anglican churchman who taught at Cambridge around the time of the American Revolution. His teachings reveal the extent to which Enlightenment rationalism was seen as compatible with the teachings of revealed religion. Lincoln had studied Paley's work, and his *Natural Theology* was the most relevant to Lincoln's theology of labor. This work sought to infer the existence and wisdom of God without recourse to the authority of revelation and through unaided reason based on the manifest contrivance, intelligence, design, and purpose in nature. It provides an Enlightenment version of Aquinas's cosmological and teleological ways to consider the existence of God. Paley states the core of his argument in these terms: "There cannot be design without a designer; contrivance without a contriver; order without choice; arrangement, without any thing capable of arranging. . . . Arrangement, disposition of parts, subserviency of means to an end, relation of instruments to an use, imply the presence of intelligence and mind."[13]

Lincoln was intellectually inclined toward rational defenses of revealed religion, which contrasted so starkly with the emotionalism of his early religious environment. Certainly this explains his similar interest in Rev. James Smith's work on the compatibility between faith and reason, *The Christian's Defense, Containing a Fair Statement and Impartial Examination of the Leading Objections Urged by Infidels, Against the Antiquity, Genuineness, Credibility and Inspiration of Holy Scripture*. Smith was a former skeptic who became a Presbyterian minister. He provided spiritual consolation to the Lincoln family after the death of their son Eddie in 1850. Smith's own skepticism as well as his lawyerly method in stating and replying to objections of skeptics seemed to have resonated with Lincoln's own intellectual character and spiritual journey. And as historian Ron White has emphasized, Lincoln's understanding of the compatibility between faith and reason was also influenced by the theology of Rev. Phineas Gurley, whose New York Avenue Presbyterian Church Lincoln attended when president. Indeed, Gurley "would become a regular visitor in the White House."[14] White explains that Gurley preached the Old School Presbyterian theology, which was "rooted itself in a rational doctrinal tradition."[15] Paley similarly provided a rational defense of revelation titled *Evidences of Christianity*, which was a best seller in England.

Paley's *The Principles of Moral and Political Philosophy*, which Lincoln had also read, articulated a view of the compatibility between faith and reason that is highly consistent with Speed's reminiscence above. In the preface of this book, Paley criticizes secular rationalist thinkers of his time who "divide too much the law of Nature from the precepts of Revelation; some authors industriously declining the mention of Scripture authorities, as belonging to a different province; and others reserving them for a separate volume: which appears much to me the same defect."[16] One suspects that Paley is referring to Voltaire and the other Enlightenment philosophes.

Paley attempted to synthesize the utilitarianism of his era with Christian theology *and ethics*, as when he explained "that what promotes the general happiness, is required by the will of God."[17] Moreover, his understanding of the "moral sense," which combined traditional Christian views of conscience with a utilitarian understanding of human inclination, would likewise influence Lincoln, who explained at Springfield on June 26, 1857, that "[w]ill springs from the two elements of moral sense and self-interest."[18] Whether Paley ultimately succeeded in reconciling his utilitarianism with Christianity is less relevant for our purposes here than his more general view of the harmony between the law of nature and the precepts of revelation, and its influence upon Lincoln's theology of labor.

As mentioned above, sources corroborate that Lincoln read Paley's *Natural Theology* "in the years preceding his election to the Presidency."[19] Indeed, Lincoln's allusions to natural theology coincide within this time frame. At Hartford, Connecticut, on March 5, 1860, after Lincoln's stunning debut at Cooper Union where he established himself as a viable Republican Party candidate, he explained: "I think that if anything can be proved by *natural theology* it is that slavery is morally wrong. God gave man a mouth to receive bread, hands to feed it, and his hand has a right to carry bread to his mouth without controversy."[20] In the same speech, Lincoln again appealed to natural theology in validating the principle of equality and the right to enjoy the fruits of one's own labor against slavery: "We think slavery is morally wrong, and a direct violation of that principle [of equality]. We *all* think it wrong. It is clearly proved, I think, by natural theology, apart from revelation. Every man, black, white or yellow, has a mouth to be fed and two hands with which to feed it—and that bread should be allowed to go to that mouth without controversy."[21]

In historical context, Lincoln's theology of labor was articulated as a response to Southern theological, scientific, and philosophical justifications of slavery and their corresponding critique of free society. Most notably, it can be seen as a reply to the mudsill theory of James H. Hammond, the proslavery theology of Presbyterian divines such as Frederick Ross, and the proslavery philosophy of George Fitzhugh. Each of these thinkers provided a comprehensive moral, political, and economic vision to defend slavery. The mudsill theory maintained that every society inevitably rested upon some bottom rung to do manual labor. South Carolina senator Hammond famously articulated this view when he said, "In all social systems there must be a class to do the mean duties, to perform the drudgery of life. . . . It constitutes the very mud-sills of society."[22] Fitzhugh from Virginia, whose work Lincoln had read in the *Richmond Enquirer,* provided a critique of free society by claiming that slavery was part of the natural order of things and that Southern slaves actually fared better than their Northern wage slave counterparts.[23] Ross was a Presbyterian minister from Huntsville, Alabama, and the author of a work titled *Slavery Ordained of God*—an allusion to Romans 13:1. Ross was indicative of a new generation of Southern clergymen who no longer apologized for slavery as a necessary evil but affirmed it as a positive good—a divine blessing to both master and slave. According to Ross, "slavery was found to be in absolute harmony with the word of God."

In a fragment that has come down to us titled "On Pro-Slavery Theology," Lincoln explicitly mentioned Ross by name and scornfully replied to his argument that slave labor was willed by God:

> The sum of pro-slavery theology seems to be this: "Slavery is not universally *right,* nor yet universally *wrong;* it is better for *some* people to be slaves; and, in such cases, it is the Will of God that they be such."
>
> Certainly there is no contending against the Will of God; but still there is some difficulty in ascertaining, and applying it, to particular cases. For instance we will suppose the Rev. Dr. Ross has a slave named Sambo, and the question is "Is the Will of God that Sambo shall remain a slave, or be set free"? The Almighty gives no audable [*sic*] answer to the question, and his revelation—the Bible—gives none—or, at most, *none* but such admits of squabble, as to it's [*sic*] meaning. No one thinks of asking Sambo's opinion on it. So, at last, it comes this, that *Dr. Ross* is to decide the question. And while he consider [*sic*] it, he sits in the shade, with gloves on his hands, and subsists on the bread that Sambo is earning in the burning sun. If he decides that God wills Sambo to continue a slave, he thereby re-

tains his own comfortable position; but if he decides that God wills Sambo to be free, he thereby has to walk out of the shade, throw off his gloves, and delve for his own bread. Will Dr. Ross be actuated by that perfect impartiality, which has ever been considered most favorable to correct decisions?

But, slavery is good for some people!!! As a *good* thing, slavery is striking perculiar [*sic*], in this, that it is the only good thing which no man ever seeks the good of, *for himself.*

Nonsense! Wolves devouring lambs, not because it is good for their own greedy maws, but because it is good for the lambs!!![24]

The fragment is quintessentially Lincoln in combining humor, storytelling, and ironclad logic in its assessment and critique of proslavery theology. Lincoln begins by summarizing the core of the proslavery argument. He then presumes the will of God as a common starting point. The difficulty, however, is in ascertaining the will of God in particular cases—for, as he would ironically note years later in his Second Inaugural Address, "both read the same Bible, and pray to the same God; and each invokes His aid against the other."[25]

After alluding to "the squabble" over interpreting the Bible, Lincoln alludes to the fundamental justice of the republican principle of consent in relation to both self-government and free labor when he humorously and effectively notes, "No one thinks of asking Sambo's opinion on it. So, at last, it comes to this, that *Dr. Ross* is to decide the question." While raising questions about the Bible as providing a definitive resolution to the slavery question, he nonetheless alludes to Genesis 3:19—"In the sweat of thy face shalt thou eat bread"— as a theological defense of free labor. Lincoln relates that Reverend Ross "sits in the shade, with gloves on his hands, and subsists on the bread that Sambo is earning in the burning sun." In addition to appealing to the republican principle of consent and God's revelation in Genesis 3:19, Lincoln likewise appeals to unaided reason and common sense. Slavery goes against natural human inclination to seek the good: "As a good thing, slavery is striking perculiar [*sic*], in this, that it is the only good thing which no man ever seeks the good of, *for himself.*" This truth is readily confirmed by universal human experience.

Finally, Lincoln concludes his satirical story with the ancient wisdom of Aesop's parable "The Wolf and the Lamb," which exposes how greedy and selfish interests attempt to justify wickedness as good: "Wolves devouring lambs, not because it is good for their own greedy maws, but because it is good for the lambs!!!" Thus this fragment characteristically combines reason, revelation, and republicanism in its critique of slave labor and vindication of free labor.

Perhaps the most common widely accepted biblical defense of slavery throughout the South was the "Curse of Ham" based upon an interpretation of Genesis 9:18–27. This section of Genesis narrates the plight of Noah's three sons—Shem, Ham, and Japheth—who were interpreted allegorically as representatives of the three races of humanity. The Bible tells us that God punished Noah's son Ham for his impudence and that the curse for this transgression was visited and concentrated upon his descendants who were interpreted allegorically as the entire black race! Indeed, at the Democratic State Convention in Jackson, Mississippi, on July 6, 1850, Jefferson Davis, future president of the Confederacy, invoked the Curse of Ham as a theological defense of slave labor. Forthrightly repudiating Lincoln's political theology of equality in the Declaration, Davis proclaimed:

> A declaration of rights made by bodies politic is construed as an essay upon the individual relations of man to man. Arguing to their own satisfaction for the unity in origin of the races of man, they draw thence the conclusion of his present equality. . . . As to him, it matters not whether Almighty power and wisdom stamped diversity on the races of men at the period of creation, or decreed it after the subsidence of the flood. It is enough for us that the Creator, speaking through the inspired lips of Noah, declared the destiny of three races of men. Around and about us is the remarkable fulfillment of the prophecy, the execution of the decree, and the justification of the literal construction of the text.[26]

In response to these proslavery justifications, Lincoln, a man of ideas, developed a theology of labor to vindicate free labor and the right to rise. His method similarly resembles John Locke's approach in the *First Treatise of Government,* which invoked the Bible and natural reason to provide a critique of Robert Filmer's defense of divine right monarchy in *Patriarcha, or the Natural Power of Kings.* Lincoln thus provides an American version of Locke's teaching in this regard.

In sum, Lincoln's theology of labor included the following elements: (1) an appeal to Genesis 3:19: "In the sweat of thy face shalt thou eat bread," (2) Paley's natural theology, and (3) the republicanism of the founders, based on the related principles of liberty, equality, and consent.

Lincoln cited Genesis 3:19 (perhaps his favorite biblical allusion against slavery) in defense of free labor as early as 1847 in the context of a tariff discussion:

> In the early days of the world, the Almighty said to the first of our race "In the sweat of thy face shalt thou eat bread"; and since then, if we except the *light* and the *air* of heaven, no good thing has been, or can be enjoyed by us, without having first cost labour. And, inasmuch [as] most good things are produced by labour, it follows that [all] such things of right belong to those whose labour has produced them. But it has so happened in all ages of the world, that *some* have laboured, and *others* have, without labour, enjoyed a large proportion of the fruits. This is wrong, and should not continue. To [secure] to each labourer the whole product of his labour, or as nearly as possible, is a most worthy object of any good government.[27]

Twelve years later, in a fragment on free labor possibly from September 17, 1859, Lincoln repeated this train of thought, invoking Genesis 3:19 against the mudsill theory:

> We know, Southern men declare that their slaves are better off than hired laborers amongst us. How little they *know*, whereof they *speak!* There is no permanent class of hired laborers amongst us. Twentyfive [sic] years ago, I was a hired laborer. The hired laborer of yesterday, labors on his own account to-day; and will hire others to labor for him to-morrow. Advancement—improvement in condition—is the order of things in a society of equals. As Labor is the common *burthen* of our race, so the effort of *some* to shift their share of the burthen on to the shoulders of *others*, is the great, durable, curse of the race. Originally a curse for transgression upon the whole race, when, as by slavery, it is concentrated on a part only, it becomes the double-refined curse of God upon his creatures.[28]

Here as elsewhere, Lincoln often included his own experience as a self-made man to validate the possibility of improvement and advancement in the race of life. He embodied the right to rise and the American Dream. In a speech in New Haven, Connecticut, he confessed: "I am not ashamed to confess that twenty five years ago I was a hired laborer, mauling rails, at work on a flat-boat—just what might happen to any poor man's son! I want every man to have the chance—and I believe a black man is entitled to it—in which he *can* better his condition—when he may look forward and hope to be a hired laborer this year and the next, work for himself afterward, and finally to hire men to work for him! That is the true system."[29]

Following Paley, Lincoln then appealed to unaided reason to infer divine purpose, contrivance, and design in adducing a natural right to free labor and to enjoy the fruits thereof. Lincoln's sense of humor comes through when he talks about the design of the hands and mouth as manifesting divine contrivance to labor:

> I hold that if there is any one thing that can be proved to be the will of God by external nature around us, without reference to revelation, it is the proposition that whatever any one man earns with his hands by the sweat of his brow [Genesis 3:19], he shall enjoy in peace. I say that whereas God Almighty has given every man one mouth to be fed, and one pair of hands adapted to furnish food for that mouth, if anything can be proved to be the will of Heaven, it is proved by this fact, that that mouth is to be fed by those hands, without being interfered with by any other man who has also his mouth to feed and his hands to labor with. I hold that if the Almighty had ever made a set of men that should do all the eating and none of the work, he would have made them with mouths only and no hands, and if he had ever made another class that he had intended should do all the work and none of the eating, he would have made them without mouths and with all hands. But inasmuch as he has not chosen to make man in that way, if anything is proved, it is that those hands and mouth are to be co-operative through life and not to be interfered with. That they are to go forth and improve their condition as I have been trying to illustrate, is the inherent right given to mankind directly by the Maker.[30]

Lincoln's humorous appeal to the natural design of the insect world as proof of a divine right to labor was likely inspired by Paley who devoted an entire chapter to insects in *Natural Theology*. Similarly Lincoln explained that the self-evident truth of equality was "[m]ade so plain by our good Father in Heaven, that all *feel* and *understand* it, even down to brutes and creeping insects. The ant, who has toiled and dragged a crumb to his nest, will furiously defend the fruit of his labor, against whatever robber assails him. So plain, that the most dumb and stupid slave that ever toiled for a master, does constantly *know* that he is wronged."[31]

The republican principles of liberty, equality, and consent constituted another element of Lincoln's theology of labor. Today we take for granted that slavery and free society are incompatible, but this was not always the case. The South cited the ancient republics of Athens, Sparta, and Rome as proof that slavery and popular government could coexist harmoniously. It was part of Lincoln's philosophical genius and political greatness to emphasize the utter incompatibility between the principle of slavery and popular government based on liberty, equality, and consent. Lincoln understood that freedom also had an economic dimension: it means free markets; the consent of the laborer; the right to enjoy the fruits of his labor; the right to rise and improve; a dynamic society that rewards people on the basis of merit rather than class, hereditary, or racial privilege; and even the right to strike. Popular government is incompatible with feudal hierarchies and fixed conditions of labor. Labor, as Lincoln would often emphasize, is prior to capital. In his Annual Message to Congress on December 3, 1861, he profoundly delved into the relationship between labor and popular government. Lincoln denounced the "effort to place *capital* on an equal footing with, if not above *labor*, in the structure of government." "It is assumed," he explained,

> that labor is available only in connexion with capital; that nobody labors unless somebody else, owning capital, somehow by the use of it, induces him to labor. This assumed, it is next considered whether it is best that capital shall *hire* laborers, and thus induce them to work by their own consent, or *buy* them, and drive them to it without their consent. Having proceeded so far, it is naturally concluded that all laborers are either *hired* laborers, or what we call slaves. And further it is assumed that whoever is once a hired laborer,

is fixed in that condition for life. Now, there is no such relation between capital and labor as assumed; nor is there any such thing as a free man being fixed for life in the condition of a hired laborer. Both these assumptions are false, and all inferences from them are groundless. Labor is prior to, and independent of, capital. Capital is only the fruit of labor, and could never have existed if labor had not first existed. Labor is the superior of capital, and deserves much the higher consideration.[32]

In this passage, Lincoln affirms the priority of labor over capital. He then emphasizes the centrality of the republican principle of consent to both free labor and self-government. Despotism in whatever form is defined by depriving others of their consent. In the case of labor, this means stealing the fruit of another person's hard-earned labor without his or her consent. Lincoln articulated what has become known as the "labor theory of value," the view that labor is prior to capital in human activity and that capital is the fruit of labor and not its permanent master. He thus eschewed the Marxist view of the inherent conflict between labor and capital as well as the Southern view of the complete and permanent submission of labor to capital. Free society was dynamic.

In conclusion, though Lincoln was not a philosopher per se, he thought quite deeply about ideas. In response to the proslavery theology and mudsill theories of the time, he developed a theology of labor to vindicate free labor and free society. This theology of labor was based on Lincoln's synthesis of biblical revelation, the republican principles of liberty, equality and consent, and unaided reason in the form of Paley's natural theology—the three Rs. Lincoln, perhaps more than anyone, has provided us with enduring expressions of the American Dream and of the right to rise. As we confront new challenges to free markets today, it would be wise to ponder Lincoln's enduring wisdom: "The prudent, penniless beginner in the world, labors for wages awhile, saves a surplus with which to buy tools or land, for himself; then labors on his own account another while, and at length hires another new beginner to help him. This, say its advocates, is *free* labor—the just and generous, and prosperous system, which opens the way for all—gives hope to all, and energy, and progress, and improvement of condition to all."[33]

Notes

1. Joshua Speed quoted in Michael Burlingame, *Abraham Lincoln: A Life*, 2 vols. (Baltimore: Johns Hopkins University Press, 2008), 2:38.

2. Allen C. Guelzo, *Abraham Lincoln: Redeemer President* (Grand Rapids, MI: William B. Eerdmans, 1999), 50–51, and Burlingame, *Abraham Lincoln*, 1:38–41, 238–40.

3. David Herbert Donald, *Lincoln's Herndon* (New York: Da Capo, 1989 [1948]), 359.

4. William E. Barton, *The Soul of Abraham Lincoln* (New York: George A. Doran, 1920), 271–72; Burlingame, *Abraham Lincoln*, 1:83–85; and Ronald C. White Jr., *A. Lincoln: A Biography* (New York: Random House, 2009), 45, 54–55, 135, 180–82.

5. See, for example, Samuel W. Calhoun and Lucas E. Morel, "Abraham Lincoln's Religion: The Case for His Ultimate Belief in a Personal, Sovereign God," *Journal of the Abraham Lincoln Association* 33, no. 1 (Winter 2012): 38–74; William Lee Miller, *President Lincoln: The Duty of a Statesman* (New York: Knopf, 2008); Douglas L. Wilson, *Lincoln's Sword: The Presidency and the Power of Words* (New York: Knopf, 2006); Joseph R. Fornieri, *Abraham Lincoln's Political Faith* (DeKalb: Northern Illinois University Press, 2003); James Tackach, *Lincoln's Moral Vision: The Second Inaugural Address* (Jackson: University Press of Mississippi, 2002); and Lucas E. Morel, *Lincoln's Sacred Effort: Defining Religion's Role in American Self-Government* (Lanham, MD: Lexington Books, 2000).

6. Reinhold Niebuhr, "The Religion of Abraham Lincoln," *The Christian Century* (February 10, 1965), 172–75.

7. Doris Kearns Goodwin, *Team of Rivals: The Political Genius of Abraham Lincoln* (New York: Simon & Schuster, 2005).

8. Fornieri, *Abraham Lincoln's Political Faith*.

9. Quoted in Michael Novak, *On Two Wings: Humble Faith and Common Sense at the American Founding* (San Francisco: Encounter Books, 2002), 37.

10. James Wilson, *Collected Works of James Wilson*, ed. Kermit L. Hall and Mark David Hall, 2 vols. (Indianapolis, IN: Liberty Fund, 2007), vol. 1, part 2, "Lectures on Law," 509.

11. William Paley, *Natural Theology* (Oxford: Oxford University Press, 1999 [1802]), ix.

12. Allen C. Guelzo notes the influence upon Lincoln of another work of Paley's, *Principles of Moral and Political Philosophy* (1785); see Guelzo, *Abraham Lincoln*, 49. Also see Gabor S. Boritt, *Lincoln and the Economics of the American Dream* (Urbana: University of Illinois Press, 1994); Harry V. Jaffa, *A New Birth*

of Freedom: Abraham Lincoln and the Coming of the Civil War (Lanham: Rowman & Littlefield, 2000); and Morel, *Lincoln's Sacred Effort.*

13. Paley, *Natural Theology*, 12.

14. White, *A. Lincoln*, 404.

15. Ibid., 403.

16. William Paley, *The Principles of Moral and Political Philosophy* (Indianapolis, IN: Liberty Fund, 2002 [1785]), xxvi.

17. Ibid., 33.

18. Abraham Lincoln, "Speech at Springfield, Illinois" (June 26, 1857), in *Collected Works of Abraham Lincoln*, ed. Roy P. Basler, 8 vols. plus index (New Brunswick, NJ: Rutgers University Press, 1953), 2:409. Hereinafter cited as *CW*; emphases in original unless otherwise noted.

19. Rufus Rockwell Wilson, *What Lincoln Read* (Washington, DC: Pioneer Publishing, 1932). Wilson states: "[W]hen asked to follow his wife's example and join the author's church [that of James Smith, who wrote *The Christian's Defense*], [Lincoln] declared that he 'could not quite see it.' Perhaps he found a stronger appeal to reason in Hitchcock's *Religious Truth*, Bailey's *Theology* and Paley's *Natural Theology*, which he procured and read in the years preceding his election to the Presidency." In a letter of December 6, 1866, Joshua Speed notes Lincoln's reading habits. Speed mentions that Lincoln read Paley, one of the few philosophers he mentions by name in the letter. See Douglas L. Wilson and Rodney O. Davis, eds., *Herndon's Informants: Letters, Interviews, and Statements about Abraham Lincoln* (Urbana: University of Illinois Press, 1998), 498–99. See also Robert Bray, *Reading with Lincoln* (Carbondale: Southern Illinois University Press, 2010).

20. Abraham Lincoln, "Speech at Hartford, Connecticut" (March 5, 1860), in *CW*, 4:3.

21. Ibid., 4:9–10.

22. Quoted in Burlingame, *Abraham Lincoln*, 1:530.

23. Burlingame, *Abraham Lincoln*, 1:461–62, and Fornieri, *Abraham Lincoln's Political Faith*, 71–91.

24. Abraham Lincoln, "Fragment on Pro-Slavery Theology" [October 1, 1858?], in *CW*, 3:204–5.

25. Abraham Lincoln, "Second Inaugural Address" (March 4, 1865), in *CW*, 8:333.

26. Quoted in Jaffa, *New Birth of Freedom*, 155–56.

27. Abraham Lincoln, "Fragments of a Tariff Discussion" [December 1, 1847?], in *CW*, 1:411–12.

28. Abraham Lincoln, "Fragment on Free Labor" [September 17, 1859?], in *CW*, 3:462–63.

29. Abraham Lincoln, "Speech at New Haven, Connecticut" (March 6, 1860), in *CW*, 4:24–25.

30. Abraham Lincoln, "Speech at Cincinnati, Ohio: Omitted Portion" (September 17, 1859), in *Collected Works of Abraham Lincoln: First Supplement, 1832–1865*, ed. Roy P. Basler (New Brunswick, NJ: Rutgers University Press, 1974), 44.

31. Abraham Lincoln, "Fragment on Slavery" [April 1, 1854?], in *CW*, 2:222.

32. Abraham Lincoln, "Annual Message to Congress" (December 3, 1861), in *CW*, 5:52–53.

33. Abraham Lincoln, "Address before the Wisconsin State Agricultural Society, Milwaukee, Wisconsin" (September 30, 1859), in *CW*, 3:478–79. He repeated this sentiment almost verbatim in Lincoln, "Annual Message to Congress," 5:52.

Part III

Lincoln at War

11

Abraham Lincoln as War President

Practical Wisdom at War

Mackubin Thomas Owens

No president in American history, before or since, has faced a greater crisis than the one Abraham Lincoln confronted in the spring of 1861. Although sections of the country had threatened disunion many times in the past, the emergency had always passed as some compromise was found. But in 1861, Lincoln, who had won the election of 1860 because of a split in the Democratic Party, faced a rebellion "too powerful to be suppressed by the ordinary course of judicial proceedings."[1] By the time of his inauguration on March 4, 1861, seven states had declared their separation from the Union and had set up a separate provisional government called the Confederate States of America.

A little over five weeks later, at 4:30 a.m. on April 12, 1861, rebel gunners opened fire on Fort Sumter in Charleston harbor. In response, Lincoln issued a call for 75,000 volunteers to serve ninety days. Denouncing the president's policy of "coercion," four more states left the Union. The ensuing war, the most costly in American history, would last for four agonizing years. When it was over, between 600,000 and 750,000 Americans had died, and the states of the South had suffered economic losses in the billions of dollars when measured in terms of today's currency.

Lincoln was entering uncharted waters as he confronted the rebellion. There were few precedents to which he could turn in response to the emergency facing the government.[2] Claiming broad emergency powers that he argued the Constitution had vested in the executive branch, he called out the militias of the loyal states, authorized increases in the size of the regular army and navy, expended funds for military purchases, deployed military forces, blockaded Southern ports, suspended the writ of habeas corpus in certain areas, authorized arbitrary arrests, and impaneled military tribunals to try civilians in occupied or contested areas. He took these steps without congressional authorization, although he subsequently explained his actions to Congress.

As he wrote to the Senate and House on May 26, 1862, "it became necessary for me to choose whether, using only the existing means, agencies, and processes which Congress had provided, I should let the government fall at once into ruin, or whether, availing myself of the broader powers conferred by the Constitution in cases of insurrection, I would make an effort to save it with all its blessings for the present age and for posterity."[3] Later he authorized conscription and issued the Emancipation Proclamation.

Lincoln justified these steps as necessary to save the Union and preserve the Constitution. As he wrote to Horace Greeley:

> I would save the Union. I would save it the shortest way under the Constitution. The sooner the national authority can be restored, the nearer the Union will be to "the Union as it was." . . . My paramount object in this struggle is to save the Union, and it is not either to save or destroy slavery. If I could save the Union without freeing any slave, I would do it, and if I could save it by freeing all the slaves, I would do it; and if I could save it by freeing some and leaving others alone I would also do that.[4]

But this often misunderstood passage conceals an important point: for Lincoln, the Union and the Constitution that he sought to save were not ends in themselves but the means to something else.[5]

Lincoln saw the Constitution principally as a framework for sharing power within a *republican government*. *This* was the real thing he aimed to preserve, because only republican government was capable of protecting the liberty of the people. Lincoln saw the Declaration of Independence as the *foundation* of such a government and the Constitution as the *means* of implementing it.

Lincoln articulated the relationship between liberty and republican government on the one hand and the Constitution on the other in a fragment that he probably composed in 1860, perhaps as the basis for some speeches he gave in New England. Here Lincoln observes that as important as the Constitution and Union may be, there is "something back of these, entwining itself more closely about the human heart. That something, is the principle of 'Liberty to all'" as expressed in the Declaration. With or without the Declaration, Lincoln continues, the United States could have declared independence, but "*without* it, we could not, I think, have secured our free government, and consequent prosperity.[6]

Lincoln refers to the Declaration's principle of liberty for all as a "word 'fitly spoken,' which has proved an 'apple of gold' to us. The *Union*, and the *Constitution*, are the *picture* of *silver*, subsequently framed around it," not to conceal or destroy the apple "but to *adorn*, and *preserve* it. The *picture* was made *for* the apple—*not* the apple for the picture. So let us act, that neither *picture*, or *apple* shall ever be blurred, or bruised or broken."[7] In other words, republican liberty was the real thing to be preserved by saving the Union and the Constitution.[8]

The *means* to preserve the *end* of republican government were dictated by *prudence*. According to Aristotle, prudence is concerned with deliberating well about those things that can be other than they are (means). In political affairs, prudence requires the statesman to be able to adapt universal principles to particular circumstances in order to arrive at the means that are best given existing circumstances.[9] For Lincoln to achieve the end of preserving the Union and thereby republican liberty, he had to choose the means necessary and proper under the circumstances. Aristotle calls prudence the virtue most characteristic of the statesman. It is through the prism of prudence that we must judge Lincoln's claim of a war power, the balance between liberty and security, his response to secession, emancipation, and the strategy employed to fight the war.[10]

Lincoln and the War Power

Don Fehrenbacher once observed that Lincoln has been described by historians as a dictator far more than any other president.[11] This is true not only of those who criticize him, but also of those who praise him. But if Lincoln was a dictator, he was one unlike any other in history. Dictatorship is characterized by unlimited, absolute power exercised in an arbitrary and unpredictable manner, with no regard for political legitimacy. A dictator doesn't go out of his way to respect legal limits as Lincoln did, despite his belief that the emergency required special measures. In addition, a dictator is not subject to the pressures of public opinion, congressional constraint, and party competition that Lincoln faced during his war presidency. Finally, a dictator doesn't risk an election in the midst of an emergency, especially one that he thinks he might lose.

As Geoffrey Perret has observed, Lincoln "create[d] the role of commander in chief," but he did not create his war power out of whole cloth.[12] Lincoln believed that the power he needed to deal with the rebellion was a part of the executive power found in the Constitution. As he wrote to James Conkling in August 1863, "I think the Constitution invests its commander-in-chief, with the law of war, in time of war."[13] In addition to the commander-in-chief clause, he found his war power in the clause of Article II requiring him to "take care that the laws be faithfully executed" and his presidential oath "to preserve, protect, and defend the Constitution of the United States."

Some constitutional scholars, such as Edward Corwin and Raoul Berger, have rejected Lincoln's claim that the commander-in-chief clause and the "faithfully execute" clause provide an inherent presidential war power.[14] But these scholars seem to take their constitutional bearings from normal times, during which the rights of the people are secure and the main instrument of majoritarian representative government is the legislature, which expresses the will of the people. During normal times, the president, although he possesses his own constitutional source of power, primarily executes the laws passed by Congress.

But in times of extraordinary emergency, the principle that *salus populi est suprema lex* (the safety of the people is the highest law) trumps all other considerations and justifies extraordinary executive powers. As Thomas Jefferson observed in a letter to Caesar A. Rodney, "in times of peace the people look most to their representatives; but in war, to the executive solely . . . to give direction to their affairs, with a confidence as auspicious as it is well-founded."[15]

This of course is the "prerogative," described by John Locke as the power of the executive "to act according to discretion for the public good, *without the prescription of the law and sometimes even against it.*"[16] Since the fundamental law that the executive ultimately must implement is to preserve society, it is "fit that the laws themselves should in some cases give way to the executive power, or rather to *this fundamental law of nature and government, viz. that as much as may be, all members of society are to be preserved.*"[17]

The prerogative is rendered necessary by the fact that laws arising from legislative deliberation cannot foresee every exigency. For the safety of the republic, the executive must retain some latitude for action. Jefferson expressed the spirit of the prerogative in a letter to John B. Colvin. Responding to Colvin's question concerning "whether circumstances do not sometimes occur, which make it a duty in officers of high trust, to assume authorities beyond the law," Jefferson wrote:

> A strict observance of the written law is doubtless one of the highest duties of a good citizen, but it is not the highest. The laws of necessity, of self preservation, of saving our country when in danger, are of higher obligation. To lose our country by a scrupulous adherence to written law, would be to lose the law itself, with life, liberty, property and all those who are enjoying them with us; thus absurdly sacrificing the ends to the means. . . . It is incumbent on those only who accept of greatest charges, to risk themselves on great occasion, when the safety of the nation, or some of its very high interests are at stake.[18]

Lincoln made the same point in his speech to Congress in special session after the attack on Fort Sumter in defense of his suspension of the writ of habeas corpus:

> The whole of the laws which were required to be faithfully executed were being resisted, and failing of execution in nearly one third of the States. Must they be allowed to finally fail of execution, even had it been perfectly clear that by the use of the means necessary to their execution some single law, made in such extreme tenderness of the citizen's liberty, that practically it relieves more of the guilty than of the innocent, should to a very limited extent be violated? To state the question more directly: are all the laws but one to go unexecuted, and the Government itself to go to pieces, lest that one be violated? Even in such a case, would not the official oath be broken if the government should be overthrown, when it was believed that disregarding the single law would tend to preserve it?[19]

As we shall see, Lincoln did not believe he had violated the law, because the privilege of the writ of habeas corpus may be suspended "when, in cases of rebellion or invasion, the public safety may require it."

Some scholars have taken issue with the idea that the prerogative should form a part of constitutional government. Sanford Levinson, for example, asks if the powers implied by the prerogative, as understood by Lincoln "mean, in effect, that it is impossible for Presidents to violate their constitutional oath, so long as they are motivated in their conduct by the sincere desire to maintain 'free government' against those whom they view as its enemies, foreign or domestic?"[20]

Lincoln answered in the affirmative. An emergency power is useless unless it is sufficient to meet the emergency. Since the magnitude and the character of the emergency determine the extent of the necessary power, the president is in the best position to determine how much power he needs. In revoking Maj. Gen. David Hunter's emancipation order in South Carolina, Lincoln stated that the decision to free slaves would depend on his determination that such a step "shall have become a necessity indispensable to the maintenance of the government." The exercise of such a power, he continued, "I reserve to myself."[21] In September 1862, Lincoln declared that an emancipation proclamation was part of his power as commander in chief, which gave him "a right to take any measure which may best subdue the enemy."[22]

But Lincoln's emphasis on preserving republican government taught him, as it should teach us, that the prerogative is limited by the will of the people, which, "constitutionally expressed, is the ultimate law for all. If they should deliberately resolve to have immediate peace even at the loss of their country, and their liberty, I know not the power or the right to resist them. It is their own business, and they must do as they please with their own."[23]

In addition, Lincoln entertained no doubt that any extraordinary powers were limited to the duration of the emergency and not applicable to normal times. His reply to Erastus Corning and a group of New York Democrats who had criticized his war measures is also the proper response to Professor Levinson:

> I can no more be persuaded that the Government can constitutionally take no strong measures in time of rebellion, because it can be shown that the same could not lawfully be taken in time of peace, than I can be persuaded that a particular drug is not good medicine

for a sick man, because it can be shown not to be good for a well one. Nor am I able to appreciate the danger apprehended by the meeting [of the New York Democrats] that the American people will, by means of military arrest during the Rebellion, lose the right of Public Discussion, the Liberty of Speech and the Press, the Law of Evidence, Trial by Jury, and Habeas Corpus, throughout the indefinite peaceful future, which I trust lies before them, any more than I am able to believe that a man could contract so strong an appetite for emetics during temporary illness as to persist in feeding upon them during the remainder of his healthful life.[24]

Lincoln faced other dilemmas as war president. One was the dual nature of the conflict: it was both a war and a domestic insurrection. As we shall see, Lincoln believed that the states could not legally secede and that accordingly, the Confederacy was a fiction. Thus he had to be careful lest the steps he took be construed as recognizing the Confederacy. This applied to his decision to blockade Southern ports, traditionally a measure taken against a belligerent, and confiscation. His concerns about the constitutionality of the two confiscation acts passed by Congress and the fact that they implied recognition of the Confederacy led him to treat emancipation as a war measure.

Lincoln's Response to the Emergency

Lincoln could have responded in a variety of ways to the action of the Southern states. He could have permitted them to leave. He could have attempted some sort of compromise. He could have bided his time, hoping that unionist sentiment in the South would reassert itself. Finally, he could have employed force to coerce the states back into the Union.

Many in the North were willing to let the Union dissolve. For instance, Horace Greeley wrote in the *New York Tribune* of November 9, 1860, that "if the Cotton States shall become satisfied that they can do better out of the Union than in it, we insist on letting them go. We never hope to live in a republic whereof one part is pinned to the residue by bayonets." Radical abolitionists, who saw the Constitution as a "covenant of death" with slaveholders, also favored disunion. But Lincoln could not accept this alternative, for all the reasons cited above.

Lincoln also rejected any compromise that permitted an extension of slavery into the federal territories. After all, this was the issue that had led to the Republicans' electoral triumph in the North. Besides, permitting further extension of the institution would undercut his own plan for convincing the slave state governments to accept his plan for gradual, compensated emancipation. In the Senate, John J. Crittenden of Kentucky cobbled together a series of amendments to the Constitution that would have, among other provisions, protected slavery in the states from any interference by the federal government and expanded the application of the Missouri Compromise line of 36° 30' from territories acquired as part of the Louisiana Purchase to all territories "now held, or hereafter acquired."[25]

But Lincoln was adamant. In a series of letters written to Lyman Trumbull, William Kellogg, Elihu Washburne, and Thurlow Weed in December 1860, Lincoln abjured them to "entertain no proposition for a compromise in regard to the extension of slavery."[26] To do so would be to put the United States on the road to becoming a "slave empire." To John Defrees he wrote: "I am sorry any republican inclines to dally with [popular sovereignty] of any sort. It acknowledges that slavery has equal rights with liberty and surrenders all we have contended for. Once fastened on us as a settled policy, filibustering for all South of us, and making slave states of it, follows in spite of us, with an early Supreme court decision, holding our free-state constitutions to be unconstitutional."[27]

In a similar vein, he wrote to James T. Hale that "we have just carried an election on principles fairly stated to the people. Now we are told in advance, the government must be broken up, unless we surrender to those we have beaten, before we take the offices . . . [I]f we surrender, it is the end of [the Republican Party] and of the government. They will repeat the experiment upon us *ad libitum*. A year will not pass, till we shall have to take Cuba as a condition upon which they will stay in the Union."[28]

Lincoln understood the risk associated with a precipitous resort to arms—thus the conciliatory tone of his inaugural address. In it, he tried to reassure the South that he had no intention of interfering with slavery where it already existed, and he also indicated that he would make no attempt to recover federal property seized by the seceded states. As he said in his inaugural address, "in your hands, my dissatisfied fellow countrymen, and not in mine, is the momentous issue of civil war."[29]

Lincoln was willing to wait. He in fact believed that there was Unionist sentiment through much of the South and that if he bided his time, that sentiment would lead the seceded states to come to their senses. But if war came, Lincoln understood the importance of having the South fire the first shot. This he was able to achieve, thanks to those Southerners who wished to prevent reconciliation.

At the time of his inauguration, only two federal installations in the seven seceded states remained in Union hands: Fort Pickens in Florida and Fort Sumter in Charleston harbor. When the commander of Fort Sumter advised Lincoln that he would not be able to hold out much longer, the president asked his cabinet and his commanding general, Winfield Scott, for their opinions about whether to hold or abandon the fort. Scott and six of the seven members of his cabinet counseled evacuating the fort.

But Lincoln rejected their advice. He believed evacuation of Fort Sumter would lessen the credibility of the government and lead to further confrontations. He chose to reprovision, but not reinforce, the fort. If the reprovisioning succeeded, the Confederacy would suffer a blow to its credibility. If the reprovisioning were opposed by force, the South would be the aggressor. Lincoln advised the governor of South Carolina that the attempted provisioning would take place. The Confederate government had its own reasons for firing on Fort Sumter, but fire it did, with the result that public opinion in the North was galvanized behind the president.[30]

Lincoln's response to secession was measured. He refused to compromise on the principles that he believed had led to the Republican electoral victory in 1860, but he did everything else he could to reassure the South that he would not interfere with their institutions and interests. Those who criticize Lincoln for "tricking" the Confederacy into firing on Fort Sumter ignore substantial evidence that Southerners desired separation with or without war and that some feared a compromise that would keep them in the Union.[31]

The Domestic Politics of Civil War:
Lincoln, His Cabinet, Radicals, and Copperheads

When critics refer to Lincoln as a "dictator," they ignore the fact that members of Congress from both parties constantly second-guessed his policies and strategy. Lincoln had to navigate the treacherous waters of partisan politics in order to prosecute the war. To do so, he developed a working coalition composed primarily of moderate Republicans and War Democrats but including

Radical Republicans when it came to attacking slavery. It is important to note that the disagreements between Lincoln and the Radicals concerned *means*, not *ends*. While he was often annoyed by Radical criticism, he understood that the differences between Radical and moderate Republicans were of far less import than those between the Republicans and Democrats. He once remarked that the difference between himself and the Radical Republican senator from Massachusetts Charles Sumner was about six weeks.[32] There was not much he could do about the "peace" wing of the Democratic Party, which veered perilously close to crossing the line from dissent to obstruction.

The composition of his cabinet reflects his approach to the problem of partisan politics. Lincoln attempted to balance regional interests within the infant Republican Party as well as maintain the loyalty of the border slave states of Missouri, Kentucky, Maryland, and Delaware.[33] He also hoped to incorporate non-Republicans, preferably from the upper South. Accordingly, he offered a portfolio to a Unionist congressman from North Carolina, John Gilmer, who rejected his offer.

Interestingly, Lincoln appointed his four main rivals for the Republican nomination in 1860 to cabinet posts: William Seward as secretary of state, Edward Bates as attorney general, Simon Cameron as secretary of war, and Salmon Chase as secretary of the Treasury. Seward and Chase still thought they should have been president.

Seward thought of himself as prime minister and took steps during the secession crisis without Lincoln's knowledge, notably assuring Confederate commissioners that Fort Sumter would be abandoned. On this occasion, Lincoln made it clear that he was the president and accordingly was responsible for administration policy.[34] Subsequently Seward became Lincoln's most loyal cabinet member.

As a member of the cabinet, Chase caused no end of problems for Lincoln. Nonetheless, despite the fact that he had no experience as a financier, he became an extremely effective secretary of the Treasury, working closely with Congress and private bankers such as Jay Cooke to fund the war while keeping the rate of inflation relatively low.[35]

Cameron's integrity was always suspect, and after he made a series of missteps, Lincoln named him ambassador to Russia, replacing him with Edwin Stanton, a War Democrat who had also been James Buchanan's attorney general.

Stanton was an effective secretary of war. Carl von Clausewitz, the nineteenth-century Prussian philosopher of war, distinguished between *preparation for war,* the mobilization of resources, and *war proper,* the development and implementation of strategy and conduct of operations and campaigns.[36] While the latter must ultimately be decisive in war, the conduct of war also depends on effectively mobilizing resources. Stanton became Lincoln's real right-hand man in the preparation for war. His great contribution to Lincoln and the Union cause was to supply the energy and vigor necessary to prosecute the war.[37] In tandem with Maj. Gen. Montgomery Meigs, the quartermaster general of the US Army, Stanton was able to tap the entrepreneurial talents of Northern businessmen, effectively mobilizing the resources necessary to prevail in a modern industrial conflict.[38]

The tensions that developed in Lincoln's cabinet were a microcosm of the difficulties the president faced in his conduct of the war as a whole. Lincoln had to constantly hold both the Radical Republicans and "Peace Democrats" at bay. The former saw Lincoln's prudential approach to the war as being too timid. The latter sought a negotiated settlement with the seceded states.

The Radicals

Despite the fact that the Radicals shared the same goals as Lincoln, many did not think he was up to the task of commander in chief. They constantly pushed for a government by cabinet, which they wanted to control by ousting the War Democrats and replacing them with more reliably antislavery Republicans.

The Radicals' attempt to wrest control of the war from Lincoln by reshaping the cabinet culminated in December 1862 during the gloomy days following the Union debacle at Fredericksburg. Aided and abetted by Treasury Secretary Chase, who had presidential aspirations, a delegation of Radicals attempted to force Lincoln to fire Secretary of State Seward, whom they claimed had influenced the president to reject such aggressive war measures as emancipation, arming black soldiers, and appointing antislavery generals.

Lincoln met with a delegation of Republican senators and listened to their complaints about Seward. Seward had submitted his resignation, but the senators did not know this. Lincoln promised to consider their claims and invited them to return the next day. They did so but were surprised to find the cabinet, minus Seward, assembled. Lincoln defended Seward and claimed that the entire cabinet had supported policy decisions for which he alone was responsible. He then turned to the cabinet for confirmation. Chase was put on the spot. He could either disagree with the president and reveal himself as disloyal to Lincoln or agree with the president, which would call his courage and commitment to the Radicals into question. He chose the latter, enraging the senators.

The next day, Chase offered his resignation to Lincoln, who snatched it from his hand. "Now I can ride," he exclaimed. "I have a pumpkin in each end of my bag." The message was clear. If the Radicals wanted to get rid of Seward, they would have to lose Chase too.[39]

The Radicals possessed many tools to force Lincoln to pursue a course of war more to their liking. One of these was the "Joint Committee on the Conduct of the War," which looked over his shoulder for the duration of the conflict, calling generals back to Washington to testify and grilling those they believed were not sufficiently committed to their own vision of the war. The committee did little good and much harm to the Union cause, not the least by demoralizing the Union's top generals. Eschewing prudence and ignoring the political conditions that Lincoln faced, the committee constantly criticized him for his timidity. Had it prevailed in forcing its policies on Lincoln, the Union cause most likely would have been lost in 1862.[40]

Of course, the Radicals' most effective method for putting pressure on Lincoln was through legislation. Thus Congress passed bills regarding confiscation of rebel property and policies for "reconstructing" the Union at the end of the rebellion. In most cases the differences between Lincoln and Congress had to do with prudence. Unlike Lincoln, Radicals in Congress often seem to have forgotten the role of consent in republican government.

A case in point was the clash between Lincoln and the Radical Republicans in Congress concerning Reconstruction.[41] Lincoln wished to restore the Union as quickly as possible with minimum federal interference in internal affairs. His theory of government held that the states were never out of the Union—he believed firmly that the Union is perpetual. Instead, individuals within the states were in rebellion. He wished to reestablish the proper relationship between the federal government and the states controlled by rebels as quickly as possible. He believed that "restoration" and suppression of the rebellion could occur simultaneously.

The Radicals, on the other hand, wished to use the full power of the federal government to effect a social revolution, extending civil and political rights to former slaves. Radical Republicans rejected Lincoln's plan for Reconstruction, which they dismissed as a "soft peace." They believed that the war must be won before Reconstruction could begin. For many Radicals, the rebellious states were disorganized communities without legitimate civil governments. Some radicals wanted to return seceded states to a territorial status, in which they would be governed by Congress.

Lincoln's plan for Reconstruction "called for establishing a tangible nucleus of loyal citizens in each seceded state—10 percent of qualified voters based on the 1860 census—who would swear an oath of allegiance. Accordingly he sought to grant amnesty or pardons to white Southerners—excluding Confederate civil officers, military officers (including those who had resigned commissions in the US Army or Navy), and members of Congress or judges who had resigned their seats or appointments (these could apply for individual pardons, which would be granted liberally)—and give those who took a loyalty oath to the government the full power to reestablish state governments. His plan implied, but did not make explicit, that the abolition of slavery was a precondition for the restoration of a state. Before the end of the war, Virginia, Louisiana, Arkansas, and Tennessee were "reconstructed" according to Lincoln's plan, but Congress refused to seat the representatives of those states.[42]

In 1864 Congress passed the Wade-Davis Act—an explicit rejection of the presidential Reconstruction. This act called for temporary rule by military government to supervise enrollment of white male citizens. It required that a majority of voters take an "ironclad" oath declaring that they had never voluntarily supported the Confederacy. Delegates to a state convention would then be selected from among the list of qualified voters. This convention was required to repudiate secession and abolish slavery prior to restoration. And of course, all slaves were to be emancipated. Lincoln employed a "pocket veto" to kill the bill.

After Lincoln's death, Andrew Johnson pursued a lenient policy of Reconstruction, but he was discredited by the irresponsible behavior of the Southern Reconstruction governments and the deference he paid to them. In effect, he became a captive of the old Confederates, whom he detested.

The Johnson state governments repealed ordinances of secession but did not repudiate secession, reestablished social control over freed slaves by means of odious Black Codes, and ignored proscriptions against unamnestied Confederates. Mississippi refused to ratify the Thirteenth Amendment, and South Carolina refused to repudiate Confederate debt. In response, Navy Secretary Gideon Welles wrote: "The entire South seem to be stupid and indiscreet, know not their friends, and are pursuing just the course which their opponents, the Radicals, desire. I fear a terrible ordeal awaits them in the future."[43]

Welles's words were prophetic. As he predicted, the conduct of Southern states and Johnson's vetoes of the Freedmen's Bureau and Civil Rights bills led to a loss of credibility on the part of the executive branch and caused a shift in Congress, which gave power to the Radicals. The election of 1866 was a disaster for Johnson. His intemperate rhetoric was matched by the Radicals' electoral strategy of "waving the bloody shirt" of the late rebellion. Republicans gained a veto-proof majority of both houses of Congress and won every Northern governorship and legislature, paving the way for Radical Reconstruction.

Copperheads

The Peace Democrats caused no end of troubles for Lincoln and his effort to prosecute the war. Some historians have discounted the influence of the "Copperheads,"[44] but it seems clear that the Northern antiwar movement was far from a peripheral phenomenon. In fact, it often crossed the line from dissent to obstruction of the war effort.[45]

Disaffection with the war in the North was widespread and the influence of the Peace Democrats on the Democratic Party was substantial, especially when things were going badly for the Union military effort. For example, the influence of the Copperheads peaked during the summer of 1864 when the likelihood of Union success in the war seemed remote. Despite Union successes in both the eastern and western theaters—the repulse of Gen. Robert E. Lee and his Confederate Army of Northern Virginia at Gettysburg and the fall of Vicksburg and Chattanooga in 1863 and the spring–summer 1864 Virginia campaign that had forced Lee into a defensive position around Petersburg—the Northern people were weary of the war and appalled by its human cost.

The Virginia Overland Campaign of May–June 1864 reflected the military philosophy of newly promoted Lt. Gen. Ulysses S. Grant, whom Lincoln had appointed general in chief of the armies of the United States on March 10, 1864. "The art of war," Grant maintained, "is simple enough. Find out where your enemy is. Get at him as soon as you can. Strike him as hard as you can and as often as you can, and keep moving on."[46]

Thus for forty days in May and June, Maj. Gen. George Meade's Army of the Potomac, accompanied by Grant, was locked in an unprecedented death struggle with Lee's Army of Northern Virginia, beginning with the hell that was the Wilderness and continuing through the bloodletting at Spotsylvania, North Anna, and Cold Harbor. While Lee, operating on interior lines, was able to parry each blow, he could never wrest the initiative from his adversary. Eventually Grant and Meade were able to sidestep Lee once more, cross the James River, and besiege Petersburg.[47]

As necessary as it may have been strategically, the human cost of the Virginia Campaign of May–June 1864 was staggering. Meade suffered fifty-five thousand casualties in addition to the loss of thousands of veteran troops whose three-year enlistments came to an end. The casualty lists that affected every town and city in the North created widespread disaffection with the war, which substantially increased the influence of the Copperheads on the Democratic Party. Democratic newspapers cited the failure of Union arms in Virginia and Maj. Gen. William Tecumseh Sherman's lack of success in Georgia as a reason for ending the war as soon as possible: "If nothing else would impress upon the people the absolute necessity of stopping this war, its utter failure to accomplish any results would be sufficient."[48]

Buoyed by disaffection with the war, the Copperheads wrote the Democratic Party platform of 1864, and one of their own, Rep. George H. Pendleton of Ohio, was the party's candidate for vice president. Although former Union major general George B. McClellan was not himself a Copperhead, he reportedly said, "If I am elected, I will recommend an immediate armistice and a call for a convention of all the states and insist upon exhausting all and every means to secure peace without further bloodshed." The Republicans feared, with good reason, that this meant that the Union, if restored at all, would be so on the basis of the old Democratic formula: "the Constitution as it is, the Union as it was"—in other words, with slavery still intact.

Thus on August 23, 1864, Lincoln drafted a short memorandum that he asked his cabinet to sign without reading. It read: "This morning, as for some days past, it seems exceedingly probable that this Administration will not be re-elected. Then it will be my duty to so co-operate with the President elect, as to save the Union between the election and the inauguration; as he will have secured his election on such grounds that he cannot possibly save it afterwards."[49] In other words, Lincoln vowed to pursue victory for as long as he was president—in those days the new president was inaugurated in March—and he expected his cabinet to support him.

It is clear that the Confederates were counting on Lincoln's electoral defeat. As the *Charleston Monitor* editorialized, McClellan's election on a peace platform "must lead to peace and our independence . . . [provided] that for the next two months we hold our own and prevent military success by our foes."[50]

Fortunately for Lincoln and the survival of the Union and the end of slavery, three military events changed the electoral landscape, resulting in his reelection. The first, Rear Admiral David Farragut's capture of Mobile, had occurred during the summer, but its importance was not recognized until later when the second event took place: Sherman's seizure of Atlanta on September 2. The trifecta was completed in October when Philip Sheridan routed Jubal Early at Cedar Creek, driving the Confederates from the Shenandoah Valley for the last time.

Although the Union survived, the historical record makes it clear that the actions of the Copperheads materially damaged the ability of the Lincoln administration to prosecute the war. The fact is that Peace Democrats actively interfered with recruiting and encouraged desertion. Indeed, they generated so much opposition to conscription that the army was forced to divert resources from the battlefield to the hotbeds of Copperhead activity in order to maintain order.[51] Many Copperheads actively supported the Confederate cause, materially as well as rhetorically.

However, in the long run, the Democratic Party was badly hurt by the Copperheads. Their actions radically politicized Union soldiers, turning into stalwart Republicans many who had strongly supported the Democratic Party's opposition to emancipation as a part of the prosecution of the war. In fact, many Union soldiers came to despise the Copperheads more than they disdained the rebels. In the words of an assistant surgeon of an Iowa regiment, "it is a common saying here that if we are whipped, it will be by Northern votes, not by Southern bullets. The army regard the result of the late [fall 1862] elections as at *least* prolonging the war."[52]

It is certain that the Union soldiers tired of hearing from the Copperheads that the rebels could not be defeated. They surely tired of being described by the Copperheads as instruments of a tyrannical administration trampling the legitimate rights of the Southern states. The soldiers seemed to understand fairly quickly that the Copperheads preferred Lincoln's failure to the country's success. They also recognized that the Copperheads offered no viable alternative to Lincoln's policy except to stop the war.

As a result, Union soldiers voted overwhelmingly for Lincoln in 1864, abandoning the once-beloved McClellan because of the perception that he had become a tool of the Copperheads. And as the Democrats were reminded for many years after the war, the Copperheads had made a powerful enemy of the Union veterans.

Vigilance and Responsibility: Civil Liberties in Time of War

The most controversial element of Lincoln's war presidency is his treatment of civil liberties.[53] Even many defenders of Lincoln argue that he overstepped constitutional bounds by declaring martial law, arbitrarily arresting civilians and trying them by military tribunal, and shutting down opposition newspapers. After the war, the Supreme Court criticized many of these measures in *Ex parte Milligan.*

The dilemma that a president faces in time of emergency was expressed by James Madison in a letter to Thomas Jefferson: "It is a melancholy reflection that liberty should be equally exposed to danger whether the government have too much or too little power." Lincoln addressed this dilemma during his speech to a special session of Congress after Fort Sumter. "Is there," he asked, "in all republics, this inherent, and fatal weakness? 'Must a government, of necessity, be too *strong* for the liberties of its own people, or too *weak* to maintain its own existence?'"[54]

Throughout the history of the American republic, there has been a tension between two virtues necessary to sustain republican government: *vigilance* and *responsibility.*[55] Vigilance is the jealousy on the part of the people that constitutes a necessary check on those who hold power lest they abuse it. As Jefferson wrote, "it is jealousy and not confidence which prescribes limited constitutions, to bind those whom we are obliged to trust with power."[56]

But while vigilance is a necessary virtue, it may, if unchecked, lead to an extremism that incapacitates a government, preventing it from carrying out even its most necessary and legitimate purposes, such as providing for the common defense. "Jealousy," wrote Alexander Hamilton, often infects the "noble enthusiasm for liberty" with "a spirit of narrow and illiberal distrust."[57]

Responsibility on the other hand is the prudential judgment necessary to moderate the excesses of political jealousy, thereby permitting limited government to fulfill its purposes. Thus in *Federalist* No. 23, Hamilton wrote that those responsible for the nation's defense must be granted all of the powers necessary to achieve that end.[58] Responsibility is the virtue necessary to govern and to preserve the republic from harm, both external and internal. The dangers of foreign and civil war taught Hamilton that liberty and power are not always adversaries, that the "vigor" of government is essential to the security of liberty.

Lincoln's actions as president during the Civil War reflected his agreement with this principle. Due to the unprecedented nature of the emergency created by the rebellion, he believed that he had no choice but to exercise broad executive power. Lincoln addressed the issue of civil liberties in wartime in the aforementioned letter to Erastus Corning, who had sent him the resolutions of the Albany Democratic Convention.[59] His arguments are as applicable today to the war on terrorism as they were in 1863 during a domestic insurrection.

The Albany Democrats had expressed loyalty to the Union but had censured the Lincoln administration for what it called unconstitutional acts, such as military arrests of civilians in the North. To the Albany Democrats' claim that they supported the use of "every constitutional and lawful measure to suppress the rebellion," Lincoln replied that he had "not knowingly employed . . . any other" in the past nor did he intend to in the future.

The Albany Democrats invoked the safeguards and guarantees for the liberties of citizens under the Constitution, observing that they "were secured substantially to the English people, *after* years of protracted civil war, and were adopted into our constitution at the *close* of the revolution." Lincoln replied that their point would have been stronger had they said that these safeguards had been adopted and applied during the civil war and during our revolution, rather than after the one and at the end of the other. "I, too," said Lincoln, "am devotedly for them after civil war, and before civil war, and at all times, 'except when, in cases of rebellion or invasion, the public safety may require' their suspension."

Lincoln then argued that those who wished to destroy the Constitution were relying on the fact that "the government would, in great degree, be restrained by the same Constitution and law from arresting their progress." If anything, Lincoln continued, he waited too long to implement emergency measures: "[T]horoughly imbued with a reverence for the guaranteed rights of individuals, I was slow to adopt the strong measures which by degree I have been forced to regard as being within the exceptions of the Constitution, and as indispensable to the public safety."

The core of Lincoln's argument was that the courts of justice are incompetent to handle cases arising out of a vast emergency. Suspension of habeas corpus is the constitutional provision that applies in such cases. The drafters of the Constitution, he continued, understood that there were emergency instances in which "men may be held in custody whom the courts, acting on ordinary rules would discharge." Habeas corpus does not discharge those proved to be guilty of a defined crime. The Constitution permits its suspension "that men may be arrested and held who cannot be proved to be guilty of defined crime, 'when in cases of rebellion or invasion the public safety may require it.'" This is because in times of emergency, arrests must sometimes be made not for what has been done, but to prevent things that probably would be done.

Lincoln pointed out that a number of still high-ranking Confederates, whose sentiments were then known, were in the power of the government when the rebellion broke out. Had they been seized, the rebellion would be weaker. But none of them had committed a crime defined in law, so they would have been discharged on the basis of habeas corpus if the writ were permitted to operate. "In view of these and similar cases, I think I shall be blamed for having made too few arrests than too many."

The Albany Democrats had called the arrests of civilians in areas where the rebellion did not exist unconstitutional. Lincoln replied that the Constitution made no such distinction. His actions, he continued, were constitutional *wherever* the public safety required them, whether to prevent the rebellion from spreading, to prevent mischievous interference with raising and supplying the armies necessary to suppress the rebellion, or to restrain agitators who sought to encourage desertion—in other words, his actions were "equally constitutional at all places where they will conduce to the public safety, as against the dangers of rebellion or invasion."

The Albany Democrats criticized the arrest and trial by military tribunal of the antiwar Ohio Democratic congressman Clement Vallandigham merely for his words. But Lincoln replied that Vallandigham was encouraging desertion from the army, upon which the nation was depending to save the Union. He noted that the Albany Democrats support the suppression of the rebellion by force. But this depends on an army, and one of the biggest problems armies face is desertion, an act so serious that it is punished by death. "Must I shoot a simple-minded soldier boy who deserts, while I must not touch a hair of a wiley [*sic*] agitator who induces him to desert?"

Lincoln said that if he is wrong on the question of his constitutional power, his error is in believing that certain actions that are not constitutional in the absence of rebellion or invasion become constitutional when those conditions exist—in other words, "that the Constitution is not in its application in all respects the same in cases of rebellion or invasion involving the public safety, as it is in times of profound peace and public security."

As noted above, Lincoln argued that the means appropriate for an emergency are not appropriate for normal times. A sick man is given medicine that would not be good for a well one. Lincoln's argument here is quintessentially prudential.

Lincoln's detractors have often embraced the "Lost Cause" narrative, which holds that while Lincoln ran roughshod over civil liberties in the North, the Confederacy adhered to a strict constitutionalism in defense of civil liberties. They have also treated Chief Justice Roger Taney as a paragon of respect for civil liberties who worked to stymie Lincoln's abuses.

But both arguments are demonstrably false. In the South, as in the North, most civilians accepted restrictions on their liberties because they believed the restrictions constituted temporary, necessary measures that ensured stability and would help win the war. Southern society was not nearly as "obsessive about liberty" as previously thought. And Taney's opposition to Lincoln stemmed from politics, not respect for the Constitution.

Mark Neely has effectively refuted the Lost Cause narrative regarding civil liberties, demonstrating that Jefferson Davis was far from the staunch defender of civil liberties and constitutionalism that he claimed to be in his history of the Confederacy.[60] Davis, like Lincoln, was committed to the survival of his country. Early on, Davis spoke of "sacred civil liberties" in an attempt to persuade the border states to secede. But as the North made inroads into the South, Davis sacrificed individual rights to the preservation of what remained of the Confederacy.

The fact is that the Confederacy, like the Union, acted "as modern democratic nations [do] in war," placing restrictions on individual liberties out of perceived military necessity. The fact is that both the Union and the

Confederacy faced the enduring dilemma of republican government: how to balance vigilance and responsibility.[61]

The portrayal of the conflict between Lincoln and Roger Taney's Supreme Court during the Civil War as a contest between a president who was more interested in preserving the Union than in respecting civil liberties and a chief justice who was a defender of civil liberties "though the walls of heaven fall" is simplistic as well. As Don Fehrenbacher has noted, Chief Justice Taney was not especially solicitous of individual liberties. His real motive in issuing *Ex parte Merryman,* which challenged Lincoln's policy of military arrests of civilians, was his attitudes toward the Union and the war. Taney did not think the Union was worth saving at all. Indeed, there is no record of any public or private statement in support of the Union cause. Instead, he sympathized with the Confederacy, favoring peaceable separation. He "considered the war a descent into madness, detested Republicans as a class, and regarded the Lincoln administration as a hateful despotism."[62]

Lincoln's Military Contribution as Commander in Chief

On the surface, Abraham Lincoln seemed ill-prepared to meet the military challenges that this crisis generated. By all measures his Confederate counterpart, Jefferson Davis, would seem to have had the edge. Davis was a graduate of the US Military Academy at West Point, he had a distinguished record during the Mexican War, he had been secretary of war during the administration of Franklin Pierce, and, as a US senator from Mississippi, he had chaired the Committee on Military Affairs.[63]

In contrast, Lincoln had served as a captain of militia during the Black Hawk War, during which he had seen no action. As a Whig congressman for only one term, Lincoln had poked fun at his own military record by way of mocking the attempt by the Democrats during the election campaign of 1848 to turn Lewis Cass of Michigan into a military hero comparable to the Whigs' Zachary Taylor:

> By the way, Mr. Speaker, did you know I am a military hero? Yes sir; in the days of the Black Hawk war, I fought, bled, and came away. Speaking of General Cass' career reminds me of my own. I was not at Stillman's defeat, but I was about as near it, as Cass was to Hull's

surrender; and like him, I saw the place very soon afterwards. . . . If Gen. Cass went in advance of me in picking huckleberries, I guess I surpassed him in charges upon the wild onions. If he saw any live fighting Indians, it was more than I did; but I had a good many bloody struggles with the mosquitoes; and although I never fainted from loss of blood, I can truly say I was often very hungry.[64]

His one term in Congress was lackluster. He gained notoriety for opposing the Mexican War, as did most Whigs, and demanding that President James Polk show the very spot upon which Mexico had provoked the conflict.[65]

What was Lincoln's role in the Union victory? Some have concluded that his contribution was minimal. Given the relative power of the North, goes the argument, Union victory was assured beforehand; Lincoln's role was superfluous at best and negative at worst—his propensity for interfering in the details of military operations was counterproductive. A variation of this view holds that Lincoln's main contribution to Union victory was to find the right general. According to this view, Lincoln had to wade through a mass of incompetents until he found Ulysses S. Grant, who led the Union armies to success.[66]

In recent years, historians have begun to give Lincoln more credit as a war leader.[67] He was responsible for establishing the policy of the Union and for developing and implementing a strategy to achieve the goals of his policy.[68] In doing so, he demonstrated flexibility and strategic acumen. He skillfully managed both his cabinet and his generals and even Congress, where he had to maintain a working majority if the war was to be won. He did not hesitate to overrule his advisers, both military and civilian. As Eliot Cohen has noted, "Lincoln had not merely a powerful intellect but an extraordinarily orderly and balanced one."[69] Historians have acknowledged that the Union's material advantage was not sufficient in itself to ensure victory. Lincoln had to make the decisions that translated this advantage into military and political success.

We sometimes forget that he also had to defeat the strategy pursued by the Confederacy. As Clausewitz reminds us, war involves an active opponent who acts and reacts to our strategy, often in unexpected ways.[70] And certainly with field commanders as talented as Robert E. Lee, Confederate armies did confound Union plans on more than one occasion.

Lincoln and Union Strategy

Strategy is a species of prudence. Like the prudent man, the strategist never loses sight of the proper end. But he must be able to adapt his actions in pursuit of that end to particular conditions. As Clausewitz wrote: "Strategy is the use of the engagement for the purpose of the war. The strategist must therefore define an aim for the entire operational side of the war that will be in accordance with its purpose. In other words, he will draft the plan of the war, and the aim will determine the series of actions intended to achieve it: in fact, shape the individual campaign and, within these, decide on the individual engagements."[71]

Strategy is a plan of action for using available means to achieve the ends of policy. The modern conception of strategy originated with two nineteenth-century theorists of war, the Baron Antoine Henri Jomini and Clausewitz, who understood strategy to be the art of assembling and employing forces in terms of time and space.[72] Within time and space, strategy does three things.

First, strategy links ends and means, ensuring that there is not a mismatch between the two. Second, strategy helps to establish a priority among ends. Since means are limited, not everything can be done. Strategy ensures that choices are made among competing ends. As Frederick the Great observed, "he who tries to defend everything ends up defending nothing." Finally, strategy helps to conceptualize resources as means. In other words, it translates raw inputs such as men and money into the divisions and fleets that will be employed for the object of war. To carry out a strategy, one must have the right tactical instrument. Even the best-conceived strategy will fail unless it can rely on the right instrument to implement it.[73]

Strategy is both a process and product. As such, it is dynamic. It must adapt to changing conditions, such as geography, technology, and social conditions.[74] A strategy that works under one set of conditions may not work under different ones. To develop and execute a strategy requires that one be able to comprehend the whole and be able to bring the right instrument to bear at the right time and in the right place in order to achieve the object of the war. In Clausewitz's formulation, strategy is the use of the engagement for the purpose of the war. The strategist must therefore define an aim for the entire operational side of the war that will be in accordance with its purpose. In other words, he will draft the plan of the war, and the aim will determine the series of actions intended to achieve it: he will, in fact, shape the individual campaigns and, within these, decide on the individual engagements.[75]

A strategy can be judged according to a number of criteria. These include (1) the adequacy of the strategy for achieving the end and its fit with the character of the war; (2) the degree to which it takes account of the strengths and weaknesses of the enemy and tactical, operational, logistical, and geographical constraints; (3) the appropriateness of the means to the achievement of the political objective; (4) the degree to which attainment of the military objective translates into the achievement of political objectives; (5) the degree to which the actual conduct of the war corresponds to the strategic conception at the beginning of the war; (6) the match between the strategy and social conditions (i.e., the degree to which the strategy fits the "genius" of the people); (7) the ability of the government to maintain public support for the war and the chosen strategy; (8) the ability of social and political factors to withstand the shock of war; and (9) the costs and risks of the chosen strategy compared to the outcome. Finally, we must always ask, *were there better strategic alternatives than the one chosen?* In terms of these criteria, Lincoln's strategy was extremely successful.

Although Lincoln had no formal military education, he learned quickly and proved to be a competent strategist. T. Harry Williams wrote that "Lincoln stands out as a great war president, probably the greatest in our history, and a great national strategist, a better one than any of his generals."[76] McPherson disagrees with Williams's claim about Lincoln as strategist, writing that "Lincoln was not a 'natural strategist.' He worked hard to master the subject, just as he had done to become a lawyer."[77]

Lincoln intuitively adhered to the old adage that in war, "the main thing is to make sure that the main thing remains the main thing." As his letter to Horace Greeley illustrated, the "main thing" for Lincoln—the goal of Union policy—was to preserve the Union. But like any good strategist, Lincoln proved willing to adapt his strategy to the circumstances in order to achieve this goal.

In a strictly military sense, Lincoln understood that the key to victory for the Union was a strategy of "concentration in time"—that is, the simultaneous application of military force at multiple points, making it difficult for the Confederacy to defend its territory.[78] Although it was not successfully implemented until 1864, Lincoln articulated the principle in early 1862, in a memo to Maj. Gen. Don Carlos Buell:

I state my general idea of this war to be that we have greater resources, and the enemy has the greater facility of concentrating
forces upon points of collision; that we must fail unless we can
find some way of making our advantage an overmatch for his; and
that this can be done by menacing him with superior forces at different points at the same time, so that we can safely attack one or
both, if he makes no changes; and if he weakens one to strengthen
another, forbear to attack the strengthened one, but seize and hold
the weakened one, gaining so much.[79]

In keeping with this principle and distressed by the immobility of his armies
in early 1862, he issued his General War Order No. 1, directing Union forces
to move in concert on Washington's Birthday, February 22, 1862.[80] And Grant
wrote that in April 1864 when he explained his intention to have all forces,
even those on the defensive, advance at the same time, Lincoln replied, "Oh,
yes! I see that. As we say out West, if a man can't skin he must hold a leg
while somebody else does."[81]

He also understood that a successful strategy required Union armies to
defeat Confederate armies. To use Clausewitz's term, Lincoln understood
that it was the Confederate army, not territory or the Confederate capital,
that constituted the Confederacy's "center of gravity." Crush the armies
and the back of the rebellion would be broken. "I think *Lee's* Army, and not
Richmond, is your true objective point."[82]

Finally, he understood the importance of the West in Union strategy. In
early 1862, Union armies had employed the Tennessee River as the "main
line of operations" to penetrate deep into western Tennessee and northern
Mississippi, turning Confederate defenses on the Mississippi River and in
Kentucky. Grant's subsequent victory at Shiloh permitted Union forces to
seize major parts of the Confederacy's one remaining east–west railroad
line and opened the way to both Vicksburg on the Mississippi River and
Chattanooga. The capture of the latter permitted Union forces eventually
to penetrate the Appalachian barrier and seize Atlanta.[83]

Emancipation as Political-Military Strategy

Of course there was a great deal more to Lincoln's strategy than the military
element. His was also a political strategy, the main weapon of which was

emancipation.[84] Emancipation struck at not only the war-making potential of the Confederacy, but also the heart of the Southern social system. The Union attack on slavery began as early as May of 1861 with Maj. Gen. Benjamin Butler's contraband policy and continued with the passage of the two confiscation acts passed by Congress in 1861 and 1862, Lincoln's Emancipation Proclamation, and the enlistment of black soldiers in the Union army. It culminated with the passage of the Thirteenth Amendment to the Constitution, which finally drove a stake through the heart of the institution.

Nonetheless, Lincoln had to tread carefully for domestic political reasons, because emancipation was denounced by conservative Democrats in the North and loyal slaveholders in the slave states that remained in the Union. Lincoln believed he needed both groups if he was to prosecute the war successfully. As James Oakes argues, "[d]uring the first year of his administration, Lincoln was discreet about his approach to slavery, but there was no mistaking the [antislavery] substance of his policies."[85]

Lincoln approached emancipation according to the dictates of prudence. Accordingly, he was denounced by the conservatives as moving too fast and by the Radicals as moving too slowly. For instance, he enraged the Radicals soon after the war began by reversing an emancipation proclamation issued in Missouri by Maj. Gen. John C. Frémont. He did so for sound reasons. First, Frémont was invoking emancipation for *political* rather than for *military* reasons. This was, Lincoln believed, unconstitutional.[86]

Second, allowing it to stand might antagonize the loyal slave states, providing them an incentive to join the Confederacy. As he continued in his letter to Orville Browning, "I think to lose Kentucky is nearly to the same as to lose the whole game. Kentucky gone, we cannot hold Missouri, nor, as I think, Maryland. These all against us, and the job on our hands is too large for us."[87]

Although born in response to the Nebraska controversy of 1854, the Republican Party inherited a coherent set of antislavery principles formulated much earlier. This antislavery consensus shaped the policies of the Lincoln administration and Congress toward slavery once the war began.

The antislavery consensus that underpinned the Republican Party was based on a number of principles: (1) that the founding generation suffused the Constitution with the principles of natural law and the law of nations, which held that man's natural condition is freedom—the Constitution is inseparable from the Declaration of Independence; (2) that the presumption of freedom recognized by the Constitution could be overridden only by local or municipal law—in other words, freedom was "national," holding sway wherever the Constitution was sovereign, such as in the federal territories and on the high seas, while slavery was "local," limited to state jurisdiction; (3) that while the Constitution placed slavery in the states where it existed beyond the reach of the federal government, the Constitution did enable the federal government to limit the expansion of slavery; and (4) that the slavery compromises of the Constitution never included the idea that slaves were property—there could be no such thing as "property in man."

Republicans firmly believed that these principles provided the basis for a federal assault on slavery once Lincoln and a Republican Congress took office, notwithstanding the fact that the Constitution prohibited the federal government from interfering with slavery in the states where it existed. To this end, the Republicans intended to ban slavery from all the western territories, abolish slavery in Washington, DC, withdraw federal protection of slavery on the high seas, and deny admission to any new slave states. Many Republicans—if not Lincoln himself—wished to prohibit federal enforcement of the fugitive slave clause of the Constitution.[88]

Lincoln, like the Republican Party in general, believed that if he could prevent the expansion of slavery into the federal territories and prevail upon state legislatures to accept gradual, compensated emancipation (funded by Congress), he could shrink slavery, making it uneconomical, and place it back on the eventual road to extinction that he believed the founders had envisioned. The outbreak of war opened a second approach for attacking slavery: military emancipation. Thus he pursued a dual approach: offers of compensated emancipation in the loyal slave states and military emancipation in the rebellious states.[89] Lincoln reasoned that the combination of military success against the Confederacy and compensated emancipation in the loyal slave states would lead to the collapse of the Confederacy, which had staked its hopes on eventually incorporating the border slave states.[90]

But neither condition came to pass. Lincoln's proposals for compensated emancipation were rejected by the border slave states, and the Army of the Potomac under McClellan was driven back from Richmond after coming close to capturing it. Lincoln concluded that stronger measures were needed to bring the war to a successful conclusion. The Emancipation Proclamation was Lincoln's response to the failure of Union arms and compensated emancipation. It also met the requirement of the second Confiscation Act for the president to emancipate the slaves whose services had been "confiscated" by Congress's actions. The time had come, as he wrote to Cuthbert Bullitt, to stop waging war "with elder-stalk squirts, charged with rose water."[91] Thus after Lee's invasion of Maryland was turned back at Antietam, Lincoln issued a Preliminary Emancipation Proclamation on September 22 that gave the Confederates one hundred days to submit to the Union or face the prospect of immediate emancipation.

As Allen Guelzo observes, the Emancipation Proclamation was Lincoln's response not only to the refusal of the loyal slave states to accept gradual, compensated emancipation, but also to his concerns about the legality of other alternatives favored by Radical Republicans in Congress, such as treatment of fugitive slaves under federal control as "contrabands of war," confiscation, and emancipation as part of martial law. All, he believed, were unconstitutional and open to legal challenge.[92]

Indeed, it was possible that even after a successful war to subdue the rebellion, a slaveholder whose property had been seized in this manner could sue successfully in federal court. "[O]nce the war emergency was over," writes Guelzo, "the federal dockets would fill up with appeals that either attacked [martial law emancipation] proclamations as unconstitutional or denied that specific cases really fell within the definitions of the proclamation."[93]

In addition, they put Lincoln in a quandary concerning the status of the Confederacy. To apply confiscation and contraband as they were understood in international law gave the Confederacy belligerent status. This was at odds with Lincoln's insistence that the states of the Confederacy could never legally leave the Union. On the other hand, if the war was only a domestic rebellion, as Lincoln held, then confiscation of slave contraband violated the constitutional prohibition against attainder.

A similar problem arose with the use of martial law to effect emancipation. For this reason Lincoln revoked Frémont's aforementioned emancipation proclamation in Missouri at the beginning of the war, arguing that to invoke emancipation for *political* rather than for *military* reasons, as Frémont had, was unconstitutional.

Guelzo observes that Lincoln did everything he could to keep emancipation out of the federal courts, fearing that if the federal judiciary under Roger Taney ever took up emancipation, the court would become in effect the guarantor of slavery, setting back the prospect for all future emancipation just as *Dred Scott* had set back the effort to prevent the expansion of slavery into the territories.[94] The fact that the *Prize Cases,* which essentially affirmed the legality of the Union's conduct of the war, were decided by a vote of only 5–4 in the midst of the war seems to confirm Lincoln's decision.[95]

Such concerns notwithstanding, Southern Unionists, loyal slaveholders, and Democrats charged that Lincoln was "revolutionizing" the war by issuing his proclamation. Lincoln did not disagree, admitting that once the proclamation took effect, "the character of the war will be changed. It will be one of subjugation and extermination."[96] But, as he wrote to another correspondent, "This government cannot much longer play a game in which it stakes all, and its enemies stake nothing. Those enemies must understand that they cannot experiment for ten years trying to destroy the government, and if they fail still come back into the Union unhurt." Lincoln took particular exception to the demand by loyal slaveholders "that the government shall not strike its open enemies, lest they be struck by accident." This demand by border-state representatives, who had recently rejected Lincoln's last proposal for compensated emancipation, had become "the paralysis—the dead palsy—of the government in this whole struggle."[97]

The stronger medicine represented by the Emancipation Proclamation was necessary because the Confederacy was just now exerting its maximum effort to mobilize its population for war. In April 1862, the Confederate congress passed a conscription act. Then, abandoning the "cordon" defense that had permitted Union armies to penetrate Confederate territory as far as northern Mississippi in early 1862, the Confederacy organized its mobilized manpower into field armies. One of these forces, Braxton Bragg's Army of Tennessee, struck Grant at Shiloh. Lee's Army of Northern Virginia drove McClellan back from the gates of Richmond. Then in the fall of 1862, the former invaded Kentucky, and the latter invaded Maryland. To a great extent, the South was able to do this only because slave labor freed white men to fight. Emancipation could undermine the slave labor system of the South, thereby undercutting the Confederate effort to mobilize its military resources.

From a military standpoint, emancipation was a war measure designed to attack the Southern economy directly.[98] As General in Chief Henry Halleck explained to Grant, "The character of the war has very much changed within the last year. There is now no possible hope of reconciliation. . . . We must conquer the rebels or be conquered by them. . . . Every slave withdrawn from the enemy is the equivalent of a white man put *hors de combat.*"[99] In addition, to the extent that slaves freed by federal troops came under control of Union forces, they could be substituted for soldiers who were required to labor, freeing them up to fight. Thus emancipation had the effect of transferring labor from South to North, increasing the fighting potential of Union armies while decreasing that of the Confederate armies. As Gideon Welles, Lincoln's secretary of the navy, recalled, the president called emancipation "a military necessity, absolutely essential to the preservation of the Union. We must free the slaves or be ourselves subdued. The slaves were undeniably an element of strength to those who had their service, and we must decide whether that element should be with us or against us."[100]

Militarily, the Emancipation Proclamation opened the way to the next logical step in this process of weakening the South while strengthening the North—enrolling blacks as soldiers in the Union army. The manpower boon to the Union was substantial. Some 180,000 black soldiers served in the Union army. They constituted 120 infantry regiments, twelve regiments of heavy artillery, ten batteries of light artillery, and seven cavalry regiments. At the end of the war, they constituted 12 percent of the Union's military manpower.[101]

While the material contribution of African Americans, both freedmen and former slaves, to Union victory was substantial, their participation in the war to achieve their own liberty was important for its own sake. Without their participation, the war to save the Union "as it was" could not have been transformed into a war to save the Union "as it should be"—that is, without slavery—and it is unlikely that African Americans could ever have achieved full citizenship and equality in the United States.[102] And Lincoln understood the psychological impact of enlisting black troops in the Union cause. As he wrote to Andrew Johnson, the Unionist governor of Tennessee, "the bare sight of fifty thousand armed, and drilled black soldiers on the banks of the Mississippi, would end the rebellion at once."[103]

Lincoln took an immense gamble by issuing the Emancipation Proclamation. It was foremost a political gamble. Those who argue that Lincoln was only "waiting for the right time" to issue the Proclamation must confront the fact that because of his action, the Republicans paid an enormous price during the 1862 elections. Lincoln put the most highly charged issue of the war before the voters in the midst of an unwon conflict. Votes for Republicans fell by 16 percent from 1860. The party suffered disastrous setbacks in Pennsylvania, Indiana, Ohio, New York, and New Jersey.

Such losses in the elections of 1862 led some to conclude that Lincoln would not issue the final Emancipation. He did so for reasons that he made clear in his annual message to Congress for 1862: "Fellow citizens, we cannot escape history. . . . The fiery trial through which we pass, will light us down, in honor or dishonor, to the latest generation. . . . The dogmas of the quiet past are inadequate to the stormy present. . . . In giving freedom to the slave, we assure freedom to the free. . . . We must disenthrall ourselves, and then we shall save our country."[104]

Similar speculation emerged during the dark days of summer 1864, when Lincoln believed he would not be reelected. Most War Democrats and many Republicans saw his commitment to emancipation as an obstacle to peace. The chairman of the Republican National Committee (and editor of the *New York Times*) told Lincoln on August 22 that party leaders thought that Lincoln would lose: "Two special causes are assigned to this great reaction in public sentiment—the want of military success and the impression . . . that we can have peace with Union [but for the impression that the war is] not for Union but for the abolition of slavery."[105]

But Lincoln refused to give in on the question of emancipation. His reasons were both military and moral, as he told two Wisconsin Republicans on August 19:

There have been men who have proposed to me to return to slavery the black warriors of Port Hudson & Olustee to their masters to conciliate the South. I should be damned in time & eternity for so doing. The world shall know that I will keep my faith to friends & enemies, come what will. My enemies say I am now carrying on this war for the sole purpose of abolition. It is & will be carried on so long as I am President for the sole purpose of restoring the Union. But no human power can subdue this rebellion without using the Emancipation lever as I have done. Freedom has given us control of 200,000 able bodied men, born and raised on southern soil. It will give us more yet. Just so much it has sub[t]racted from the strength of our enemies. . . . My enemies condemn my emancipation policy. Let them prove by the history of the war, that we can restore the Union without it.[106]

Earlier he had expressed the same sentiments in an angry letter to James Conkling: "And then there will be some black men who can remember that, with silent tongue, and clinched teeth, and steady eye, and well-poised bayonet, they have helped mankind on to this great consummation; while, I fear, there will be some white ones, unable to forget that, with malignant heart, and deceitful speech, they strove to hinder it."[107]

Lincoln and His Generals

Eliot Cohen has demonstrated that Lincoln's presidency was by no means the model of the "normal" theory of civil-military relations, wherein the civilian authority establishes the goals of the war and then steps out of the way to permit the generals to implement what they believe to be the best military measures to achieve those goals.[108] Lincoln was an activist commander in chief who "interfered" with his generals by constantly asking questions and goading them to perform more aggressively.[109]

Lincoln intuitively understood that civilian leaders cannot simply leave the military to its own devices during a conflict because war is an iterative process involving the interplay of active wills. In this he reflected an intuitive understanding of Clausewitz, who wrote that "the political objective is the goal, war is the means of reaching it, and means can never be considered in isolation from their purpose. . . . Therefore, it is clear that war should never be thought of as *something autonomous* but always as an *instrument* of policy."[110]

Thus Lincoln understood that what appears to be the case at the outset of the war may change as the war continues, modifying the relationship between political goals and military means. The fact remains that wars are not fought for their own purposes but to achieve policy goals set by the political leadership of the state.

Perhaps the most important challenge Lincoln faced in the area of civil-military relations was that early in the war his generals pursued the war they wanted to fight rather than the one their commander in chief wanted them to fight. The clearest example of this problem was Maj. Gen. George McClellan, who disagreed with many of Lincoln's policies and in fact may have attempted to sabotage them.

There is perhaps no more remarkable document in the annals of American civil-military relations than the letter McClellan gave to Lincoln when the president visited the Army of the Potomac at Harrison's Landing on the James River in July 1862. McClellan, who had been within the sound of

Richmond's church bells only two weeks earlier, had been driven back by Lee in a series of battles known as the Seven Days'.

McClellan's letter went far beyond the description of the state of military affairs that he had led Lincoln to expect. Instead, McClellan argued against confiscation of rebel property and interference with the institution of slavery: "A system of policy thus constitutional and conservative, and pervaded by the influences of Christianity and freedom, would receive the support of almost all truly loyal men, would deeply impress the rebel masses and all foreign nations, and it might be humbly hoped that it would commend itself to the favor of the Almighty." McClellan continued that victory was possible only if the president was pledged to such a policy. "A declaration of radical views, especially upon slavery, will rapidly disintegrate our present Armies" making further recruitment "almost hopeless."[111]

Advice from a general, no matter how inappropriate, is one thing. But for a general to act on his own without consulting his commander in chief smacks of insubordination. In early June 1862, while the Army of the Potomac was still moving toward Richmond, McClellan had designated his aide, Col. Thomas Key, to represent him in prisoner-of-war negotiations with the Confederates, represented by Howell Cobb. But McClellan went far beyond the issue at hand, authorizing Key to investigate the possibility of peace between the sections.

In response to Cobb's assertion that Southern rights could be protected only by independence, Key replied that "the President, the army, and the people" had no thought of subjugating the South but only desired to uphold the Constitution and enforce the laws equally in the States. McClellan apparently thought it was part of his duty to negotiate with the enemy on the terms for ending hostilities and to explain to that enemy the policies and objectives of his commander in chief without letting the latter know that he was doing so.

McClellan did not try to hide his efforts at peace negotiations from Lincoln. Indeed, he filed Key's report with Secretary of War Stanton and asked him to give it to the president. Stanton acceded to McClellan's request but reminded him that "it is not deemed proper for officers bearing flags of truce in respect to the exchange of prisoners to hold any conference with the rebel officers upon the general subject of the existing contest."[112]

McClellan's generalship was characterized by a notable lack of aggressiveness. He was accused of tarrying when John Pope's Army of Virginia was being handled very roughly by Lee at Second Manassas. Indeed, one of his corps commanders, Fitz-John Porter, clearly serving as a surrogate for McClellan, was court-martialed for his alleged failure to come to Pope's aid quickly enough. A month later, McClellan was accused of letting Lee slip away to fight another day after Antietam, and after another bout of inactivity, Lincoln relieved him.

Although there is little evidence to support the Republicans' charge that his lack of aggressiveness arose out of a near-treasonous sympathy for the South, McClellan's language and that of some of his officers was often intemperate. McClellan wrote his wife that "I have commenced receiving letters from the North urging me to march on Washington & assume the Govt!!"[113] He also wrote her about the possibility of a "coup" after which "everything will be changed in this country so far as we are concerned & my enemies will be at my feet."[114]

He did not limit the expression of such sentiments to private correspondence with his wife. Lincoln and his cabinet were aware of the rumors that McClellan intended to put "his sword across the government's policy." McClellan's quartermaster general, Montgomery Meigs, expressed concern about "officers of rank" in the Army of the Potomac who spoke openly of "a march on Washington to 'clear out those fellows.'"[115] Such loose talk did not help McClellan or his army in Lincoln's eyes.

Lincoln understood that he must take action in order to remind the army of his constitutional role. He did so by disciplining Maj. John Key, aide-de-camp to Major General Halleck and brother of McClellan's aide, the aforementioned Col. Thomas Key. Lincoln wrote to Major Key stating that he had learned that the latter had said, in response to a query from a brother officer as to "why . . . the rebel army [was not] bagged immediately after the battle near Sharpsburg [Antietam]," that "that is not the game. The object is that neither army shall get much advantage of the other; that both shall be kept in the field till they are exhausted, when we will make a compromise and save slavery."

Lincoln dismissed Major Key from the service, despite pleas for leniency (and the fact that his son had been killed at Perryville), writing in his record of the event that "it is wholly inadmissible for any gentleman holding a military commission from the United States to utter such sentiments as Major Key is within proved to have done."[116] He remarked to his secretary, John Hay, "that if there was a 'game' ever among Union men, to have our army not take an advantage of the enemy when it could, it was his object to break up that game." At last recognizing the danger of such loose talk on the part of his officers and soldiers, McClellan issued a general order calling for the subordination of the military to civil authority. "The remedy for political errors, if any are committed, is to be found only in the action of the people at the polls."[117]

It is easy to criticize McClellan, but his view of the war was not uncommon during its early phases. Even Lincoln deplored the potential resort to a "remorseless revolutionary struggle" against the South. But by the summer of 1862, he realized that the Confederacy would not relent unless the character of the war changed. There were substantial political risks for Lincoln and the Republicans, but he concluded that the only way to save the Union was to ratchet up the pressure. The successful Union generals were those who adapted to the changing circumstances. McClellan was not one of them.

One of the enduring fictions of the Civil War is that early in the war Lincoln had to weed out incompetent generals before he found Grant and Sherman, while the Confederates were blessed from the outset with superior talent. The fact is that there was only one successful Confederate army—the Army of Northern Virginia under Lee. Its western counterpart, the Army of Tennessee, was consistently defeated by Union forces.

So why did it take Lincoln so long to find his general? Why did Lincoln rely on McClellan rather than Grant or Sherman in 1862? The answer is that Grant's greatness was not apparent in 1862. Neither was Sherman's. In fact, in 1862 there was little difference between McClellan and Grant concerning how to conduct the war. But Grant changed his view after the bloodletting at Shiloh. He realized that the South could only be subdued by hard fighting. McClellan still believed in "soft" war.

In addition, neither Grant nor Sherman acquitted themselves particularly well in battle during the early phases of the war. Grant had won a victory at Belmont, Missouri, and captured Forts Henry and Donelson. He was also the victor at Shiloh, but both he and Sherman had been badly surprised at that battle. Grant's army was very nearly destroyed. Thus it is unfair to both Lincoln and McClellan to compare the latter in 1862 to Grant and Sherman in 1864. Under the circumstances that prevailed at the beginning of the conflict, McClellan was Lincoln's only real choice.[118]

Most of Lincoln's personnel choices make a great deal of sense when examined in context. Lincoln's first general in chief was Winfield Scott, recognized as the greatest American soldier between Washington and Grant.[119]

But Scott, who had conducted a brilliant campaign that culminated in the capture of Mexico City during the Mexican War, was old and infirm when the Civil War began. Scott formulated the first Union strategy, the so-called Anaconda Plan, which provided the framework for the conduct of the war. But Lincoln was dissatisfied with Scott's advice regarding Fort Sumter, and the old general clearly lacked the necessary vigor to provide the required military leadership.

Lincoln replaced Scott as general in chief with McClellan. The latter's record was exemplary. He was first in his class at West Point, had served with distinction during the Mexican War, had been sent as an observer of the Crimean War, and after resigning his commission had risen to president of the Illinois Central Railroad. At the outbreak of the war, McClellan had been offered command of the military forces of several states. He chose Ohio. He had defeated Confederate forces under Lee in western Virginia (now West Virginia), becoming the Union's first military hero. Accordingly, Lincoln appointed him both general in chief (overall commander of all Union armies) and commanding general of the Army of the Potomac (command of a single field army). When Lincoln expressed concern that both jobs were too much for one man, McClellan replied, "I can do it all."[120]

But Lincoln was right. As a field commander, McClellan could not properly carry out his tasks as general in chief, so Lincoln replaced him with Henry Halleck in the spring of 1862. Halleck was a true military intellectual who was commander of the Department of Missouri when Lincoln tapped him for general in chief. It was he who formulated the plan to use the Tennessee River as the "main line of operation" by which Union forces outflanked Confederate forces on the Mississippi River and in Kentucky. But as general in chief, Halleck was a disappointment to Lincoln, acting primarily as a conduit for communications between Lincoln and his generals.

Lincoln replaced Halleck with Grant in 1864. Grant was by far the Union's most successful field commander. After snatching victory from the jaws of defeat at Shiloh in April 1862, he led his Army of the Tennessee to victories at Corinth and Iuka in the fall of that year, and after a masterful campaign captured Vicksburg in July 1863. He subsequently was elevated to commander of Union armies in the West, in which capacity he oversaw the capture of Chattanooga in November of 1863. As general in chief, Grant implemented Lincoln's strategy of concentration in time. During the Virginia Campaign of spring–summer 1864 and the siege of Petersburg, he made his headquarters in the field with the Army of the Potomac, largely because Lincoln had never quite forgiven its commander, George Meade, for failing to pursue Lee more vigorously after Gettysburg.[121]

One of Lincoln's great strengths as commander in chief was his decisiveness in relieving failed generals. In this he differed greatly from the Confederate president. In 1862 he relieved not only McClellan, but also John Pope after Second Manassas, Don Carlos Buell as commander of the Army of the Ohio (later renamed the Army of the Cumberland), and Ambrose Burnside, McClellan's successor, after the disaster at Fredericksburg. In 1863 he relieved Joseph Hooker as commander of the Army of the Potomac early in the Gettysburg campaign and William S. Rosecrans after his Army of the Cumberland was mauled at Chickamauga. Lincoln described him as "confused and stunned, like a duck hit on the head."[122]

In contrast, Jefferson Davis left Braxton Bragg in command of the Army of Tennessee long after his leadership was compromised by the opposition and resentment of his subordinate commanders. Davis's attitude toward his generals was driven by personality. One of the reasons Davis did not relieve Bragg was gratitude: he believed that Bragg had saved his life during the Mexican War. On the other hand, Davis fought with generals Joseph Johnston and P. G. T. Beauregard over supposed personal affronts.[123]

Lincoln never let pride, sentiment, or his personal opinion of an officer get in the way of his assessment of that officer's military potential. He was willing to accept a great deal from his generals if they would give him victory. This is illustrated by two cases. On one occasion, Lincoln visited McClellan at his headquarters. McClellan was not present when the president arrived, so Lincoln waited. When McClellan returned, he went directly upstairs, although he knew Lincoln was there. Sometime later, McClellan sent an orderly to advise Lincoln that the general had retired for the evening.[124] When John Hay criticized the president for permitting such an affront, Lincoln replied that "it was better at this time not to be making points of etiquette and personal dignity."[125]

An even more striking example is the letter that Lincoln sent to Maj. Gen. Joseph Hooker when he appointed him commanding general of the Army of the Potomac in early 1863:

> I have placed you at the head of the Army of the Potomac. Of course
> I have done this upon what appear to be sufficient reasons. And yet I

think it best for you to know that there are some things in regard to which, I am not quite satisfied with you. I believe you to be a brave and a skillful soldier, which, of course, I like. I also believe you do not mix politics with your profession, in which you are right. You have confidence in yourself, which is a valuable, if not an indispensable quality. You are ambitious, which, within reasonable bounds, does good rather than harm. But I think that during Gen. Burnside's command of the Army, you have taken counsel of your ambition, and thwarted him as much as you could, in which you did a great wrong to the country, and to a most meritorious and honorable brother officer. I have heard, in such a way as to believe it, of your recently saying that both the Army and the Government needed a Dictator. Of course it was not *for* this, but in spite of it, that I have given you command. Only those generals who gain successes, can set up dictators. What I now ask of you is military success, and I will risk the dictatorship. The government will support you to the utmost of its ability, which is neither more nor less than it has done and will do for all commanders. I much fear that the spirit which you have aided to infuse into the Army of criticizing their Commander, and withholding confidence from him, will now turn upon you. I shall assist you as far as I can, to put it down. Neither you, nor Napoleon, if he were alive again, could get any good out of an army, while such a spirit prevails in it.

And now, beware of rashness. Beware of rashness, but with energy, and sleepless vigilance, go forward, and give us victories.[126]

One of the major challenges Lincoln faced with regard to his choices for high command was to satisfy the demands of different groups within the electorate whose support he needed to prosecute the war, especially War Democrats and German Americans. For instance, one of the reasons that Lincoln did not sack McClellan sooner was that such a move would have agitated the Democrats, who revered him as an obstacle to what they took to be the radical policies of the Republicans and their abolitionist allies. These, the Democrats believed, were destined to ruin the Union and lose the war.

On occasion, this need for balance created problems. For example, in the fall of 1862, Grant was preparing for a move south along the Mississippi Central Railroad to capture Vicksburg. Meanwhile, John McClernand, a

War Democrat and friend of Lincoln's from Illinois, convinced the president to permit him to raise an independent command in the Northwest also for action against Vicksburg. McClernand argued that Grant was moving too slowly and that raising the new force would rekindle the patriotism of the Northwest in the wake of the unpopular preliminary Emancipation Proclamation.

When Grant got wind of McClernand's actions, he telegraphed General in Chief Halleck for clarification of his authority. Halleck assured Grant that he had control of all troops in his department and then organized McClernand's force into two corps subordinate to Grant. McClernand complained to Lincoln, but the president backed Grant.[127]

In general Lincoln performed effectively as a military leader. He understood what had to be done and then found the generals who could implement his vision. The Union may have possessed a material edge over the Confederacy, but it was necessary to develop and implement a strategy that would translate this advantage into victory. This Lincoln did.

Prudence and War

What can we say about Abraham Lincoln as war president? First and foremost, that he saved the Union. It is hard to imagine that anyone else among his contemporaries could have done what he did. Many were willing to let the Union go to pieces. Who knows how many "confederacies" there would now be on the North American continent had the view of James Buchanan and the Peace Democrats prevailed? Who knows when slavery would have ended? Who knows what would have become of a world without a United States to oppose a Hitler and a Stalin?

Many others would have pursued policies that lacked any element of consent. As Lincoln remarked on numerous occasions, public sentiment is critically important in a republic. In the absence of public sentiment, legislators cannot pass laws and presidents cannot execute them. Lincoln could have avoided war by making another of the base concessions that politicians had been making for several decades. But that would only have postponed the day of decision, making it unlikely that republican government could survive in North America and, since the United States was the "last, best hope of earth," making it unlikely that republican government could survive *anywhere*.

Lincoln's war presidency teaches us that, as important as institutions may be, by themselves they do not save republics when they are threatened. Lincoln's war presidency teaches us the necessity of prudence for successful democratic statesmanship. Lincoln's war presidency teaches us that citizens of a democratic republic respond to strong, principled leadership in time of crisis.

Lincoln set a high standard for leadership in time of war. He called forth the resources of the nation, he appointed the agents of victory, both civilian and military, he set the strategy, he took the necessary steps to restrain those who would cooperate with the disunionists, and he provided the rhetoric that stirred the people. Yet he did these things within a constitutional framework.

In our time, we face issues similar to those that confronted Lincoln. Once again we face the perennial tension between vigilance and responsibility as the United States is the target of those who would destroy it. In all decisions involving trade-offs between two things of value, the costs and benefits of one alternative must be measured against the costs and benefits of the other. At a time when the United States once again faced an adversary who wished nothing less than its destruction, President George W. Bush correctly took his bearing from Lincoln, whose war presidency taught that prudence dictates that responsibility trumps vigilance in time of war. If those responsible for the preservation of the republic are not permitted the measures to save it, there will be nothing left to be vigilant about.

Notes

An earlier version of this essay was published as "Abraham Lincoln: Leadership and Democratic Statesmanship in Wartime," *Orbis* (January 2009). Used by permission of the Foreign Policy Research Institute.

1. Abraham Lincoln, "Proclamation Calling Militia and Convening Congress" (April 15, 1861), *Collected Works of Abraham Lincoln,* ed. Roy P. Basler, 8 vols. plus index (New Brunswick, NJ: Rutgers University Press, 1953), 4:332. Hereinafter cited as *CW.*

2. James M. McPherson, *Tried by War: Abraham Lincoln as Commander in Chief* (New York: Penguin, 2008), 4–5.

3. Abraham Lincoln, "To the Senate and House of Representatives" (May 26, 1862), in *CW,* 5:241. Cf. Abraham Lincoln, "Message to Congress in Special Session" (July 4, 1861), in *Abraham Lincoln: His Speeches and Writings,* ed. Roy P. Basler (New York: Da Capo Press, n.d.), 594–609. Hereinafter

cited as *AL*. Since this collection is more accessible than *CW*, I will cite *AL* whenever possible.

4. Abraham Lincoln, "To Horace Greeley" (August 22, 1862), in *AL*, 652.

5. This passage is usually cited as an illustration of the claim that Lincoln was not really interested in the fate of slavery. But as numerous historians have shown, Lincoln had already begun work on an emancipation proclamation. At a minimum, such a presidential proclamation was required by the Second Confiscation Act, which Lincoln signed on July 17, 1862.

6. Abraham Lincoln, "Fragment: The Constitution and Union" [1860?], in *CW*, 4:169.

7. Proverbs 25:11: "A word fitly spoken is like apples of gold in pictures [or frames] of silver."

8. A number of writers have commented on the importance of this fragment for understanding Lincoln's actions as war president. See Herman Belz, *Lincoln and the Constitution: The Dictatorship Question Reconsidered* (Fort Wayne, IN: Louis A. Warren Lincoln Library and Museum, 1984), 19–20, and Walter Berns, "Constitutional Power and the Defense of Free Government," in *Terrorism: How the West Can Win*, ed. Benjamin Netanyahu (New York: Farrar, Straus and Giroux, 1986), 154.

9. Aristotle, *Aristotle's Nichomachean Ethics*, trans. Robert C. Bartlett and Susan D. Collins, book V (Chicago: University of Chicago Press, 2011).

10. On Lincoln's constitutionalism, see Daniel Farber, *Lincoln's Constitution* (Chicago: University of Chicago Press, 2003), and Mark E. Neely, *Lincoln and the Triumph of the Nation: Constitutional Conflict in the American Civil War* (Chapel Hill: University of North Carolina Press, 2011).

11. Don E. Fehrenbacher, "Lincoln and the Constitution," in *The Public and Private Lincoln: Contemporary Perspectives*, ed. Cullom Davis (Carbondale: Southern Illinois University Press, 1979), 127.

12. Geoffrey Perret, *Lincoln's War: The Untold Story of America's Greatest President as Commander in Chief* (New York: Random House, 2004), xiii.

13. Abraham Lincoln, "To James C. Conkling" (August 26, 1863), in *AL*, 721.

14. Edward S. Corwin, *Total War and the Constitution* (New York: Knopf, 1947), and Raoul Berger, *Executive Privilege: A Constitutional Myth* (Cambridge, MA: Harvard University Press, 1974).

15. "To Caesar A. Rodney," in *Jefferson: Writings*, ed. Merrill Peterson (New York: Library of America, 1984), 1218.

16. John Locke, *Second Treatise of Civil Government*, various editions, chap. 15, "Of Prerogative," sec. 160 (emphasis added).

17. Ibid., sec. 159 (emphasis added).

18. "To John Colvin," in Peterson, *Jefferson: Writings*, 1231–33.

19. Lincoln, "Message to Congress in Special Session," 600–601.

20. Sanford Levinson, "Abraham Lincoln as Constitutionalist: The Decision to Go to War," unpublished manuscript.

21. Abraham Lincoln, "Proclamation Revoking General Hunter's Order of Military Emancipation of May 9, 1862" (May 19, 1862), in *CW*, 5:222.

22. Abraham Lincoln, "Reply to Emancipation Memorial Presented by Chicago Christians of All Denominations" (September 13, 1862), in *CW*, 5:421.

23. Abraham Lincoln, "Response to a Serenade" (October 19, 1864), in *AL*, 761.

24. Abraham Lincoln, "To Erastus Corning and Others" (June 12, 1863), in *AL*, 705.

25. Phillip Shaw Paludan, *The Presidency of Abraham Lincoln* (Lawrence: University Press of Kansas, 1994), 32–33.

26. Abraham Lincoln, "To William Kellogg" (December 11, 1860), in *AL*, 565.

27. Abraham Lincoln, "To John Defrees" (December 18, 1860), in *AL*, 566–67.

28. Abraham Lincoln, "To James T. Hale" (January 11, 1861), in *CW*, 5:172.

29. Abraham Lincoln, "First Inaugural Address" (March 4, 1861), in *AL*, 588.

30. Paludan, *Presidency of Abraham Lincoln*, 49–67; James M. McPherson, *Battle Cry of Freedom: The Civil War Era* (Oxford: Oxford University Press, 1988), 264–75; and Russell McClintock, *Lincoln and the Decision for War: The Northern Response to Secession* (Chapel Hill: University of North Carolina Press, 2008).

31. On whether Lincoln "tricked" the Confederates into firing on Fort Sumter, see, e.g., Charles W. Ramsdell, "Lincoln and Fort Sumter," *Journal of Southern History* 3 (August 1937): 259–88; Richard Nelson Current, *Lincoln and the First Shot* (Philadelphia: Lippincott, 1963); Kenneth M. Stampp, *The Imperiled Union: Essays on the Background of the Civil War* (New York: Oxford University Press, 1980); and McClintock, *Lincoln and the Decision for War*.

32. James Oakes, *Freedom National: The Destruction of Slavery in the United States, 1861–1865* (New York: Norton, 2013), xxi. For the argument that Lincoln and the Radicals were closer than normally portrayed, see James Oakes, *The Radical and the Republican: Frederick Douglass, Abraham Lincoln, and the Triumph of Antislavery Politics* (New York: Norton, 2008). For the contrary view, see T. Harry Williams, *Lincoln and the Radicals* (Madison: University of Wisconsin Press, 1965 [1941]). Williams argues that the typical Radical was not a "normal political type," calling the Radicals "Jacobins"—true revolutionaries whose program differed substantially from that of Lincoln.

33. On building the cabinet, see Paludan, *Presidency of Abraham Lincoln*, chap. 2. The definitive study of Lincoln's cabinet is Doris Kearns Goodwin,

Team of Rivals: The Political Genius of Abraham Lincoln (New York: Simon & Schuster, 2006).

34. Abraham Lincoln, "Reply to Secretary Seward's Memorandum" (April 1, 1862), in *AL*, 590–91.

35. For a succinct treatment of the Northern war economy and Chase's work as financier of the war, see McPherson, *Battle Cry of Freedom*, 442–50.

36. Carl von Clausewitz, *On War*, ed. and trans. Michael Howard and Peter Paret (Princeton, NJ: Princeton University Press, 1976), 131–32.

37. See Benjamin P. Thomas and Harold M. Hyman, *Stanton: The Life and Times of Lincoln's Secretary of War* (New York: Knopf, 1962).

38. Cf. Allan Nevins, *The War for the Union*, 4 vols. (New York: Charles Scribner's Sons, 1959–1971), especially volumes three and four, and Herman Hattaway and Archer Jones, *How the North Won: A Military History of the Civil War* (Urbana: University of Illinois Press, 1983).

39. McPherson, *Battle Cry of Freedom*, 574–75, and Paludan, *Presidency of Abraham Lincoln*, chap. 8.

40. See Bruce Tap, *Over Lincoln's Shoulder: The Committee on the Conduct of the War* (Lawrence: University Press of Kansas), and Bill Hyde, ed., *The Union Generals Speak: The Meade Hearings on the Battle of Gettysburg* (Baton Rouge: Louisiana State University Press, 2003).

41. On Reconstruction, see, e.g., Kenneth M. Stampp, *The Era of Reconstruction, 1865–1877* (New York: Knopf, 1965); Eric Foner, *Reconstruction: America's Unfinished Revolution, 1863–1877* (New York: Harper & Row, 1988); Michael Perman, *Emancipation and Reconstruction*, 2nd ed. (Wheeling, IL: Harlan Davidson, 2003 [1987]); and Michael Les Benedict, *The Fruits of Victory: Alternatives in Restoring the Union, 1865–1877* (Lanham, MD: University Press of America, 1986).

42. Abraham Lincoln, "Proclamation of Amnesty and Reconstruction" (December 8, 1863), in *AL*, 738–41.

43. Stampp, *Era of Reconstruction*, 76.

44. The most prominent of the skeptics has been the late Frank Klement, who argued that what Lincoln called the Copperhead "fire in the rear" was mostly "a fairy tale," a "figment of Republican imagination" made up of "lies, conjecture and political malignancy." Frank Klement, *The Copperheads in the Middle West* (Chicago: University of Chicago Press, 1960); *The Limits of Dissent: Clement L. Vallandigham and the Civil War* (New York: Fordham University Press, 1998); and *Lincoln's Critics: The Copperheads of the North* (Shippensburg, PA: White Mane Books, 1999).

45. Jennifer L. Weber, *Copperheads: The Rise and Fall of Lincoln's Opponents in the North* (New York: Oxford University Press, 2006).

46. John H. Brinton, *Personal Memoirs of John H. Brinton: Civil War Surgeon, 1861–1865* (Carbondale: Southern Illinois University Press, 1996 [1914]), 239.

47. For a concise treatment of the Virginia Overland Campaign of 1864, see Mark Grimsley, *And Keep Moving On: The Virginia Campaign, May–June, 1864* (Lincoln: University of Nebraska Press, 2002).

48. Cited in McPherson, *Battle Cry of Freedom,* 771.

49. Abraham Lincoln, "Memorandum concerning His Probable Failure of Re-election" (August 23, 1864), in *CW,* 7:414. See also John G. Nicolay and John Hay, *Abraham Lincoln: A History,* 10 vols. (New York: Century, 1890), 9:221.

50. Cited in McPherson, *Battle Cry of Freedom,* 772.

51. Robert W. Coakley, *The Role of Federal Military Forces in Domestic Disorders, 1789–1878* (Washington, DC: Center of Military History, US Army, 1988), 227–67.

52. Cited in Weber, *Copperheads,* 69.

53. See, e.g., J. G. Randall, *Constitutional Problems under Lincoln,* rev. ed. (Urbana: University of Illinois Press, 1951); Paul Finkelman, "Civil Liberties and the Civil War: The Great Emancipator as Civil Libertarian," *Michigan Law Review* 91 (1993); Mark E. Neely Jr., *The Fate of Liberty: Abraham Lincoln and Civil Liberties* (Oxford: Oxford University Press, 1991); Farber, *Lincoln's Constitution*; and Frank J. Williams, "Abraham Lincoln, Civil Liberties, and the Corning Letter," *Roger Williams University Law Review* 5, no. 2 (Spring 2000). Jonathan White's splendid book is must reading for understanding the complexities regarding how a republic deals with treason and disloyalty: *Abraham Lincoln and Treason in the Civil War: The Trials of John Merryman* (Baton Rouge: Louisiana State University Press, 2011).

54. Lincoln, "Message to Congress in Special Session," 598.

55. See Karl-Friedrich Walling, *Republican Empire: Alexander Hamilton on War and Free Government* (Lawrence: University Press of Kansas, 1999), 6–12.

56. Draft of the Kentucky Resolution, October 1798, in Peterson, *Jefferson: Writings,* 454.

57. Hamilton to James Duane (September 3, 1780), in *The Papers of Alexander Hamilton,* 26 vols., ed. Harold G. Syrett and Jacob E. Cooke (New York: Columbia University Press, 1961), 2:404.

58. Alexander Hamilton, *The Federalist Papers,* ed. Clinton Rossiter (New York: Penguin, 1999), essay no. 23, 149–51.

59. Lincoln, "To Erastus Corning and Others," 699–708.

60. Mark E. Neely, *Southern Rights: Political Prisoners and the Myth of Confederate Constitutionalism* (Charlottesville: University of Virginia Press, 1999). See also Daniel Sutherland, ed., *Guerrillas, Unionists, and Violence on the Confederate Home Front* (Fayetteville: University of Arkansas Press, 1999).

61. We should not be surprised that the Confederacy's commitment to civil liberties in wartime was no greater than that of the North. The fact is that, the Lost Cause narrative's portrayal of the South as united against Yankee tyranny notwithstanding, dissent was widespread within the seceded states.

While Lincoln faced opposition primarily from Peace Democrats or Copperheads, Unionists in the South did many of the same sorts of things that Copperheads did in the North. Some Unionists, like their Copperhead counterparts up North, limited their dissent to political opposition. As Daniel Sutherland writes, "the most staunch wartime Unionists—the so-called 'tories'—endorsed Union political ideology, encouraged hostility to the Confederacy, and sought to end the war at all costs." Sutherland, *Guerrillas, Unionists, and Violence on the Confederate Home Front*, 4.

Unionist sentiment was most prevalent in eastern Tennessee, western Virginia, and western North Carolina, but there were also Unionist enclaves in northern Louisiana, Mississippi, and Alabama, as well as in central Texas. It is a little recognized fact that, with the exception of South Carolina, every seceded state provided at least one regiment of white troops to the Union cause.

As the war dragged on and the appalling human and material cost of the war began to mount, even many loyal Confederates began to turn against it. As in the North, conscription constituted a flash point. It is sometimes forgotten that the South turned to conscription a year earlier than the North did. The exemption of large slave owners from the draft, the "20 [slave] law," fed dissent and led to the often-voiced complaint that the conflict was "a rich man's war, but a poor man's fight."

Desertion was a problem for both sides, but as the war began to turn against the South, it became an epidemic in the Confederacy. Confederate generals, including the gentlemanly Robert E. Lee, did not hesitate to shoot deserters, but even the prospect of such a punishment did not stanch the loss of manpower to the Confederate cause.

Attempts by the Confederate government to do so, along with other efforts to suppress dissent in the seceded states—including intimidation by Confederate soldiers, local militias or "home guards," conscription and impressment agents, and "watchful secessionist neighbors"—often erupted into guerrilla warfare carried out against not only progovernment civilians but also rebel military units.

62. Fehrenbacher, "Lincoln and the Constitution," 130–31.

63. On Jefferson Davis, see William C. Davis, *Jefferson Davis: The Man and His Hour: A Biography* (New York: HarperCollins, 1991).

64. Abraham Lincoln, "The Presidential Question: Speech in the United States House of Representatives" (July 27, 1848), in *AL*, 242.

65. Abraham Lincoln, "The War with Mexico: Speech in the United States House of Representatives" (January 12, 1848), in *AL*, 202–15.

66. See Kenneth P. Williams, *Lincoln Finds a General: A Military Study of the Civil War*, 5 vols. (New York: Macmillan, 1949–1958). Although T. Harry Williams praises Lincoln as a strategist as well as a sound judge of men, his book *Lincoln and His Generals* (New York: Knopf, 1952) belongs primarily in this category.

67. McPherson, *Tried by War*, and Eliot A. Cohen, "Lincoln Sends a Letter," chap. 2 of his *Supreme Command: Soldiers, Statesmen, and Leadership in Wartime* (New York: Free Press, 2002).

68. On the relationship between strategy and policy, see Mackubin Thomas Owens, "Strategy and the Strategic Way of Thinking," *Naval War College Review* (Autumn 2007). In their military history of the United States, Allan Millett and Peter Maslowski define defense policy as "the sum of the assumptions, plans, programs, and actions taken by the citizens of the United States, principally through governmental action, to ensure the physical security of their lives, property, and way of life from external military attack and domestic insurrection." Allan R. Millett and Peter Maslowski, *For the Common Defense: A Military History of the United States of America*, rev. ed. (New York: Free Press, 1994 [1984]), xiii. For the purpose of this chapter, *policy* refers primarily to such broad national goals as interests and objectives, *strategy* to the alternative courses of actions designed to achieve those goals within constraints set by material factors and geography.

69. Cohen, *Supreme Command*, 22.

70. "War is not the action of a living body on a lifeless mass . . . but always the collision of two living forces." Clausewitz, *On War*, 77.

71. Ibid., 177.

72. On the origins of modern strategy, see Azar Gat, *The Origins of Military Thought: From the Enlightenment to Clausewitz* (Oxford: Clarendon Press, 1989).

73. Mackubin Thomas Owens, "Thinking about Strategy," in *Strategy and Force Planning*, 3rd ed., ed. Strategy and Force Planning Faculty (Newport, RI: Naval War College Press, 2000), 426–34.

74. Williamson Murray and Mark Grimsley, "On Strategy," in *The Making of Strategy: Rulers, States, and War*, ed. Williamson Murray, Elvin Bernstein, and MacGregor Knox (Cambridge: Cambridge University Press, 1994).

75. Clausewitz, *On War*, 177.

76. Williams, *Lincoln and His Generals*, vii.

77. McPherson, *Tried by War*, 4.

78. Archer Jones, *Civil War Command and Strategy: The Process of Victory and Defeat* (New York: Free Press, 1992), 99.

79. Abraham Lincoln, "To Don C. Buell" (January 13, 1862), in *CW*, 5:98.

80. Abraham Lincoln, "President's General War Order No. 1" (January 27, 1862), in *CW,* 5:111–12.

81. Ulysses S. Grant, *Personal Memoirs of U.S. Grant* (New York: Library of America, 1990 [1885]), 486.

82. Abraham Lincoln, "To Joseph Hooker" (June 19, 1863), in *CW,* 6:257.

83. For a succinct but complete treatment of the Civil War in the western theater (the Mississippi to the Appalachians), see Steven E. Woodworth, *Decision in the Heartland: The Civil War in the West* (Westport, CT: Praeger, 2008).

84. This is the realm of "grand strategy," which is designed to bring to bear all the elements of national power—military, economic, and diplomatic—in order to secure the nation's interests and objectives.

85. Oakes, *Freedom National,* 283.

86. Abraham Lincoln, "To Orville Browning" (September 22, 1861), in *CW,* 4:531.

87. Ibid., 532.

88. Oakes, *Freedom National,* 1–48 and *passim.* In June 1859 Lincoln wrote Gov. Salmon P. Chase regarding Ohio's Republican Party platform, which called for the "repeal of the atrocious Fugitive Slave Law":

> Although I think congress has constitutional authority to enact a Fugitive Slave law, I have never elaborated an opinion upon the subject. My view has been, and is, simply this: The U.S. constitution says the fugitive slave "shall be delivered up" but it does not expressly say who shall deliver him up. Whatever the constitution says "shall be done" and has omitted saying who shall do it, the government established by that constitution, *ex vi termini,* is vested with the power of doing; and congress is, by the constitution, expressly empowered to make all laws which shall be necesary and proper for carrying into execution all powers vested by the constitution in the government of the United States. This would be my view, on a simple reading of the constitution; and it is greatly strengthened by the historical fact that the constitution was adopted, in great part, in order to get a government which could execute it's own behests, in contradistinction to that under the Articles of confederation, which depended, in many respects, upon the States, for its' execution; and the other fact that one of the earliest congresses, under the constitution, did enact a Fugitive Slave law. [Misspellings and capitalization in original.]

Abraham Lincoln, "To Salmon P. Chase" (June 20, 1859), in *CW,* 3:386. See also Abraham Lincoln, "To Salmon P. Chase" (June 9, 1859), in *CW,* 3:384.

89. Oakes, *Freedom National,* 34–42.

90. Abraham Lincoln, "Message to Congress on Gradual Abolishment of Slavery" (March 6, 1862), in *CW,* 5:144–46. Cf. Allen C. Guelzo, *Lincoln's*

Emancipation Proclamation: The End of Slavery in America (New York: Simon & Schuster, 2004). On the dual approach for attacking slavery during the war, see Oakes, *Freedom National.*

91. Abraham Lincoln, "To Cuthbert Bullitt" (July 28, 1862), in *AL,* 650. On the relation between the two confiscation acts passed by Congress and Lincoln's Emancipation Proclamation, see Oakes, *Freedom National,* 225–35.

92. Guelzo, *Lincoln's Emancipation Proclamation,* 29–59.

93. Ibid., 54.

94. Ibid., passim.

95. For an excellent and complete account of Lincoln and the Supreme Court in wartime, see Brian McGinty, *Lincoln and the Court* (Cambridge, MA: Harvard University Press, 2008).

96. T. J. Barnett, in *Recollected Words of Abraham Lincoln,* ed. Don E. Fehrenbacher and Virginia Fehrenbacher (Stanford, CA: Stanford University Press, 1996), 23.

97. Abraham Lincoln, "To August Belmont" (July 31, 1862), in *CW,* 5:350–51.

98. On the Emancipation Proclamation as a war measure, see Burrus M. Carnahan, *Act of Justice: Lincoln's Emancipation Proclamation and the Law of War* (Lexington: University Press of Kentucky, 2007). John Fabian Witt has demonstrated how the Lincoln administration's attempt to regulate the conduct of war by issuing General Orders 100—the "Lieber Code"—also advanced the Union war effort and supported emancipation. The Lieber Code was "not just a humanitarian shield . . . [but] also a sword of justice, a way of advancing the Emancipation Proclamation and of arming 200,000 black soldiers who would help end slavery once and for all." John Fabian Witt, *Lincoln's Code: The Laws of War in American History* (New York: Free Press, 2012), 4.

99. Halleck to Grant (March 31, 1863), in *The War of the Rebellion: A Compilation of the Official Records of the Union and Confederate Armies,* ser. 1, vol. XXIV, pt. 3, 157; hereinafter cited as *OR.*

100. Gideon Welles, "The History of Emancipation," *The Galaxy* 14 (December 1872), 842–43.

101. See Dudley Taylor Cornish, *The Sable Arm: Black Troops in the Union Army, 1861–1865* (Lawrence: University Press of Kansas, 1987 [1957]).

102. The importance of former slaves fighting for their freedom is revealed by examining a story recounted by the Greek historian Herodotus. At the beginning of Book Four of *The History,* Herodotus tells of the return of the nomadic Scythians from their long war against the Medes, during which time the Scythian women had taken up with their slaves. The Scythian warriors now find a race of slaves arrayed against them.

Having been repulsed repeatedly by the slaves, one of the Scythians admonishes his fellows to set aside their weapons and take up horsewhips. "As long as they are used to seeing us with arms, they think that they are our equals and that their fathers are likewise our equals. Let them see us with whips instead of arms, and they will learn that they are our slaves; and, once they have realized that, they will not stand their ground against us."

The tactic works. The slaves are bewildered by the whip-wielding Scythians, lose their fighting spirit, and flee in terror. The implication of Herodotus's story is clear. There are natural masters and natural slaves. A slave has the soul of a slave and lacks the manliness to fight for his freedom, especially if a master never deigns to treat him as a man. Herodotus, *The History*, trans. David Grene (Chicago: University of Chicago Press, 1987), 280.

The Scythian view is reflected in a comment by Howell Cobb of Georgia: "The day you make soldiers of niggers is the beginning of the end of the revolution. If slaves will make good soldiers our whole theory of slavery is wrong." *OR*, ser. 4, vol. III, 1009–1010. Thus their performance under arms was important to make it clear that blacks were not the natural slaves that Southerners, and in fact many Northerners, believed them to be.

103. Abraham Lincoln, "To Andrew Johnson" (March 26, 1863), in *CW*, 6:149–50.

104. Abraham Lincoln, "Annual Message to Congress" (December 1, 1862), in *AL*, 668.

105. Abraham Lincoln, "Henry J. Raymond to Lincoln" (August 22, 1864), in *CW*, 7:517–18.

106. Abraham Lincoln, "Interview with Alexander W. Randall and Joseph T. Mills" (August 19, 1864), in *CW*, 7:507. Cf. Abraham Lincoln, "To Charles D. Robinson" (August 17, 1864), in *CW*, 7:499–501.

107. Lincoln, "To James C. Conkling," 720–24. Cited passage at 723–24.

108. Cohen, *Supreme Command*, chap. 1. The "normal theory" of civil-military relations is developed by Samuel P. Huntington in *The Soldier and the State: The Theory and Politics of Civil-Military Relations* (Cambridge, MA: Harvard University Press, 1957), especially chapter 4. For another critique of Huntington, see Peter D. Feaver, *Armed Servants: Agency, Oversight, and Civil-Military Relations* (Cambridge, MA: Harvard University Press, 2003).

109. See, e.g., Lincoln's letter of February 3, 1862, to McClellan in which he asked for a detailed response to a number of questions about McClellan's plan. *CW*, 5:118–25.

110. Clausewitz, *On War*, 87–88; emphasis in original. Of course, the claim that Lincoln possessed a Clausewitzian understanding of war and the relationship between policy and strategy has been criticized by those who observe that

Lincoln was not familiar with Clausewitz's works. The military theorist most read by Americans at the time was the Baron Antoine Henri Jomini. But one is reminded of a story about Winston Churchill. On one occasion, his friend F. E. Smith gave him a copy of Aristotle's *Nichomachean Ethics*. Later Smith asked Churchill what he thought of the work. Churchill replied that he found it interesting but was amazed at how many of Aristotle's points he had already worked out on his own before reading the book. The point of this anecdote is that while Clausewitz may have described strategy, he did not "invent" it any more than Aristotle "invented" ethics. Any reader of Thucydides understands that the Greeks had the concept of strategy although not necessarily the name. Thus it is possible for Lincoln to have had a Clausewitzian understanding of war and strategy without actually having read Clausewitz.

111. McClellan to Lincoln (July 7, 1862) in *Civil War Papers of George B. McClellan, 1860–1865,* ed. Stephen B. Sears (New York: Ticknor and Fields, 1989), 344, and *OR,* ser. 1, vol. XI, pt. 1, 73.

112. For coverage and discussion of this entire issue, see Joseph Cullen, *The Peninsula Campaign of 1862: McClellan and Lee Struggle for Richmond* (Harrisburg, PA: Stackpole Books, 1973), 69–76, and *OR,* ser. 1, vol. XI, 1052–61.

113. McClellan to Mary Ellen McClellan (July 11, 1862), in Sears, *Civil War Papers,* 351.

114. McClellan to Mary Ellen McClellan (August 10, 1862), in ibid., 390.

115. "General M. C. Meigs on the Conduct of the Civil War," *American Historical Review* 26 (1920–1921), 294.

116. Abraham Lincoln, "Record of Dismissal of John J. Key" (September 26–27, 1862), in *CW,* 5:442–43.

117. *OR,* ser. 1, vol. XIX, pt. 2, 295–96.

118. See Thomas J. Rowland, *George B. McClellan and Civil War History: In the Shadow of Grant and Sherman* (Kent, OH: Kent State University Press, 1998).

119. John Eisenhower, *Agent of Destiny: The Life and Times of Winfield Scott* (New York: Free Press, 1997); Timothy D. Johnson, *Winfield Scott: The Quest for Military Glory* (Lawrence: University Press of Kansas, 1998), and Allan Peskin, *Winfield Scott and the Profession of Arms* (Kent, OH: Kent State University Press, 2003).

120. Stephen W. Sears, *George B. McClellan: The Young Napoleon* (New York: Ticknor and Fields, 1988).

121. On some of the difficulties Meade faced, see Eric J. Wittenberg, J. David Petruzzi, and Michael F. Nugent, *One Continuous Fight: The Retreat from Gettysburg and the Pursuit of Lee's Army of Northern Virginia, July 4–14, 1863* (New York: Savas Beatie, 2008).

122. Tyler Dennett, ed., *Lincoln and the Civil War in the Diaries and Letters of John Hay* (New York: Da Capo, n.d. [1939]), 106.

123. William Davis, *Jefferson Davis;* Steven E. Woodworth, *Jefferson Davis and His Generals: The Failure of Confederate Command in the West* (Lawrence: University Press of Kansas, 1990); and James I. Robertson Jr., "Braxton Bragg: The Lonely Patriot," in *Leader of the Lost Cause: New Perspectives on the Confederate High Command,* ed. Gary W. Gallagher and Joseph T. Glatthaar (Mechanicsburg, PA: Stackpole Books, 2004).

124. Perret, *Lincoln's War,* 110.

125. Fehrenbacher and Fehrenbacher, *Recollected Words,* 208. The Fehrenbachers judged as inauthentic a similar anecdote related by Perret (ibid., 111) that when McClellan did not attend a meeting with the president, Lincoln responded, "Never mind. I will hold McClellan's horse if he will only bring us success." *Recollected Words,* 332.

126. Abraham Lincoln, "To Joseph Hooker" (January 26, 1863), in *CW,* 6:78–79.

127. McPherson, *Battle Cry of Freedom,* 577–78; Abraham Lincoln, "To John A. McClernand" (January 22, 1863), in *CW,* 6:70–71; and Grant, *Personal Memoirs,* 282–95.

12

Lincoln's Executive Discretion

The Preservation of Political Constitutionalism

Benjamin A. Kleinerman

Both Abraham Lincoln's exercise of executive power and his defense of that exercise are the most paradoxical aspects of his presidency. Summing up one of the essential paradoxes, Wilfred Binkley writes: "Surely no one could have guessed that in this harassing critic of the war policy of President [James K.] Polk there lurked even the possibility of a war President who was to deal with Congress and the Constitution at times in a manner more imperious than any President before or since."[1] That is, in the first place, Lincoln's exercise of executive power, or what might be called a "prerogative" power, is paradoxical because it seems to contradict the Whiggish aversion to a strong executive that characterized his earlier political career. Of course, there would be no paradox if Lincoln simply abandoned his earlier Whiggishness in favor of an embrace of that power he now possessed. But I will suggest that Lincoln, in a certain sense, always remains a Whig, despite the fact that he was willing to exercise *and defend* a far-reaching discretionary executive power during the Civil War.[2]

The second paradox of Lincoln's exercise of executive power is related to the first. Lincoln is frequently considered one of the presidents most aware of and even committed to the Constitution.[3] Yet this same president seemed to violate the Constitution in a myriad of different manners.[4] Again, as with his Whiggishness, this paradox would simply be a contradiction if Lincoln chose simply to abandon his constitutional devotion once he became president. This is true even if we excuse Lincoln's abandonment of the Constitution by pointing to the necessities of winning the Civil War. I will suggest further that this paradox remains a contradiction even if we attempt to excuse or explain away Lincoln's abandonment of the Constitution by his embrace of the doctrine of the "adequate Constitution."[5] Formulated as it was by many of the Radical Republicans during and after the Civil War—as a doctrine of nearly unlimited governmental power to do what is necessary to preserve the Union and make it prosper—the doctrine of the adequate Constitution no longer remains meaningfully constitutional.[6] Instead, Lincoln's exercise of extensive presidential discretion remains paradoxical precisely because he came to understand it as fully compatible with and, in fact, demanded by his commitment to a limited Constitution.

This claim introduces another important paradox within Lincoln's exercise of executive prerogative. Many scholars have sought to defend Lincoln's actions by noting and applauding his deference to Congress.[7] For instance, Louis Fisher, one of the most famous advocates of congressional power over and against a powerful president, points to Lincoln as his guiding example.[8] For Fisher, Lincoln's continuing devotion to the Constitution is evidenced by his deference to Congress during the Civil War. One can find, however, a very different claim in the earlier work of Wilfred Binkley and Edward Corwin. For instance, Binkley writes: "The high-water mark of the exercise of executive power in the United States is found in the administration of Abraham Lincoln. No President before or since has pushed the boundaries of executive power so far over into the legislative sphere."[9] I will suggest that Binkley and Corwin are much closer to the truth about both Lincoln's exercise of executive power and his defense of that exercise. And those scholars who attempt to defend Lincoln's constitutionalism by noting his deference to Congress must simply ignore much of what he actually did and said after his initial speech to Congress in emergency session in July 1861—a speech in which he did seem to have a deferential tone. Instead, Lincoln adopted a rather "aggressive" stance concerning both the independence of his power relative to Congress and the existence of presidential powers not possessed by Congress.[10] Thus evidence of his commitment to constitutionalism cannot derive from his deference to Congress. Again, if a commitment to constitutionalism requires deference to Congress, then Lincoln's position is not paradoxical—it is contradictory. I will suggest, however, that the paradox lies in Lincoln's belief that *precisely* his commitment to constitutionalism required that he remain both independent of Congress and that he possess powers that Congress does not possess. In other words, the seeming "aggressiveness" of his arguments regarding the scope of executive power followed from his commitment to the limiting aims of a Constitution.

The final paradox in Lincoln's political thought stems from the nature of his constitutionalism itself. Especially in this age of judicial supremacy, we are accustomed to thinking of the Constitution as independent of politics. Further, the realm of politics is thought to occur in opposition to the realm of constitutional judgment. This judgment about the role the Constitution plays in political life is reflected even in those scholars who are some of Lincoln's strongest defenders.[11] Unlike many who do not take seriously Lincoln's constitutional devotion, they see that Lincoln possessed what Allen Guelzo calls a "near-religious reverence for the rule of law."[12] But that reverence is typically translated only into an abiding political prudence about that which would survive constitutional scrutiny and that which would not. So Guelzo can only make sense of Lincoln's political prudence in regard to the constitutionality of the Emancipation Proclamation by suggesting that "he was convinced (and with good reason) that [all other methods of freeing the slaves] would [not] survive challenges in federal court."[13] So, for Guelzo, Lincoln's relation to the Constitution remains essentially adversarial. He would have gone further, if he could have, but he was politically prudent enough to realize that he could not. The constitutional opposes and constrains the political. Scholars such as Guelzo, as much as they should be applauded for recognizing Lincoln's prudence, still fail to see that Lincoln could be, at one and the same time, both political and constitutional. He was political precisely because he was so committed to the Constitution, and he was so committed to the Constitution precisely because he was so political. For Lincoln, the bounds of the Constitution make politics possible. So, in response to Chase's request that he extend the Emancipation Proclamation to areas already under federal control, Lincoln responds: "If I take the step must I not do so, without the argument of military necessity, and so, without any argument, except the one that I think the measure politically expedient, and morally right? Would I not thus give up all footing upon the constitution or law? Would I not thus be in the boundless field of absolutism?"[14]

Politics occurs in the adjudication of and compromise with competing political opinions. The Constitution makes politics possible because it forecloses certain opinions from simply being forced upon others in the "boundless field of absolutism." The Constitution seeks democratic deliberation as a good independent of the good being sought through democratic deliberation. Thus, for instance, Lincoln did not seek gradual and compensated emancipation primarily because he was concerned that no other form of emancipation would withstand constitutional or judicial scrutiny. He sought it because he thought that a legislative solution to the problem of slavery within the states where it existed would produce the most favorable solution to the problem. The founders did not "solve" the slavery problem in the Constitution merely because they could not; they also thought the problem was best solved by the states themselves. Paradoxically, then, as I will argue, Lincoln's exercise of an extraordinary amount of executive power, including in the Emancipation Proclamation itself, aimed to preserve the realm of constitutional politics because it aimed partially to foreclose members of Congress from simply abandoning the Constitution because of their belief about the power that the war conferred on them.

Additionally, however, Lincoln's understanding of the Constitution as fundamentally political led him to very different arguments concerning his use of executive power than many of those who supported him offered. Where their arguments tended to be legalistic, Lincoln's arguments remained political, couching his interpretation of the Constitution in the rhetoric of political persuasion. In attempting to defend his actions as executive, he does so politically rather than legally, making reference to the Constitution because its status as a bound on political life makes it an essential "landmark" that establishes what can and cannot be done politically.

Lincoln's "Whiggishness"

The paradox at the heart of Lincoln's conception of executive power best emerges by considering first the "Whiggish" arguments he made earlier in his political career. The allegations of hypocrisy, made both in Lincoln's own time and from subsequent scholars, stem from the aversion to a strong executive that characterized Lincoln's earlier political thought—an aversion he shared with Whig Party doctrine at the time.[15] David Donald attempts to rescue Lincoln from the charges of hypocrisy by suggesting that Lincoln was, in fact, a "Whig in the White House" insofar as he combined a strong deference to the legislature in policy matters with a strong assertion of power in military matters—a combination Donald claims was intrinsically Whiggish.[16] Although Donald is correct that Lincoln remained a Whig insofar as he, for the most part, adopted a principled willingness to allow Congress to legislate on domestic matters as it saw fit without his interference, Donald's claim that Whig doctrine also embraced a strong presidency in wartime is based almost entirely on one speech made by John Quincy Adams. The problem with his reliance on this one speech is that it ignores the substantial evidence in their reaction to the Mexican-American War of a strong Whig aversion to a strong presidency in wartime as well. In fact, many of the allegations of Lincoln's hypocrisy arise from his remarks as a member of the House of Representatives during this period.

In the first place, as a member of the House of Representatives, Lincoln states with uncommon clarity the principle underlying the Whig aversion to excessive presidential involvement in domestic legislative matters, leaving them instead to be decided by Congress. In the 1848 election, the Democrats criticized Zachary Taylor for his unwillingness to stake out a position on any of the important domestic policy issues of the day. Lincoln characterizes their criticism: "But gentlemen on the other side are unanamously [*sic*] agreed that Gen. Taylor has no other principles. They are in utter darkness as to his opinions on any of the questions of policy which occupy the public attention." In response, Lincoln admits and then celebrates Taylor's unwillingness to stake out a position on questions of policy: "The people say to Gen. Taylor 'If you are elected, shall we have a national bank?' He answers '*Your* will, gentlemen, not *mine*' 'What about the Tariff?' 'Say yourselves.' 'Shall our rivers and harbours be improved?' 'Just as you please.'" In response to the Democratic claim that this doctrine of noncommittal by the presidential candidate contains no principle, Lincoln says: "[T]o us it appears like principle, and the best sort of principle at that—the principle of allowing the people to do as they please with their own business." He continues later: "We prefer a candidate, who, like Gen. Taylor, will allow the people to have their own way, regardless of his private opinions." Taylor's unwillingness to stake out positions on these issues, Lincoln suggests, follows from the Whig doctrine that formulating domestic policy was Congress's concern rather than the president's. By this argument, the presidential veto exists only to be used if a bill is clearly unconstitutional. Quoting Thomas Jefferson, Lincoln says the veto is "'chiefly for cases, where [members of Congress] are clearly misled by error, ambition, or interest.'"[17]

In explicating this theory, we begin to see the germs of the very same constitutional understanding that I will suggest continues with Lincoln into and throughout his presidency—a constitutional understanding that, paradoxically, led him to assert that much more strongly the independence of the executive branch in fulfilling its particular functions. At the heart of the Whig doctrine of presidential deference is a defense of politics—a type of politics that is made impossible by excessive presidential involvement in legislation. Voicing the opinions of the Democrats, Lincoln says: "'The President is as much the representative of the people as Congress.'" Lincoln responds: "In a certain sense, and to a certain extent, he is the representative of the people. He is elected by them, as well as congress is. But can he, in the nature [of] things, know the wants of the people, as well as three hundred other men, coming from all the various localities of the nation? If so, where is the propriety of having a congress?" The existence of Congress makes possible political deliberation between a wide range of different and even competing interests. To transfer legislative responsibilities to the president, Lincoln argues, "is clearly to take it from those who understand, with minuteness, the interests of the people, and give it to one who does not, and can not so well understand it." Of course, one might respond that so long as "a Presidential candidate avow his opinion upon a given question, or rather, upon all questions, and the people, with full knowledge of this, elect him, they thereby distinctly approve all those opinions." But Lincoln claims this is a "pernicious deception." Measures would be "adopted or rejected, contrary to the wishes of the whole of one party, and often nearly half of the other."[18]

For Lincoln, the decisive problem with both the Democratic approach to presidential elections and presidential leadership after the election is that it forecloses the political adjudication, compromise, and deliberation that are only possible in a body composed of representatives from a wide variety of sections of the country and political points of view. By creating a legislature independent of the president, the Constitution guarantees this political process. Lincoln suggests that the Democrats' position "of laying down, in advance, a platform—a set of party positions, as a unit" forces the people to accept a whole variety of things "however unpalatable some of them may be." On the other hand, the Whigs are "in favor of making Presidential elections, and the legislation of the country, distinct matters; so that the people can elect whom they please, and afterwards, legislate just as they please."[19] In other words, just as, as we will see, the president proclaiming the slaves free in areas where there was no military necessity to do so would have brought us into the "boundless field of absolutism," there is something absolutist about the president ruling in domestic policy, even or especially if he was elected democratically. For the Whigs, democratic self-government requires more than occasional elections—it requires the people's active participation in the process of governing themselves, which is only possible at the federal level through Congress.

As much as Lincoln asserts the independent power of the executive branch during the Civil War, he does so in response to an internal rebellion, during a time when the South has abandoned, in Lincoln's words, "ballots" in favor of "bullets." The power he exercises aims to restore the possibility of politics rather than to overrun the political sphere. In fact, as the war comes to a close, Lincoln emphasizes that his power as executive will recede with the close of the war—that is, the realm of politics will necessarily enlarge, and thus what one might call the "apolitical" power of the executive will recede. Moreover, to the extent that he does intrude on the powers of the legislature more than one would expect given his earlier Whig principles, he does so primarily because he thinks the legislature is attempting to exercise executive powers it both does not and should not possess constitutionally. That is, Lincoln "intrudes" on Congress only because he thinks its members have intruded on him, claiming for themselves, in the words of Sen. Charles Sumner, "all that belongs to any government in the exercise of the right of war."[20] But, just as it would be tyrannical and absolutist for the executive to usurp the political functions of the legislature, so too Lincoln suggests that a legislature attempting to exercise the "war power" would also be tyrannical. Lincoln's "Whiggish" argument suggests only that the president should defer to the legislature when the legislature is exercising political power.

Of course, the deeper charge concerning Lincoln's hypocrisy stems from his arguments against Polk's actions in the Mexican-American War. Lincoln, along with many other Whigs, charges that Polk "unnecessarily and unconstitutionally" commenced the war with Mexico by charging into Mexican territory without congressional authorization.[21] President Polk claimed the war began in self-defense because the American troops were fired upon by Mexico in territory that we had claimed. The essential dispute between the Whigs and the Democrats concerned the question whether there was actually any dispute about the possession of the territory where the hostilities began. Lincoln suggests in one of his speeches on this question that there is simply no evidence whatsoever that the land claimed by Polk as ours was ever understood by anyone else other than Polk to have been ours. For Lincoln,

Polk simply marched "an army into the midst of a peaceful Mexican settlement" and "frighten[ed] the inhabitants away," without any congressional declaration of war or authorization whatsoever.[22]

The decisive problem with Polk's action Lincoln best states not in any of his public speeches but in a private letter to William H. Herndon. He writes: "The provision of the Constitution giving the war-making power to Congress, was dictated, as I understand it, by the following reasons. Kings had always been involving and impoverishing their people in wars, pretending generally, if not always, that the good of the people was the object. This, our Convention understood to be the most oppressive of all Kingly oppressions; and they resolved to so frame the Constitution that no one man should hold the power of bringing this oppression upon us. But your view destroys the whole matter, and places our President where kings have always stood."[23] As Lincoln's discussion of past kings implies, the Constitution separates the power to bring the country to war from the power to conduct it because, as James Madison wrote years before as Helvidius, war is "the true nurse of executive aggrandizement." Although the executive might benefit from war insofar as, again quoting Madison, "laurels are to be gathered; and it is the executive brow they are to encircle," Lincoln emphasizes the extent to which the country as a whole will not.[24]

The problem is, however, that, once in progress, war does not admit of that calm judgment required for the people truly to know what benefits them and what does not. As Lincoln says in one of his speeches in the House of Representatives, Polk trusted "to escape scrutiny, by fixing the public gaze upon the exceeding brightness of military glory—that attractive rainbow, that rises in showers of blood—that serpent's eye, that charms to destroy."[25] By giving to Congress the power to declare war in order for it to begin, the Constitution forces deliberation during the peaceful period in which real deliberation is still possible. As the Whigs found out during the Mexican-American War, once a war has begun it is exceedingly difficult to oppose it without seeming to oppose the troops in combat and even the country itself. In opposing Polk's entrance into Mexico, Lincoln keeps trying to draw a distinction between "the cause of the President in beginning the war, and the cause of the country after it was begun," but that he had to emphasize this distinction over and against an opposition who suggested that there was "no distinction between them" suggests much about the difficult rhetorical situation the Whigs faced.[26]

Although Donald is not right insofar as he suggests that an aggressive presidency was fully compatible with Whig doctrine, he is right that Lincoln's actions during the Civil War do not show that he simply abandoned the Whig doctrine—although he does dissent from the radical Whig doctrine displayed by some of the congressional Republicans during the war. He may remain a Whig because his war is so substantially different than the war he criticizes Polk for creating. Lincoln emphasizes that Polk "unnecessarily and unconstitutionally" began the war, and his public speeches ask Polk to defend the necessity of the war's beginning by showing that American troops were, in fact, fired upon first. Based on the logic of Lincoln's speeches, if Polk could have shown this necessity, then the war would not have begun unnecessarily. So too, then, Lincoln's constitutional complaint would also have been answered. Lincoln opposes Polk's decision because there was no necessary reason why the Constitution had to be circumvented. In the Civil War, by contrast, in the first place, there was insufficient time for Lincoln to have waited for Congress to meet to declare war. In the second place, it is not clear that it would have been constitutionally appropriate for Congress to have declared war even if it could have. As Lincoln understands the situation—and his understanding might be the only constitutional justification for war in the first place—the United States is not warring with an independent state; it is at war because of an internal rebellion within the states. To declare war with the Confederacy may be to imply that the Confederacy enjoys status as an independent nation. As I will explore further, this is why Lincoln comes to think the powers of the president must enlarge even more in this particular war. Both his constitutional oath "to preserve, protect, and defend the Constitution"—an oath only he takes—and his constitutional duty to "take Care that the Laws be faithfully executed"—a duty only he possesses—have placed on him a particular responsibility to restore the Union and with it the applicability of both the Constitution and the laws in the Confederacy. In other words, where Polk began the Mexican-American War under no pressing constitutional necessity but for "some strong motive" other than his constitutional duty, Lincoln will argue that he is brought into the Civil War entirely because of his constitutional duties. The president's power is enlarged by this particular war because normal politics, in which congressional power is greatest, has been circumvented. The president's power is necessarily greatest during extraordinary times when the law must be restored.

The Adequate Constitution and the Congressional Republicans

To understand the situation Lincoln faced in regard to the preservation of the Constitution during the Civil War, it is essential to understand the position of the Radical Republicans in Congress. The problem with many of the previous constitutional studies of Lincoln's use of executive power during the Civil War is that they have failed to incorporate the alternative constitutional understanding advocated by the Radical Republicans who, although they were of the same party as the president, constituted one of the most formidable opponents to the more moderate approach Lincoln favored. Moreover, contrary to what some scholars have implied, they were not concerned about constitutional limitations even as Lincoln was not.[27] Instead, the situation was precisely the opposite: Lincoln was concerned about constitutional limitations even as they were not. Although Thaddeus Stevens was one of the most radical of the Radical Republicans, his understanding of the Constitution and its applicability to the war provides us with the best beginning point. Summarizing and quoting from Stevens's position, George Anastaplo writes: "Thaddeus Stevens, one of the radical abolitionist leaders in Congress, had proclaimed that there was no longer any Constitution and reported that he was weary of hearing the 'never-ending gabble about the sacredness of the Constitution.'"[28]

Stevens indicates the sentiments of many of the Radical Republicans who had become thoroughly disenchanted with the very idea of a limiting Constitution. Disenchanted with a Constitution that, in the hands of men such as Chief Justice Roger B. Taney and President James Buchanan, seemed to foreclose both positive change and necessary action, many in the North had turned away from the Constitution entirely. Part of this disenchantment stemmed initially from the position of a vast majority of the abolitionists. As Thomas Schneider characterizes their position, quoting from Henry David Thoreau: "The error of 'all men of expediency' . . . lay in considering not whether a law 'is right, but is it what they call constitutional.'"[29] William Lloyd Garrison summed up their feelings about what the abolitionists regarded as a "Covenant with Death" when he said: "To Hell with the Constitution."[30] But the frustrations with governmental inactivity in the face of Southern aggression were causing this disenchantment to spread in the North to both members of Congress and ordinary citizens. The San Francisco newspaper *Daily Alta California* declared: "We are at war, and we must make war effectively, without regard to paper cobwebs."[31] Expressing a similar sentiment, a volunteer army officer in 1861 wrote: "The people . . . have been brought to regard the Constitution . . . as an almost invincible barrier to its [the nation's] acknowledged welfare . . . and all have set themselves to finding a method by which to overreach it."[32] A substantial amount of the Northern public had grown tired of constitutional limitations, first for having forced them to sacrifice their moral sensibilities on the altar of the constitutional settlement on the question of slavery and then in seeming to frustrate and impede the government's response to the secession of a vast portion of the country.

In fact, given a substantial portion of the public's frustration with the idea of any constitutional limitations, one can imagine that, had Lincoln been a different kind of man, a man more like Thaddeus Stevens or some of the others in Congress at the time, a real dictatorship might have emerged from this crisis. This is to say that, given the constitutional temperament of the North, constitutional prudence demanded that Lincoln navigate the country away from simply abandoning the Constitution even as the situation demanded that he exercise powers outside of its typical boundaries. One could lose the Constitution both by failing to exercise the necessary powers *and* by exercising them in such a way that the Constitution would not return in full at the conclusion of the conflict.

Of course, not all the Republicans in Congress were as open as Stevens in their simple rejection of the Constitution. Instead, many of them embraced what is often called the adequate Constitution, according to which the Constitution must not be overreached—it must be reinterpreted. Illustrating the thesis of the adequate Constitution, Timothy Farrar, the former partner of Daniel Webster, published an article in which he insisted that the Constitution had been misinterpreted since the founding. Instead of restraining the government, the Constitution should be understood as fully adequate "to the exigencies of government and the preservation of the Union." According to Farrar, the full potential of the Constitution "has not hitherto been exhibited and proved in practice, nor fully asserted and insisted on by its friends, even in theory."[33] In Farrar's hands, the Constitution was no longer, as Hyman writes, a "checkrein against which officials must struggle." The difficulty is, however, that, while Farrar is, to some extent correct—that the Constitution should not be interpreted as a checkrein—it is also a *constitution* that aims to limit government even as it empowers it. For the Constitution truly to be adequate, it must find a way of doing both at the same time.

Hyman writes: "The Civil War became a cram course in unexplored aspects of the Constitution."[34] Up to that point in American history, there was probably no part of the Constitution that had been more unexplored than its capacity to respond to an emergency situation, especially a situation as grave as the Civil War. In part, the debate was between those like Taney and Buchanan who held that the Constitution was simply too great a restraint on government to admit of the power that would be necessary to bring the South back into the Union and those like Farrar and others who saw the Constitution as fundamentally a document of powers that did admit of much more power than had ever been conceived previously. But this was not the only debate. Most scholars have failed to take note of another important debate within the adequate Constitution argument itself. This debate took shape in the Senate during Congress's attempt to pass the Second Confiscation Act in the spring of 1862. Where the first debate revealed only that the Constitution might be thought adequate to meet the exigencies it now faced, this second debate explores the structural solution to the problem that the first solution introduces. That is, does Congress or the president possess the "war power" that has been activated by the adequate Constitution?[35]

Proposed well before Lincoln began indicating he would issue the Emancipation Proclamation, the Second Confiscation Act was tremendously controversial in part because many thought it would change the aims of the war from a limited effort to restore the Union to a revolutionary effort to free the slaves. But the legislation was controversial for reasons that extended beyond the issue of slavery. Many of its critics in Congress claimed this bill was essentially a bill of attainder, explicitly prohibited by the Constitution. It declared the guilt of and punished those in the rebellion without giving them a trial. It also, its critics claimed, violated the Fifth Amendment's guarantee that no person "be deprived of life, liberty, or property, without due process of law."

To defend the legislation, Charles Sumner made an argument very similar to that which we already saw from Thaddeus Stevens. The Constitution is simply inapplicable to war. It "is made for a state of peace, and not for the fearful exigencies of war." If you seek to "moderate [war] by constitutional limitations . . . you take from war something of its efficiency."[36] To defend their argument that Congress possessed this war power rather than the president, Sumner and others articulated an argument that combined this willingness to go beyond the Constitution in war with a legalistic argument that the president must be regulated by the "rule of law" in his conduct of the war. For instance, Benjamin Wade says: "The president cannot lay down and fix the principles upon which the war shall be conducted. . . . It is for Congress to lay down the rules and regulations by which the Executive shall be governed in conducting the war."[37] Thus Phillip Shaw Paludan has suggested that in advancing what we will soon find is one of the most "Whiggish" arguments ever made in defense of the supremacy of Congress over all other branches, Congress was merely aiming to provide "legal procedures to replace personal fiat." He suggests that this concern for the rule of law provides evidence of a much deeper concern for constitutionalism among the Radical Republicans than historians had thought previously.[38]

Paludan's suggestion, however, confuses a concern for the "rule of law" with a concern for constitutionalism. Although these Radical Republicans chose—or perhaps were forced because of their position as legislators—to emphasize the rule of law in arguing for their power over and against the president, this does not prove that their emphasis stemmed from a constitutional concern. As Walter Murphy has recently argued, there is a difference between constitutionalism and what he calls "constitutionism." Where the former stems from a concern for true limitations on the arbitrary power of government, the latter pretends that governmental power is not arbitrary by giving it a "legal" pedigree.[39] If the Second Confiscation Act, as initially proposed by Congress was truly a bill of attainder, then it is arbitrary and unconstitutional regardless of whether or not it is called the "rule of law." In fact, as we will see, given the exigencies of war, especially an extraordinary war such as the Civil War, Lincoln understood the exercise of executive "personal fiat"—so long as it was truly responding to military necessity—as far more constitutional than a congressional "rule of law."

To defend Congress's supremacy over the president, these Radical Republicans moved to an argument much more Whiggish than anything Lincoln ever articulated earlier in his political career. In some ways, it was an argument so Whiggish that it, in and of itself, departed from the constitutional order of separated and independent powers. Spearheaded by the theoretical arguments articulated by Sidney George Fisher, many of these Republicans argued that the president "is only the instrument of Congress."[40] William Riker shows how Fisher's argument was both the theoretical backbone of the Radical Republican claims and how he came to this position. Fisher's original aim was to justify Lincoln's suspension of the writ of habeas corpus as an extension of Congress's power—the same ad interim argument so many scholars continue to make in defense of Lincoln's action.[41] Notably, Fisher's original impetus was in the form of a response to Horace Binney, who had suggested that the suspension of the writ of habeas corpus was wholly an executive power.[42] To ground this justification, especially in the face of the claim that it was the executive's power to exercise, Fisher arrived at a position of absolute congressional supremacy: "The whole power of the people, within the sphere of the General Government, does and must, in the nature of things reside in Congress, and the security of the people consists in their control over Congress by the ballot box."[43] To justify the position that Congress could suspend the writ of habeas corpus during war, Fisher arrives ultimately at the position that Congress has complete supremacy in both war and peace.

The problem for Lincoln was that Congress's Whiggishness was leading it to the argument that it had complete supremacy over the president in conducting the war. Benjamin Wade suggests that Congress's supremacy is so absolute that it has the right "to interfere with the command of a general in the field before the enemy."[44] Jacob Howard says Congress may direct "the entire use which he [the president] shall make of the military forces of the country." Admittedly, where the boundary lies between Congress's legislative power and the president's independent executive power has never been clear—one might even go so far as to suggest that it is intentionally unclear so that the boundary emerges from political contestation—but these Republican claims that they have complete control of the president's power solves this problem of boundaries by essentially eviscerating them. In doing so, they went further than merely regulating the executive's discretion—they attempted to exercise it on their own. And in the congressional attempt to exercise the realm of discretionary executive power, we can see why it is not simply unconstitutional to do so: it is also unwise.

In providing the executive with an independent realm of power, the Constitution partially aims to ensure that the branch responsible for the success of war also has the means to prosecute it. But the reason is deeper than this and relates to the problems that inhere in any congressional attempt to exercise, on its own, the discretion necessary in a military engagement. Under the claim of wartime necessity, many in Congress wanted the Second Confiscation Act to decree that all enemy property shall be seized. But to be rationally and constitutionally related to "wartime necessity," the decision whether to seize enemy property must follow from the actual exigencies of the battlefield. It is impossible for the legislature to wield this power in a way that actually relates to the necessities of the battlefield. Inevitably such legislation will tend to be much more far-reaching than that which the executive would have done on its own. And in trying to exercise this discretion, so far from being more constitutional because less arbitrary and more "legal," such legislation is inevitably much less constitutional because it is much more arbitrary in its exercise. The arbitrariness of power exercised because of "wartime necessity" should be limited as much as possible. So, where Congress during the Civil War was using the claim of "wartime necessity" to justify a vast amount of otherwise unconstitutional legislation, the executive's use of the "war power" was actually much more limited. Although Congress can anticipate what powers might become necessary and provide for these in advance, the claim of necessity is inherently a matter of action and singularity. Its logic demands that one wants only those actually responsible for action on the battlefield to wield such power, both because they can most clearly see when it really is necessary and because they can most clearly be held responsible for its misuse. The authority to pass a law permitting the exercise of the extraordinary power of confiscation stems solely from the necessities of war. Only the executive, as commander in chief during the war, can determine these actual necessities.

Lincoln's willingness to stand up to the aggression of this Congress, both through his "spokesman" Orville Browning—one of the major dissenters to the legislation—and through his threatened veto when the legislation was finally passed, does not necessarily stem then from a departure from his own Whiggish political principles. As we saw in the previous section, Lincoln's earlier political principles were based upon an aversion to absolutism and a concomitant conviction that real politics could only take place in the legislature. For Lincoln, however, this decision by Congress to attempt to use its majority stature and the "necessities" of the war to justify the confiscation of all rebel property beyond the owners' lifetime also smacked of absolutism. By circumscribing the legislation that the legislature could legitimately pass, the Constitution aims to preserve political debate within the legislature. Political debate can only take place between two sides for whom losing on any particular issue does not mean the loss of one's ability to win on the next issue. The Constitution forecloses things such as bills of attainder because it aims to preserve political debate, rather than allowing political debate to degenerate into absolutist rule. For the same reason that Lincoln thinks it is essential that the South not be allowed to resort to "bullets" when it loses in "ballots," he also thinks it important that Congress not be allowed to use the claim of "wartime necessity" to pass vindictive legislation that forecloses the possibility of politics returning at the conclusion of the war. Though these radical Republicans understand themselves as more completely Whiggish in giving so much power to Congress, Lincoln would suggest that the power they are attempting to exercise damages not only the efforts of the war but also the standing of Congress itself. It damages the standing of Congress because it turns Congress from a political body in which adjudication, compromise, and debate can take place, into an absolutist body in which the losers are stamped on by the majority power of the winners.

Lincoln's Understanding of a Presidential War Power

There are two essential challenges to articulating and understanding Lincoln's full position on his possession of a presidential war power. First, there is very good evidence that his position changed or, as Corwin writes, "underwent a gradual stiffening" over the course of the war.[45] For this reason, we cannot trust that what he says early in the war remains his position by the end of the war. Second, Lincoln is famously unwilling to elaborate fully his position on a whole variety of issues, including his understanding of a presidential war power, or is uninterested in doing so. Thus we must piece together his position from what little he did say about it, while supplementing his position with the much fuller position that Orville Browning and a couple of other senators were presenting in the Senate in 1862.

To see that Lincoln's position changed, we must first see where he started. In his message to Congress in special session on July 4, 1861, Lincoln justifies certain controversial measures he had taken in the interim period before Congress had met by suggesting "these measures, whether strictly legal or not, were ventured upon, under what appeared to be a popular demand, and a public necessity, trusting, then as now, that Congress would readily ratify them." He continues: "Nothing has been done beyond the constitutional competency of Congress."[46] In this message, he seems here to hold the Radical Republican position articulated later in the war that subsumes all executive action into the ultimate authority of Congress. It is this argument that has caused many scholars to conclude that Lincoln was ultimately deferential to Congress, justifying his exercise of power only ad interim, in lieu of Congress's being unable to meet. As I will suggest, even if Lincoln held something closer to this position at the beginning of the war, he abandoned it by the middle of the war. Before even showing that his position changed, however, one must first recover his actual argument. And one of the problems is that previous scholars have used this argument in ways that Lincoln did not seem to intend. For instance, in ascribing the ad interim argument to Lincoln, Louis Fisher connects Lincoln's argument in this passage to his attempt to justify the suspension of the writ of habeas corpus. He claims that Lincoln believed "that his actions (especially suspending the writ of habeas corpus) were not 'beyond the constitutional competency of Congress.'"[47] But Lincoln does not, in fact, connect this argument to the suspension of the writ of habeas corpus at all. His justification for that comes two paragraphs later and takes a very different form. Instead, Lincoln offers this argument only to justify the measures that he had just discussed immediately before: the call for volunteers and, most problematically, the "large additions to the regular Army and Navy." Given that the Constitution explicitly gives to Congress the power "to raise and support Armies," "to provide and maintain a Navy," and "to provide for calling forth the Militia," Lincoln's decision to do all three on his own without Congress's prior consent is clearly constitutionally problematic. Given the Constitution's plain meaning on this point, Lincoln must offer the ad interim argument in order to justify his actions.

It is striking then that Lincoln chooses not to offer this argument in the next section in which he justifies the suspension of the writ. Instead, he offers here two arguments. First, whereas he had previously justified his actions by claiming his actions may or may not be legal—and even if illegal, they will become legal once Congress ratifies them—he now suggests that he may have simply violated the law in authorizing the suspension of the writ.[48] But this violation of one law is justified now not by Congress's post hoc ratification but by the necessity of preserving the government itself: "Are all the laws, but one, to go unexecuted, and the government itself go to pieces, lest that one be violated?" Moreover, Lincoln now finds the constitutional justification not in Congress's power but in his own: "Would not the official oath be broken, if the government should be overthrown, when it was believed that disregarding the single law, would tend to preserve it?" In other words, where he had grounded his previous actions, such as the calling up of volunteers and the enlargement of the army and the navy, in the "constitutional competency of Congress," he now justifies the suspension of the writ by his own constitutional competency as it flows from his oath of office.

In the second argument, Lincoln backs off from the suggestion that he broke the law: "It was not believed that this [the prior] question was presented. It was not believed that any law was violated." Where the first argument justified his action in breaking the constitutional law according to which only Congress could suspend the writ, this second argument raises the possibility that the Constitution should be interpreted as giving him the power rather than Congress. He says: "The Constitution itself, is silent as to which, or who, is to exercise the power." This silence then must be read in light of common sense: "as the provision was plainly made for a dangerous emergency, it cannot be believed that the framers of the instrument intended, that in every case, the danger should run its course, until Congress could be called together; the very assembling of which might be prevented, as was intended in this case, by the rebellion."[49] Following this claim, however, Lincoln backs off from the apparent conclusion that the power to suspend belongs solely to the president by saying: "Whether there shall be any legislation upon the subject, and if any, what, is submitted entirely to the better judgment of Congress." After pointing in the direction that the Constitution must be understood as giving this power to the president, Lincoln seems to retreat to a position that sounds similar to the one with which he justified the expansion of the military: he is merely acting as Congress would have were they able to meet at the time. It is worth noting, however, that where the prior position seemed to ask and even require Congress to ratify his actions, this position leaves that judgment entirely to Congress. In other words, in this case, Lincoln implicitly raises the possibility that his actions can stand on his own constitutional authority with or without Congress's ratification. But, as he will articulate the position later in the war, this independent constitutional authority, although it does not require Congress's ratification for it to exist, is and must be susceptible to congressional judgment after its exercise. Although Congress does not grant the power, it does judge it.

It is on this question that Lincoln's position "stiffens" over the course of the war. He progressively abandons his seeming willingness to defer to Congress on these questions. He adopts instead a position that he never states openly but that is reported to have been said by him in John G. Nicolay and John Hay's biography: "I conceive that I may in an emergency do things on military grounds which cannot be done constitutionally by Congress."[50] To see why Lincoln came to this position, we should first see that part of his first statement on this question from which he most significantly departs. In his first discussion of his actions, Lincoln justifies them by citing a "popular demand, and a public necessity." In doing so, he echoes a Jeffersonian understanding of prerogative according to which acts of questionable constitutionality can and should be justified by public approval.[51] As democratically respectable as this position might sound, it is this position that Lincoln comes to abandon over the course of the war, and it is because he abandons this position that Lincoln also comes to think that he possesses emergency powers not possessed by Congress.

The primary reason Lincoln comes to think he possesses these powers rather than Congress relates again to this distinction between what is political and what is not. Although the powers necessary to return the country to a state of peace and to preserve the Constitution can and should be judged politically, they are not in and of themselves political powers. And if they are exercised politically, they smack of the absolutism that Lincoln thinks effectively forecloses actual politics. Military powers, the powers of force, the powers that have made the executive expand so much during this war must be exercised solely in terms of the force necessary to make their very exercise no longer necessary. As such, they cannot and should not be exercised based on a popular demand because the people cannot determine well what "war powers" are actually necessary to be exercised; they can and should, however, judge that necessity after the fact. What might be called the "apolitical" might of the executive should not be exercised through the people, but it should be judged by the people. Near the end of the war, in a letter to one of his generals, Benjamin F. Butler, Lincoln articulates this principle in regard to a conflict over power between the newly formed civil and military authorities in Norfolk. Lincoln writes:

> If you, as Department commander, find the cleansing of the City necessary to prevent pestilence in your army—street lights, and a fire department, necessary to prevent assassinations and incendiarism among your men and stores—wharfage necessary to land and ship men and supplies—a large pauperism, badly conducted, at a needlessly large expense to the government, and find also that these things, or any of them, are not reasonably well attended to by the civil government, you rightfully may, and must take them into your

> own hands. But you should do so *on your own avowed judgment*
> *of a military necessity, and not seem to admit that there is no such*
> *necessity, by taking a vote of the people on the question.*[52]

In other words, the only judgment as to what is and is not military necessity must be made by the military commander, not by popular judgment. To allow the people to take a vote on any question of military necessity is, Lincoln suggests, "to admit that there is no such necessity." The judgment of military necessity can only be made by those responsible for military matters. Because the people are not responsible for military matters, they cannot judge what is necessary for them. Lincoln continues: "Nothing justifies the suspending of the civil by the military authority, but military necessity, and of the existence of that necessity the military commander, and not a popular vote, is to decide." Although one could take this argument to indicate a threatening and dangerous militarism in Lincoln's thought, Lincoln thinks it will have the opposite effect. By preserving the distinction between that which is necessary for military matters and that which can be done by civil authorities, Lincoln hopes to preserve the realm of politics independent of the realm of war and force. Of course, as we can see in this letter, Lincoln fully understands that the realm of war and force can spill over into the political realm in its application—under the claim of military necessity, Butler may build street lights, clean the city, expel the paupers, and so forth. But for Lincoln, all of these things preserve the distinction between the civil and the military, at least in theory, because they are still justified solely by military necessity, as determined by the commanding officer. Once the military realm begins holding popular votes to determine what the people want the military to do, then the distinction is destroyed in both theory and practice. Now the political realm has essentially been subsumed by the military realm. In Lincoln's model, the argument of military necessity, as applied by an officer in the field, brackets what can be done by the military; the theoretical argument brackets the practical application because, while "military necessity" might be far-reaching, it necessarily stops at those things that cannot be credibly related to military necessity. In the model he is here criticizing, the public's vote on what is and is not "military necessity" has no longer a credible relation to actual military necessity. By submitting the question to a vote, the brackets erected by Lincoln's distinction are effectually eviscerated insofar as there is no credible way by which the public can determine what is and is not a matter of "military necessity." In other words, requiring that the military commander, and only the military commander, determine what is military necessity maintains the connection between the claim and its actuality in practice—a connection sufficiently strong that its adequacy can be judged—whereas allowing the public to make this determination turns the claim into a mere legal fiction. Whereas the former makes possible that "whatever is not within such necessity should be left undisturbed," the latter could potentially leave nothing undisturbed because there is no longer any effectual principle to determine what is and is not a matter of "military necessity."[53] In a certain sense, then, the apparently aggressive claims made here on behalf of military necessity protect the political in their very aggressiveness. If the political subsumes the realm of war and force, then it is no longer really political. By insisting on a distinct realm of war and force apart from the political, Lincoln's argument paradoxically protects the political as distinctly political.

Of course, one might suggest that Lincoln's position here stems not from a constitutional calculation but from a political one. His worry may be that, if allowed to vote, the public will not vote to create and sustain the martial law that is necessary in the region. However, the public had already in fact voted to create martial law when he wrote this letter. General Butler had notified Lincoln back in February of 1864 that he contemplated taking a popular vote on the question of martial law. Lincoln blames himself for not objecting then. He writes: "I probably should have [objected], had I studied the subject as closely as I have since done." In other words, his position is still evolving on the relation between military necessity and the public so that even in February of 1864 he has not yet fully seen that precisely because this is a matter of military necessity, it should not be decided by the public. By August of 1864, however—which is, I would suggest, not coincidentally around the same time as he claims for himself powers Congress does not possess—Lincoln has fully seen this connection. Thus he writes definitively: "I now think you would better place whatever you feel is necessary to be done, on this distinct ground of military necessity, openly discarding all reliance for what you do, on any election."[54] Precisely by *openly* placing everything that he does on the *distinct* ground of military necessity, the general ensures that the ground itself remains distinctly military, rather than obfuscating the distinction between what can be done by military authorities and what can be done by political authorities. To allow an election to determine that which is military necessity is to allow military necessity to become a political question. While Lincoln hopes that the full range of the political will return at the conclusion of this war, the war will have been fought for nothing if that range now encompasses a political ability to use military measures for political ends.

Lincoln thinks the existential danger to a regime during a war like this comes not so much from the military itself as from the public becoming militaristic. Precisely because, as Lincoln said years before in his Whiggish speech in defense of the power of Congress over domestic matters, Congress more clearly represents the people, he came to think that it should not possess the war power. Precisely its populist credentials make it a problematic vessel for a power that should never be understood as finding its roots in the popular will.

In a letter to Matthew Birchard and others, a letter that followed up on their own follow-up to his letter to Erastus Corning and others, Lincoln most fully articulates why he thinks the president in particular should be responsible for exercising the extraordinary powers that this war required. He responds to their question: "You ask, in substance, whether I really claim that I may override all the guarrantied [*sic*] rights of individuals, on the plea of conserving the public safety—when I may choose to say the public safety requires it." He suggests in response that, "divested of the phraseology calculated to represent me as struggling for an arbitrary personal prerogative," this question "is either simply a question who shall decide, or an affirmation that nobody shall decide, what the public safety does require, in cases of Rebellion or Invasion." Given, he argues, that the language of the Constitution rejects the possibility that nobody shall decide, the question becomes only *who* is to make the decision when "the decision is to be made, from time to time." Whereas in his message on July 4, 1861, Lincoln had seemed to equivocate in response to this question, there is no longer any equivocation. He writes: "I think the man whom, for the time, the people have, under the constitution, made the commander-in-chief, of their Army and Navy, is the man who holds the power, and bears the responsibility of making it."[55] Because the president is responsible for conducting the war and because the overriding of the guaranteed rights of individuals can only follow from the necessities of war, then it follows, Lincoln suggests, that the president must be responsible for determining when those rights must be overridden. For Congress to do so would be to separate the responsibility from the power;

because Congress is not responsible for conducting the war, it should not have the power to make decisions relating to the war's conduct. As I have argued elsewhere, this does not mean that Congress cannot bracket and delimit the executive's discretion, but it does mean that it should not attempt to exercise that discretion on its own.[56] Since the discretionary power arises because of the war, it follows that he who is responsible for conducting the war must also be responsible for exercising the discretionary power necessary for its conduct. Power must be connected to responsibility, or else power will be exercised irresponsibly.

In the Constitution, the connection between power and responsibility is, however, always enforced by some other independent power capable of holding responsible he who does not exercise his power responsibly. Thus, so as to make good on his implicit claim that he was not, in fact, struggling for an "arbitrary personal prerogative," Lincoln immediately emphasizes the external control that exists on his responsibility to make these important wartime decisions. Lincoln writes: "If he uses the power justly, the same people will probably justify him; if he abuses it, he is in their hands, to be dealt with by all the modes they have reserved to themselves in the constitution."[57] That an external control exists on his responsibility distinguishes the power from prerogative insofar as the latter's reminiscence of the "royal prerogative" implies that the power cannot be judged. A prerogative simply exists by right in the president.[58] Instead, this power does not exist by right in the president. The power exists only in "cases of Rebellion or Invasion" and only "in its application." That is, the power comes into existence only in the case of the exigency that requires it be exercised. The power exists neither prior to nor after it has actually been exercised. Because of the conditionality of its existence, it is and must be rightfully susceptible of judgment. By giving the president the war-making power, the Constitution ensures that it is exercised responsibly. By giving Congress the power to judge the exercise of the war-making power, the Constitution also ensures responsibility—it ensures that a president who abuses this power will be "dealt with" either through impeachment or through not being reelected.

It is the distinction between the absolute existence of a power and its conditionality that explains Lincoln's otherwise curious insistence that Matthew Birchard and others have misstated his position. They represent his position as "'the constitution is different in time of insurrection or invasion from what it is in time of peace & public security.'" He writes in response:

"A recurrence to the paper will show you that I have not expressed the opinion you suppose. I expressed the opinion that the constitution is different, *in its application,* in cases of Rebellion or Invasion, involving the Public Safety, from what it is in times of profound peace and public security."[59] The Constitution only changes in those situations when it is necessary for it to change—it only changes "in its application." Contrary to what many were saying in Congress at the time, cases of rebellion or invasion do not create an entirely new constitutional order during which much that was not permitted before becomes so. Instead, cases of rebellion or invasion simply change the applicability of otherwise inviolable constitutional rules and only in ways that apply directly to that which military necessity requires.

The Emancipation Proclamation

Perhaps the most important illustration of this distinction comes in the Emancipation Proclamation. Whereas the peacetime Constitution was understood simply to prevent the emancipation of the slaves within the Southern states, by the middle of the war Lincoln arrived at the opinion that he could now emancipate the slaves as a matter of military necessity. He arrives at this position, however, after having resisted emancipation when initiated by both Maj. Gen. John C. Frémont and Maj. Gen. David Hunter earlier in the war and while continuing to resist emancipation by legislative proclamation even after he has already issued his own emancipation.

Early in the war, when General Frémont emancipates the slaves within his military jurisdiction, Lincoln revokes the emancipation. His reasons for doing so, at that point in the war, were partially political. As he writes in his letter to Orville Browning explaining his decision: "The Kentucky Legislature would not budge till that proclamation was modified. . . . [T]he very arms we had furnished Kentucky would be turned against us. I think to lose Kentucky is nearly the same as to lose the whole game."[60] But as important as this political calculation was to Lincoln's decision, he insists in the first place on the *principle* by which he revokes this emancipation. He writes: "Genl. Fremont's proclamation, as to confiscation of property, and the liberation of slaves, is *purely political,* and not within the range of *military* law, or necessity." He continues: "The proclamation in the point in question, is simply 'dictatorship.' It assumes that the general may do *anything* he pleases—confiscate the lands and free the slaves of loyal people, as well as of disloyal ones."[61] Precisely because this power exists only as a matter of military necessity, it is bracketed and limited by that very necessity. He writes: "If a commanding General finds a necessity to seize the farm of a private owner, for a pasture, an encampment, or a fortification, he has the right to do so, and so hold it, as long as the necessity lasts; and this is within military law, because within military necessity. But to say that the farm shall no longer belong to the owner, or his heirs forever; and this as well when the farm is not needed for military purposes as when it is, is purely political, without the savor of military law about it." Although military necessity empowers the general to take many actions beyond the ordinary purview of the law, the very terms on which the general is empowered also impose a limit on that power. Taking an action beyond that limit transforms the power from an apolitical exercise of the military into a "purely political" action that takes place in the "boundless fields of absolutism" or "dictatorship."

As important as this letter is as an insight into Lincoln's constitutional principles, it also indicates the extent to which Lincoln's thinking had still not fully evolved on these questions. In this letter, in contrast to his later understanding, Lincoln seems to indicate that "law-makers" could settle the question of slavery. He writes: "That must be settled according to laws made by law-makers, and not by military proclamations." If Lincoln means here that state legislatures must settle the question of slavery and/or that Congress must settle it by a constitutional amendment, then it is in keeping with his later position. If Lincoln means here that Congress could and should settle the question of slavery simply through making laws, then he departs from this position. By the end of the war, even after he has issued his own Emancipation Proclamation, he continues to insist strenuously on the inability of Congress simply to pass a law emancipating all of the slaves. In other words, his thinking evolves further in the direction that is implied by, but not yet fully developed, in this letter. If military necessity is a necessarily limiting principle in wartime, then Congress is even more limited by it than the executive branch. Where, as Lincoln later writes in his letter to Matthew Birchard and others, the executive is capable of deciding what amounts to military necessity because he holds both the power over the military and the responsibility for the exercise of such decisions—thus he can also be held responsible if he exercises this power poorly—Congress possesses neither the power nor the responsibility. And if Congress attempts to exercise this power, it is even more "simply dictatorship" than when exercised in an unnecessary manner by a military commander in the field.

On its own terms, this letter also indicates one of the lingering questions about Lincoln's own Emancipation Proclamation that cannot be fully answered in terms of the constitutional framework I have established here. In the letter, after his discussion of the use of farms and the return of the farm when it is no longer necessary for the war, Lincoln writes that "the same is true of slaves. If the General needs them, he can seize them, and use them; but when the need is past, it is not for him to fix their permanent future condition." Lincoln's actual Emancipation Proclamation also justifies itself on the grounds of military necessity, but unlike his articulation of this principle in this letter, Lincoln there says: "All persons held as slaves within any state, or designated part of a state, the people whereof shall then be in rebellion against the United States shall be then, thenceforward, and *forever* free."[62]

One might ask, how could Lincoln justify the military necessity of freeing the slaves *forever*?[63] In a certain way, Lincoln responds to this question in his August 26, 1863, letter to James C. Conkling. Lincoln writes: "Negroes, like other people, act upon motives. Why should they do any thing for us, if we will do nothing for them? If they stake their lives for us, they must be prompted by the strongest motive—even the promise of freedom. And the promise being made, must be kept."[64] In other words, Lincoln came to see both that the Emancipation Proclamation was only meaningful as a military measure to the extent that it held out a meaningful promise to the slaves who would revolt in its name—such as permanent freedom—and that a promise of this sort must be kept once it is made.

The constitutional justification for Lincoln's actual Emancipation Proclamation actually comes most clearly in his letter to Horace Greeley— a letter he composed after he had already decided that he would issue the Proclamation but had not yet found the right time to do so. Although this letter is rightly interpreted by historians as an eminently political document—Michael Burlingame described it as "greasing the wheels" for the Emancipation Proclamation, which would come soon thereafter—it is also more than that. In their exclusive emphasis on the political nature of the letter, historians such as Burlingame and Guelzo tend to miss the essential constitutional arguments that are at the core of this important letter. Although the letter is political, it is also constitutional. It aims to show in a political manner the nature of Lincoln's constitutional authority with regard to slavery. In their emphasis on the politics of this letter, historians tend to get the relationship backward. Lincoln's political approach follows from his constitutional understanding, rather than his constitutional understanding following from his political approach. In other words, he does not choose the constitutional argument he makes in this letter in order to justify himself politically; he chooses the constitutional argument because he thinks this is the proper principle of constitutionalism. That this principle of constitutionalism dictates a moderate political approach follows from the moderate and nonabsolutist nature of the Constitution itself.

Thus the constitutional argument brackets the whole letter. He begins the substantive argument by writing: "I would save the Union. I would save it the shortest way under the Constitution." He ends the letter by writing: "I have here stated my purpose according to my view of *official* duty; and I intend no modification of my oft-expressed *personal* wish that all men every where could be free."[65] As I have developed more fully elsewhere, this distinction between his official duty and his personal wish is critically important for Lincoln.[66] Because he is aiming to avoid the pure dictatorship he describes in his earlier letter to Browning, he cannot simply act on his personal wish to destroy slavery. His power and authority flow only from his constitutional duty. As such, what he does about slavery must follow from his constitutional duty to preserve the Union. In the same way that the general's actions regarding a farm he encounters in his military movement are conditioned by the wartime necessity, so too Lincoln's actions regarding slavery are conditioned by the necessity that he preserve the Union. As he writes, his "paramount object in this struggle is to save the Union, and is not either to save or to destroy slavery." His subsequent argument follows from his understanding of his constitutional responsibility: "If I could save the Union without freeing any slave I would do it, and if I could save it by freeing all the slaves I would do it; and if I could save it by freeing some and leaving others alone I would also do that."[67] In both emphasizing the distinction between his personal wish and his constitutional responsibility and emphasizing—even overly so—the distinction between his approach to slavery and his constitutional concern for the preservation of the Union, Lincoln highlights the constitutional nature of this argument. Unlike many in the North who would abandon such constitutional scruples in favor of moral righteousness, Lincoln's moderation consists in emphasizing his constitutional responsibilities even as he is about to issue the proclamation that would change the nature of the war.

In accordance with my argument so far, the actual Emancipation Proclamation transforms from an act in which Lincoln seems to be merely putting into effect the power of Congress, into an act in which Lincoln rests entirely on his own authority as president. The first draft of the Emancipation Proclamation begins by mentioning the Second Confiscation Act and, as such, seems to rest his power to emancipate the slaves on this act of the legislature. Although even here Lincoln also mentions his power as commander in chief, the emphasis seems to be on his expression of the will of the legislature rather than his own authority. In the Preliminary Emancipation Proclamation, by contrast, he makes his power much more central. He begins by writing: "I, Abraham Lincoln, President of the United States of America, and Commander-in-Chief of the Army and Navy thereof, do hereby proclaim and declare." Where the first draft seems to derive his power from an act of Congress, this proclamation centralizes his own authority to issue the Emancipation Proclamation. But, here again but later in the document, he draws attention to the acts of Congress that are relevant to this power. His final and official Emancipation Proclamation never so much as mentions Congress, much less an act of Congress. Moreover, where his previous statements had seemed only to imply that this power derived from his office, the final Emancipation Proclamation made it very clear: "Now, therefore I, Abraham Lincoln, President of the United States, *by virtue of the power in me vested* as Commander-in-Chief, of the Army and Navy of the United States." Because Lincoln came to see the Emancipation Proclamation exclusively in terms of his own "war power," he disconnected it from any act of Congress. It follows entirely from his power to determine what is a "fit and necessary war measure for suppressing said rebellion"—a power that his responsibility to conduct the war and to preserve the Union imposes entirely on him. Although Congress can, should, and, under Lincoln's leadership, did encourage the various state legislatures to create programs of gradual and compensated emancipation, Congress itself does not have the power to issue a legislative edict freeing the slaves. Congress had never been understood to possess this power prior to the war and, although many in Congress want to claim that the "war power" gives them it now, Lincoln arrives at the position that the war changes nothing with regard to Congress's legislative power. Where the actual conduct of the war requires from the executive nonlegislative proclamations such as the Emancipation, Congress cannot claim the same "war power" because it is not responsible for the actual conduct of the war. As Lincoln writes in his letter to James Conkling: "You say it is unconstitutional—I think differently. I think the constitution invests its Commander-in-Chief, with the law of war, in time of war."

In a fragment Lincoln wrote at the end of August 1863, he reflects on the lessons of this war. Although never published, these fragments are often important indications of Lincoln's internal monologues. Lincoln used them as opportunities to work out an argument in its detail and complexity, although the conclusion of them often ends up indicating Lincoln's arresting clarity as he penetrates through the detail and complexity straight to the heart of the matter. In this case, Lincoln reflects on what would happen if those in the rebellion were to announce a cessation to their fighting. Lincoln contemplates that he probably "should answer . . . 'You began the war, and you can end it.'" He then goes on to contemplate the meaning of the war: "This war is an appeal, by you, from the ballot to the sword; and a great object with me has been to teach the futility of such appeal from a fair election, but to the next election."

For Lincoln, the import of this war lies in both preserving self-government and in proving that self-government is not, as he says in his first inaugural, "too weak to maintain its own existence." Paradoxically, by exercising the tremendous powers of the sword, Lincoln aims to prove the futility of the appeal "from the ballot to the sword." As Lincoln knew so well from his reflections as a Whig earlier in his political career, war's danger to self-government lies as much internally—it tempts us with the "boundless fields of absolutism"—as it does externally. To be, as he writes to James Conkling, "worth the keeping," the Union must exercise the power it needs without destroying the very foundations of limited government. As Lincoln writes in a letter to Edwin M. Stanton in 1864: "While we must, by all available means, prevent the overthrow of the government, we should avoid planting and cultivating too many thorns in the bosom of society."[68]

Because our more recent experience is with the "thorns" that emerge from a powerful executive power, the tendency is to assume that the thorns have always come from this direction. By revisiting Lincoln's understanding of executive power during the Civil War, we cast light not only on his preeminent concern for the politics that can only emerge within a limited constitution. Lincoln's historical example also provides a useful countervailing argument against the current tendency to place all of our constitutional faith in the need for a preeminent Congress. Lincoln teaches us the usefulness of an independent executive, even or especially in severe crises like the Civil War. Rather than destroying the political sphere by subverting the Constitution to the absolutist whims of a radical Congress, the independent and "apolitical" war power of the executive allowed Lincoln to preserve politics as a sphere independent from that which was necessary to win the war. This is not to suggest, however, that, with a different administration in a different situation, absolutism could not come from the executive. Just as Congress could exercise its legislative power in an absolutist manner, so too could the executive usurp the legislative powers of Congress. The presidential usurpation of legislative power is as absolutist, if not more so, as Congress's exercise of unconstitutional power. On the other hand, the executive exercise of power, even in vast amounts, is not necessarily a sign of absolutist ambitions. If the Constitution does not give certain powers to Congress, then the president is not usurping them. Instead, because the president's exercise of certain kinds of "war power" is both more responsible—in the sense that it can be more precisely related to the actual necessities of war—and more accountable—because the president can be impeached for their abuse—these powers should be understood as his to exercise if the need arises to exercise them.

This is neither to argue that Congress has no role in demarcating the limits of these powers nor to argue that the powers themselves should be understood as unquestionably the executive's to exercise.[69] It is to argue, however, that Lincoln's example shows us that we should be wary of going too far in our efforts to strip the executive of all independent power. The excellence of the United States Constitution lies in its decision to separate powers into independent branches of power with independent functions, allowing each branch to exercise its function while providing other branches the power to judge the exercise of that function. Although Lincoln remains a Whig insofar as he always understands Congress as possessing the legislative power, he remains a constitutionalist in his understanding that the legislature does not possess all of the powers of government.

Notes

1. Wilfred E. Binkley, *President and Congress* (New York: Knopf, 1947), 110.

2. As will become clear, my suggestion that Lincoln remains a Whig is very different from David Donald's similar suggestion. See David Donald, "Abraham Lincoln: Whig in the White House," in his *Lincoln Reconsidered: Essays on the Civil War Era* (New York: Vintage Books, 1961). For a critique of Donald's argument from a different angle, see Stephen B. Oates, "Abraham Lincoln: Republican in the White House," in *Abraham Lincoln and the American Political Tradition*, ed. John L. Thomas (Amherst: University of Massachusetts Press, 1986).

3. I have developed in other work the extent to which Lincoln remained committed to the Constitution throughout the Civil War even as he exercised a great deal of discretionary executive power. Most important, both his rhetoric and his actions made possible the restoration of a peacetime Constitution at the conclusion of the war. See Benjamin A. Kleinerman, "Lincoln's Example: Executive Power and the Survival of Constitutionalism," *Perspectives on Politics* 3, no. 4 (2005).

4. For an examination of the numerous constitutional questions and problems raised by Lincoln's presidency, see J. G. Randall, *Constitutional Problems under Lincoln*, rev. ed. (Gloucester, MA: Peter Smith, 1963). For a more recent examination that relates more immediately to some of the issues raised in this chapter, see Mark G. Neely Jr., *Lincoln and the Triumph of the Nation: Constitutional Conflict in the American Civil War* (Chapel Hill: University of North Carolina Press, 2011).

5. For a discussion of the doctrine of the adequate Constitution, see, for instance, Harold M. Hyman, *A More Perfect Union: The Impact of the Civil War and Reconstruction on the Constitution* (New York: Knopf, 1973), 124–30.

6. For a description of the departure from a limiting Constitution to an unlimited one in the case of one of the more important political thinkers of the time, see William Riker, "Sidney George Fisher and the Separation of Powers during the Civil War," *Journal of the History of Ideas* 15, no. 3 (June 1954).

7. See, for instance, David Gray Adler, "The Constitution and Presidential Warmaking: The Enduring Debate," *Political Science Quarterly* 103, no. 1 (Spring 1988).

8. Louis Fisher said this at a conference, "Presidential Power in America: Post 9/11," held at the Massachusetts School of Law (October 2006).

9. Binkley, *President and Congress,* 126. See, also, Edward Corwin, *The President: Office and Powers, 1787–1984,* 5th ed., ed. Randall W. Bland, Theodore T. Hindson, and Jack W. Petalson (New York: New York University Press, 1984), 167.

10. For the fullest development of Lincoln's attitude toward Congress during the Civil War and its attitude toward him, see Nathaniel W. Stephenson, *Lincoln: An Account of His Personal Life, Especially of Its Springs of Action as Revealed and Deepened by the Ordeal of War* (Indianapolis, IN: Bobbs-Merrill, 1922). Some recent scholarship has also investigated the Civil War confiscation debate between Congress and the president. See Silvana R. Siddali, *From Property to Person: Slavery and the Confiscation Acts: 1861–1862* (Baton Rouge: Louisiana State University Press, 2005), and Daniel W. Hamilton, *The Limits of Sovereignty: Property Confiscations in the Union and the Confederacy during the Civil War* (Chicago: University of Chicago Press, 2007). However, these treatments of the issue have failed to pay attention to the centrality of the issue of separation of powers in the debate; see Benjamin A. Kleinerman, *The Discretionary President,* 196.

11. See, for instance, Allen C. Guelzo, *Lincoln's Emancipation Proclamation: The End of Slavery in America* (New York: Simon & Schuster, 2004).

12. Ibid., 5.

13. Ibid., 6.

14. Abraham Lincoln, "To Salmon P. Chase" (September 2, 1863), *Collected Works of Abraham Lincoln,* ed. Roy P. Basler, 8 vols. plus index (New Brunswick, NJ: Rutgers University Press, 1953), 6:429. Hereinafter cited as *CW;* emphases in original unless otherwise noted.

15. See Daniel Walker Howe, *The Political Culture of the American Whigs* (Chicago: University of Chicago Press, 1979), 87–89.

16. Donald, "Abraham Lincoln."

17. Abraham Lincoln, "Speech in the U.S. House of Representatives on the Presidential Question" (July 27, 1848), in *CW,* 1:502–5.

18. Ibid., 1:504–5.

19. Ibid., 1:506.

20. Quoted in Binkley, *President and Congress,* 116.

21. Abraham Lincoln, "Speech in the United States House of Representatives: The War with Mexico" (January 12, 1848), in *CW,* 1:432.

22. Lincoln, "Speech in the U.S. House of Representatives on the Presidential Question," 1:514.

23. Abraham Lincoln, "To William H. Herndon" (February 15, 1848), in *CW,* 1:451–52.

24. Alexander Hamilton and James Madison, *The Letters of Pacificus and Helvidius (1845) with the Letters of Americanus: A Facsimile Reproduction* (Delmar, NY: Scholars' Facsimiles & Reprints, 1976), 89–90.

25. Lincoln, "Speech in the United States House of Representatives: The War with Mexico," 439.

26. Lincoln, "Speech in the U.S. House of Representatives on the Presidential Question," 515.

27. See Michael Kent Curtis, *Free Speech, "The People's Darling Privilege": Struggles for Freedom of Expression in American History* (Durham, NC: Duke University Press, 2000).

28. George Anastaplo, *Abraham Lincoln: A Constitutional Biography* (Lanham, MD: Rowman & Littlefield, 1999), 207.

29. Thomas E. Schneider, *Lincoln's Defense of Politics: The Public Man and His Opponents in the Crisis over Slavery* (Columbia: University of Missouri Press, 2006), 2.

30. For both an excellent discussion of the tendency to view the Constitution as entirely distinct from, and even in opposition to, the egalitarian aims of the abolitionists and a persuasive argument that Lincoln attempts to join these to one another, see Phillip Shaw Paludan, "Emancipating the Republic: Lincoln and the Means and Ends of Antislavery," in *"We Cannot Escape History": Lincoln and the Last Best Hope of Earth*, ed. James M. McPherson (Urbana: University of Illinois Press, 1995).

31. Quoted in Leonard P. Curry, *Blueprint for Modern America: Nonmilitary Legislation of the First Civil War Congress* (Nashville, TN: Vanderbilt University Press, 1968), 78.

32. Quoted in Harold M. Hyman, "Reconstruction and Political-Constitutional Institutions: The Popular Expression," *New Frontiers of the American Reconstruction*, ed. Harold M. Hyman (Chicago: University of Illinois Press, 1966), 20.

33. Quoted in Hyman, *More Perfect Union*, 129.

34. Ibid., 131.

35. I explore this debate and the answers to it much more fully in my book *The Discretionary President*.

36. US Congress, "Congressional Globe" (Washington, DC: Blair and Rives, 1834–1873), 37th Cong., 2nd sess., 1862, 2964.

37. Quoted in Phillip Shaw Paludan, *A Covenant with Death: The Constitution, Law, and Equality during the Civil War* (Urbana: University of Illinois Press, 1975), 36.

38. Ibid., 36–37. For a useful discussion of both the prior historical consensus and the growing tendency to rethink it, see Michael Les Benedict, "Preserving the Constitution: The Conservative Basis of Radical Reconstruction," *Journal of American History* 61 (June 1974).

39. Walter F. Murphy, *Constitutional Democracy: Creating and Maintaining a Just Political Order*, Johns Hopkins Series in Constitutional Thought (Baltimore: Johns Hopkins University Press, 2007), 6.

40. Congress, "Congressional Globe," 2964.

41. See, for instance, David Gray Adler, "Constitution and Presidential Warmaking," in *The Constitution and the Conduct of American Foreign Policy*, ed. David Gray Adler and Larry N. George (Lawrence: University Press of Kansas, 1996), and Mark J. Rozell, "Executive Prerogative and American Constitutionalism," in *Abraham Lincoln, Contemporary: An American Legacy*, ed. Frank J. Williams and William D. Pederson (Campbell, CA: Savas Woodbury, 1995).

42. Horace Binney, *The Privilege of the Writ of Habeas Corpus under the Constitution*, 2nd ed. (Philadelphia: C. Sherman & Sons 1862).

43. Quoted in Riker, "Sidney George Fisher," 407.

44. Congress, "Congressional Globe," 2930.

45. Corwin, *President*, 167.

46. Abraham Lincoln, "Message to Congress in Special Session" (July 4, 1861), in *CW*, 4:429.

47. Louis Fisher, *Presidential War Power* (Lawrence: University Press of Kansas, 1995), 38–39.

48. If Lincoln believed he simply violated the law, he would be in agreement with Taney in his *Merryman* decision. For the best discussion of the importance of *Merryman*, see Jonathan W. White, *Abraham Lincoln and Treason in the Civil War: The Trials of John Merryman* (Baton Rouge: Louisiana State University Press, 2011).

49. Lincoln, "Message to Congress in Special Session," 4:430–31.

50. John G. Nicolay and John Hay, *Abraham Lincoln: A History*, 10 vols. (New York: Century, 1890), 9:120. See also Michael Burlingame, *Abraham Lincoln: A Life*, 2 vols. (Baltimore: Johns Hopkins University Press, 2008), 2:660. Michael Les Benedict claims that Lincoln could not have said this and Hay must have "misconstrued his words." In contrast to my argument here, Benedict attempts to show that Lincoln justified his actions wherever he could by reference to Congress's power rather than his own. See Michael Les Benedict, "The Constitution of the Lincoln Presidency and the Republican Era," in *The Constitution and the American Presidency*, ed. Martin L. Fausold and Alan Shank (Albany: State University of New York Press, 1991), 268–69.

51. For the best presentation of Jefferson's view of prerogative, see Jeremy D. Bailey, *Thomas Jefferson and Executive Power* (Cambridge: Cambridge University Press, 2007).

52. Abraham Lincoln, "To Benjamin F. Butler" (August 9, 1864), in *CW*, 7:487–88 (emphasis added).

53. Ibid., 7:488.

54. Ibid.

55. Abraham Lincoln, "To Matthew Birchard and Others" (June 29, 1863), in *CW,* 6:303.

56. See Kleinerman, *Discretionary President.* See also David J. Barron and Martin S. Lederman, "Commander in Chief at the Lowest Ebb: Framing the Problem, Doctrine, and the Original Understanding," *Harvard Law Review* 121, no. 3 (January 2008), and David J. Barron and Martin S. Lederman, "Commander in Chief at the Lowest Ebb: A Constitutional History," *Harvard Law Review* 121, no. 4 (February 2008).

57. Lincoln, "To Matthew Birchard and Others," 6:303.

58. This is why it does not seem accidental that Lincoln only refers to his exercise of discretionary executive power with the term "prerogative" in this letter as a way of rejecting the very term.

59. Lincoln, "To Matthew Birchard and Others," 6:302.

60. Abraham Lincoln, "To Orville H. Browning" (September 22, 1861), in *CW,* 4:532.

61. Ibid., 531.

62. Abraham Lincoln, "Preliminary Emancipation Proclamation" (September 22, 1862), in *CW,* 5:434. Lincoln quotes this passage verbatim in his Final Emancipation Proclamation on January 1, 1863; see ibid., 6:29.

63. I thank Dennis Foster of Virginia Military Institute for raising this question in the draft stage of this chapter.

64. Abraham Lincoln, "To James C. Conkling" (August 26, 1863), in *CW,* 5:434.

65. Abraham Lincoln, "To Horace Greeley" (August 22, 1862), in *CW,* 5:388–89.

66. See Kleinerman, "Lincoln's Example."

67. Lincoln, "To Horace Greeley," 5:388.

68. Abraham Lincoln, "To Edwin M. Stanton" (March 18, 1864), in *CW,* 7:255.

69. For a fuller development of both of these points, see Kleinerman, *Discretionary President.*

Part IV

Lincoln and Modern-Day America

13

Lincoln and the Progressives

Ronald J. Pestritto and Jason R. Jividen

In many respects the Barack Obama presidency has become a unifying force
for both conservatives and liberals. Conservatives seem united in looking
aghast at what they consider to be the radical and comprehensive remaking
of American national government—a remaking that seems to reject not only
the American constitutional order, but to exceed even the ambitions of the
New Deal and Great Society in its extension of governmental authority into
the private sphere. Yet the developments since 2009 have been in the making
for the better part of the twentieth and now twenty-first centuries, as the
Constitution appears to have become nothing more than an afterthought
in national policy debates. The very idea of constitutionally limited government—even the energetic variety of it envisioned by its federalist framers—
seems an anachronism today when a speaker of the House of Representatives
doesn't think that the constitutionality of one of the most far-reaching pieces
of legislation in a generation is a "serious question." Conservatives appear
to have come together in realizing, too late, that the founders' Constitution
has been pushed aside and that this has led to a government that strikes
them as more European, and more socialistic. Liberals too have united and
have done so under the banner of Progress. In fact, those who once called
themselves "liberals" now embrace the term "progressive." The most influential think tank on the Left today, founded by former Bill Clinton aide John
Podesta, is the Center for American Progress. The title of Podesta's popular
book is *The Power of Progress: How America's Progressives Can Once Again
Save Our Economy, Our Climate, and Our Country.* And one thing, at least,
seems to unite liberals and conservatives with one another: both camps are
pointing to America's original Progressive Era as the source (at least the most

proximate one) for our current expansion of government and abandonment of constitutionalism. Some conservatives have been making this connection for some time, but the Left now seems very much to have consciously embraced its progressive roots.[1] When today's liberals refer to themselves as "progressives," they do so not merely because "progressive" is a nicer way of saying "liberal" (a term that those on the Left have avoided since it became a dirty word in the 1980s). When pressed about this term, those on the Left make clear, as Hillary Clinton did during the 2008 presidential primary campaign, that by "progressive" they mean to connect themselves with the American progressive movement that was at its height at the turn of the twentieth century.

Within conservatism, however, the unity ends at the identification of the progressives as the source of our limitless government. For while conservatives agree that progressive ideas and policies have served as a springboard for modern American liberalism, they disagree as to whether the progressives introduced big government into the American political tradition or merely capitalized on something that had been smuggled into the American tradition much earlier. While some conservatives contend that it was the progressives who imported a foreign philosophy of government into the American tradition and used it to pursue a fundamentally new direction in American politics, a rather eclectic alliance of libertarians and paleoconservatives has emerged to point the finger not only at the progressives themselves, but also at Abraham Lincoln.

The nature of the libertarian/paleoconservative critique of Lincoln has been explored in a recent book by Thomas L. Krannawitter, who summarizes the essence of it this way: "The major premise is that the Confederate South was fighting for limited government, trying to protect the states' rights from an overbearing national government. The minor premise is that Lincoln opposed the Confederacy by opposing secession. The conclusion, therefore, is that Lincoln opposed limited government. And by so opposing the rights of states, which served as powerful checks against an intrusive national government, Lincoln effectively paved the way for the big government we have today."[2]

This argument that the transformation to unlimited national government came with Lincoln and was then seized upon by opportunistic liberals in the twentieth century has been buttressed by the fact that liberals today like to portray Lincoln as a champion of their cause. Krannawitter provides the example of Barack Obama, who wrote in 2006 that "Lincoln's 'basic insight' was 'that the resources and power of the national government can facilitate, rather than supplant, a vibrant free market.'" As Obama saw it, however, this "insight" had to wait for the opportunity of the Great Depression to find an outlet for expression. Krannawitter explains that, "according to Obama, Lincoln first envisioned the principles of New Deal liberalism, while Franklin Roosevelt put them into practice."[3] These assumptions about Lincoln as the originator of progressive liberalism underlie much of Thomas DiLorenzo's neo-Confederate/libertarian attack on Lincoln.[4] They have also given rise to comments such as this from the economist Walter Williams: "Abraham Lincoln opened the door to the kind of unconstrained, despotic, arrogant government we have today, something the framers of the Constitution could not have possibly imagined."[5]

Finally, to the list of those who see Lincoln as a source of progressivism and subsequent iterations of liberalism in American political development, we can add the progressives themselves. It is a common feature of Progressive Era writings to point to Lincoln as a guide and inspiration. Theodore Roosevelt proclaimed, for example, in his 1913 address "The Heirs of Abraham Lincoln" that "we progressives and we alone are to-day the representatives of the men of Lincoln's day who upheld the hands of Lincoln"; he claimed that "Lincoln and Lincoln's supporters were emphatically the progressives of their day."[6] In order to understand how and why progressives claimed Lincoln's legacy, we must first understand the general aims of the national progressive movement. These aims were grounded in an appeal to move beyond the principles of the American founding.

The Principles of Progressivism

Progressives drew on a peculiar account of American history and Lincoln's role in it in making their own multifaceted argument that America needed to move beyond the principles of its founding generation. The progressives knew that their policy agenda required an active and centralized national government—not one that was energetic merely within the context of its constitutionally defined ends (after the fashion of Hamilton's vision in *Federalist* No. 23, for instance) but one that instead expanded its very ends and purposes to fit the prevailing sentiment of the day. They knew that the political philosophy of the American founding, resting as it did on a natural account of individual liberty that was to be secured through the Constitution's careful arrangement and limitation of governing institutions, needed to be either discredited or recast in a light more congenial to progressive aims. While there is much discrediting of the founding in progressive speeches and writings, the more astute progressives also sought to recast it in a light favorable to their cause—relying, when useful, on Lincoln to help in the effort. The effort consisted of promoting a vision of both the Declaration of Independence and the Constitution as reinterpreted through a progressive lens.

With respect to the Declaration, progressives objected most to its universal account of individual rights and of the purpose of legitimate government. Under such an account, they knew, government could not redefine itself as it wished from age to age, and it would run up against the inviolable status of man's natural rights even when fueled by a robust majority will. In *Liberalism and Social Action,* the progressive intellectual John Dewey lamented what he called the "crisis" in modern liberalism that came from the founding generation's lack of "historic sense" and from too many of his contemporaries who refused to abandon the founders' universalism.[7] Woodrow Wilson, who was a prolific progressive scholar long before he entered public life, attempted to discredit the Declaration by exaggerating its abstractness and equating its natural-rights doctrine with that of the French Revolution, notwithstanding the revulsion of most of the founders to that revolution and the decisive differences between its principles and those of America's own. This was a sleight of hand for which Wilson engaged not only Lincoln but Edmund Burke, as we shall soon show. Progressives, in general, understood the important relationship between the Declaration and the Constitution, seeing that the institutional arrangement contained in the Constitution was made necessary by the natural-rights doctrine of the Declaration.[8] Because of the proposition that the permanent end of government is to secure the citizens' natural rights, the greatest threat in democratic government is faction. The political science of the Constitution was designed to mitigate the problem of faction and did so, progressives believed, in a manner that would forever prevent it from being used as a tool of progressive liberalism.

The more academic progressives such as Wilson and Dewey therefore sought a recasting of the American founding grounded in the idea of historical contingency. To the founding's ahistorical notion of human nature they opposed the historical argument that the ends, scope, and role of just government must be defined by the different principles of different epochs and that it is therefore impossible to speak of a single form of just government for all ages. This was a conscious reinterpretation, as Wilson even suggested in one speech that the Declaration ought to be understood by excluding from it the principled arguments of the first two paragraphs. In a 1911 address Wilson remarked that "the rhetorical introduction of the Declaration of Independence is the least part of it. . . . If you want to understand the real Declaration of Independence, do not repeat the preface."[9] It was this assertion of historical contingency over the permanent principles of American constitutionalism that animated the main tenets of progressive scholarship.

In terms of invoking Lincoln for the sake of this progressive vision, the speeches of Theodore Roosevelt are more familiar than the scholarship of Wilson or Dewey. In making his claim on Lincoln, Roosevelt was deeply influenced by having read Herbert Croly's *The Promise of American Life.* Thus we will begin with Croly's understanding and use of the Lincoln legacy, which will point the way to Roosevelt's reliance on Lincoln as a champion of the progressive cause. The final part of the chapter will return to the argument of Wilson, whose firm reliance on Lincoln is less well known but particularly illuminating for those who would seek to understand both how progressivism serves as a foundation for modern American liberalism and how Lincoln has justly or unjustly been caught up in the development of modern liberalism.

Herbert Croly's Lincoln and *The Promise of American Life*

Among the several reasons for the progressives' adoption of Lincoln's legacy, the chief one is Lincoln's role in the Civil War. The progressive narrative here accords very closely with today's libertarian/neo-Confederate critics of Lincoln: that the founding established a decentralized form of government that exalted individuals and states over the central government, that Lincoln was a great champion of centralization as an end in itself, and that the post–Civil War government was a transformation of and departure from the original. This "new" conception of government, necessitated by history and championed by Lincoln, represented a paradigm shift in the American political tradition and served as the springboard for progressivism in subsequent decades.

In *The Promise of American Life,* Croly attempted to articulate and defend the ends of progressivism; his account of Lincoln's place in American political history was crucial to this effort. For Croly, Lincoln served as an enduring example of leadership that transcended merely local and individualistic politics for the sake of a living national idea. Lincoln was the first legitimate politician, Croly claimed, to reveal fully the promise of American national life.[10]

According to Croly, the Jeffersonian, "democratic" tradition of local government and individual rights and the Hamiltonian, "nationalist" tradition of efficient central government and leadership had always been the most common reference points in American political discourse. Croly contended that the political problem throughout American history had been the persistent failure to bring these principles together.[11] Traditionally, Croly argued, Americans had embraced the Jeffersonian tradition of individualism, equal rights, and local self-government at the expense of a coherent national idea. In a predominantly agrarian economy, where individual effort was more likely to reward one with prosperity, the common, national interest and the individual interest often coincided. However, with the rise of modern industry and the increase of economic specialization, the average American could no longer achieve political, economic, and spiritual satisfaction merely through the sweat of his own brow. The Jeffersonian tradition, more applicable to a predominantly agrarian existence, had proven inadequate to address the problems facing Americans in a new, industrial economy where individual social and economic mobility were hampered by changing conditions.[12] American democracy would now need a model of leadership that would show reformers and average citizens how to transcend local and particular interests in favor of coherent national policy. Croly offered Lincoln as the best model for this purpose, suggesting that all of Lincoln's thoughts ultimately "looked in the direction of a higher level of human association."[13] Croly continued:

> It is this characteristic which makes him a better and, be it hoped, a more prophetic democrat than any other national American leader. His peculiar distinction does not consist in the fact that he was a "Man of the People." ... Lincoln's peculiar and permanent distinction as a democrat will depend rather upon the fact that his thoughts and his actions looked towards the realization of the highest and most edifying democratic ideal. *Whatever his theories were,* he showed

by his *general outlook and behavior* that democracy meant to him more than anything else the *spirit and principle of brotherhood.*[14]

According to Croly, the "Union might well have been saved and slavery extinguished without [Lincoln's] assistance; but the life of no other American has revealed with anything like the same completeness the peculiar moral promise of genuine democracy." Croly thus promoted the promise of a democracy dedicated not to the security of individual natural rights, but directed instead toward the realization of human brotherhood in the nation as a whole.[15]

Croly's Lincoln as "More than an American"

Lincoln had the kind of character, Croly argued, that made him a truly national man, and it was Lincoln's character that mattered to Croly much more than his words or deeds. He described Lincoln as "more than an American," asserting that Lincoln was not merely a pioneer democrat and man of the people, but also an embodiment of the coming national identity.[16]

Lincoln's role in the slavery dispute was a manifestation, Croly argued, of his national character. When Lincoln confronted the problem of slavery, he made it "plain that a democratic nation could not make local and individual rights an excuse for national irresponsibility." Lincoln, Croly reasoned, "began to emancipate the American national idea from an obscurantist individualism and provincialism." Even though the Constitution had tolerated slavery, Croly argued that the institution had been a threat to the American nation. Antebellum political parties had failed to adequately address the slavery crisis because they were far too willing to sacrifice the national, common good for mere self-interest. The Democrats believed the slavery question to be only a matter of local or state importance, and the Whigs, despite their Hamiltonian roots and professed sympathy for the national ideal, were all too willing to compromise away their principles for political gain.[17] According to Croly, Lincoln's leadership offered the solution to this failure. The institution of slavery had to be gradually reduced to insignificance, or it would tear the nation apart. By proclaiming that a house divided against itself cannot stand, Lincoln suggested that slavery was a national problem that required a truly national solution. For the first time, Croly argued, an American politician had publicly claimed that the American nation was a "living principle" rather than a mere "legal bond."[18]

And it was Lincoln's character that mattered most. Croly conceded, as mentioned above, that the Union might well have been saved and slavery extinguished without Lincoln. For Croly, what Lincoln really offered was an example of human excellence, of the qualities necessary for disinterested leadership to transcend the self-interested, local concerns of the average American in favor of a complete national vision. Yet for Croly to offer Lincoln as a model for progressive reformers, he needed to recast Lincoln in the progressive mold. Croly had to offer a discussion of Lincoln that diverted attention from Lincoln's own political principles.

Croly's Misuse of Lincoln

One particularly clear example of Croly's propensity to invoke Lincoln in a manner contrary to Lincoln's own principles comes in Croly's discussion of human nature. Croly believed that the average American's hope for better things to come, his faith in the promise of American life, was rooted in his shared desire for social amelioration, something that could only be realized through a stronger, more focused, more efficient national government. Such a government "would not be dedicated either to liberty or to equality in their abstract expressions, but to liberty and equality, in so far as they made for human brotherhood." He assumed that human nature could be shaped in such a way that individuals might routinely sacrifice self-interest for the sake of the common good. In contradistinction to *The Federalist*, which thought men capable of self-government but carefully circumscribed the scope of popular government due to the permanent inclination to factiousness within man's nature, Croly made a more utopian assumption about the perfectibility of human nature. He thus had faith that human government could be entrusted with the achievement of actual material equality, as opposed to securing a merely "abstract" equality of rights. While Croly admitted that the extent to which human nature could be "modified by social and political institutions of any kind is, at best, extremely small," he concluded that democracy nevertheless "must stand or fall on a platform of possible human perfectibility" and "cannot be disentangled from an aspiration toward human perfectibility, and hence from the adoption of measures looking in the direction of realizing such an aspiration." For Croly, progressive reform and the pursuit of human brotherhood as the end of American democracy simply assumes—indeed it must assume—a malleable human nature that can be improved through the social planning of administrative experts.[19]

Despite Croly's attempt to incorporate the Lincoln example into this progressive vision of man, Lincoln held a very different understanding of human nature, perhaps best expressed in his 1864 "Response to a Serenade." Reflecting upon the difficulty of holding elections during the war, Lincoln suggested: "The strife of the election is but human-nature practically applied to the facts of the case. What has occurred in this case, must ever recur in similar cases. *Human-nature will not change. In any future great national trial, compared with the men of this, we shall have as weak, and as strong; as silly and as wise; as bad and good.* Let us, therefore, study the incidents of this, as philosophy to learn wisdom from, and none of them as wrongs to be revenged."[20] In Lincoln's thought, there is no overcoming man's nature to advance to new heights of civic association. There is no assumption that history will culminate in the perfection of human nature through social planning. The enduring problems of political life are rooted in our enduring and necessarily imperfect human nature, and like the American founders, Lincoln understood that limited, constitutional government is structured in light of this observation. For Croly, however, Lincoln exemplified the promise of American life through his "general outlook and behavior," "whatever his theories were." That is to say, whatever Lincoln might have identified as his own political principles and reasoning is of no real consequence. Ultimately, in light of the progress of history, Croly claimed to understand Lincoln better than Lincoln understood himself and sought to appropriate the Lincoln image while rejecting Lincoln's principles.[21]

This rejection of Lincoln's principles is also evident in Croly's discussion of natural rights. Despite his attempt to invoke the Lincoln image, Croly explicitly turned away from the natural-rights principles that served as the foundation of Lincoln's political thought. "The ideal of a constructive relation between American nationality and American democracy," Croly wrote, "is in truth equivalent to a new Declaration of Independence. . . . There comes a time in the history of every nation, when its independence of spirit vanishes, unless it emancipates itself in some measure from its traditional illusions."[22] Croly called for a refounding of our fundamental moral and political ends, contending that American democracy must free itself from the illusory notion that its purpose is to secure the natural and equal rights of individuals. "Belief in the principle of equal rights," Croly argued, "does not bind, heal, and unify public opinion. Its effect rather is confusing, distracting, and at worst, disintegrating."[23] Yet Lincoln, Croly's ideal statesman, claimed the opposite view. Responding to the Southern slave interest's denial of the principles of the Declaration, Lincoln suggested: "Public opinion, on any subject, always has a '*central idea*' from which all its minor thoughts radiate. That 'central idea' in our political tradition, at the beginning was, and until recently has continued to be, 'the equality of men.'" For Lincoln, the self-evident truth that all men are created equal—that is, that they are equally endowed with natural and inalienable rights—is "the electric cord" that "links the hearts of patriotic and liberty-loving men together."[24]

While Lincoln and Croly would agree that the equality of all men had served as the central idea informing American public opinion, they profoundly disagreed as to the real meaning of equality. For Croly, if the purpose of American government is merely to secure our equal natural rights, then "democracy becomes an invitation to local, factional, and individual ambitions and purposes." According to Croly, "of all perverted conceptions of democracy, one of the most perverted and dangerous is that which identifies it exclusively with a system of natural rights. Such a conception of democracy is in its effect inevitably revolutionary, and merely loosens the social and national bond." For Croly, the notion of natural rights necessarily places undesirable limitations on the power of national government to address social problems.[25] Public opinion must be redirected toward a new understanding of democracy, based not upon the idea that the purpose of government is to secure natural rights, but rather upon the idea that "genuine democracy" must necessarily be dedicated to securing human brotherhood. Croly's effort to seize the Lincoln image is frustrated by the fact that Lincoln's moral and political reasoning is fundamentally rooted in the very natural-rights principles that Croly himself rejects. For Croly to offer up Lincoln as a model for contemporary progressive reform, he had to recast Lincoln's example in terms of a progressive unfolding of American history and an abandonment of the very principles beneath Lincoln's own understanding of free government and democratic statesmanship.

Theodore Roosevelt's Abraham Lincoln

After reading Croly's *The Promise of American Life* in 1909, Theodore Roosevelt was convinced that the founders' political science had become obsolete in light of changing historical and economic circumstances. The progress of history had led to the necessity of a stronger, more efficient national government, unhampered by institutional mechanisms such as federalism and separation of powers. The new aim of government, Roosevelt believed, was not to secure the natural and inalienable rights of individuals, but rather the material and spiritual well-being of the entire community.[26] Roosevelt thus sought to transform the American polity into what he described as a "real" or "genuine" democracy.

There can be no real democracy without "economic democracy," wrote Roosevelt—that is, a democracy in which citizens are afforded the equal opportunity to become intellectually, morally, and materially fit to be their own masters.[27] In modern, industrial America, where people were increasingly tied not to the land but to the factory, Roosevelt contended that equality of opportunity could not be secured without an increase in the role of the national government in providing that security though social and economic legislation aimed at reining in powerful special interests. Moreover, Roosevelt suggested, this object could not be attained without a corresponding increase in the people's direct control over their elected representatives, court decisions, and the Constitution itself. In his political rhetoric, Roosevelt frequently appealed to Lincoln as a "pure democrat" who would have supported increased legislation for social and industrial justice on the principle that the people are the rightful masters of their public servants and the Constitution.

"Equality of Opportunity"

In his debates with Stephen Douglas, Lincoln claimed that the slavery question was a manifestation of "the eternal struggle between . . . two principles—right and wrong—throughout the world." One, Lincoln claimed, "is the common right of humanity, and the other is the divine right of kings. It is the same principle in whatever shape it develops itself. It is the same spirit that says: 'You toil and work and earn bread, and I'll eat it.'" In his 1913 address, "The Heirs of Abraham Lincoln," Roosevelt suggested that the Progressive Party platform "is but an amplification of this statement of Lincoln's."[28]

Roosevelt sought to connect Lincoln's expression of equal natural rights with his own vision of "equality of opportunity." In his "New Nationalism"

speech, Roosevelt claimed that in "every wise struggle for human better-
ment one of the main objects, and often the only object, has been to achieve
in large measure equality of opportunity." The "essence of the struggle" is
always "to equalize opportunity, destroy privilege and give to the life and
citizenship of every individual the highest possible value both to himself and
to the commonwealth. That is nothing new." Roosevelt suggested that while
we might not achieve perfect equality in this struggle, we could achieve a
"practical equality of opportunity," which promises that "every man will have
a fair chance to make of himself all that in him lies . . . unassisted by special
privilege of his own and unhampered by the special privilege of others."
This "equality of opportunity means that the commonwealth will get from
every citizen the highest service of which he is capable."[29] In "The Heirs of
Abraham Lincoln," Roosevelt explained how Lincoln could be a source for
this vision of equality. He claimed that the purpose of the Progressive Party
was none other than Lincoln's purpose, declared in Lincoln's Message to
Congress in Special Session of July 4, 1861, to "elevate the condition of men,"
to "lift artificial weights from all shoulders," to "clear the paths of laudable
pursuit for all," and to "afford all, an unfettered start, and a fair chance, in
the race of life."[30] For Lincoln, the artificial weights of chattel slavery were to
be lifted by emancipation and the free labor system. For Roosevelt, government must lift the artificial weights as they existed in his day in the form of
"wage slavery" practiced by modern industry. But, Roosevelt argued, the
"real issue" confronting the Progressive Party was the same basic issue that
confronted Lincoln: the struggle between the rights of man and the tyrannical principle that it is one man's duty to labor and another man's right to
enjoy the fruits of that labor.[31]

Yet the "New Nationalism" speech illustrates how far Roosevelt actually
departed from Lincoln's principles: "We grudge no man a fortune in civil life
if it is honorably obtained and well used. It is not even enough that it should
have been gained without doing damage to the community. We should
permit it to be gained only so long as the gaining represents benefit to the
community. This, I know, implies a policy of a far more active governmental
interference with social and economic conditions in this country than we
have yet had, but I think we have got to face the fact that such an increase
in governmental control is now necessary."[32] According to Roosevelt, the
"central condition of progress" is to "take from some one man or class of
men the right to enjoy power, or wealth, or position, or immunity, which

has not been earned by service to his or their fellows" and redistribute these goods to "men who have earned more than they possess." For Roosevelt, government must determine the acceptable use of property and must respect property rights if, and only if, it is deemed socially useful to do so. When Roosevelt urged that every man must "have a fair chance to make of himself all that in him lies . . . unassisted by special privilege of his own," that "special privilege" included property deemed useless to the common good if left in private hands.[33]

Roosevelt's effort to claim the Lincoln inheritance for his "practical equality of opportunity" departs from Lincoln's principles. For Lincoln, the principles of the Declaration suggest that all human beings are equally endowed with natural and inalienable rights. To whatever extent one man is superior to another in accidental characteristics or talents, he may indeed fare better in securing his advantage in the world, but no one can claim a right by nature to rule over another without the other's consent. In everyday practice this equality means that a man should be able to eat the bread that he has earned. Lincoln's understanding of natural equality is central to his defense of free labor, in that the origin of private property consists in the natural and equal right that each human being has to his body, to the labor of that body, and to the fruits of that labor.[34] Lincoln consistently maintained this Lockean understanding that all men are equally entitled, so far as it is possible, to eat the bread that they earn by the sweat of their own brow.[35]

Far from implying the redistribution Roosevelt advocated in "New Nationalism," Lincoln's pursuit of equality suggests the justice of an equality of rights but not an equality of rewards. For Lincoln, free labor ensures that all have an equal right to pursue happiness under the rule of law, while understanding that unequal rewards will necessarily result. We recall Madison's proclamation in *Federalist* No. 10 that the first object of government is the protection of the "different and unequal faculties of acquiring and possessing property."[36] Lincoln's understanding of equality accords directly with this Madisonian principle and thus diverges sharply from Roosevelt's redistributionism. This is why Lincoln could suggest to the New York Workingmen's Association in 1864 that "property is the fruit of labor—property is desirable—it is a positive good in the world. That some should be rich, shows that others may become rich, and hence is just encouragement to industry and enterprise. Let not him who is houseless pull down the house of another; but let him labor diligently and build one for himself, thus by example assuring that his own house shall be safe from violence when built."[37]

Roosevelt obscured the distinction between equality of rights and equality of rewards that was so crucial to Lincoln's understanding of equality. He also denied the very foundation of Lincoln's views on free labor—that by nature, nothing should come between a man's hand and his mouth. For Lincoln this meant that, insofar as it is possible, government should exalt and protect the rights of private property.

Direct Democracy

For Roosevelt, if government is to secure "practical equality of opportunity," the people must have increased and more direct control over the power of government. Roosevelt's opponents had criticized the progressives for seeking to incorporate elements of direct democracy into American republicanism. Roosevelt responded by pointing to Lincoln:

> Our opponents have especially objected to our doctrine that the people have the right to control all their servants, judicial, executive, and legislative alike. Well, listen to Abraham Lincoln. He assailed his opponents because they "made war upon the first principle of popular government, the rights of the people," because they "boldly advocated" "the denial to the people of the right to participate in the selection of public officers except the legislative," and because they argued "that large control by the people in government" is the "source of all political evil." Mind you, I am quoting from Lincoln's words uttered over fifty years ago. They are applicable in letter and in spirit to our opponents to-day. They apply without the change of a word to those critics who assail us because we advocate the initiative and the referendum and, where necessary, the recall, and because we stand for the right of the people to control all their public servants, including the judges when the judges exercise a legislative function.[38]

Roosevelt referred here to Lincoln's Annual Message to Congress of December 1861. Lincoln did indeed suggest in this address that the Confederate "insurrection is largely, if not exclusively, a war upon the first principle of popular government—the rights of the people." According to Lincoln, in "the most grave and maturely considered public documents" of the Confederacy "we find the abridgment of the existing right of suffrage and the denial to the people of all right to participate in the selection of public officers except the legislative boldly advocated, with labored arguments to prove that large control of the people in government is the source of all political evil. Monarchy itself is sometimes hinted at as a possible refuge from the power of the people."[39] But nothing in this address suggests that Lincoln's support for the sovereignty of the people envisioned the initiative, referendum, or the right of the people to recall public officials. Rather, Lincoln was speaking of elections, and he understood the right of people to control all their public servants to consist in their right to exercise their voice through established, constitutionally structured modes of consent. Consider the following from Lincoln's First Inaugural Address: "By the frame of the Government under which we live . . . [the] people have wisely given their public servants but little power for mischief; and have, with equal wisdom, provided for the return of that little to their hands at very short intervals. While the people retain their virtue and vigilance, no administration, by any extreme of wickedness or folly, can very seriously injure the Government in the short space of four years."[40]

Put another way, extraconstitutional mechanisms such as the recall were unnecessary in Lincoln's view of government because, unlike the progressives, Lincoln conceived of the ends of government in limited terms. Lincoln spoke here of the executive, yet the principle could clearly apply to other elected officials. According to Lincoln (who does not mention impeachment here), elected officials may be "recalled" in the usual constitutional way: through elections coming at fixed intervals.[41]

Drawing on Lincoln, Roosevelt took particular issue with his critics' opposition to the progressive call for "the people to control all their public servants, *including the judges* when the judges exercise a legislative function."[42] Although Roosevelt did not support proposals for the recall of judges in New York, he did suggest that such measures might be necessary in some states, and he claimed that progressives took a Lincolnian "attitude" when they supported the recall of judges.[43] Lincoln, however, never said anything about the "return" of unelected officials, nor did anything in his speeches and writings suggest that he thought that the "right" to *recall* public servants, including judges, was a necessary inference from the idea that the people have the right to *control* those servants. Yet Roosevelt went further than merely to suggest that Lincolnian principles would require the popular recall of judges. He also suggested that Lincolnian principles required the popular recall of judicial decisions. Critics of the Progressive Party, Roosevelt claimed, were "especially fond of denouncing our attitude toward the courts, and above all, our demand that the people shall be made the masters of the courts as regards constitutional questions." In response, Roosevelt reminded us that Lincoln had once suggested, in an 1859 speech in Cincinnati, that "the people of these United States are the rightful masters both of Congresses and courts, not to overthrow the Constitution, but to overthrow the men who pervert the Constitution." According to Roosevelt, this was the progressive position.[44]

Lincoln did assert in Cincinnati that the people are the "rightful masters of both Congresses and courts." However, if we consider Lincoln's statement in its fuller context, we find that Roosevelt failed to convey Lincoln's thoughts accurately:

> I say that we must not interfere with the institution of slavery in the states where it exists, because the constitution forbids it, and the general welfare does not require us to do so. We must not withhold an efficient fugitive slave law because the constitution requires us, as I understand it, not to withhold such a law. But we must prevent the outspreading of the institution, because neither the constitution nor general welfare requires us to extend it. We must prevent the revival of the African slave trade and the enacting by Congress of a territorial slave code. We must prevent each of these things being done by either Congresses or courts. The people of these United States are the rightful masters of both Congresses and courts not to overthrow the constitution, but to overthrow the men who pervert that constitution.
>
> *To do these things we must employ instrumentalities. We must hold conventions; we must adopt platforms if we conform to ordinary custom; we must nominate candidates, and we must carry elections.*[45]

Roosevelt obscured, in other words, the fact that Lincoln sought to address the slavery problem *through established constitutional and political means.* Nothing in Lincoln's remarks in Cincinnati or in the whole of his statements on slavery extension (pertaining, for example, to *Dred Scott,* the African slave trade, the Fugitive Slave Law, or a national slave code) suggests that a right to recall judges or judicial decisions by popular vote ought to follow from Lincoln's principles. In order to address unwise policies or erroneous decisions made by congresses or the courts, and to demonstrate that the people are the rightful masters of both, Lincoln urged that the people must speak through the established electoral process and established, constitutionally structured, representative institutions.

Nevertheless, Roosevelt contended that there was an "exact parallelism" between Lincoln's attitude toward the courts and the progressive support for the recall of judicial decisions by popular referendum. This argument became the dominating theme in "The Heirs of Abraham Lincoln" and was voiced frequently by Roosevelt during the 1912 presidential campaign. In "The Recall of Judicial Decisions," he defended his opposition to several New York State Court of Appeals decisions that he believed had frustrated the ability of legislatures to foster social and industrial justice. Roosevelt asserted that the recall of judicial decisions by popular referendum was "*precisely and exactly* in line with Lincoln's attitude toward the Supreme Court in the Dred Scott case, and with the doctrines he laid down for the rule of the people in his first inaugural as President" and that his position differed "in *no essential way* . . . from the principles laid down and acted upon by Abraham Lincoln in this matter."[46] But Roosevelt and Lincoln really did differ in an "essential way" on this question, in that they fundamentally disagreed about the means by which erroneous or irresponsible judicial decisions could be addressed. This concrete disagreement may be why Roosevelt focused on Lincoln's "attitude" toward the court rather than the specific details of his opinions on *Dred Scott.*

Roosevelt did correctly claim that Lincoln "would not have the citizen conform his vote" to the "decision of the Supreme Court [in *Dred Scott*] nor the member of Congress his" and that Lincoln would oppose making it a "rule of political action for the people."[47] But this, of course, does not suggest anything close to "judicial recall," as much as Roosevelt tried to conflate the two in his 1912 Speech to the Ohio Constitutional Convention:

It was Lincoln who appealed to the people against the judges when the judges went wrong, who advocated and secured what was practically the recall of the Dred Scott decision. . . . Lincoln actually applied in successful fashion the principle of the recall in the Dred Scott case. He denounced the Supreme Court for that iniquitous decision . . . and appealed to the people to recall the decision—the word "recall" in this connection was not then known, but the phrase exactly describes what he advocated. He was successful, the people took his view, and the decision was practically recalled. It became a dead letter without the need of any constitutional amendment.[48]

Roosevelt conflated the "exact" conception of judicial recall with its "practical" equivalent, illustrating the inherent difficulty in his appeal to Lincoln in support of this mechanism of direct democracy. To assert that Lincoln appealed to the people when the judges went wrong is not accurate in the sense that Roosevelt suggested. Lincoln appealed to the people insofar as he appealed to established constitutional and political means to deal with a decision he judged to be erroneous and irresponsible. He did this, above all, by urging the people to elect more Republicans to office, to change the makeup of the court, and to convince the court itself to reverse the *Dred Scott* decision.[49]

Roosevelt's claim that *Dred Scott* became a dead letter, with no need of constitutional amendment to overcome it, would also have us forget Lincoln's unwavering belief that emancipation would ultimately require constitutional amendment. For Roosevelt, judicial recall, "practical" or otherwise, was simply a quick and easy method of controlling and amending the Constitution. Roosevelt's reliance upon institutions of direct democracy was predicated upon his belief, characteristic of progressivism generally, that the problem of faction had been overcome by historical development and changing economic conditions. Roosevelt suggested that "there are sincere and well-meaning men of timid nature who are frightened by the talk of tyranny of the majority. These worthy gentlemen are nearly a century behind the times. It is true that De Tocqueville, writing about eighty years ago, said that in this country there was great tyranny by the majority. His statement may have been true then, although certainly not to the degree he insisted, but it is not true now."[50] Constitutional and political institutions that had originally been designed to moderate and structure democratic rule were thus deemed obsolete in light of the progress of history.

On the question of majority tyranny, Roosevelt compared his contemporary opponents to Lincoln's opponent, Stephen Douglas. Roosevelt claimed that, just as Douglas had denounced Lincoln for publicly disagreeing with the *Dred Scott* decision, contemporary opponents of judicial recall were denouncing the progressives for resisting the courts.[51] Yet Roosevelt had far more in common with Douglas than with Lincoln. Like Roosevelt's vision of direct democracy, Douglas's doctrine of "popular sovereignty" was premised on the idea that majority tyranny was impossible. Popular sovereignty illustrates the dangers of unmitigated majority rule in which there are no longer any overarching moral or constitutional limits placed upon the objects to which a majority might consent. Lincoln's devastating critique of popular sovereignty in his debates with Douglas suggests that, despite Roosevelt's attempt to adopt Lincoln as the precursor to progressive reform, there is no better critic of Roosevelt's dismissal of majority tyranny than Lincoln himself.

Roosevelt's dismissal of the concept of majority tyranny is fundamental to his attempt to redefine the ends and means of American democracy. Breaking sharply with the political theory of the American founding, Roosevelt came to believe that any interest that did not actively and consciously serve the common good as defined by the government was necessarily a "special interest" that must be "driven out of politics."[52] For Roosevelt, direct democracy offered an efficient means of doing so, and he sought to connect the Lincoln image with his call for progressive reform. But Lincoln had more in common with the American founders than he did with Roosevelt. The founders' political science was based upon the idea that while a multiplicity of interests would help to control the effects of faction, the problem of faction could not be driven out of political life, for its causes were sown in the nature of man.[53] Likewise, although Lincoln certainly believed that self-interest could not serve as the sole standard of right action, he understood that our natural selfishness and our natural love of justice stand in "eternal antagonism."[54] Thus institutional arrangements designed to temper and moderate the demands of factious majorities were both necessary and desirable, and always would be. In order to argue that such institutional restraints were no longer necessary, progressives relied on a rather peculiar account of American history and of Lincoln's role in it. This is where Woodrow Wilson's vision of American political development becomes crucial to understanding the progressive reliance on Lincoln's legacy.

Wilson's Use of Lincoln

Wilson employed a narrative of Lincoln's role in American history as part of his effort to recast the Constitution in progressive terms. Wilson's many writings on American history, often overlooked by scholars, provide the clearest picture of this narrative. To understand American constitutionalism properly, Wilson contended that the single most important historical lesson to learn was that American history represented a triumph over the narrow individualism of the founding. America, he claimed, had evolved into a genuine nation. He elaborated: "Our life has undergone radical changes since 1787, and almost every change has operated to draw the nation together, to give it the common consciousness, the common interests, the common standards of conduct, the habit of concerted action, which will eventually impart to it in many more respects the character of a single community."[55]

Wilson urged that the Constitution be read in light of these centralizing developments and that the power of the central government be expanded accordingly. The nation overcame its difficulties, he reasoned, not by sticking to its original principles, but by submitting to progress and growth, by adopting new methods and new political ideas to meet new historical circumstances. History would continue to bring improvement to America precisely to the extent that it was willing to let go of its original principles. Without Lincoln and the Civil War, the old order would have continued and America could not have taken the steps necessary to mature. As Wilson summarized in his book *The State,* the "Civil War completes the Union," by which he meant that the last vestiges of the old order, which had stood in the way of progress, were swept away by the conflict.[56]

Wilson saw American development in the first half of the nineteenth century as a struggle between the forces of originalism, which wanted to keep the country fragmented, and the forces of union, led by Abraham Lincoln, which were on the side of progress. These two main forces contended for decades in a conflict that led up to, and was decisively resolved by, the Civil War. To understand the significance of Lincoln and the union issue to Wilson's conception of American politics and to understand why Wilson was no Southern partisan, it is vital to know that, for Wilson, it was the *Southerners* who were the constitutional originalists. Wilson foreshadowed today's libertarians and neo-Confederates: the forces of states' rights and secession, as Wilson understood them, represented the founders' Constitution as it was originally intended to be—one that placed strict limits on the sphere of federal authority. Those who favored national unity and the cause of the North, then, were the progressives. Lincoln and the progressive, prounion forces advocated a departure from the original constitutional understanding and an embrace of national unity and expanded national government. The prounion forces were progressive because they wanted to adjust political principles to the advances and new circumstances brought about by history. They understood that America was growing and evolving, and they wanted to read the Constitution accordingly. The Southerners, according to this narrative, had the correct view of the original Constitution, and they wanted the country to stick to it. Secession, therefore, was not an attack on the Constitution but rather a movement of reactionary forces who wanted to restore original constitutionalism in a fight against progress.

In his short history of America in the nineteenth century, *Division and Reunion,* Wilson expressed his approval of Daniel Webster's prounion argument—"that the Constitution had created, not a dissoluble, illusory partnership between the States, but a single federal state, complete in itself." But he made clear that this interpretation, however much he embraced it, was probably *not* the view of those who framed the Constitution: "It may, nevertheless, be doubted whether this was the doctrine upon which the Union had been founded." While the states' rights view of the Southerners may have been the one that most accurately reflected original intent, it was inferior historically and contrary to the march of progress, since "Webster's position was one toward which the greater part of the nation was steadily advancing."[57] Wilson explained in a subsequent essay that, in spite of its inferiority, Calhoun's "doctrine of the ultimate sovereignty of the States was not new. It had once been commonplace to say that the Union was experimental, to speak of circumstances in which the contracting States might deem it best to withdraw." The historically inferior understanding of federal power that animated the founding generation was simply a reflection of the particular historical environment in which it grew up—one where it was simply more common for the focus to be on the states and their primacy.[58] In the face of this undue attachment to original forms, those who favored a national union adopted what might be called today a "living constitution" understanding of government. Wilson explained: "The legal theory upon which [secession] was taken was one which would hardly have been questioned in the early years of the government. . . . But constitutions are not mere legal documents:

they are the skeleton frame of a living organism; and in this case the course of events had nationalized the government once deemed confederate."[59] In the dialectical contest between the forces of the old order and those of the new, history inevitably and necessarily decided things in favor of the side representing progress. Wilson commented in a letter on the war that "*I think the North was wholly right then,* and that the South paid the inevitable penalty for lagging behind the national development, stopping the normal growth of the national constitution."[60]

Statesmanship and Leadership

Lincoln, according to this Wilsonian narrative, was the agent of historical progress; he helped the country shed its original principles by acting as a man of his times—by his willingness to embrace the new spirit of a new age. It was for this very reason that Wilson put Lincoln in the same category as Edmund Burke, whom Wilson considered to be the best model for statesmanship. In a view of Burke that was too exclusively influenced by the *Reflections on the Revolution in France,* Wilson considered Burke's greatest virtue to be his historical pragmatism—that Burke was guided in his statesmanship, as Wilson saw it, by whichever way the historical winds seemed to be blowing at the time. Like Wilson's Lincoln, Wilson's Burke did not theorize about what politics ought to be in form; he did not conjure up abstract principles of political justice to serve as guides to political action. Instead, he constantly adjusted to fit changing circumstances. In his 1893 essay on Burke, Wilson identified a series of key issues that Burke confronted during his career. Wilson contended that Burke approached each of these issues in a consistent manner: he "had no system of political philosophy" but was guided instead by the circumstances of each case.[61]

In addition to his alleged Burkean antipathy to abstract principles in politics, Lincoln represented to Wilson the ideal model of presidential leadership. This was a model where the president was to tap directly into the people's opinion and thus circumvent the Constitution as the principal source of presidential power and the separation of powers system as the principal means of checking that power. For Wilson, Lincoln contrasted very favorably with several earlier presidents, especially Thomas Jefferson, who Wilson believed did not sufficiently seek out a close connection to public opinion.[62] Wilson praised Lincoln, by contrast, for serving as a man of the people, for embodying the spirit of the masses. Yet he also praised Lincoln for standing out in front of the masses, for seeing their own will more clearly than they were able to see it themselves:

> A great nation is not led by a man who simply repeats the talk of the street-corners or the opinions of the newspapers. A nation is led by a man who hears more than those things; or who, rather, hearing those things, understands them better, unites them, puts them into a common meaning; speaks, not the rumors of the street, but a new principle for a new age; a man in whose ears the voices of the nation do not sound like the accidental and discordant notes that come from the voice of a mob, but concurrent and concordant like the united voices of a chorus, whose many meanings, spoken by melodious tongues, unite in his understanding in a single meaning and reveal to him a single vision, so that he can speak what no man else knows, the common meaning of the common voice. Such is the man who leads a great, free, democratic nation.[63]

Much in the same terms that Croly would later employ in *The Promise of American Life,* Wilson described Lincoln as the perfect American. Like Andrew Jackson, he was a man of the people and came from the frontier. But unlike Jackson, Lincoln was able to interpret the true spirit of the American people and to understand that the American future was one of nationalization. In this respect, Lincoln was the leader for whom the time was ripe. He was the agent of change that the progress of history required. "To the Eastern politicians," wrote Wilson, Lincoln "seemed like an accident; but to history he must seem like a providence."[64] Displaying the qualities necessary for any modern leader, Lincoln used popular rhetoric to affect the people, then pull them in the direction of his vision for their future. "He was vastly above [the people] in intellectual and moral stature," Wilson wrote of Lincoln. "He gained an easy mastery over them, too, by cultivating, as he did, the directer and more potent forms of speech."[65]

The Progressive Abuse of Lincoln

In sum, progressives painted a picture of Lincoln that depicted him as an icon for their movement: as a new man for new times who seized on the circumstances of the day as a justification for abandoning constitutional government, as a visionary centralizer who used public opinion leadership to redefine the scope of government, and as a man who would not be guided by theories or principles—who refused to hold the nation back or be bound by a stubborn adherence to the outmoded doctrines of the Declaration and Constitution. The picture of Lincoln painted by Wilson, Croly, and Roosevelt is, in other words, very much like the one painted of him by the libertarians and neo-Confederates of our own day. And in both cases, the picture is almost entirely at odds with the reality of Lincoln's words and deeds. The progressive characterization of Lincoln—particularly Wilson's narrative of Lincoln as a man unconcerned with the original theory of American government—is at such sharp variance with the reality even a cursory review of Lincoln's speeches would have revealed that one is initially at a loss for an explanation. More closely examined, the progressives' encounter with Lincoln fits a pattern they employed when celebrating the key figures of America's political tradition: their celebrations are almost exclusively historical and biographical and carefully avoid any reference to—or commemoration of—ideas or principles.

In this respect, progressive accounts of the founders are remarkably different from Lincoln's own accounts. If progressive accounts can be identified by their avoidance of the founders' principles, Lincoln's primary reason for calling to mind the founders was to recover their principles and bring them to bear on the debates of his own day. In attacking the doctrine of popular sovereignty in the Kansas-Nebraska Act and in contending against the denial of black citizenship in *Dred Scott,* Lincoln's mode was to call to mind the founders for the purpose of calling to mind the principles of the Declaration and Constitution.[66] It was Chief Justice Roger B. Taney's view, after all, that the founders had merely been men of their time—that their principles merely reflected the racial animus prevalent in the latter part of the eighteenth century. In refuting this assertion, Lincoln talked not so much about the founders as representatives of their age but instead explicated the abstract equality doctrine of the founding, paying careful attention to what it meant and what it did not mean, and bringing it to bear on the central questions of the 1850s. As Lincoln explained in his speech on the *Dred Scott* case, the value of the Declaration's equality doctrine did *not* come from its relevance at the time it was written but precisely from its applicability across generations: "The assertion that 'all men are created equal' was of no practical use in effecting our separation from Great Britain; and it was placed in the Declaration, not for that, but for future use."[67]

It was in emphasizing the historical and biographical approaches that progressives could write romantically of men of the founding era or of Lincoln, while at the same time offering consistently sharp criticisms of the actual principles espoused by the founders or by Lincoln. Wilson, for example, devoted a significant portion of his scholarly career—about ten years—to writing histories and biographies, and it is no accident that these are the works where the key figures of America's past are most celebrated and held up for admiration. When it comes to the other categories of Wilson's scholarly work—his writings on the principles of government and administration or his various treatments of American political institutions—there is no celebrating of past figures, documents, or ideas. In fact, any references to the critical figures or documents of American history in these works are normally for the purpose of showing how they are outmoded and how they are inadequate when measured against the more historically advanced ideas and systems of Europe. It was in this way that Wilson wrote an entire biography of George Washington that says very little, if anything, about Washington's conception of government. And it was in the same way that several progressive commentators on Lincoln could celebrate his leadership of the Union during the Civil War, without once attempting to come to terms with Lincoln's own explanation of that leadership or Lincoln's own understanding of the war's causes and aims. Coming to terms with these things would, of course, have led progressives to uncover much about Lincoln that would have cast him not as an iconic progressive but—to use the progressive phraseology—as a reactionary.

Lincoln as Burke

Wilson's understanding of Lincoln as a model Burkean statesman serves as an excellent illustration of how Lincoln was adopted for the progressive cause. By this characterization of Lincoln as Burke, Wilson meant, as explained above, that Lincoln's greatest virtue was his liberation from any overarching set of principles—his willingness to go in the new direction for the country that history was bringing about, unbounded or unlimited by any abstract notions of constitutionalism or natural right. Leaving aside the problematic reading of Burke inherent in Wilson's view, the relevant point for us is that Wilson simply denied that Lincoln was guided by abstract principles: "What commends Mr. Lincoln's studiousness to me," wrote Wilson, "is that the result of it was he did not have any theories at all.... Lincoln was one of those delightful students who do not seek to tie you up in the meshes of any theory."[68] In reality, of course, Lincoln's statesmanship is characterized by the quality exactly opposite to the one which Wilson asserts here. Lincoln's letter to Henry L. Pierce in 1859 immediately comes to mind, in which Lincoln commended Jefferson and the Declaration for precisely the abstractness that Wilson claimed he never exhibited: "All honor to Jefferson—to the man who, in the concrete pressure of a struggle for national independence by a single people, had the coolness, forecast, and capacity to introduce into a merely revolutionary document, an abstract truth, applicable to all men and all times."[69]

To show that Lincoln, contrary to Wilson's assertion, was indeed guided by a certain abstract theory of politics does not suggest that he was a kind of ideologue, after the fashion of the French revolutionaries who carried out their atrocities in the name of some demented version of natural justice. Rather, Lincoln's model of statesmanship relied upon prudence, as his Temperance Address from 1842 shows. The accomplishment of moral reform in politics requires, as Lincoln explained, both a commitment to a "theory" or moral principle and an understanding of and appeal to the prevailing tradition and popular conventions.[70] Wilson's objection to this understanding of statesmanship was its mooring in any kind of principle that might transcend history. Such a mooring stood as an obstacle to the progressive agenda to remake American government, not just in its means but in its ends.

Historical Contingency

Both in Lincoln's celebration of the "abstract" quality of Jefferson's Declaration and in his remark from the *Dred Scott* speech that the principles of the Declaration were "for future use," we see a quality that pervades his major speeches and writings: a rejection of the historical contingency that infused the political philosophy of Wilson, Croly, Roosevelt, and other progressives. Recalling Wilson's admonition, previously mentioned, to "not repeat the preface" of the Declaration, we see that Lincoln celebrated precisely that part of the document that Wilson wished had never been written and that Wilson denigrated as a mere "rhetorical introduction." It was this mere "rhetorical introduction" from which Wilson wanted to free American government, whereas Lincoln put it at the heart of the most pressing political disputes of his own time. In contending against the doctrine of popular sovereignty espoused by Stephen Douglas and implemented in the Kansas-Nebraska Act, the crux of Lincoln's argument was that the doctrine contradicts the "spirit of seventy-six," which spirit is enshrined in that part of the Declaration that Wilson would have us disregard. In fact, Lincoln took the passage of Kansas-Nebraska as sad evidence that many Americans had already gone down the path that Wilson would later urge them to take—to disregard the equality and natural-rights principles of the Declaration and deny their applicability beyond their own age. Lincoln lamented that "we have been giving up the old for the new faith."[71] Yet Wilson championed Lincoln precisely because Lincoln was a man, according to Wilson, who happily gave up the old for the new faith—who promoted "a new principle for a new age."[72] In the Kansas-Nebraska speech, however, Lincoln famously drew on the old principles of the old age and made fairly clear what ought to befall those who would replace the old with the new faith:

> When Pettit, in connection with his support of the Nebraska bill, called the Declaration of Independence "a self-evident lie" he only did what consistency and candor require all other Nebraska men to do. Of the forty odd Nebraska Senators who sat present and heard him, no one rebuked him. . . . If this had been said among Marion's men, Southerners though they were, what would have become of the man who said it? If this had been said to the men who captured Andre, the man who said it, would probably have been hung sooner than Andre was. If it had been said in old Independence Hall, seventy-eight years ago, the very door-keeper would have throttled the man, and thrust him into the street.[73]

While Wilson seemed to think Lincoln was the kind of man who bent with the historical winds and gave up the old faith for the new, Lincoln arguably would have thought Wilson the type of man who would have been throttled by the doorkeeper of Independence Hall and kicked out onto the street. The contrast could not be clearer. While Wilson urged us to disregard the Declaration, Lincoln urged a return to it: "Let us re-adopt the Declaration of Independence, and with it, the practices, and policy, which harmonize with it." While Wilson's solution for the imperfections of American republicanism was to bury the principles of the Revolution, Lincoln's was to resurrect them: "Our republican robe is soiled," he wrote, "and trailed in the dust. Let us re-purify it. Let us turn and wash it white, in the spirit, if not the blood, of the Revolution."[74]

The Purpose of Statesmanship

Such a contrast also helps bring to light the broader problem with the progressive characterization of Lincoln's statesmanship. As Wilson understood it, Lincoln embraced the cause of union as a consequence of having perceptively read the trends of history. The cause of the Union in the Civil War represented, in the eyes of progressives, the historical triumph of nationalization and centralization over originalism. The essence of Lincoln's statesmanship was the keenness of his vision of where history was going and the fact that he did not let adherence to outdated principle interfere with his steering the nation down the historically appointed path. A key quality of Lincolnian statesmanship, according to progressives, seems to have been that Lincoln did not take the principles of the Declaration and the law of the Constitution too seriously or at least that he was willing to read them flexibly or organically. Not only does such an estimation fly in the face of Lincoln's actual dedication to the principles and law of the founding, as demonstrated above, but it also misunderstands what Lincoln himself saw as the task of statesmanship. What most disturbed Lincoln in the 1850s was not the actual practice of slavery in those states where it already existed (while he abhorred this, he said repeatedly that nothing could be done about it at the time as a matter of law)[75] but the notion that it could be extended into new territories without doing violence to the principles of the founding. It was what Lincoln referred to as the principle of "indifference" in his Kansas-Nebraska speech—the idea that the establishment of slavery through popular sovereignty was a matter on which our founding principles were neutral—that clearly caused Lincoln the greatest consternation. He would, therefore, certainly have been appalled to see Roosevelt champion the purely majoritarian principles of popular sovereignty, to attribute them to Lincoln, and to confuse them with those of America's founders.

The state of affairs in the 1850s indicated to Lincoln that many Americans had ceased both to understand their fundamental law and to practice an attachment to it. The goal of his statesmanship, then, seems not to have been—as progressives suggested—the liberation of America from its fundamental law but rather a reintroduction of America to this law and an encouragement to renew devotion to it. This is why Lincoln called for Americans to "re-adopt the Declaration of Independence." He worried not that Americans would be held back by a commitment to this old document but rather that they had become corrupted by abandoning it. The principle of "indifference" represented, for Lincoln, "a dangerous dalliance for a free people—a sad evidence that, feeling prosperity, we forget right—that liberty, as a principle, we have ceased to revere."[76] The task of the statesman under such circumstances—where the people have detached themselves from their fundamental law—is not to go with the historical trends, as progressives urged, but to do as the young Lincoln did in his Lyceum Speech in 1838. In it Lincoln called not for a progressive remaking of our political institutions but for a perpetuation of them. Such a perpetuation was to be effected by encouraging a devotion to the law—both to the ordinary civil and criminal law and to the fundamental law of the Constitution:

> Let every American, every lover of liberty, every well wisher to his posterity, swear by the blood of the Revolution, never to violate in the least particular, the laws of the country; and never to tolerate their violation by others. As the patriots of seventy-six did to the support of the Declaration of Independence, so to the support of the Constitution and Laws, let every American pledge his life, his property, and his sacred honor;—let every man remember that to violate the law, is to trample on the blood of his father, and to tear the character of his own, and his children's liberty.[77]

Lincoln saw it as a task of statesmanship to encourage a devotion to the fundamental law, and this devotion took on a religious tone, encouraging a kind of worship of the law and of the great men who had promulgated it. As Lincoln went on to exhort: "Let it become the *political religion* of the nation, and let the old and the young, the rich and the poor, the grave and the gay, of all sexes and tongues, and colors and conditions, sacrifice unceasingly upon its altars." The old images of the founders and the founding had served as "pillars of the temple of liberty," but as time had passed they had come in need of being reestablished through this political religion.[78]

The contrast between this Lincolnian exhortation for political religion and Wilson's own reflections on the occasion of the Fourth of July in 1907 speaks directly to the essential difference between the two. Wrote Wilson: "We are not bound to adhere to the doctrines held by the signers of the Declaration of Independence. . . . We are not here to worship men or a document. . . . Neither are we here to indulge in a mere rhetorical and uncritical eulogy. Every Fourth of July should be a time for examining our standards, our purposes, for determining afresh what principles, what forms of power we think most likely to effect our safety and happiness."[79]

Much of the difference at work here comes from the starkly different accounts of American history that underlie the progressives' political thought as opposed to Lincoln's. In one important respect, the two sides agreed in their assessments of mid-nineteenth-century America: Americans had indeed distanced themselves from the principles of the founding. Yet the similarity ends there. For the progressives, this state of affairs was a positive development, proof that history was a force for progress. Under this narrative the losing side in the conflict—the South—stood for the old principles of the founding, and Lincoln, as the leader of the victorious North, was to be celebrated precisely for his role in overcoming America's origins. For Lincoln, on the other hand, the events of the 1850s were sad evidence that America had lost sight of its founding. His speech on the *Dred Scott* decision makes this very point, taking Taney to task for assuming a moral superiority in the prevailing sentiments of the 1850s as opposed to those of the founding era. Taney had made a progressive assumption about the course of American history—suggesting that it was the founding generation that had had a less just and historically inferior conception of human freedom and concluding that the founders, consequently, had not intended to include blacks in their vision of natural or civil rights. Lincoln, by contrast, held up the principles of the founding as the standard of justice from which America had strayed. "In those days," said Lincoln, "our Declaration of Independence was held sacred by all, and thought to include all; but now, to aid in making the bondage of the negro universal and eternal, it is assailed, and sneered at, and construed, and hawked at, and torn, till, if its framers could rise from their graves, they could not at all recognize it."[80] Both *Dred Scott* and the Kansas-Nebraska Act were evidence of a growing ignorance of the political theory of the founding.[81] This move away from the founding was not progress to Lincoln. The South did not, as progressives contended, represent to Lincoln the founding order that had to be overcome. Rather, the conflict between North and South was the result of a house that had become divided over its founding principles and the question of whether or not the nation should, as Lincoln believed, return to them.

Presidential Leadership and Lincoln's Legacy

This difference between the progressives' Lincoln, who was an integral part in America's move away from its original constitutionalism, and the real Lincoln, whose statesmanship was animated by a drive to return the country to its original ideas, emerges clearly in the debate over Lincoln's conception of presidential leadership. While the debate over the propriety of Lincoln's actions during the Civil War is beyond the scope of this chapter, Lincoln's own understanding of those actions offers a useful contrast to the Wilsonian vision for presidential leadership (previously explained). For Wilson, the great promise of presidential leadership was in its prospects for transcending the Constitution. Because Wilson worried that the Constitution's separation-of-powers system would stand as a barrier to the expansive government favored by progressives, he looked to the presidency—and especially to the president's popularity—as the means of surmounting the barrier. The whole point of presidential leadership, for Wilson, was to move the country beyond the Constitution. This is exactly the charge leveled against Lincoln by today's libertarian/neo-Confederate critics, and it is one of the reasons they characterize Lincoln as a founder of American progressivism. Yet while Wilson saw the president's popularity as a mode of overcoming the Constitution (he contrasted the "political" and "constitutional" aspects of the presidency, as previously explained), Lincoln saw popular rhetoric—or an appeal to "fashion," as he termed it in his Temperance Address—as a means of pointing the people back to their fundamental principles.[82] All of Lincoln's great speeches have this quality. Furthermore, Lincoln understood preservation of the Constitution as the primary aim of his presidential statesmanship, even in those cases where his actions may arguably have violated the letter of the Constitution's law. As he explained in an 1864 letter to Albert Hodges: "By general law, life and limb must be protected; yet often a limb must be amputated to save a life; but a life is never wisely given to save a limb. I felt that measures, otherwise unconstitutional, might become lawful, by becoming indispensable to the preservation of the Constitution, through the preservation of the Nation."[83]

For Lincoln, the cause of the nation and the cause of the Constitution were indistinguishable. For Wilson, and for his progressive brethren generally, the vitality of the nation required moving beyond the Constitution. This is the fundamental difference between the two camps, and it is why the progressive claim to Lincoln's legacy ought seriously to be questioned.

Notes

Ronald J. Pestritto gratefully acknowledges a fellowship research grant from the Earhart Foundation, which supported his work on this chapter, and Jason R. Jividen thanks the Earhart Foundation for a graduate fellowship grant, which supported early work on material in this chapter. Pestritto also acknowledges Fordham University Press for granting permission to incorporate into this chapter parts of his "Contesting the Legacy of Lincoln and the Civil War in the Progressive Era," in *Constitutionalism in the Approach and Aftermath of the Civil War,* ed. Paul D. Moreno and Johnathan O'Neill (New York: Fordham University Press, 2013), 183–201. Portions of this chapter are also adapted from arguments presented in Jason R. Jividen's *Claiming Lincoln: Progressivism, Equality, and the Battle for Lincoln's Legacy in Presidential Rhetoric* (DeKalb: Northern Illinois University Press, 2011) and J. David Alvis and Jason R. Jividen's *Statesmanship and Progressive Reform: An Assessment of Herbert Croly's Abraham Lincoln* (New York: Palgrave Macmillan, 2013). Jividen thanks Northern Illinois University Press and Palgrave Macmillan for their permission to draw upon these works here.

1. See Ronald J. Pestritto, *Woodrow Wilson and the Roots of Modern Liberalism* (Lanham, MD: Rowman & Littlefield, 2005). See also John Marini and Ken Masugi, eds., *The Progressive Revolution in Politics and Political Science: Transforming the American Regime* (Lanham, MD: Rowman & Littlefield, 2005); Charles R. Kesler, "Separation of Powers and the Administrative State," in *The Imperial Congress: Crisis in the Separation of Powers,* ed. Gordon S. Jones and John A. Marini (New York: Pharos Books, 1988), 20–40; and Charles R. Kesler, "The Public Philosophy of the New Freedom and the New Deal," in *The New Deal and Its Legacy,* ed. Robert Eden (New York: Greenwood, 1989).

2. Thomas L. Krannawitter, *Vindicating Lincoln: Defending the Politics of Our Greatest President* (Lanham, MD: Rowman & Littlefield, 2008), 290.

3. Ibid., 293.

4. See, for example, DiLorenzo's defense of the Confederacy as the model of limited government in *The Real Lincoln: A New Look at Abraham Lincoln,*

His Agenda, and an Unnecessary War (Roseville, CA: Prima Publishing, 2002), 273–74.

5. Walter Williams, "Why the Civil War," syndicated column published December 2, 1998, http://econfaculty.gmu.edu/wew/articles/98/civil-war.htm, accessed on June 27, 2014.

6. Theodore Roosevelt, "The Heirs of Abraham Lincoln," Speech at the Lincoln Day Banquet, New York City (February 12, 1913), in *Works of Theodore Roosevelt*, ed. Hermann Hagedorn, 20 vols. (New York: Charles Scribner's Sons, 1926), 17:359–60. Hereinafter cited as *Works*.

7. See John Dewey, *Liberalism and Social Action* (Amherst, NY: Prometheus Books, 2000 [1935]), 37–60, esp. 40–43.

8. Put another way, the founders were careful to be guided not only by ideas but by the experience of political development, as can be seen in *Federalist* No. 9 with its dependence upon the historical "improvements" in the science of politics, as well as in *Federalist* No. 85 with reference to David Hume's exhortation to rely upon experience. And the founders also understood that experience would allow continued improvement to the institutional means by which the fixed ends of American government could be achieved, writing as they did in *Federalist* No. 82: "'Tis time only that can mature and perfect so sound a system." This argument of *The Federalist* is why, in part, Harvey Mansfield has written that the universal ideas of the Declaration are made particularly American through the prudence of the Constitution, which turns Americans into a "constitutional people." It is in this way that the Americans distinguish themselves from the "revolutionary" people of France. See Harvey C. Mansfield, "The Unfinished Revolution," in *The Legacy of the French Revolution*, ed. Ralph C. Hancock and L. Gary Lambert (Lanham, MD: Rowman & Littlefield, 1996), 33, and Harvey C. Mansfield, *America's Constitutional Soul* (Baltimore: Johns Hopkins University Press, 1991), 1–17.

9. Woodrow Wilson, "An Address to the Jefferson Club in Los Angeles" (May 12, 1911), in *Papers of Woodrow Wilson*, 69 vols., ed. Arthur S. Link (Princeton, NJ: Princeton University Press, 1966–1993), 23:33–34. Hereinafter cited as *Papers*.

10. Croly's use of Lincoln is treated at length in J. David Alvis and Jason R. Jividen, *Statesmanship and Progressive Reform: An Assessment of Herbert Croly's Abraham Lincoln* (New York: Palgrave Macmillan, 2013).

11. Herbert Croly, *The Promise of American Life* (New York: Capricorn Books, 1964 [1909]), 27–51.

12. Croly, *Promise*, 17, 100–105, 182–85. See David Levy, *Herbert Croly of the New Republic: The Life and Thought of an American Progressive* (Princeton, NJ: Princeton University Press, 1985), 99–101.

13. Croly, *Promise*, 93–94; cf. Herbert Croly, "The Paradox of Lincoln," *The New Republic* (February 18, 1920), 350–53.

14. Croly, *Promise*, 94 (emphasis added).

15. Ibid., 89, 207.

16. Ibid., 89–99. See Alvis and Jividen, *Statesmanship and Progressive Reform*, 36–46.

17. Croly, *Promise*, 86.

18. Ibid., 86–88.

19. Ibid., 207, 399–400, 454.

20. Abraham Lincoln, "Response to a Serenade" (November 10, 1864), in *Collected Works of Abraham Lincoln*, ed. Roy P. Basler, 8 vols. (New Brunswick, NJ: Rutgers University Press, 1953), 8:101 (emphasis added). Hereinafter cited as *CW*.

21. See Alvis and Jividen, *Statesmanship and Progressive Reform*, 81–82.

22. Croly, *Promise*, 278–79.

23. Ibid., 185.

24. Abraham Lincoln, "Speech at a Republican Banquet, Chicago, Illinois" (December 10, 1856), in *CW*, 2:385, and Abraham Lincoln, "Speech at Chicago, Illinois" (July 10, 1858), in *CW*, 2:500.

25. Croly, *Promise*, 80–81. See Edward A. Stettner, *Shaping Modern Liberalism: Herbert Croly and Progressive Thought* (Lawrence: University Press of Kansas, 1993), 48–49; David K. Nichols, "The Promise of Progressivism: Herbert Croly and the Progressive Rejection of Individual Rights," *Publius: The Journal of Federalism* 17, no. 2 (Spring 1987): 31; and Alvis and Jividen, *Statesmanship and Progressive Reform*, 66–74.

26. Jean M. Yarbrough, "Theodore Roosevelt and the Stewardship of the American Presidency," in *History of American Political Thought*, ed. Bryan-Paul Frost and Jeffrey Sikkenga (Lanham, MD: Lexington Books, 2003), 537, 542. See Theodore Roosevelt, "The New Nationalism," Speech at Osawatomie, Kansas (August 31, 1910), in *Works*, 17:5–22, and Theodore Roosevelt, "Limitation of Governmental Power," Address at the Coliseum, San Francisco (September 14, 1912), in *Works*, 17:306–14.

27. Theodore Roosevelt, "Progressive Democracy," a review of Herbert Croly's *Progressive Democracy* and Walter Lippmann's *Drift and Mastery* (November 18, 1914), in *Works*, 12:232–39.

28. Abraham Lincoln, "Reply: Seventh Debate with Stephen A. Douglas at Alton, Illinois" (October 15, 1858), in *CW*, 3:315, and Roosevelt, "Heirs of Abraham Lincoln," 17:363.

29. Roosevelt, "New Nationalism," 17:8–10.

30. Abraham Lincoln, "Message to Congress in Special Session" (July 4, 1861), in *CW*, 4:438.

31. Roosevelt, "Heirs of Abraham Lincoln," 17:362–66. Cf. Theodore Roosevelt, "Washington and Lincoln: The Great Examples," in *Works*, 19:56–58; Abraham Lincoln, "Address before the Wisconsin State Agricultural Society, Milwaukee, Wisconsin" (September 30, 1859), in *CW*, 3:478–81; Abraham Lincoln, "Speech at New Haven, Connecticut" (March 6, 1860), in *CW*, 4:24; and Abraham Lincoln, "Annual Message to Congress" (December 3, 1861), in *CW*, 5:52.

32. Roosevelt, "New Nationalism," 17:13–14.

33. Ibid., 9–10. See Yarbrough, "Theodore Roosevelt," 545, and Ronald J. Pestritto, "Why Progressivism Is Not, and Never Was, a Source of Conservative Values," Claremont Institute (August 2005), http://www.claremont.org/publications/pubid.439/pub_detail.asp, accessed October 25, 2009.

34. See George Anastaplo, *Abraham Lincoln: A Constitutional Biography* (Lanham, MD: Rowman & Littlefield, 1999), 234, 330n473; Harry V. Jaffa, *How to Think about the American Revolution: A Bicentennial Cerebration* (Durham, NC: Carolina Academic Press, 1978), 45; and Harry V. Jaffa, *A New Birth of Freedom: Abraham Lincoln and the Coming of the Civil War* (Lanham, MD: Rowman & Littlefield, 2000), 300.

35. See, for example, Abraham Lincoln, "Speech at Springfield, Illinois" (June 26, 1857), in *CW*, 2:405–6; Abraham Lincoln, "Speech at Springfield, Illinois" (July 17, 1858), in *CW*, 2:520; and Abraham Lincoln, "Reply: First Debate with Stephen A. Douglas at Ottawa, Illinois" (August 21, 1858), in *CW*, 3:16. Cf. John Locke, *The Second Treatise of Government: An Essay concerning the True Original, Extent, and End of Civil Government* in *Two Treatises of Government*, ed. Peter Laslett (Cambridge: Cambridge University Press, 1988), esp. sec. 54.

36. James Madison, *Federalist* No. 10, in Alexander Hamilton, James Madison, and John Jay, *The Federalist*, ed. Jacob E. Cooke (Hanover, NH: Wesleyan University Press, 1982), 58. See Jaffa, *How to Think*, 45.

37. Abraham Lincoln, "Reply to New York Workingmen's Democratic Republican Association" (March 21, 1864), in *CW*, 7:259–60. In one of the few works to critically examine the progressives' claim to Lincoln's legacy, Steven Hayward suggests that they rejected his understanding of natural rights and equality. See Steven Hayward "The Children of Abraham," *Reason* 23 (May 1991): 26, 29. Also see Jaffa, *How to Think*, 45.

38. Roosevelt, "Heirs of Abraham Lincoln," 17:364–65.

39. Abraham Lincoln, "Annual Message to Congress," 5:51.

40. Abraham Lincoln, "First Inaugural Address" (March 4, 1861), in *CW*, 4:270.

41. See Judd Stewart, "Abraham Lincoln on Present-Day Problems and Abraham Lincoln as Represented by Theodore Roosevelt," Letter to the Members of the Ohio State Constitutional Convention, Columbus, Ohio (February 1912), Illinois State Historical Society, 8.

42. Roosevelt, "Heirs of Abraham Lincoln," 17:364–65 (emphasis added).

43. See ibid., 373–74; cf. Theodore Roosevelt, "The Right of the People to Rule," Address at Carnegie Hall, New York City (March 20, 1912), in *Works*, 17:164.

44. Roosevelt, "Heirs of Abraham Lincoln," 17:367; cf. Abraham Lincoln, "Speech at Cincinnati, Ohio" (September 17, 1859), in *CW*, 3:460.

45. Lincoln, "Speech at Cincinnati, Ohio," 3:460–61 (emphasis added).

46. Theodore Roosevelt, "The Recall of Judicial Decisions," Address at Philadelphia, Pennsylvania, April 10, 1912, in *Works*, 17:195 (emphasis added). Also see Roosevelt, "Right of the People," 17:163–64.

47. Roosevelt, "Heirs of Abraham Lincoln," 17:369. See Abraham Lincoln, "Speech at Springfield, Illinois" (July 17, 1858), in *CW*, 2:516.

48. Theodore Roosevelt, "A Charter of Democracy," Address before the Ohio State Constitutional Convention at Columbus, Ohio (February 21, 1912), in *Works*, 17:121, 139.

49. See, for example, Lincoln, "Speech at Chicago, Illinois," 2:495.

50. Roosevelt praised Bryce's statement that the "once dreaded danger" of majority tyranny had disappeared from American life. See James Bryce, *The American Commonwealth*, 3 vols. (London: Macmillan, 1888), 3:143. For Roosevelt it is not that the problem of tyranny as such had disappeared but rather that the tyrannies from which men, women, and children were suffering in "real life" were tyrannies by the minority of wealthy special interests. See Roosevelt, "Recall of Judicial Decisions," 17:202, and Roosevelt, "Right of the People," 17:152.

51. Roosevelt, "Heirs of Abraham Lincoln," 17:367–68.

52. Yarbrough, "Theodore Roosevelt," 548. See Roosevelt, "New Nationalism," 17:5–22.

53. See James Madison, *Federalist* No. 10, in Hamilton, Madison, and Jay, *The Federalist*, 58–59.

54. Abraham Lincoln, "Speech at Peoria, Illinois" (October 16, 1854), in *CW*, 2:271; cf. Lincoln, "Response to a Serenade," 8:101.

55. Woodrow Wilson, *Constitutional Government in the United States* (New York: Columbia University Press, 1908), 46–47.

56. Woodrow Wilson, *The State: Elements of Historical and Practical Politics* (Boston: D. C. Heath, 1898), 480.

57. Woodrow Wilson, *Division and Reunion: 1829–1889* (New York: Longmans, Green, 1901 [1893]), 44–47.

58. Woodrow Wilson, "State Rights" (December 20, 1899), in *Papers,* 11:311–12.

59. Wilson, *Division and Reunion,* 211.

60. Woodrow Wilson, "To Hermann Eduard von Holst" (June 29, 1893), in *Papers,* 8:271–72.

61. Woodrow Wilson, "Edmund Burke: The Man and His Times" (August 31, 1893), in *Papers,* 8:334–36.

62. Woodrow Wilson, "An Address on Thomas Jefferson" (April 16, 1906), in *Papers,* 16:363.

63. Woodrow Wilson, "Abraham Lincoln: A Man of the People" (February 12, 1909), in *Papers,* 19:42.

64. Woodrow Wilson, "A Calendar of Great Americans" (September 15, 1893), in *Papers,* 8:378–79.

65. Wilson, *Division and Reunion,* 216.

66. Lincoln, "Speech at Peoria, Illinois," 2:247–83.

67. Abraham Lincoln, "Speech at Springfield, Illinois" (June 26, 1857), in *CW,* 2:406.

68. Wilson, "Abraham Lincoln," 19:39.

69. Abraham Lincoln, "Letter to H. L. Pierce and Others" (April 6, 1859), in *CW,* 3:376.

70. Abraham Lincoln, "Temperance Address Delivered before the Springfield Washington Temperance Society" (February 22, 1842), in *CW,* 1:271–79.

71. Lincoln, "Speech at Peoria, Illinois," 2:275.

72. Wilson, "Abraham Lincoln," 19:42.

73. Lincoln, "Speech at Peoria, Illinois," 2:275.

74. Ibid., 2:276. See also Abraham Lincoln, "Speech in Independence Hall, Philadelphia, Pennsylvania" (February 22, 1861), in *CW,* 4:240, where Lincoln suggested, "[A]ll the political sentiments I entertain have been drawn, so far as I have been able to draw them, from the sentiments which originated and were given to the world from this hall. I have never had a feeling politically that did not spring from the sentiments embodied in the Declaration of Independence."

75. See, for example, Lincoln, "Reply: First Debate with Stephen A. Douglas," 3:16. This statement was repeated in Lincoln's First Inaugural Address; see Lincoln, "First Inaugural Address," 4:262–63.

76. Lincoln, "Speech at Peoria, Illinois," 2:274.

77. Abraham Lincoln, "The Perpetuation of Our Political Institutions: Address before the Young Men's Lyceum of Springfield, Illinois" (January 27, 1838), in *CW,* 1:112.

78. Ibid., 1:112, 115; emphasis in original.

79. Woodrow Wilson, "The Author and Signers of the Declaration of Independence" (July 4, 1907), in *Papers,* 17:251.

80. Lincoln, "Speech at Springfield, Illinois," 2:404.

81. Abraham Lincoln, "'A House Divided': Speech at Springfield, Illinois" (June 16, 1858), in *CW,* 2:461–69.

82. Lincoln, "Temperance Address," 1:277.

83. Abraham Lincoln, "Letter to Albert G. Hodges" (April 4, 1864), in *CW,* 7:281.

Contributors

John Channing Briggs is the John Gleason McSweeney Family Chair in Rhetoric and Teaching Excellence, professor of English, and director of the University Writing Program at the University of California, Riverside. He is the author of *Lincoln's Speeches Reconsidered* and *Francis Bacon and the Rhetoric of Nature.*

Michael Burlingame is the Chancellor Naomi B. Lynn Distinguished Chair in Lincoln Studies at the University of Illinois Springfield and Sadowski Professor of History Emeritus at Connecticut College. He is the author of *The Inner World of Abraham Lincoln* and editor of twelve books, including *Abraham Lincoln: The Observations of John G. Nicolay and John Hay; Dispatches from Lincoln's White House;* and *Lincoln Observed: Civil War Dispatches of Noah Brooks.* His most recent publications are *Abraham Lincoln: A Life,* a two-volume biography that garnered the prestigious Lincoln Prize, and *Lincoln and the Civil War.*

Joseph R. Fornieri is professor of political science at the Rochester Institute of Technology and director of its Center for Statesmanship, Law, and Liberty. He is the author of *Abraham Lincoln's Political Faith,* editor of *The Language of Liberty: The Political Speeches and Writings of Abraham Lincoln,* and coeditor of *Lincoln's American Dream: Clashing Political Perspectives.* His most recent publication is *Abraham Lincoln, Philosopher Statesman.*

Allen C. Guelzo is the Henry R. Luce Professor of the Civil War Era and director of the Civil War Era Studies Program at Gettysburg College. He is a three-time winner of the Lincoln Prize for *Abraham Lincoln: Redeemer President; Lincoln's Emancipation Proclamation: The End of Slavery in America;* and *Gettysburg: The Last Invasion.*

Jason R. Jividen is associate professor of politics in the McKenna School at St. Vincent College, where he also serves as a fellow in civic and constitutional affairs for the Center for Political and Economic Thought and director of the Aurelius Scholars Program in Western Civilization. He is the author of *Claiming Lincoln: Progressivism, Equality, and the Battle for Lincoln's Legacy in Presidential Rhetoric* and *Statesmanship and Progressive Reform: An Assessment of Herbert Croly's Abraham Lincoln.*

Fred Kaplan is distinguished professor emeritus of English at Queens College and the Graduate Center of the City University of New York. He is the author of *Lincoln: The Biography of a Writer*, which earned an honorable mention for the Lincoln Prize in 2009. His previous biographies include *The Singular Mark Twain; Gore Vidal; Henry James: The Imagination of Genius; Charles Dickens;* and *Thomas Carlyle.* His most recent publication is the critically acclaimed *John Quincy Adams: American Visionary.*

Steven Kautz is associate professor of political science at Michigan State University and associate dean for academic and student affairs of the College of Social Science. He is the author of *Liberalism and Community* and coeditor of *The Supreme Court and the Idea of Constitutionalism.*

Benjamin A. Kleinerman is associate professor of political theory and constitutional democracy at James Madison College at Michigan State University and was the Garwood Visiting Fellow in the *James Madison Program in American Ideals and Institutions* at Princeton University for 2011–2012. He is the author of *The Discretionary President: The Promise and Peril of Executive Power* and coeditor of *Extra-Legal Power and Legitimacy: Perspectives on Prerogative.*

Thomas L. Krannawitter is director of the Defenders of the Declaration program of the Leadership Program of the Rockies and has taught at Colorado Christian University, Hillsdale College, and Claremont McKenna College. He is the author of *Vindicating Lincoln: Defending the Politics of Our Greatest President.*

Lucas E. Morel is the Class of 1960 Professor of Ethics and Politics at Washington and Lee University. He is the author of *Lincoln's Sacred Effort: Defining Religion's Role in American Self-Government* and editor of *Ralph Ellison and* *the Raft of Hope: A Political Companion to Invisible Man.* He is working on a forthcoming book, *Lincoln and the American Founding.*

Mackubin Thomas Owens is professor of national security affairs at the US Naval War College. He is the editor of *Orbis: A Journal of World Affairs,* coeditor of the fourth edition of *Strategy and Force Planning,* and author of *U.S. Civil-Military Relations after 9/11: Renegotiating the Civil-Military Bargain* and is working on a forthcoming book, *Sword of Republican Empire: A History of American Civil-Military Relations.*

Ronald J. Pestritto is graduate dean and the Charles and Lucia Shipley Chair in the American Constitution at Hillsdale College. He is the author of *Woodrow Wilson and the Roots of Modern Liberalism,* editor of *Woodrow Wilson: The Essential Political Writings,* and coeditor of *American Progressivism: A Reader.*

Matthew Pinsker is the Brian Pohanka Chair of Civil War History at Dickinson College. He is the author of *Lincoln's Sanctuary: Abraham Lincoln and the Soldiers' Home* and *Abraham Lincoln* in the American Presidents Reference Series by CQ Press. He is working on a forthcoming book, *Boss Lincoln: Understanding Lincoln's Partisan Leadership.*

Diana J. Schaub is professor of political science at Loyola University Maryland. She is a coeditor of *What So Proudly We Hail: The American Soul in Story, Speech, and Song,* author of *Erotic Liberalism: Women and Revolution in Montesquieu's "Persian Letters,"* and a contributing editor to *The New Atlantis: A Journal of Technology & Society.*

Clarence Thomas is an associate justice of the United States Supreme Court. He is the author of *My Grandfather's Son: A Memoir.* Before his appointment to the Supreme Court, he served on the US Court of Appeals for the District of Columbia and as chairman of the US Equal Employment Opportunity Commission (1982–1990).

Index